PLANTS HAVE SO MUCH TO GIVE US,
ALL WE HAVE TO DO IS ASK

PLANTS HAVE SO MUCH TO GIVE US, ALL WE HAVE TO DO IS ASK

ANISHINAABE BOTANICAL TEACHINGS

MARY SIISIP GENIUSZ

EDITED BY WENDY MAKOONS GENIUSZ

ILLUSTRATIONS BY ANNMARIE GENIUSZ

University of Minnesota Press
Minneapolis
London

The University of Minnesota Press gratefully acknowledges the generous assistance provided for the publication of this book by the Margaret W. Harmon Fund.

Published by the University of Minnesota Press
111 Third Avenue South, Suite 290
Minneapolis, MN 55401–2520
http://www.upress.umn.edu

Library of Congress Cataloging-in-Publication Data
Geniusz, Mary Siisip.
Plants have so much to give us, all we have to do is ask: Anishinaabe botanical teachings / Mary Siisip Geniusz; edited by Wendy Makoons Geniusz; illustrations by Annmarie Geniusz.
Includes bibliographical references and index.
ISBN 978-0-8166-9673-4 (hc)—ISBN 978-0-8166-9676-5 (pb)
1. Ojibwa Indians—Ethnobotany. 2. Ojibwa Indians—Ethnobotany—History—Sources. 3. Ojibwa Indians—Folklore. 4. Ethnobotany—North America. 5. Plants, Useful—North America. 6. Medicinal plants—North America. I. Geniusz, Wendy Djinn. II. Geniusz, Annmarie Fay. III. Title. IV. Title: Anishinaabe botanical teachings.
E99.C6G47 2015
581.6'3097—dc23   2015012241

Printed in the United States of America on acid-free paper

The University of Minnesota is an equal-opportunity educator and employer.

30   29   28   27   26   25   24   15   14   13   12   11   10   9

Nimaamaayag miinawaa nindaanisag nimiinaag ow mazina'igan.

To my mothers and daughters I give this book.

Spring Tea Poem

To you I would serve cedar tea
mixed with a touch of April
distilled from shy green stems,
the frosted perfume of spring
rain along with a dollop
of honey and ice

—Keewaydinoquay Peschel

Contents

Preface

Wendy Makoons Geniusz

Plants Have So Much to Give Us, All We Have to Do Is Ask is written by a Native woman, Mary Siisip Geniusz, my mother, who demonstrates the strength and vitality of *Anishinaabe-bimaadiz-iwin,* the Anishinaabe way of life, in her frequent references to contemporary life. This book does not lament the loss of our old ways, nor does it present a laundry list of how the Anishinaabe use plants. It is a detailed account of important teachings from *Anishinaabe-gikendaasowin,* Anishinaabe knowledge, and it will be a valuable contribution to Anishinaabe cultural revitalization. Throughout this book, my mother shares teachings she received from the late Keewaydinoquay, an *Anishinaabe-mashkikiiwikwe,* Anishinaabe/Ojibwe medicine woman, and ethnobotanist who was her first teacher of Anishinaabe-gikendaasowin. According to Keewaydinoquay's teachings, plants are thought of as beings with their own histories, stories, beliefs, and ways of life. Anishi-naabe protocols require us to introduce plants just as we would introduce another human being, and this is what my mother does in this text. It is filled with stories, teachings, culinary and medicinal recipes—some from Anishinaabe traditions, some from the author's own life, and some from other traditions. I welcome and encourage readers to learn more about these cognizant beings who can be of such help to us if only we ask.

This scholarly text comes from a rich educational tradition, which is just as complex and has just as many protocols and levels of learning as non-Native educational systems. This book exem-plifies the Biskaabiiyang approach to research, which I describe in my book, *Our Knowledge Is Not Primitive: Decolonizing Anishi-naabe Botanical Teachings.* Following Biskaabiiyang research methodologies, we, as Anishinaabe people, conduct our own scholarly research and create resources presenting our knowledge to the world in ways that will be beneficial to our communities, our families, and ourselves. To do this, we need to look at how colonization has negatively impacted our opinions of our people, our knowledge, and ourselves. Only from that perspective can we begin to conduct research that will be useful to our fellow Anishinaabeg, our own lives, and the rest of the world. My mother first told me about the Biskaabiiyang methods of research; she learned about them in her courses for the Masters of Indigenous Knowledge/Philosophy Program at the Seven Generations Education Institute, which is nestled between Couchiching First Nations Reserve and Fort Francis, Ontario, on Agency One Land.

I watched my mother experience the Biskaabiiyang process of looking back at herself and evaluating how she had personally been affected by colonization before returning to the teachings she was given by Keewaydinoquay and then synthesizing them into written form. She struggled when writing this book because the effects of colonization on her own mind told her that it contained knowledge that would be dismissed by those raised with value systems from non-Native cultures. I believe that readers of this book, regardless of their backgrounds, will go through a decolonizing process themselves as they read this book and explore another system of keeping knowledge. To readers looking at this book through the blinders of colonization, the connections to plants that my mother makes on many levels, involving so many senses, may seem irrelevant or misplaced in scholarly work. To read this book and view it as the scholarly work that it is, readers will have to ignore the image that dominant culture frequently portrays of "primitive" Native people, cultures, stories, and knowledge keeping systems. Our people are not childlike, our cultures are not limited to the creation of fire and stone tools, our stories are not fairytales meant only to entertain children, and our knowledge is not simplistic. When we ignore these misconceptions, we are in a more open state of mind to accept the idea that plants are other beings with whom we can interact and communicate, and their stories and talents, from the trivial to the essential, are vital to our continued interactions with them.

Keewaydinoquay

Keewaydinoquay always said that the year of her birth was not recorded until many years after the event, but officially her birth year is 1918; this is also the year her mother wrote on a letter addressed to her own father (Keewaydinoquay's grandfather) as a year that she gave birth.* Keewaydinoquay spent much of her childhood in an Anishinaabe village on Cat Head Bay, on the tip of the Leelanau Peninsula in Lower Michigan. Like many Michigan tribes in the first half of the twentieth century, the band into which Keewaydinoquay was born was not federally recognized at the time of her birth. She began her training as a medicine woman when she was approximately nine years old and was apprenticed to Nodjimahkwe, a well-respected mashkikiiwikwe in the village.

Keewaydinoquay had a lifelong interest in all kinds of education. She was an elementary and secondary teacher for years, and she held several master's degrees. In 1976 she began working on a doctorate in biology at the University of Michigan, but although she completed the coursework for the degree she was not able to pass the required German proficiency examination and therefore could not take her preliminary exams or write her dissertation. She was teaching at the University of Wisconsin–Milwaukee when my mother met her in the early 1980s. My mother was her student, her teaching assistant, and eventually her *oshkaabewis*, her traditionally trained Anishinaabe apprentice. With this book my mother fulfills her promise to Keewaydinoquay that she would preserve and pass on this knowledge.

My Role as Editor

My mother had already written a complete book-length manuscript when I joined her as editor of this project. I reorganized the original manuscript and suggested additions and deletions, but this book is entirely my mother's work, and it is her voice that readers hear. The majority of my contribution concerns Ojibwe words, phrases, and plant names. Readers do learn about me, however: I am the child my mother refers to in various stories as "my daughter Makoons."

Plant Names

Ojibwe plant names are used throughout this book. All of the Ojibwe plant names that Keewaydinoquay gave to my mother are here, plus in some cases names from other sources are used, especially for plants for which Keewaydinoquay did not know an Ojibwe name. The names from other sources are included

* Helen Hornbeck Tanner told me about this letter during an interview when I was writing an article about Keewaydinoquay's life (Geniusz 2005). The letter was in her possession at that time.

out of respect for Keewaydinoquay, who always tried to use as many Ojibwe names as possible in her lectures. Whenever possible, Ojibwe plant names have been retranscribed into the double vowel writing system and translated. Occasionally Keewaydinoquay remembered only an English translation for an Ojibwe name, and these are included in quotation marks in the section headings. When a plant name refers to the spirit of a plant or a formal greeting to a plant (such as Nookomis Giizhik, My Grandmother Cedar), it is capitalized; otherwise it is not. English common names and scientific names are also provided for identification purposes; in the section headings, these names appear on their own lines so that readers will not confuse them with translations of Ojibwe names. More detailed information on these names is included in the book's glossary.

Ojibwe Names

Ojibwe names, also called Indian names, appear throughout this text. Out of respect for these names and the people known by them, no attempt has been made to standardize their spelling; the spellings in this book follow how the individuals choose to spell their own names or how other texts spell these names.

Notes

Keewaydinoquay was the source of most of the information in this book. She was an expert on Anishinaabe culture and medicine, and this book acknowledges that. For areas in which Keewaydinoquay was not an expert (for example, stories about how other peoples work with these plants), notes have been added for verification and to provide sources for further information. We intend no disrespect for Keewaydinoquay; we simply know that she would want all the information in the book to be accurate.

Acknowledgments

The knowledge that has been recorded in these pages has come to us through countless generations of the Gete-anishinaabeg, the Old Ones, our ancestors, and the Aadizookaanag, the spirits who hold our teachings, including those of the plants, trees, and animals who brought this knowledge to our ancestors. We first and foremost would like to say Miigwech, thank you, to all of them.

We also respectfully say Miigwech to Keewaydinoquay, who so graciously brought these teachings to us, her ancestral teachers, and all those who taught them including: MidéOgema, her grandfather, and Nodjimahkwe, her herb mother and teacher.

Finally, we would like to say Miigwech to the elders who took their time to help us create the most accurate list of Ojibwe words possible for this book. They are introduced here as they asked to be identified. Miigwech to the late Kenneth Johnson Sr., from Seine River First Nation in Ontario, Canada; the late George McGeshick Sr., from the Mole Lake Sokaogon Band of Lake Superior Ojibwe and Chief of the Chicaugon Chippewa of Iron River, Michigan; Dora Dorothy Whipple, Leech Lake Elder; Ma-nee Chacaby, a two-spirit elder from Animikiiwiikwedong, Thunder Bay, Ontario; and a woman who wished to be identified only as "Rose, an elder from Canada."

Introduction

I was a teaching assistant to Keewaydinoquay, The Woman of the Northwest Wind, when she was teaching ethnobotany of the Great Lakes Native Americans and philosophy of the Great Lakes Native Americans at the University of Wisconsin–Milwaukee, in the 1980s. After having been her student in these courses and working for her as a teaching assistant, in charge of the ethnobotany lab sessions and the philosophy discussion sessions, I then became her *oshkaabewis*,[1] at which time I was formally bound to her for the purpose of learning Anishinaabe medicinal knowledge and lifeways.

Keewaydinoquay was a wonder as a teacher and the warmest, most generous person I have ever known. She was the kind of teacher who changes people for the better. She transformed how I viewed much of life. Working for and with her was one of the truly great honors of my lifetime.

We worked together for years, side by side, in a little university professor's office that was crammed with books and various ethnobotanical specimens and crafts made from plants. There was always a steady stream of undergraduates with questions and appointments as well as the daily routine of university teaching. Kee[2] was a popular teacher, and one of my main functions as a teaching assistant was to try to keep demands on her time down so that she could prepare for lectures and have the time for writing her own ethnobotanical research. As the demands of students and various other community commitments claimed more of her time, I used to beg her to find time to write. I would say, "Old One, we really must find more time for you to write. That is so very, very important. So much of your ethnobotany is not written

1 Keewaydinoquay translated oshkaabewis as "medicine helper." She said the job was like that of an apprentice who is bound to a master to learn a craft and also like a novice who is learning ceremony and the rites of Spirit.

2 Keewaydinoquay called herself by this abbreviation of her name and encouraged others to do so too. To me she was and is Kee or Grandmother or the Old One.

anyplace else." She would always say, "Yes, I really must do that." Then she would laugh and go on with the endless community- and school-related functions that ate so into her time. I would keep begging her to write. She would always agree and then there never was enough time.

Once when we had this discussion (and it was one we had many, many times), she looked over her shoulder at me, with a funny little smile on her lips. She said, "You know, Mary, I really don't have to worry about that [leaving a record of botanical teachings]. I have you. And you will do it for me."

I was shocked. I said, "Oh, no! No way! How could I ever write down all that you have taught me? If you want the job done at all you will just have to do it yourself."

"No," she said. "You are sworn to me, and you will do it."

I said, "But I am not half the scholar you are. You are the one with all of the academic background. You hold what Nodji- mahkwe[3] taught you and a lifetime of reading and study since then. How could you expect me to preserve what you know, when I know so little of it?"

Now, at the time of this writing, Keewaydinoquay is gone on the four-day journey to the Other Side, my children are grown, and I am rapidly aging. I face the same quandary that my *mashkikiiwikwe*, medicine woman, faced: how to manage not to die until I have transmitted the knowledge that she gave me, that she held from Nodjimahkwe and the ancestral teachers down the ages, as well as that which I have learned along the way myself. Each generation has this task. And it is no minor thing. I fully expect to have to account for my life decisions that made/make it possible for me to fulfill my part in the on-going of Anishinaabe knowledge. Every generation has this responsibility. Our knowledge is ancient in this land, *mashkikiiwinini, medicine man,* or mashkikiiwikwe to oshkaabewis, master to student, in unbroken line down the eons.

For a number of years I was not pleased with the idea of having to write this account of the ethnobotanical teachings that Kee gave to me. I would say to her, "But if you would just write your own knowledge down I would not have to write it."

She would respond, "My writing it or not writing it will not get you out of the obligation to write down what you have learned from me and what you have done with that knowledge. It is just how our knowledge has always grown."

3 In the 1920s, Keewaydinoquay was apprenticed to the noted medicine woman Nodjimahkwe, of Cat Head Bay Village on the Leelanau Peninsula of Michigan. The descent of Nodjimahkwe's knowledge can be traced back for four hundred years. See chapter 1 for more information.

When Keewaydinoquay started talking like that, a person just put her head down and said, "Yes, Grandmother." What else was there to say?

In the Anishinaabe worldview that Keewaydinoquay labored so to explain to me, *mashkikiiwikwewag,* medicine women, or *mashkikiiwininiwag,* medicine men, take *oshkaabewisag,* apprentices, in order to pass on the knowledge their teachers entrusted to them and also the knowledge that the oshkaabewisag have gleaned since they left their teachers. Master to apprentice, new master to new apprentice down the ages, that is how knowledge is kept from one generation to the next and how it grows within the culture. The taking of apprentices, their education and empowerment, is a duty a mashkikiiwikwe /mashkikiiwinini owes both to their own teachers and to the knowledge itself, so that the Anishinaabeg may retain what they have gathered over thousands of years in this land. The knowledge with which one is gifted during one's years of training is precious, but it must also be augmented with what one gathers along the way. Without growth, all things die. Knowledge that stagnates soon dies, drying up like a mud puddle in the sun or silted over like a stream with too slow a flow.

The oshkaabewisag, once they are on their own, acquire knowledge by working with the plants, making and administering medicines, observing the effectiveness of different medicines, and by the continual adjustments necessary to maintain the health of those for whom they are responsible and the harmony from which comes all health and well being of the individual, the group, the Anishinaabeg, and ultimately all of creation. In time, the oshkaabewisag, too, take on helpers, teaching them in payment for their physical, mental, and spiritual help.

In the actual teaching, when such knowledge is passed from one person, one generation, to the next, the stories that one has gathered along with the plants must also be taught, for story is one of our most powerful methods of storing knowledge. Because of that, the stories in Anishinaabe culture are the documentation of the validity of what one has to say. No one will believe a medicine person who cannot offer a personal story about the making and administering of a particular plant cure, about the effectiveness of that medicinal cure. If such a person has no first-hand experience of the cure, the story of his or her own teacher, ancestral teachers, or a close personal acquaintance, would be the next best thing. But the testimony of personal experience is always best and is given more credence. What non-native science and medicine dismisses as "anecdotal," and therefore "suspect," is in the Anishinaabe way the highest possible degree of credible information. It is like hearing about a land one has not seen for oneself: we take the word of someone who has been there, who has seen the lay of the country and can talk about the dangers or delights of the place. Personal experience is just valued more than so-called "objective" or "depersonalized" testimony. To us, source is all.

Our stories of those cures are therefore heavier on the family-type stories than Nodjimahkwe's stories were, because she was a practicing community doctor for her village, often the only medicinal help available to her tribal members at the time. So, when reading these stories that I include, as per Anishinaabe tradition, in this account, readers will hear about the time goldthread helped my little daughter to swallow food after a long illness, and the time equisetum and boneset mended my husband's broken leg. These stories are necessary in our way; they tell the reader that I have actually used the medicines I was taught to use and what I learned by such usage. One learns something. One utilizes that knowledge, and one then has more knowledge to pass on to another person. Anishinaabe knowledge grows like crystals in rock. The process is slow, and it is beautiful. And sometimes it grows into gems of treasure.

In the actual writing of this book, I have presented one plant at a time. This is the way I was taught, and the way Kee was taught, too. I try to cover the plant's physical characteristics, something of where one can expect to find it in the wild, and also as much as possible about the plant's life with the Anishinaabeg. Names are very important to the Anishinaabe worldview, so I give English common names, scientific names for identification purposes, and at least one Anishinaabe name, if available, for the plant. I also tell as many of the stories of the plant as I was taught or that I have found in my own studies, because story is such an important aspect of Anishinaabe culture. Story to us is a living being. It is said that stories existed before even our world was created. It is one of the differences in worldview between Anishinaabe culture and non-native mainstream culture. I will explain more about the vital importance of story in the teaching of ethnobotany later in the text.

In writing, I have also used published, non-native sources, especially for identification purposes. Keewaydinoquay always emphasized that in ethnobotany there is no room for a mistake because "dead is dead, and there is no degree of 'deadness.'" One must be sure of identification of plants to use them safely. When I was learning, I had Kee. She showed me the plants in classroom settings, using published books for identification, photographic slides in classroom lectures, or actual plant specimens in the ethnobotany lab. Or, she took me and the rest of her students on plant walks around the university campus or on her island in Lake Michigan. I had her instruction for years, but the readers of this book may not have that advantage of one-on-one instruction. To try to fill the gap, I have used printed and online non-native texts to try to give readers the fundamentals for identification that they will need to actually experience the plants about whom[4] I write. Line drawings are also provided, to give readers an idea of the typical growth pattern of these plants and help them with their identification. However, it is a very poor substitute for having someone show a person the plants. I would encourage anyone who actually wants to use the information in this book to acquire several of the readily available field guides to plants, or to get acquainted with online sources such as the U.S. Department of Agriculture's Plant Database.[5] Where possible I have also quoted plant experts and medical experts on possible complications that may arise from the use of the plants. In my classes, I always stress the fact that plants contain real, physical chemicals that actually do affect the body. I always urge my students to check with their own physicians if they are going to ingest the plants and to get used to using up-to-date professional databases for the latest scientific discoveries on the effects of the use of plants, especially if there is proof that the use of a plant may change or counter the effectiveness of a prescribed medicine.

I have also used non-native sources to alert readers to environmental issues, such as pollution, of which anyone wishing to utilize plants in our modern world must be aware. The world has changed, and so must we if we are to be able to continue to achieve the benefits of balance, health, and long life. Achieving *Anishinaabe-bimaadiziwin,* which Keewaydinoquay always called "Life in the Fullest Sense," was the reason my teacher said that she taught the ancestral usages of plants. She thought it was a marvelous way to help people achieve and live the fullest, happiest, best life possible now as it has always been for the People.[6] The plants have so much help to give us.

To help facilitate the actual usage of the plants described in the book, I have included a Recipes section with information that

4 Plants are alive and cognizant beings in Anishinaabe culture; that mindset occasionally affects my use of the English language.

5 The database, available at http://plants.usda.gov, is an excellent source for identification of plants. It can be searched by common or by scientific name of the plants. eFlora's Flora of North America project is also very helpful: http://www.efloras.org.

6 Kee used "the People" in reference to humankind and/or the Anishinaabeg.

a person wishing to utilize the virtues that the plants have to share with us might need. I have included recipes for foods and medicines. Keewaydinoquay always said that there was nothing like actually getting one's hands on the plants to really learn them. She was a firm believer in using all of the senses to acquire and to fix the knowledge thus acquired, so that a person would actually utilize it in their lives. Once one has tasted cedar tea, mixed kinnikinnick, made a skin cream or lip balm, one then knows the plants involved on a much deeper and more intimate level than if one limits one's exposure to the material by simply reading about it.

Ode'imini-giizis 2014

Invocation

This is the song Keewaydinoquay taught me to sing, as a way of showing respect, before I told a story that I suspected was an Aadizookaan—a story that is considered a cognizant being and that knows when it is being told.

> Hey oh way
> I tell a story,
> A story from the Ancient Ones
> Hey oh way
> I place Asemaa for their
> spirits
> Hey oh way
> I tell a story.
> Listen! And Learn!

A Note on Botanical Usage

This is not a medical text. Readers should not use the instructions in this book in place of modern medicine. The author does not hold a medical degree, and she wants all readers to know that she cannot, nor has she ever undertaken to, diagnose an illness or treat anyone but her immediate family. She would never tell anyone not to use modern medicine, nor would Keewaydinoquay, whose traditional Anishinaabe medicinal teachings are shared in this text, have told anyone that either. Keewaydinoquay said, "When you are ill, use any and all means available to get well." She used modern MD doctors as well as chiropractors, massage therapists, dentists, and so on. The authoress often had to make her appointments with such professionals, and even drove her to some of those appointments. Keewaydinoquay did not set herself up as a physician.

The teachings in this book are not sacred, secret, or Midewiwin teachings. Keewaydinoquay always said that even in her childhood, in the early twentieth century, every Ojibwe grandmother knew these things. This book is filled with teachings that would best be described as "over the counter type" cures.

As is explained in this book, according to Anishinaabe culture, before taking anything from the natural world one must remember to give thanks to the being who is asked to make the sacrifice and ask that being's permission. Therefore, before using any of the instructions in this book or before picking any botanical material, one should make an offering of asemaa, sacred tobacco or kinnikinnick.

1

Traditional Anishinaabe Teaching about Plants

"The Year the Roses Died"

~~~~~~

Gichi-mewinzha gii-oshki-niiging akiing, a very long time ago, when the earth was new, there was a horrible year that was remembered as "The Year the Roses Died." In that long-ago time a large number of animals depended on the roses for their food. But that spring there were no roses, not on the wide prairie, not in the mountain meadows nor in the most hidden forest glade. The roses were gone. When the animals realized the roses were really not going to grow that spring, there was a great outcry and a call for a council meeting to determine what had happened and, most important, "who did it?"

The *waawaashkeshiwag,* the deer, lowering their antlered heads with great dignity, said that they knew it was the *bineshiinyag,* the little birds, who were responsible, because they had seen them eating the flowers.

The bineshiinyag flew to a branch in the middle of the clearing and chirped, "We may have eaten a few flowers, but it was really the *aamoog,* the bees, who were responsible, because they ate the pollen."

The aamoog buzzed angrily. "We did taste a little of the pollen but it is really the *memengwaag,* the butterflies, who are responsible, because they left their eggs on the roses, and their caterpillars hatched and ate all of the leaves."

The memengwaag flitted. "We had to have some nursery for our children, and they were hungry when they were born, but it was really the waawaashkeshiwag who ate the stems."

The waawaashkeshiwag said, "We ate a few of the stems, but it was *Waabooz,* Rabbit, who dug up and ate the roots."

All of the animals turned and looked at Waabooz, and then they all jumped him. They grabbed his tail and broke it off, and that is the reason why to this day *waaboozoog,* rabbits, have such tiny tails. Then *Ma'iingan,* Wolf, grabbed one ear, and *Ma'iinganens,* Coyote, grabbed the other. *Esiban,* Raccoon, grabbed one of his back legs, and *Ginebig,* Snake, wrapped his long body around the other. And they pulled and they pulled while Waabooz howled. That is the reason why to this day his ears are so long and his legs are so stretched out.

They probably would have killed Waabooz, but *Makwa,* Black Bear, rose up on his hind legs, swaying side to side, and growled, "All right! Drop the waabooz! I don't like him much either, but Creator must have had some purpose for him, or Creator wouldn't have bothered creating him."

Just then the *Manidoo,* Spirit, whose job it was to watch over that place, rose up and said, "What seems to be the problem?"

"Well," said Makwa, softening his growl to show respect, "you see, Your Honor, it has been determined that Waabooz is responsible for the disappearance of the roses."

The Manidoo said, "Killing the Waabooz will not bring back the roses. You all noticed that the roses were in trouble, and you all decided to take your own shares even if it meant killing the roses forever. There is no honor in this. This is not keeping creation in balance as you were told to do in the Beginning Time."

All the animals hung their heads because they knew that the Manidoo was right.

"Well," said the Manidoo. "I will bring the roses back, but this time I am going to give them protection so you won't be tempted to eat them up entirely again. And I am also going to leave Waabooz as he is so that you will always be reminded of the disgrace of forgetting the balance."

So now, when we see the thorns on the roses and the poor misshaped waabooz, we are reminded of the Year the Roses Died.

Mii iw, Miigwech, That's it, thank you.

The Primacy of Plants

The story of "The Year the Roses Died" embodies the teaching of the place of plants in the order of life on *Gidakiiminaan,* our Earth, whom we call *Ninga,* "my own mother." We are told that humankind was the last created, the youngest, and therefore the most dependent of all the different forms of life. This is really no different from what non-native science teaches. Plants are the source of life on this planet. Without plants, the rocks would not break down into soil. Without plants to take the sunlight into their own bodies and by the use of chlorophyll trap the light of the sun into a usable form of energy, no animal life could survive. Plants take in carbon dioxide and make oxygen for all animals to breathe. If plants are not here, neither are we. We are all in this life together and to survive we must all survive.

The Anishinaabeg have always believed that the ultimate good is a bountiful land that could and would supply all that humankind needs to sustain life. This planet of ours has four orders of life. The first created, the elder brothers[1] are the Earth forces: the minerals, the rocks, the wind and the rain and the snow and the thunder beings and all of the rest of the beings we refer to as weather, and the *Aadizookaanag,* the Grandfathers and Grandmothers, our ceremonies, songs, and traditional stories. The second created, the second brothers, are the plants: the trees, the greeners and the non-greeners. The third created are the nonhuman animals, the four-leggeds, the flyers, the creepers and the crawlers and those who swim. The fourth created, the youngest brothers, and therefore the most vulnerable, are human beings. All four orders of life are interconnected. None can survive without the others except for those of the first order, and if they had to survive alone they would not be happy because they could not do as Creator directed everyone to do in the Beginning Time. They could not take care to see that all of life continued as Creator had intended.

This philosophy sees humankind as the weakest because they alone need all three of the other orders of life to survive at all. Humans are not at the top of the order of creation. Humans are not the lords of this earth. We are at the bottom because we are the most dependent.

Modern society does not think much about the other orders of life. Perhaps that started to happen when we no longer had to hunt for our meat and till the soil for our vegetables and grains. When we removed ourselves from the lives of our ancestors and found other ways, more artificial ways of being, we could begin to disregard the harmony that has sustained us this far. Safe in cities, getting our meat in cellophane-wrapped packages in the supermarket and our fruit and vegetables and our grains in paper bags, we could forget about our elder brothers the animals and the plants. But we forget them to our peril, for we cannot survive without them. Only the rocks and the thunder beings and those other life-forms of the first created order can survive alone. We are the babies of this family of ours. We are the weakest because we are the most dependent. We should remember that more often, or the time will come when the rocks and the thunderers will be grieving and here on this beautiful planet all by themselves.

[1] For "brothers," read "brothers and sisters." Language changes constantly. When I was a child learning English, we understood that the name of our species was "man." It did not imply that only males were meant. It meant that our kind of animal was called "man," and that it included both male and female. Personally, I resist attempts to change the language for the political interests of one particular group or another. I miss the female part of our language that is being eliminated by well meaning folk who think that by calling a woman who writes poetry a "poet" instead of a "poetess" we will somehow eliminate the very real discrimination against women that exists in our time. If I thought that women would be instantly granted full citizenship and economic rights if I stopped saying "shepherdess," "inheritrix," or "seamstress," I would of course do so. I just do not think the problems we face are that simple. To destroy the female parts of the language to hasten an undefined political end just seems dumb to me. I also think it is a smokescreen to keep women from demanding change. In my time I have seen brilliant women spend their life's energy trying to have the Bible rewritten into gender-neutral language, when they could have been working on the social conditions that affect women. This problem is one of English, not our Anishinaabe language. In *Anishinaabemowin,* the Ojibwe language, there is no "he" or "she." The third person singular is both male and female. The person speaking and the person listening are supposed to be smart enough to know which is implied. Further, in Anishinaabemowin, the *Manidoog,* spirits, are neither and both male and female.

We are all in this together. For one part of creation to survive it must all survive. I have nightmares about the glaciers melting in Alaska and the permafrost in the Northwest Territories. How different our fates would be if those who now have the power on Turtle Island knew and believed the legends. Sometimes I wonder where the people who have the power expect to go if they succeed in destroying this land? Do they think they will just find another place to pillage the way their ancestors found the Americas? They might be in for a shock if they intend migrating to Mars or even further. They might read about the scientific experiments that were worked on the international space station. One experiment told about salamanders who were born and grown in space. There was something wrong with their nervous system. Some scientists speculate that the salamanders were somehow affected because they were cut off from the electrical pulses that the Earth gives off. Removed from here they did not make it elsewhere. We are all children of this same Great Mother. As Kee always said, "Blessings and balance. Balance and blessings, for from balance comes all blessings."

I know for myself, in my own life, all of the Anishinaabe lessons on the interconnectedness of all things goes beyond vague ecological fears and/or popular sentiments. I know from pure personal observations over the past half century and more that my personal actions have repercussions in my own life as well as in the lives of those around me. I know that if I kick someone in a fit of temper at noon, I can expect to be kicked myself. And the kick that I get back will come quickly, and it will not be in proportion to the kick I dealt. I will be lucky if the kick I get does not break my leg, and I usually get it before the sun goes down. I also know that my own health and the health of those I love are intimately connected to my actions. I do not just mean that if I do not feed my family enough vegetables they will get more colds. I mean that my respect for power, traditions, and ceremonies, or my lack thereof, will result in the health and the "luck" of me and mine. This has been brought home to me most forcefully in regard to my own health. Once I participated in a ceremony that I was worried was not being performed properly. Within hours I had pneumonia, and it became double pneumonia before I put two and two together and made amends. My health problems occurred even though the "fault" and/or misdeeds of the people involved were in no way my doing. I am sure that I have often simply stepped in all innocence into the disharmony created by others. I am always, however, grateful to take the harm on myself because I have my daughters and my husband and many other people whom I love. If harm is to come to one of us I am glad if it comes to me and not them. Our old ways tell us that health is directly connected to the harmony of creation. One does not always gather only what one personally sows. Sometimes we gather what others around us have planted and nurtured. Innocence is not protection!

This worldview that tells me I can get sick because someone else creates disharmony by lack of respect for power is not the worldview of the greater society. It does, however, come close to the branch of physics called quantum mechanics. My favorite quote about that discipline says, "If anyone tells you they understand quantum mechanics, they are lying." Periodically I try to understand it myself, even though there was a definite lack of non-native mathematics and sciences in my education. The part of it that I find similar to our *Anishinaabe-inendamowin*, Anishinaabe mindset or worldview, is the experiments on subatomic particles that seem to suggest that the attitude of the researchers can have a direct effect on the subatomic particles that they are studying. If they measure them, the particles will react in the way the researchers are expecting them to. It seems that the very act of observing the particles has a direct result on their actions. "If you build it he will come." "If you measure it, it will do what you are expecting it to do." It might be a stretch, but to me it tends toward our Anishinaabe view of reality that the actions and even the thoughts of the person can "change" reality, and not just the reality of the person doing the thinking or the acting. *It can change all reality.*[2]

All of the above taken together means for me that reality is not concrete. It is fluid. And that fluidity is influenced by personal actions, words, and thoughts. Ripples go out from our deeds and our words, spoken or unspoken. What we do, even what we think, changes what happens. It changes reality for everyone. No wonder we are in such a mess. If all that is true, I guess we are pretty lucky to still be treading water in the world. It does behoove one, however, to be eternally thankful to Those Who Protect Us. Without Them? . . . It is not even to be imagined!

2 Kee often made the comparison between Anishinaabe philosophy and subatomic particles in her lectures.

How Do We Know This? or the Descent of Our Knowledge

When reading this account of the ethnobotany of the Anishi-naabeg it may occur to the reader to ask, "How do these people know this stuff?" Some of the information has been in the literature of plants since Early Contact Days with Europeans, but much of it is not in the literature at all. Some of it is hinted at in dusty ethnology reports in the basements of research libraries, but the rest of the information simply is not reported in the professional literature at all.

So where did the authoress get all of this? I got all of the information contained in these pages, with the exceptions that are clearly marked with footnote citations, from Keewaydinoquay. I am not proud of my ignorance, but when I came to Kee I knew one plant, a dandelion, and then I was only sure of that identification if the plant was in bloom and growing on my front lawn. Other than that I was a clean slate that Kee wrote upon at her leisure. And where did Kee get her knowledge? She was apprenticed in the old way to Nodjimahkwe of Cathead Point Village, Leelanau Peninsula, Michigan, circa 1920s, an old and honored Anishinaabe mashkikiiwikwe, when Kee was nine years of age. She continued to work with and for her mashkikiiwikwe until Nodjimahkwe's death.

So, where did Nodjimahkwe get her information? Kee was present in Nodjimahkwe's kitchen in the late 1920s or early 1930s, when a researcher who said he was from the Smithsonian Institution interviewed Nodjimahkwe and was given the descent of her knowledge. In the old days an apprentice learned to recite the names of her teacher's teacher's teachers, and Nodjimahkwe could recite hers, and mine, back four hundredyears. Kee said she had always meant to commit the list to memory, but she never did. She always thought she had the time to do it later, until Nodjimahkwe died. But Kee always took comfort in the fact that she thought the list was safe in the keeping of the Smithsonian Institution.

Any way I look at this, it spells a very old tradition. Kee always said that the real value of our medicinal knowledge was the fact that it had been tried and tested on human subjects, not rats, and that it had been gathered and retained for thousands of years. Indians are nothing if not a pragmatic people. They do not keep what is not valuable. To have retained and kept and utilized knowledge for that long a time, it stands to reason that the People down through the ages thought it valuable because it was effective in making their lives and the lives of their children easier.

But where did the *Gete-Anishinaabeg,* the Old-time Indians, get the information that they passed along in this manner? There is a lot of academic speculation on that question. I can say absolutely, however, that it was not gathered by the use of what is called The Doctrine of Signatures. That is a European idea and concept that says that people learned medicine knowledge by observing the shape of plants and deciding by such observation that a certain plant or part of a plant would cure a certain part of the human body because the shape of the plant's leaf or root, etc. was similar in shape to that corresponding part of the person. The Doctrine of Signatures says God put a "signature" or "writing" or "clue" to the benefit of a certain plant within the growing structure of that plant that a person could read as if it were written in a book. This is a doctrine that Medieval and Renaissance Europeans believed in, and it is perpetuated down to the present day in the herbals that those early botanists wrote.

But that is not how the Anishinaabeg learned this medicinal knowledge. Kee always said that if one followed that doctrine in our land they would soon graze themselves into an early grave. She said if a person believed that and simply turned their apprentices loose to go try out the plants in the forest, they would very quickly be in need of a new batch of apprentices. A single bite of Water-Hemlock, *Cicuta maculata,* will kill. The mushrooms called Destroying Angel, *Amanita virosa,* and Death Cap, *Amanita phalloides,* both would kill with great effectiveness if a person just ate them willy-nilly. Kee always said, "There is no place in ethnobotany for a mistake. Dead is dead, and there is no degree of 'deadness.'" One has to know what plant one is taking to use as medicine or as food. To just go merrily along trusting to the idea that one will know a poison by the way that it looks would be to invite disaster.

So if our people did not use the Doctrine of Signature to decide which plants would cure what human ills, how did they know? How did they accumulate this knowledge to pass it along for their descendants to follow? I was taught that there is both a spiritual aspect of this kind of discovery and a practical, physical part of it, too. One is a spiritual idea and one is a physical idea. The spiritual idea is that the mashkikiiwininiwag and the mashkikiiwikwewag of old were gifted with this knowledge by direct spirit gift when they were told these things in their dreams and in vision. Do I believe that? Of course I do. Once one has had vision one believes in it absolutely. But was that the only way or the final way that the plants were known to be effective? No! One gets the idea in vision or dream, but one then tests the knowledge. In the old days it was considered a fine and brave thing to be the one to offer to test such knowledge for the good of all of the People. Often old people would offer themselves as human subjects to test the particular plant or medicine. Now Anishinaabeg are practical people. If a plant killed Grandfather, of course, one did not also then feed it to the new babe. And this accumulated medicinal knowledge was tested and retested on human beings probably for millennia. Absolutely none of the modern, scientifically discovered, tested, and approved medicinals can say the same.

So how was this knowledge kept after it was gathered in this method? It was kept by means of the master–apprentice model of education, where a trained and practicing medicine person would take an oshkaabewis who was gifted with the knowledge bit by bit in return for their help in the gathering and preparing of medicines and in the physical cures of the patients. One can think of it as very similar to the modern way of teaching medical doctors who work as residents in hospitals after a period of instruction to learn the practical and finer parts of their craft from other professionals. This master–apprenticeship model was, in some parts of Anishinaabe country, directed and controlled by the Midewiwin. One could think of the Midewiwin as corresponding to the accreditation program of the American Medical Association.[3]

3 The Midewiwin is concerned with the spiritual and mental health of the People as well as their physical well-being, or as we would say, it is concerned with the total health of the patient and the People and Creation.

This knowledge was also encoded and preserved in our Aadizookaanag. Our Aadizookaanag are our "Library of Alexandria," our "Library of Congress," the repository of our oldest and most valuable knowledges, encoded and transmitted to us in easily remembered forms that Their knowledge and wisdom may be kept by all of the People for the benefit of the People down through the centuries and for centuries into the future.

Talking to Plants

It is not an easy task to put all of the philosophy, mindset, and worldview of a people into a few words, let alone to do so on behalf of a whole people. Nevertheless, I must try to describe enough of Anishinaabe-inendamowin for my readers to understand the place of the blessed plants in the universe as our people traditionally thought about them.

All things created are alive. Some of the things created by humans are combinations of many beings. But the beings whom Creator made are all alive. They are different life-forms. They reproduce and grow differently than humans. They talk differently than humans. They Pass Over[4] differently than humans. Rocks are a good example. Their life span is so very much longer than ours; it is no wonder we are such different beings. The rocks are the bones of our Mother the Earth. Their language and ways of being are very much different from ours. I often think about how the rocks must view us. We are so temporary in this world. Our whole lifetimes are so short compared to that of a rock. Do they even know we are here unless we talk to them? Are we just a momentary buzzing in the perception of something that has existed for so many, many eons? How does a rock multiply? One can think about it as rock-sex. They do break apart and come together again to create more of their kind. One can begin to understand that by watching, really watching, a lake. Watching and truly seeing the world around us might help us realize that we have a purpose in the world, too. And it might help us realize how much harm humans can do to the balance when they see themselves as the only beings on this planet. Kee spoke of the rocks' teaching that was given one Summer Solstice to the People. The rocks said, "You humans are so very slow to learn!"

Creator created balance in the beginning. There is not much interest in Anishinaabe-inendamowin in the nature of Creator. It just does not matter much to the Anishinaabeg what Creator is, whether male of female or both or neither. The People just did not think it necessary to explain Creator. What is necessary is to acknowledge Creator and the idea of balance that Creator wove into the fabric of our universe.

All the parts of creation have special jobs. Each species has special jobs. Each individual has special jobs. All of the different orders of life, all of the different species, and individuals have both a physical and a spiritual purpose. And all of the jobs are necessary if the whole of creation is to be kept in balance.

The plants always know their place in the cycle of life. They are always willing to serve their fellow beings, for we are all brothers and sisters in the cycle together. The plants are closer than we to Creator because they were created before mankind. They are willing to give themselves to maintain the harmony, but they are owed the honor of being *asked* for their sacrifice.

Whenever it is necessary to change the balance as we find it, we have to talk to the individuals involved to get their consent to the change. We have to talk to the rocks if we want to crush them into gravel to make our walkway. We have to ask the earth if we

[4] Passing Over is the traditional way of speaking about death. Kee always said, "There is no death. There is just a change of form."

want to place our home in a certain place. We have to talk to the plants if we want to obtain their help in the healing of ourselves or of another being.

In the beginning one might feel silly talking to a plant. But one will soon get used to the idea. It will even get to be fun. Nodjimahkwe said that the trick is just to think about the plants or the individual rocks or the individual animals as the other "persons" that they are.

When one accepts the gift of the plant one is asking that plant to become him or her. Speak to the plant and tell it who needs it. Ask before taking. Promise that the plant's grandchildren will live after it and that you will protect them in that place. To fulfill this promise, one must know how that plant reproduces. Never take the only individual plant of its kind in an area, for the plant is trying to establish itself there. If one feels that one does not have a choice, that a death will occur if one does not take that plant, then one is morally obliged to see to it that the plant is reintroduced and protected in the spot from which one took it. But, usually, if there is one plant in an area there will be others, too. Just look and make sure before taking the plant; then you will know how much you personally owe to that plant. It is always wise to know the price before one incurs the debt.

One time Kee was spending the winter alone on *Minis-kit-igaan*, Garden Island, in the middle of Lake Michigan. As luck would have it, she slipped and broke her leg. As she had no means of calling the mainland for help, she had to set the leg herself. She had some dried boneset (*Eupatorium perfoliatum*) in her cabin, so she made it into tea, and she drank all of it. Then as soon as she could get around again on a crutch, she stripped the island of growing boneset. At the time she felt she had no choice but to take all of the boneset she could find, because she had to heal the leg if she was to get by until she could get medical help. But after that she spent the rest of her life purposely sowing boneset all over the island. Her friends and students who heard that story would send her envelopes full of boneset seed, which she would lovingly take out to her island and sow in spots she thought boneset would like. In her need she took the boneset, but she well repaid her debt.

When taking a plant be sure to ask for both a spiritual as well as a physical healing for oneself or one's patient. Nodjimahkwe said the reason people would go to "The House of Many Windows," the hospital, and come back seeming to be cured, only to just get sick again, was because the healer had only worried about the physical and not the spiritual healing of the person. The plants have both spiritual and physical healing to offer. It is just necessary to ask for the help they can give. Talking to a plant is valuable because it will make one feel connected to the plant, to the cycle, and to the balance. If one feels connected, one's patient will feel connected, too.

Really talk to the plant. In the fall, after the seeds fall, if one wants to take a catnip plant (*Nepeta cataria*), one should explain why, in the way one would explain if one wanted another human being to give blood to save a loved one. Say, "Little Catnip Plant, will you please give your being and your life for the well-being and the life of the children of my family?" It is considered better if one can tell the plants which person they will be making well. One could say, "Little Catnip Plant, will you please send your spirit along for the healing of my little daughter, Makoons?" Then one gives the plant *asemaa*, tobacco (Real Indian Tobacco is *Nicotiana rustica*) or kinnikinnick[5] to honor it[6] and says, "I promise not to take so much of you that you will not continue in this spot. Your grandchildren will live after you." Once one has asked one can usually proceed to collect the material one needs with the confidence that the plant people will send their spirits along to heal both the patient's physical and spiritual being.

Still, one has to be prepared for the possibility that when one asks permission to harvest a particular plant the answer may be "no." One time a student of Keewaydinoquay wanted to pick a plant when they were out gathering together. He made the offering as he had been instructed to do, and he asked the plant to please come along to make a tea. But while he was talking to the plant a bee flew out of the flower and dropped dead at his feet. He ran back to Kee visibly shaken and asked her what it meant. She went back with him to see the plant herself. When she saw the plant, she told him that he had been attempting to pick the wrong plant. The one he had been intending to take as a healing tea was a deadly poison. The student was instructed to put down more kinnikinnick to thank both the plant for its warning and the bee for the sacrifice of its life to preserve his.

Another time Kee asked the cattails if she could have some of them as she wanted to weave a mat to show her students how Anishinaabeg wove cattails in the traditional society. Each step she took into the "shallow" water where the cattails were growing became deeper. The waves went wild. The cattails got slippery,

5 Kinnikinnick or kinnick is a mixture of native plants that are used in prayer as an offering to spirit. A longer explanation for making kinnick is offered in the chapter on bearberry and in the recipes section.

6 The reader will find references to individual plants using "it" throughout this book. The decision to use this pronoun was a difficult one to make, as English speakers often assume "it" is used only in reference to inanimate objects. In Anishinaabe belief, the plants referred to here as "it" are considered animate, cognizant beings.

until they slipped right out of her hands. Then the whole plants started to lay themselves flat down into the water. Kee decided to get out of there, and it was not a moment too soon. Before she got back to dry land, the waves were almost over her head. She realized that she had asked, but the answer had been "No!"

Indigenous or Imported?

I was once in an ethnobotany class being taught by a Euro-American who thought he understood the Great Lakes Anishi-naabe mindset and culture enough to teach a university class on the plants used by our indigenous peoples of this area. To show the class the plants, he took us on a field trip to an overgrown area near campus, between the railroad tracks and the Milwaukee River.

As we were walking along, taking notes about the plants as he pointed them out and lectured us, one of the kids in the class said, "Hey! Isn't that a daylily (*Hemerocallis fulva* and *Hemerocallis flava*)? Can't you eat daylilies?"

The teacher replied, "Yes. It is a daylily, but I wouldn't touch it. It is an introduced plant. It isn't indigenous to North America." And with a sniff he lead the class on down the trail.

I stopped and looked around. Every white kid had dutifully followed the Euro-American teacher down the path while every Indian kid in the class hung back, dropped to their knees, and were digging the daylily bulbs out of the sandy soil with their fingers, pens, and/or pocket knives. The bulbs disappeared into numerous backpacks and the smiling Indian students ran to catch up with the group. I all but laughed myself sick.

That was the difference for me, right there. The Euro-American sniffs and says "Not real Indian," and the real Indians were taking home supper and enough bulbs to plant in their backyards, too. Indian folk are pragmatic. Intellectual games, like distinguishing which are "real Indian" herbs and which are plants introduced to this continent in the past five hundred years, are simply not as important as obtaining food.

Birch is a circumboreal plant with many species. It grows all across Northern Europe and across Russia to the Pacific. Because of the fact that it grows in Europe and Asia, an attempt has even been made to say that it is an introduced plant in North American.[7] That idea would be laughable if it was not character-istic of the way North American Indian ethnobotany has been

7 While I was working for Kee, she was given a Ph.D dissertation to read that tried to make the point that birch trees are not indigenous to North America. She loved it. She thought it was a great joke. She said, "I suppose the Europeans taught us to make birch bark canoes and birch bark wigwams and birch bark baskets, too."

traditionally treated by European academics. One wonders if they are even aware of why it is that they insist that every useful plant, every worthwhile thing in their ken, really originated in their own homelands in Europe.

I myself am an immigrant. I was born and lived as a child in Canada. I know the temptation to remember the homeland as a better place than the land one is living in here. I know how for years one can never quite give up the idea of going home again. With my family, it was tea that we missed and memorialized. Tea just did not taste the same in Wisconsin. Part of that was the water. The water in Wisconsin is harder and does taste different than it did in my home in Canada. The tea itself was different, too. For years one could only buy Lipton, a far inferior tea to the fine imported English teas of my childhood. Every time we would go home again we would fill our suitcases with tea bags to take back to Wisconsin. To this day my family in Canada sends me tea at Christmastime. It is a part of "home" I cherish.

This same "pining for the homeland" is, I am convinced, the reason that European academics have for generations insisted that all of the useful plants were brought here either intentionally or unintentionally by the European settlers of North America. Kee would always laugh and say, "Ya, this whole continent must have been just solid rock, not a plant in sight, before the Europeans came here. It must have been a pretty empty, sad place all right. Not a leaf. Not a blade of grass. Not a tree."

In actuality many of the plants that are common in North America are simply also common in Europe and Asia. This last wave of immigration from the "Old World" in the last five hundred years since the European invasion of the Americas is not the only time new peoples have come onto Turtle Island.[8] And people from the Americas have gone the other way, too. The native peoples of Alaska still visit their family members who are only a short boat trip across the Arctic waters in Siberia. Since people have gone back and forth for millennia, the plants must have done the same. Whenever medicine people move they make sure the plants they are going to need come with them.

Indian people and the rest of the twenty-first-century inhabitants of this continent have to deal with twenty-first-century North America. We have to deal now with the land as it is. It would be helpful if the people who have the power in the land now stopped bringing in other foreign species,[9] but if they cannot or will not, we still have to deal with what comes here. It would

8 Turtle Island is North America. After the Great Flood, the world was recreated by our Great Uncle Naanabozho from a paw full of mud that was brought to him from the depths by the muskrat. Naanabozho placed the mud on top of a great, grandfather turtle, and he caused it to grow into our world. The Great Turtle is still holding the world up, but if he tires another turtle swims underneath him, lifting him up, helping him to hold up our Turtle Island.

9 I think that the worst thing the non-natives have intentionally brought here is the Japanese ladybug. It was purposely brought here in the 1970s to be sold to organic gardeners with the understanding that it would kill bugs in gardens without the use of pesticides. Those ladybugs did do that, but they also bite people. I remember the time when little children loved ladybugs. They were pretty, and they were harmless, and one could sing a little nursery rhyme to them to get a wish. Now ladybugs are the enemy.

10 Virginia A. Smith, "Fruit of the vine: Kudzu extract may help binge drinkers cut consumption in half, study hints," *Milwaukee Journal Sentinel,* 18 May 2005, 3A.

11 For more information on the array of uses of kudzu, see Foster and Duke, 192.

12 Emerson, *Fortune of the Republic.* Quoted in *Oxford Dictionary of Quotations,* 207.

help, though, if everyone adopted a more indigenous philosophy about plants and started to utilize the virtues that different plants have to share with us. If the people in the South started to eat the kudzu (*Pueraria montana* var. *lobata*) the way people in parts of Asia do, or weave it into baskets, or use this plant in any of the array of possible uses for it, they would not have to spend money on huge eradication projects. McLean Hospital, in affiliation with Harvard, released a study that says that if an extract of the roots of kudzu is given to binge drinkers for as little as one week it reduces their beer consumption by one half, totally without side effects.[10] Surely there are enough binge drinkers in the South to eradicate the kudzu in a very short time if they started to use it the way it has been used in Chinese medicine for hundreds of years.[11]

If the people in the Midwest started to utilize purple loosestrife (*Lythrum salicaria*), they would find it is useful as an emergency food, that it can be made into a recreational alcoholic drink, that it will tighten skin to counteract wrinkles, and that it can be used to give a sheen to blond hair. It also brightens and soothes eyes, making them less puffy. It is an intestinal disinfectant that is helpful in treating diarrhea and food poisoning. It has a number of other potentially vital medicine applications (Bremness, 186). If all of that were commonly known, there would be a run on purple loosestrife that would soon root out the last of the plants that now are threatening to displace many of the native, wetland species. If one uses a "weed," it is not a problem.

Ralph Waldo Emerson said, "What is a weed? A plant whose virtues have not been discovered."[12] Personally I think a "weed" is a plant growing where the ignorant do not want it to grow.

The Use of Story in Ethnobotany

While writing up these ethnobotany notes and trying to record the information that was so freely given by my own teacher, Keewaydinoquay, and by my ancestral teachers through her instruction, I have thought about the place of Story in the teaching of this knowledge. I have gone back and forth on it, as I believe my teacher also did, trying to get the right balance of Story to other information.

When Kee was teaching at the University of Wisconsin–Milwaukee, she dearly loved to include the specific stories that had traditionally been told about specific plants that she was presenting to her students. She often bewailed the fact that she had so little time in a semester course to give her students all that she thought they should have to keep themselves and their future families in health as well as to preserve the knowledge for the future, what she always called "The ongoing of the People." Some semesters she told one story and some she told others. And usually she had to abridge the stories for the sake of an hourlong class in which she also had to lecture on the medicinal and other virtues that the plants have to share.

"I wish I could tell this one properly," she would say. "But this is supposed to be a botany class and not a folklore class." Then she would shrug and tell the story she wanted to tell anyway. She just thought that the stories were simply too important to leave unshared even if it meant abridging the much-abused syllabus yet again.

Because I worked for her for a number of years[13] I was able to hear the different stories, some told only once, some offered every semester. I quickly caught on that I was in a unique position and took careful note, especially of the stories that Kee thought essential to the teaching of a particular plant.

Now, as I sit to write down those stories, I am faced with Kee's dilemma again. How much to share? How many stories to include? Which ones to tell in outline form for brevity's sake and which ones to put into as complete a form as I am capable of rendering?

And, since I started working with Kee and in the years that have passed since that instruction, I have accumulated more and more stories. What do I do with them?

I was pondering this recently, and I had a dream. Dreams, of course, are most important in our way of being. They often bring insights that we struggle with in waking life. They are direct contact with our Helpers, the Grandmothers and Grandfathers, our contacts with Other-than-Human Power. Once one has been trained to trust one's dreams, one often finds them very, very helpful in life's quandaries.

In the dream of which I speak, I was working on cattails. I was in my office at my computer, trying to write about all of the things Kee had told me about them. The room was full of cattails. They were growing all around me as I sat at my keyboard. I was trying to decide if I should include the Naanabozho story of the "Dancing Cattails." Kee had not told me that story in

[13] I was her teaching assistant and lab assistant for both the ethnobotany and the philosophy courses, teaching discussion groups and lab sessions in our ethnobotany lab.

14 Roger Thomas was a Bad River Ojibwe and a Ph.D candidate in anthropology who taught courses in Ojibwe language and native cultures and storytelling at the University of Wisconsin–Milwaukee from the 1990s until his death in 2012.

15 By "Dream Sanctioned" I mean that I was instructed to do this and given permission to share this by my dreams.

her ethnobotany classes nor in personal instruction. I had first come upon it when I was studying Ojibwe language with Roger Thomas.[14] And the story itself does not actually say, at least it does not say to me, a virtue that cattails have to share with Anishinaabeg. But in the dream I decided that I should include the story with my notes.

Upon waking I knew I had to write the "Dancing Cattails" story and include it in the chapter on cattails. I trust my dreams. I have been carefully prepared to tell the difference between the random sorting of the day's events that dreams can be and a Power Dream that is to be taken more seriously. I do know the difference, and I always try to take freely offered gifts, both for their own value and so as not to insult Those Who Gift Us. So, the "Dancing Cattails" story is in this book. But that decision opens more questions. I include this particular story because of the Dream Sanction.[15] But how about the others? It does not take me long to decide that just because I personally cannot see a direct reason why the story was told and kept down through the ages, that does not mean that there is no reason. I know that some of our stories are very obvious teachings encoded in a form that makes them easy for anyone to understand. "Naanabozho and the Squeaky-Voice Plant" actually tells us that the *Lycopodiaceae* have three virtues to share with Anishinaabeg: 1) instruction by example in why one must not be arrogant about one's place in the scheme of things; 2) that all creation must survive for the proper balance that Creator intended; and 3) that the squeaky-voice plant has a medicine to keep people from madness and wild behavior. But not all of our teaching stories are so transparent. Some of them do not spell out the lesson in so straightforward a manner. Some are the kind that one can ponder over a lifetime until, when one has read or heard it told for the fiftieth time, one suddenly "understands" it. Suddenly it makes sense. Suddenly one sees connections that are so obvious that one has a flash of shame that one did not "see" it sooner. As with all literature, one can only understand as one's experience has prepared the ground for one's cognition. So? What do I do about the stories? I put them in, of course. Just because I do not personally understand does not mean that there is not profound truth and instruction encoded there that a wiser or more experienced person might find.

And I have precedence for this discussion. When Kee left teaching at the University of Wisconsin–Milwaukee, she took a research grant to work at the Newberry Research Library in Chicago. She told me she was off to find more of the plant teaching stories. She intended at the time to spend her retirement writing those stories, to restore them to access for use in teaching about the plants. I do not know what new-ancient stories she found in her hunt, but at least she left me the "direction." If Kee thought it was valuable to find and repatriate the stories to what she always thought was their original purpose, I think so too.

Therefore I have decided to include the stories Kee told me as well as the ones I have found over the years and the ones I find specifically for these writings.[16] She always said, "Stories are alive, and they go where they wish." If they come to me, I intend to pass them along.

[16] Stories not from Kee are identified with notes.

2

Indinawemaaganag

All of My Relatives

"How Cedar and Bearberry Came into the World"

Gichi-mewinzha, gii-oshki-niiging akiing, A very long time ago, when the world was new, Baambiitaa-binesi, the busybody, was busily flying around watching everything. Whenever he saw anything unusual he would drum out the news on the nearest tree for all to hear. One day he saw that the Anishinaabeg were having trouble. Remembering that Creator had admonished all creatures in the beginning to live the best life they could and to help each other along the way, Baambiitaa-binesi knew he should report this problem as soon as possible. He beat out the news, and all of the upper-air creatures assembled to decide what they should do. It was not as if they actually liked the Anishinaabeg. They had no fur, nor feathers. They could not fly. They really could not do much of anything, but still there was the Creator's admonishment to help each other. But this was a big problem, and the upper-air creatures felt that they needed the advice and help of the rest of the animals if they were going to be able to solve it. So, they tried to get the attention of the on-earth creatures and the under-earth creatures. But there was a new problem: The on-earth and the under-earth creatures did not trust the upper-air creatures. Whenever the *migiziwag,* eagles, tried to get the attention of the *giigoonyag,* fish, the giigoonyag would dive down deep in the water. Whenever the *gekekwag,* hawks, tried to get the attention of the *waaboozoog,* rabbits, the waaboozoog dove into their burrows. Whenever the *gookooko'oog,* owls, tried to talk to the *waawaabiganoojiinyag,* mice, the waawaabiganoojiinyag hid. After all, the little creatures knew that part of the reason they had been put on Earth was to feed the other creatures.

So the upper-air creatures decided to get the attention of *Amik,* Beaver, because he was always busily working and always around. But Amik said, "Can't stop now. Gotta get this dam in place. Gotta get this aspen stockpile in before winter comes."

Finally *Ogiishkimanisii,* Kingfisher said, "I will get his attention." So, he swooped down and creased the top of Amik's head, and it is the truth that even today if Amik's head is wet one can easily see the part in his hair where Ogiishkimanisii creased his head to get his attention. Amik stopped working. "Okay, "he said, "What is it?" The upper-air creatures explained to him about the trouble that the Anishinaabeg were having and how they thought that they needed the help of all of creation to solve this problem.

"Why don't they just get busy and get to work and everything will be okay?" asked Amik, "Well, all right. I'll tell the under-earth creatures, and maybe they'll be able to come up with something to help these Anishinaabeg."

The under-earth creatures are not just the worms and snakes and the little creepy things. They are all of the animals who live and sleep part of the year under the ground. Amik told them about the trouble, and they decided to call a great council meeting to discuss what to do.

The first problem was where to have the meeting. Some wanted to have it in the Hall of the Eternal Fire, but others said, "Oh no! I'm afraid to go there. There is a strange smell in that place, and I'm afraid I might go to sleep and never wake up if I sleep there." So after some discussion it was decided to hold the meeting in the Hall of Winter Slumbers.

It was a huge council, for all of the under-earth creatures sent representatives. It took a very long time for everyone to speak, as is the case in all Anishinaabeg councils to this day because everyone has a right to be heard. But finally everyone had their say. Most really did not know what to do, and some even insisted that Anishinaabeg should help themselves. Only *Gichi-makwa*, the Great Black Bear, and *Nigig*, Otter, kept insisting that they just had to do something because Creator would want it done.

Finally the council decided that if Gichi-makwa and Nigig were so concerned, they should be the ones to help by first opening a line of communication with the Anishinaabeg. That meant that they needed a path of communication, and Gichi-makwa and Nigig were assigned to open that path. Nigig is very good at digging, but even he could not dig all the way up to the surface of the Earth. Gichi-makwa is very strong but even he could not push his way up through the earth either. So they sat down to think.

They decided that they needed a tool, a tree to push up on the ground and push through to the on-earth place. First they tried an *azaadi*, poplar, but it was too brittle, and it snapped. Then they tried a *mitigomizh*, oak. It was very strong, but it was far too heavy. Poor Nigig could not even lift up his end, and Gichi-makwa even with his great strength could not do it alone. So they sat down and gave it another thought. "What we need is a tree that is strong but light of weight. It should be oily so we can spin it around in the earth, and it won't get stuck." They went on to describe all of the properties that we now know exist in Grandmother Cedar. But where were they going to get such a wonderful tool?

Finally Nigig said, "Hey, we are going about this all wrong. We are doodem animals, and like all Creator's children we have the right to call on Creator whenever we need help." So, they put down their Asemaa and they told Creator what they needed. And Creator gave them the cedar tree.

Meanwhile up on the surface of the Earth, Baambiitaa-binesi was in the neighborhood, and he saw a great trembling of the ground. He beat out the message for all to hear, and the other birds called "Well, if the earth is trembling, you'd better get out of there quick because you know what that means. BOOM!"

"No, no," said Baambiitaa-binesi, "I don't think it is like that. There is no smoke or steam."

"Well, okay, "said all the rest of the birds. "You watch and keep us informed."

So Baambiitaa-binesi did, and suddenly he saw a bit of green pop up. He beat out the message, "It's green. It's a tree. It's a new tree. It's different from all the other trees. Its foliage is all flat, and its cones are all squished. It smells very good." And it is true that the foliage of Nookomis-giizhik is very flat, and its cones are all squished. People say that is because it was pushed out of the ground. Suddenly up popped the whole cedar tree and right behind it came Gichi-makwa and Nigig.

"Howa!" said Gichi-makwa, "That was hard! Now where are these Anishinaabeg? Hear they can't fly, can't fight, have no fur, no fangs, no claws. Don't have much of anything."

Nigig said, "Let's get busy and see what they need. I want to get back to the water. My fur is drying out. Hey, look over there down on the beach. There's a group of them just milling around, bumping into trees. Boy, they don't really know what they are doing, do they?"

As Gichi-makwa and Nigig walked along the dune line, trying to catch a glimpse of the Anishinaabeg down on the beach, a line of cedar trees sprang up in their footsteps. When Gichi-makwa sat down and slid down the embankment, a line of *makwa-mis-komin,* bearberry, sprung up in the grove his bottom had made in the sandy soil.

Down on the beach they found a little Anishinaabe man-child in his *dikinaagan,* cradle board, where his parents had left him in their fright, trying to get away from the two doodem animals. He was just wailing and crying for all he was worth. Gichi-makwa waddled over to him and looked into his wide open, crying mouth, and said "Well, here is the kid's trouble. He doesn't have a last berry. Look at that! Look in the back of his mouth! He doesn't have a last berry."[1]

Nigig said, "Why would he want a berry? Personally I think fish are ever so much nicer."

Gichi-makwa said, "No! No! He needs a last berry. It is the one that keeps all the other berries down so he won't be hungry."

"Well," said Nigig, "if you think the kid needs one, give it to him so we can get back before my fur totally dries out."

So, Gichi-makwa looked around and grabbed a bright red berry off the bearberry plant that was growing down the dune onto the beach where he had slid. He popped that berry into the child's gapping mouth.

"There, "Gichi-makwa said, "at least we took care of that problem."

The baby was totally surprised by the berry being popped into his mouth. He stopped crying and started swallowing and swallowing and swallowing trying to get the berry down. And that is why babies to this day lie for hours just swallowing and swallowing. They are still trying to get the berry down.

Gichi-makwa and Nigig finally found a group of Anishinaabeg and explained to them that there is a way to communicate with all of creation and with Creator, too, a way for all of creation to live in harmony and respect and that way is Grandmother Cedar.

"Nookomis-giizhik: The Cedar Song"

As sung by Keewaydinoquay

Ojibwe verse	English verse
giwaabamaa giizhik	behold the cedar
mitig azhitwaa	the holy tree
onesenodaawaan	come let her breathe you
bimaadiziwin	new life within
gaa-noojimowaad	we call her saving tree
anishinaabeg	she saves the people
nindinaa nookomis	we say nookomis
nindabandendam	we show respect

refrain	**refrain**
nookomis sa giizhik	nookomis sa giizhik
gichitwaawendaagoziwin	gichitwaawendaagoziwin

My Grandmother Cedar: Nookomis-giizhik
White Cedar
Thuja occidentalis

In the Beginning Time, when humankind was in trouble, Bear and Otter asked for and were given the cedar tree, to open up the line of communication between man and the rest of creation. In the Aadizookaan of the "Creation of Cedar and Bearberry" we are told that Grandmother Cedar opened and maintains that line of communication. It is through the use of these two plants that Anishinaabeg can still obtain the help needed in times of trouble to ask for assistance from the rest of creation as well as help from their Guardians, the Grandfathers and the Grandmothers, and the rest of the *Manidoog,* spirits, and *Gichi-manidoo,* Creator God. It is through the Hole in the Cedar that one calls for help through the Hole in the Day, Hole in the Sky, and Hole in Heaven, the four levels of the Anishinaabe view of reality.

Grandmother Cedar has within her very growth pattern the symbol of balance. It is very easy to see in Anishinaabe country, for cedar trees are one of the principle trees of our woodlands. The upper shape of the cedar tree is a mirror image of the root structure. A cedar will grow up as it grows down. One can see this for oneself on those shorelines where erosion has washed away the soil. One can see the shape of the cedar under the earth, how it reproduces in kind the exact shape of the cedar above the surface. If a cedar is twenty feet tall, it will also have twenty-foot roots. The roots will be in the same position as the branches, a mirror image of them, in fact. MidéOgema, Keewaydinoquay's paternal Crane Clan grandfather, said that if a mother bird nested on one branch of a cedar, a mother rabbit would dig a nest for her children on the mirror image root, too. A cedar tree goes up as it goes down. If one were a spirit and could see the above Earth as well as the under the Earth, one could see this, too. Grandmother Cedar has within her very growth the balance of creation, and she ties the four levels of our physical world to the four levels of the Spirit world. Calling for help with cedar is available to Anishinaabeg in several forms. The use of kinnikinnick, of which Grandmother Cedar is a necessary ingredient, is a very prevalent custom among Native peoples across the breadth of Turtle Island. It is almost a Pan-Indian idea[2] that prayer is most effective when accompanied by the incense of asemaa and/or kinnikinnick.

2 One exception to this is among the tribes of the American Southwest where Sacred Corn Meal stands in the place of asemaa and kinnikinnick to carry one's prayers into the Spirit World.

My Grandmother Cedar: Nokomis Giizhik (*Thuja occidentalis*)

3 Kee said the use of the asinaagan was the original way asemaa and kinnikinnick were offered in the Great Lakes area. She said the use of the Sacred Pipe is a tradition now adopted by most native people, but it is an imported Plains-culture idea that we got from the Dakota. She was a pipe carrier, but she prayed with her asinaagan. She preferred the asinaagan because she thought the pipe-carrier tradition became too elitist and tended to create hierarchy in a group that was unseemly. She said anyone could pick up a rock and use it to pray. Kee always asked to be buried with her asinaagan. I hope they did that for her.

4 See the Recipes section for instruction on making Anishinaabe kinnikinnick.

A man or a woman holds an *asinaagan,* a stone dish, in an outstretched palm.[3] Within this stone dish is kinnikinnick. Flame is applied to the herb mixture, and the resulting fire is fanned and encouraged by human breath. The smoke ascends. This act is a physical rendition of a mental process of a metaphysical reality. It is prayer made physical. It is communication with the Divine rendered into a form in which it is perceivable by all five of the senses. The hand of the person who makes this gesture is outstretched, palm open, fingers slightly curved, cradling the asinaagan. The outstretched, open hand is in the position of blessing, both giving and receiving. The cradling fingers are the person's flesh encircling the stone, taking the very act of prayer within the space of the body. The asinaagan is a dish of stone. The stone is the Abiding Rock, the rib of Our Mother the Earth. It is the bedrock of our physical reality upon this planet.

The kinnikinnick is a mixture of pleasant-smelling herbs, the most pleasing of the abundant flora, the most pleasing to human and therefore, hopefully, the most pleasing to the Divine.[4] The content of the herbal mixture may vary either to suit personal taste or cultural dictates or to meet the perception of a particular ceremonial occasion; but two specific herbs will be utilized: cedar and bearberry (*Arctostaphylos uva-ursi*). Bearberry is included because it is sanctified by the tradition that it is the special gift of Bear, the great doodem animal, to sustain the life of humankind. Cedar is included because it is the Sacred Tree of Life of the Anishinaabeg.

The fire that lights the herb is symbolic of the fire of the sun, which in turn is symbolic of Gichi-manidoo, the Great Mystery. Through fire the herbs become an offering most pleasing to Creator God and to the accompanying Spirit World. The breath of the supplicant that fans the fire is the prayer, but the continued blowing of the breath is dependent upon the person inhaling. Thus the blessing is both drawn in and returned to the person, to be inhaled and expelled again in the circle of honor and love, Creator for person and person for Creator.

All five of the senses of the one involved in the act are engaged once the kinnikinnick is alight. The eyes see the smoke. The ears hear the crackling of the fire. The nose and the sense of smell as well as the tongue and the sense of taste are engaged as the herbs' fragrances are released by the fire. The hand and the face both feel the warmth of the fire and the gentle breeze of the person's own breath. By the act of lighting an asinaagan and burning the sacred herbs, the person makes physical the mental prayer and sends it off and out to the metaphysical, the World of the Spirit and ultimately to Gichi-manidoo.

Another form in which Grandmother Cedar is used to confer blessing and aid to the Anishinaabeg is through Sacred Cedar Oil. Throughout all of life Sacred Cedar Oil is of help to the Anishinaabeg. At the moment of birth, the Anishinaabe child is greeted with it. The father or the medicine woman present at the birth covers his or her hands with Sacred Cedar Oil and, even before the cord is cut, places his or her hands over the face of the child. The babe's first breath is through the wonderful aroma of cedar. The person says, "Greetings, New Little Soul! Walk in honor among the People." Cedar oil is a stimulant. It will compel the babe to breathe without the spank that is common now to begin a life. It was thought in the old days that a new life should be started with blessings and not with violence. Cedar oil is also poured on the child to clean him or her. Cedar oil is a wonderful emollient that is very good for the skin.

In the naming ceremony when a child's feet are first placed upon the Sun Trail of their ancestors, Sacred Cedar Oil is used to

5 The Final Journey is the four-day journey to the Land of Souls that the dead must make.

6 Rub it into the scalp across the entire head and don't forget the bottom of your feet and between your toes.

bless all of the openings of the child's body, that only good may come to the child by those ways. When a body is prepared for the Final Journey,[5] this ceremony is done again, that a person may journey on protected still by Grandmother Cedar.

Sacred Cedar Oil is also much used in the Sweat Lodge. People cover themselves from head to toe[6] with it to keep the skin from being dried or burned by the heat of the Grandfather Rocks. Cedar surrounds a person in the Sweat as the foliage is also laid between the poles and the covering of the lodge, and on the floor, and it is also in the water used to sprinkle on the Grandfather Rocks to produce the steam. In a community sweat, an honorable, good woman is assigned the job of Cedar Woman. She is the one responsible for the gathering of the cedar boughs to build the lodge, for seeing to the placement of the ring of cedar that marks the place before the poles are dug in, and she must see to it that a line of cedar boughs is placed to tie the lodge to a nearby standing, living cedar tree and to the fire. She is the one who sees to the proper making of the cedar tea that is used to sprinkle the Grandfather Rocks. Inside of the sweat, one sits in a warm, dark, cedar 'womb' waiting on vision, healing, and blessings.

In times of stress throughout a person's life, Sacred Cedar Oil is placed on the Life Spot, the hollow at the base of a person's throat through which all of the impulses of life pass. In old photographs of Indian people one can see large button, shell, or bone necklaces being worn to cover that most vulnerable of spots. Those Gete-Anishinaabeg wore those necklaces for more than decoration. In a fight, one protects one's life spot because a well placed knife, arrow, stick, tooth, or claw could finish a fight very quickly if one did not. Those old necklaces were shields. Nowadays, at any time of stress we put a drop of Sacred Cedar Oil on the lifespot and say, "I give thanks for the gift of life, and I unite myself with the ongoing of the People."

In Anishinaabe culture, Grandmother Cedar is still venerated for the help she gives to us. Kee often said that only in recent times would an Anishinaabe have said, "Cedar" without the honorific title of "Nookomis, My Grandmother." That started to happen only with the employment of large numbers of Anishinaabeg in the lumbering business. One could not make war on one's own grandmother and chop her down with an ax! The mindset had to change if that was the only way to make a living.

In Anishinaabe culture it is not only blood relations who are called "Nookomis, My Grandmother." and "Nimishoomis, My

Grandfather." These are general terms of respect and affection given to the old. It was once a good thing to be old. Few people lived to age. It meant that one had great skills and powerful medicine and medicine helpers. The elderly were/are living libraries of the People, and they were/are treasured as such.

This ancient veneration for Grandmother Cedar is still seen today. Many Indian families hang wreaths of cedar on their doors. Nowadays it is usually done at Christmastime, when European North Americans hang greens, too, but do not be surprised to see the same "Christmas" cedar wreath still hanging on the door come spring. The Indians who live in such a house see the cedar as conferring a blessing upon the dwelling.

If evil is feared, yarrow (*Achillea millefolium*) and sweetgrass (*Hierochloe odorata*) are added to the cedar in the wreath hanging on the door. It is said that evil will not cross a threshold were yarrow is hung. But, one must never drive out one evil and leave a void. If there is such a spot, a greater evil may take the opportunity to fill that void. Sweetgrass is hung because, as yarrow discourages the evil, sweetgrass encourages/attracts the good. And Grandmother Cedar is there to balance the two. As Kee used to say, "Blessings and balance. Balance and Blessings, for from balance comes all Blessings."

If an Anishinaabe family does not hang cedar on their door, one can be sure that they will have hung cedar boughs above the baby's dikinaagan, which itself will have been made of cedar, or they will have slipped a piece of foliage under the mattress of the baby's crib. If a child or an adult is worried in the night by bad dreams, a piece of cedar, perhaps tied to a dream catcher, will be hung over their sleeping place. Here, too, yarrow and sweetgrass may be hung if the problem is severe.

In the modern day powwow, many of the ancient ceremonial uses of Grandmother Cedar are still utilized. An outdoor powwow will often have a bower made of cedar through which the dancers enter the circle on the east side of the ground. Or a sheltering roof of cedar boughs may be laid over the drum area in the center of the circle. Someone may be sent around with a bough of cedar to shake a cedar infusion on the crowd and/or the participants in the ceremony before the dancing begins. Grandmother Cedar confers her blessings as she always has done for the Anishinaabeg.

Traditional Anishinaabe Advice to Youth

There is really no part of an Anishinaabe life that is not made better by the presence of Grandmother Cedar. In the old lifestyle cedar was very much in evidence in all of the material culture. In the days of the Gete-Anishinaabeg very young children were taught to recite a little teaching that Keewaydinoquay called: "Traditional Anishinaabe Advice to Youth." This teaching says:

> If in the future you should find yourself separated from the People, if you should be carried away by an alien tribe into a distant land, or if you should fall asleep on a night march and wake to find yourself alone, or if you should be blown off course in your canoe to an unknown shore, here is what you must do: Climb to a high place. Find a hill or climb a tree. Look out over the countryside. If you can see the white gleam of Nimishoomis-wiigwaas, Grandfather Birch, and the tall spires of Nookomis-giizhik, Grandmother Cedar, relax! You are safe! You are with your relatives! Between them Grandmother and Grandfather will provide everything you need for life, and they will get you home again in this life or the next.

Such an incredible claim that two trees could provide all a person needed to sustain life may seem impossible, but there was a time when all of a person's future education was focused on making good that promise. A child would be raised with the skills necessary to enable him or her to utilize the help and blessings offered by these two trees in obtaining everything one would need to live and live Anishinaabe-bimaadiziwin too.

In addition to the very real aid Grandmother Cedar has to help the Anishinaabeg in their spiritual lives, she also has many, many gifts to offer for their physical life. In a survival situation such as described in the "Advice to Youth," water and food must be first on the list of life needs. If one sees over the countryside where a line of cedar are growing, one will know to go there to look for water. Grandmother Cedar likes to have her feet in water. In a pinch one can even eat cedar and birch. The inner bark of both have edible starch. Of the two, birch tastes best, but both have enough starch to keep a person alive until he or she can find better tasting food.

Cedar is one of the easiest natural cordage.[7] The cordage can be produced in weights from string to thick cord. It usually is not used for fine work, although some people still make necklaces to

7 The strongest natural cord can be made from stinging nettles (*Urtica dioica*). Gather them with gloves to avoid being stung by them, then just hang them to dry. Drying will render the stinging hairs on the plant inoperative. Break down the stalks. The dried, woody outer layer will break away, and one is left with fiber. Soak the fibers before spinning them against your leg to form a cord.

remind the wearer of the blessings that Grandmother Cedar has to share with Anishinaabeg. The outer bark of cedar will strip off very easily. It is easy to take from a standing tree, but a dead tree that has fallen into a swamp is best because then one does not even have to soak the bark to make a rope. One can take a long piece of cedar bark, pull the inner bark free off the outer bark with one's hands, and roll the fibers of the inner bark against one's leg to make a very quick and moderately strong fiber. If one wants to use it for a fishing line, one should braid three thin pieces for better results. It might not hold a pike but it should be strong enough for bottom feeders, perch or bluegills, and even very little fish can be fine eating if one knows how to prepare them. It would also be strong enough to use as a rabbit snare to obtain a tasty supper. A braided piece of cedar rope would make a quick, if somewhat temporary, bow string. One might get four or five good pulls on a yew bow with one, and that should be enough for a good try at a deer. With a deer, one has plenty of meat, deer skin for clothing, and a very good bow string with the sinew of the back and hind leg of the deer for one's future hunting needs.

One can make very tasty teas with both cedar and birch. Cedar tea has a very pleasant taste and is very high in vitamin C. It has the property of being able to settle stomach gas and is therefore nice to drink after a fish supper so that one does not taste fish all evening.[8]

Once one has food and water in a survival situation, one is able to think about a camp. Fire for warmth and comfort is the gift of these two trees, too. The best fire drills are made of cedar. One makes a hole with a small v shape in a flat piece of cedar. Then one spins an upright piece of cedar in the hole by means of a bow. When one has smoke, one blows the spark into a flame and catches it in dried tinder of cedar bark fiber, fed by little pieces of birch bark. A quick and sure firestarter that many campers and sportsmen still carry in their pockets is a little roll of birch bark with a piece of cedar rope. The combination will start a fire even in wet weather. In the days when people traveled by canoe and had to make stops at portages and at numerous camping spots, little pieces of smoldering cedar rope, often carried inside of polyporous shelf fungi, was taken along from camp to camp to hasten the set up of new camps and the hasty making of meals.

After one has one's fire started and supper is cooking, one can start thinking about improving the camp itself. In this

8 Pregnant women should avoid this tea, because a very strong cedar tea may be an abortifacient. Kee always said this to her students, but she told me that one would have to drink gallons of very strong tea to have it effect most pregnancies, and a woman would most probably vomit long before she got enough to have that effect. But Kee loved little babies and would never have harmed a child even by chance, so she told her students this just in case.

undertaking, cedar again is useful. The inner bark of cedar can be cut into strips and woven into many useful items for a forest home. The different layers of the inner bark, when split by an expert craftsperson, will yield different colors according to the depth of the tissues cut. One can obtain golden-green to red with fresh bark from a standing tree. The colors will darken over time because of the tannin in the bark until they are varying shades of brown and almost black. Since cedar bark also has mold-retarding chemicals in it, cedar bags and baskets retard the growth of molds and the spoilage of food stored in them; therefore they were and are of great use when one has to keep food without refrigeration. Many people also kept and keep fine leather goods, boots and moccasins, and other powwow regalia in cedar bags for the same reason that Grandmother Cedar can be trusted to keep our treasures safe.

The Anishinaabeg also use mats as floor covering in wigwams, for the sides of summer wigwams, and to line graves. While a floor mat of cedar does take longer to make than a reed or cattail one, such a mat does last longer because it is tougher and will not break down underfoot and from the moisture or the forest floor as readily as will a cattail mat. When teaching about cedar mats, Keewaydinoquay used to tell the story found in the next section.

"The Lady of the Red and Black Wigwam"

Gichi-mewinzha, a very long time ago, there was among the Anishinaabeg a very skilled weaver who made herself a beautiful lodge with wonderfully woven cedar mats. She had such skill that she was able to achieve a vivid red and an equally vivid black color in the split bark from which she wove mats to cover her floors and mats to cover the outside of her wigwam. She was soon spoken of with respect by the People for her wondrous skill and the beautiful patterns that she wove into her mats. People started to call her "The Lady of the Red and Black Wigwam."

This skilled weaver had a very vain and selfish daughter-in-law who wanted that lodge and the fame of being its owner. Her mother-in-law would have taught her how to weave such mats herself, but the daughter-in-law was far too lazy to apply herself to the work of learning, and anyway, she had another plan in mind.

When the weaver aged and was nearing her death, she asked that the mats from her famed wigwam be taken down and used to line the walls of her "Passing Over Place"[9] Her daughter-in-law, not wanting to lose the mats, nor the honor of being the Lady of the Red and Black Wigwam, convinced the People after the old lady's death that the weaver had changed her mind: "At the very end, poor Mother-in-Law decided that it would be a great pity to waste the mats. She wanted me to have them, the dear old soul." Even before the weaver was buried, the daughter-in-law took possession. To keep the people of the village from even thinking of removing the mats, she did not budge, not even to attend her mother-in-law's funeral, which was a great disgrace, as the weaver had ever been a kind and loving mother to her son's wife.

When the village buried the weaver with all honor and ceremony, all present saw a crow swoop down on the little sacred fire on the weaver's grave, which had been lighted to comfort her soul on its final journey. The crow snatched up a burning firebrand and flew over the famed Red and Black Wigwam and dropped it on the roof. The grasping, undutiful daughter-in-law was burned to death. The same crow then swooped down on the daughter-in-law's children and marked their cheeks with its claws. The children carried the scars all of their lives, and their children were born with the same dreadful scars marking their cheeks, too. Mii'iw. Miigwech.

———————

Keewaydinoquay would always laugh when she finished that story and say she was not sure if people told the story just for the fun of the grisly ending or to point out that a person's punishment for misdeeds in this life are not always borne only by the person who commits the offense. But, she said, it also points out the great honor a fine craftsperson was given in the old society. It makes plain that cedar mats were customarily used in the home and later in the grave. Grandmother Cedar cradled the People all of their lives, from the time her wood was used to make their *dikinaaganan*, cradleboards, until her bark lined their final homes.

It is not just the bark of cedar which has always been helpful to the People. The wood is also. The wood is straight-grained and can be split into straight, thin pieces. It also has a chemical in it that makes it resistant to decay when it is in a damp place. For that reason it is a good wood for docks. Sometimes it has lasted far longer than its users intended. There are old pilings in some harbors that are still visible in the water and have been

9 "The Passing Over Place" is the traditional name for the grave because that is the place where one "passes over to the Spirit World." It is also called the "Paying Back Place" because it is there that a person has the opportunity to repay the Earth for all the sustenance that has been given to that person throughout his or her lifetime. In the traditional society cedar mats were much used to line graves, so that a person might finish their life as they had begun it and lived it, surrounded by Grandmother Cedar.

there for well over a hundred years, since they were first placed there during the lumbering days, when log boats tied up to those docks. The pilings have outlasted their docks and the industry that needed them, and are now considered a hazard to navigation. They will often have to be removed with dynamite.

Cedar wood is also widely used where moisture might rot lesser woods. It is still widely used for fence posts and for mine-shaft timbers. It was traditionally used to line wells, for bridges over marshy land, and for water buckets. Cedar is the essential wood for the making of what are called "birch bark canoes," but in reality they should be called "cedar canoes" because cedar is the wood used for all of the ribs and gunnels. This tree really will "get you home again."

When cedar does rot, it usually rots from the inside out. This in traditional culture made it much in demand, because it is relatively easy to clean out even a large log of cedar. Drums are made from cedar logs, especially *Gwiiwizens,* Little Boy, the water drum, that most sacred of the Midewiwin drums. Feather boxes, bowls used for the cutting of kinnikinnick, and bread bowls are also made with cedar logs.

Cedar Medicines

Cedar is an ingredient in many, many medicines. In medicines in which cedar is not an ingredient, a minute particle of cedar foliage is customarily added, to impart Grandmother's blessing.

There are several deodorant medicines in cedar. It is a great breath freshener. Chew the tips of the foliage for a quick and effective way to freshen one's breath on a way out to a date. A light tea made of the foliage is good after a fish supper. It will keep one from tasting fish in one's mouth all night. Cedar also makes a good vaginal wipe. This was something that in the old days a girl was taught when she became a woman. One pulls two pieces of the foliage over each other, in opposite directions, thereby releasing the oil in the leaves. This oil was the part used as a wipe. Cedar is also a great air freshener, either chopped fresh or burned to purify the air. In a sickroom a kinnikinnick with a lot of dried cedar foliage was burned on an asinaagan and fanned around the patient. It is said to kill a lot of germs and bacteria on contact.

Cedar has great medicine for the skin. Kee always taught her students the following recipe to make "Cedar-Lemon Balm," a general skin care product: Mix 1½ cups well-chopped cedar foliage and 1½ cups of chopped lemon, skin and all, but with seeds removed. One can chop the cedar and lemon by hand or use a food processor or grinder. One knows he or she has the right mix of cedar and lemon when one tastes the mixture and it tastes both lemony and "cedary." If one can taste too much lemon, one adds more cedar. Add bear grease[10] or Crisco,[11] enough to make a spreadable product. Add to this a little olive oil for healing and about 10 drops of benzoin as a preservative. Benzoin resin is the bark of the benzoin tree from Southeast Asia. Add a teaspoon or so of glycerin. One can bottle the balm now, or one can squeeze it through cheese cloth to take out the solid parts. It will be a smooth, fragrant salve that is especially good to rub on the bottoms of one's feet at night before one goes to bed to relieve hardened skin on tired feet.[12] In the old days, before the people of the Great Lakes area had access to lemons, common wood sorrel, *Oxalis acetosella,* or yellow wood sorrel, *Oxalis stricta,* were used in this recipe. Wood sorrels are low-growing plants with clover-like foliage that love cool, moist woodland glades.

Cedar is also the main ingredient in "Cedar Wart Medicine." One can make this medicine at any time of the year, even in the dead of winter, but cedar foliage has differing amounts of oil at different times of year and growing conditions; it may be necessary to add a little olive oil to the chopped foliage if one takes it in winter or from a dry tree. To make this medicine: Chop the foliage, that has been separated from the little twigs, in a blender or a coffee grinder. A sharp knife works too. Add cider vinegar. Mix until the pulp is mushy and sticky. It should smell of both cedar and vinegar. Put a glob of the medicine on a planter's wart, the kind that grows on the base of one's foot after one carelessly walks across a public shower room at the health club. Put the medicine on at night and cover with a bandage to keep it moist. This is a very mild compound with some acid in the cedar and the vinegar, but not enough to harm good skin. It does take a while to attack the wart, usually a week or two or even longer for an old, well-established wart, but it is a gentle medicine so one can still continue to use one's foot during the treatment. Small warts will melt away with this medicine. Very old warts are different. For an old "seed" wart, after one gets the top off with this poultice, one has to get the root out too. Sometimes one can just wiggle it gently back and forth with one's fingernails and it will come out on its own.[13] If it does not come loose, gather the sundew

10 Kee's mother, Sarah Good Cook, preferred porcupine grease because it has no odor or taste. She also used porcupine grease when she made birthday cakes for the same reason.

11 In our modern world, where bears are so harassed and harried, we have found Crisco a great substitute for bear grease. Other solid shortenings would work, but Kee thought Crisco gave the finished product a particularly nice texture.

12 Personally, I put a clean pair of socks over my feet when I use this medicine at night, so that I do not get little bits of foliage on the sheets. I hate gritty sheets!

13 Personally, I have had success doing this "wart wiggling" while soaking in a tub.

14 This is an endangered plant in some states. It is a good idea to check http://plants.usda.gov for information on endangered species before gathering. That is one thing our ancestors did not have to worry about, but, if we want the plants to be here for our grandchildren, we do have to think about such things now.

plant, *Drosera intermedia*, a little insectivorous plant that grows in sphagnum bogs.[14] It traps insects in the sticky drops on its leaves and digests them for food. Gather the sundew fresh. They have tiny leaves. The hairs on the leaves look like they have dew on them. Squeeze the leaf and get the juice on and into an old seed wart. It will actually eat away the root of the wart, and it may get a little of the surrounding tissue as well. If it does eat a little good skin around the wart that is a good thing because it may prevent the wart from regrowing in the same spot.

"The Birch Tree, the Maple Tree, and Naanabozho"

~~~~~~

One time Naanabozho was walking along the shore when he started to feel hungry, so he decided to see if he could find something to eat. He went up to a *wiigwaasi-mitig,* the paper birch tree, and said, "*Aaniin,* hello, brother! Can you tell me why you were created? Of what use are you to my kind?"

The wiigwaasi-mitig replied, "Oh, Naanabozho. Aaniin! You ask why was I created? Well, I don't think you would understand if I did tell you."

"Of course I would," Naanabozho insisted, "I have been to a lot of places, and I understand a lot of very complicated things about the world. I am sure I would understand you." After he had coaxed the tree for some time, the wiigwaasi-mitig finally said, "I was created to help the Anishinaabeg. They can take my bark to fashion *makakoon,* birch bark boxes, to hold their food or water or possessions. They can store things in my bark for later use."

As he was listening to the wiigwaasi-mitig, Naanabozho noticed *Ininaatig,* a sugar maple tree, nearby was leaning over to hear what the wiigwaasi-mitig was saying, "Howa!" said Naanabozho, "And why were you created, Ininaatig? Surely you can do something more than just listen to other peoples' conversations."

Ininaatig, to cover his embarrassment on being caught listening to other people talking, said, "Yes, I do have a purpose. There is something I can do for the Anishinaabeg, too, but it is rather complicated. I doubt you would know how to do it, Naanabozho."

Naanabozho insisted he was a very clever fellow who felt sure he could do most anything if necessary. After a little coaxing and flattering, he convinced Ininaatig to admit, "I have a food gift for our little brothers the Anishinaabeg. In the early spring, like now, when the days are warm and the nights still cold, I have wonderful sweet syrup that flows out of my bark."

"Good!" said Naanabozho, "I am hungry. I think I will test both of you trees to see if you are telling the truth.

Wiigwaasi-mitig, give me some of your bark for a dish, and Ininaatig, give me some of your sweet syrup." He cut a piece of bark from the wiigwaasi-mitig and fashioned it into a *makak*, birch bark container. Then he bore a hole in the ininaatig and caught the thick syrup that flowed out to the bark. He tasted it, and it was really very good. So, he drank and drank and drank the syrup until he could hold no more. But then he started to feel rather sick to his stomach for he had eaten far too much of the sweet syrup. He sat down under the trees and groaned for a while, then he started to get angry.

"You tricked me!" he screamed. "You knew that I would feel like this, but you did not bother to warn me. Ininaatig, you are just too dangerous for my poor nephews the Anishinaabeg as you are now. But I will fix that!"

So Naanabozho ran down to the river, and he scooped up a makak full of water. He raced back up the hill, climbed the ininaatig, drilled a big hole in the trunk and poured in the water. He kept pouring makak after makak full of water into the poor ininaatig until the sap that ran from the bark had only a faint taste of maple syrup.

"There!" said Naanabozho, "That will take care of that problem. My nephews will not be tempted to eat so much of you that they become sick if they have to work hard boiling your sap down to make syrup."

Then he turned to Wiigwaasi-mitig and said, "And for not warning me, Wiigwaasi-mitig, you will be punished, too. From now on the Anishinaabeg will make many useful things from your bark. They can make *jiimaanan*, boats, to travel over the water, or they will use your bark as a roof for their *wiigiwaaman*, lodges, or they can make makakoon to store things in. There will be many, many things the Anishinaabeg will be able to make with your bark if they are skilled. They will always be stripping you!"

While all of this was going on, a little *bineshiinh*, bird, was sitting on a branch watching Naanabozho and laughing at the trouble that Ininaatig and Wiigwaasi-mitig were having. Naanabozho caught the little bineshiinh and threw him against Wiigwaasi-mitig were he was smashed into the bark. To this day one can see him there. Mii' iw. Miigwech.

My Grandfather Birch: Nimishoomis-wiigwaas, Wiigwaasi-mitig
Birch (White or Paper Birch)
Betula papyrifera

The second most sacred tree to the Anishinaabeg is the Paper, White, or Canoe Birch, which, along with Cedar, is so prevalent in the whole Great Lakes area. It is considered to be sacred because it comes from the air, being a gift given by the Thunderbirds and endowed by them with many virtues to share with the Anishinaabeg.

Grandfather Birch has pitied the Anishinaabeg, and he gives so much for the ongoing of the People. Even the names of the three modern tribes who make up the People of the Three Fires, all of whom call themselves Anishinaabeg (or a slight variant on that word), come from principle gifts that Grandfather Birch shares with us. Kee taught that the name Ojibwe was associated

My Grandfather Birch: Nimishoomis-wiigwaas (*Betula papyrifera*)

with *ozhibii'ige,* he or she writes, and that is still the name for the tribe in sign language. It refers to the ancient, pre-Contact, writing system that the Anishinaabeg have that works by conveying thoughts, not words or sounds. The Sacred Scrolls of the Midewiwin, which record the ancient songs and ceremonies, are written on rolls of birch bark. The Potawatomi, the *Boodewaadamii,* whose name comes from *boodawe,* he or she builds a fire, are the Keepers of the Sacred Fire of the nation. It is Grandfather Birch who shares his wondrous bark for the lighting of fires. The Ottawa or *Odaawaa,* which comes from the word *adaawe,* he or she trades, were the middlemen, the traders of the Anishinaabe nation. They traveled the whole length and breath of *Anishinaabewaki,* Indian Country, in the great trader canoes made of the bark of Grandfather Birch. All three branches of the Anishinaabeg take their modern tribal names and identities from the gifts freely shared with them and their ancestors by the tree they have always called Grandfather.

Before the People came to the Great Lakes Region, on what some researchers and Native scholars call the Great Miigis Migration, from the ancestral land of Waabanaaki, said to have been an island in the far eastern sea, they made ceramics, clay pots for cooking. But once they arrived here in the "Land Where the Food Grows on the Water," where they found *manoomin,* wild rice, they abandoned ceramics in favor of birch bark vessels. It is much quicker to make a makak than it is to dig the clay, work it into a vessel, before one builds a fire to lay a bed of coals to fire a clay pot. And, once made, a birch bark bowl will take an awful lot of rough handling that would crack ceramic. Makakoon can be made to order to accomplish the task of most any vessel required in the camp, for harvesting, or cooking, or storing of food and/or other possessions. Although makakoon are quick to make in comparison to a ceramic pot, they are by no means one-time dishes. Once used they can be washed, dried, and used again and again.

To make a makak a person takes the bark of Grandfather Birch, either from a standing tree or from one cut for the purpose or one recently blown over in a storm. The best and easiest time to take bark is in the late spring when the sap is rising. In the Upper Peninsula of Michigan that is usually mid to late June. In the more southern areas in Wisconsin and Michigan the sap usually rises as much as a month earlier. In a cool valley or on the north side of a hill, the sap in the trees may be further delayed. A spring that has been unusually warm or unusually cool may also affect the time to take the bark. One simply has to observe the trees in one's area and adjust the harvest time to the trees' needs.

A skilled craftsperson can take the bark from a standing tree without killing the tree. They just have to be careful not to cut too deep and not to girdle the tree. The tree will be able to heal itself, but it will never regrow the beautiful, gleaming, white bark of its former condition; therefore, one would not take bark from the one carefully grown and preserved shade tree on one's own front lawn.

It is easiest to work bark as soon as it has been taken from the tree, but it is also possible to work the bark at a later period. The resins between the layers of the bark will harden once the bark is removed from the tree. No amount of soaking in water will soften the bark to restore it to the pliable condition that it had as soon as it was harvested. Warmth is what is needed to resolidify the resins and make the bark soft again, so that it can be bent without cracking. There are people so skilled at working birch bark that they can hold a sheet of bark over an open fire, either a camp fire or a gas stove, but one has only a few seconds between having pliable bark and having a flame in one's hand. It is far safer for a craftsperson to iron the bark with an electric iron. If the bark is older, it may take several minutes of ironing before the resins are soft enough, but if one keeps the iron moving, as one would do when ironing a shirt, one can achieve a bendable bark without scorching the material. Some people resoften the resins in birch bark by plunging the bark into boiling water. That will work very nicely, too, but one might need a rather large kettle to accomplish the job if one is making a large makak or a canoe.

Once the bark is soft and bent into the desired shape, one laces up the sides, the seams or the rim with *wadab,* the split root of the black spruce or balsam fir, or with *wiigob,* the inner bark of the basswood tree. Both wadab and wiigob can be harvested, prepared green by removing the outer bark, splitting the material into the desired thickness, rolling, drying, and storing the material for future use. When one wishes to use the wadab or wiigob, one can resoften them and bring them back to a pliable condition by soaking them in warm water. To sew the birch bark, one pokes a hole in the bark with an awl[15] and pulls the lacing material through the hole.

A very skilled craftsman could make an almost airtight makak. Nodjimahkwe, Keewaydinoquay's herb mother, had a makak that was airtight. She used it to store her most important medicine.

15 In pre-Contact times, before the People had access to metal for use as an awl, the thorns of honey locust trees or hawthorn trees were used for this purpose, or a sharpened animal bone, especially a split and sharpened rib bone of a deer.

If a completely waterproof makak is desired, one melts the sap of a conifer tree. The sap of any of the native fir, spruce, or pines can be used for this purpose. A little crushed charcoal is added to the liquefied sap, and the mixture is dabbed or "painted" on the seams. This step would not be done if one intended to place the makak directly on a fire, however, as it would make the vessel catch fire.

Amazingly, although birch bark is very flammable, it is possible to place a makak directly on a bed of coals to cook food directly. The top of the vessel may catch fire, but it will not burn below the level of the water inside. If one doubts, this try putting water in an unwaxed paper cup, filling it with water, and placing it in a fire. The water will boil away before the cup burns. The same thing happens with a makak. When making a makak to be used directly on a fire, one bends the bark with the orange, inside bark on the outside and the white, outer bark on the inside of the vessel.

Although it is possible to place a makak directly in a fire, it was not often done in the old days, before the People traded for iron pots. Usually a person cooked supper by heating igneous rocks in a hot fire and then slipping them one by one into a makak holding stew or soup. It takes only a few rocks to bring such a supper to a boil and to keep it there until the dish is cooked. If a few ashes were inadvertently added to the pot as well, they were either overlooked or welcomed as an addition of seasoning to the finished product. A few ashes add a salty taste to food.

One does not have to craft a traditional makak to do a quick job. To make a quick carrying container, which would help if one just happens to find a stand of ripe berries while one is about on another task, is a very simple project. One just takes a piece of bark, rolls it into a funnel, cup shape, and secures the sides by means of a split twig from the same birch tree. One takes a short twig, about one-quarter to one-half inch thick, makes a slit in the cut end and slips it onto the folded piece of bark, the way one slips a clothes-peg on a line to hang clothes. Howa! Instant berry bowl!

A similar cone-shaped makak has several other uses in traditional Anishinaabe technology. At sugaring time in the early spring, many little cones were made, sewn with wiigob, and used to mold sugar cakes given as treats to the children of the family. If such cakes were not molded in a birch cone, they were also sometimes formed in the upper mandible of a duck.

Cone-shaped birch *makakoon,* containers, were also used in medicine. A large birch cone was made that would cover a patient's nose and mouth. A hot coal would be put in the end of the cone, on top of a layer of sand or moss to keep the coal from burning through the bark too readily, and herbs would be put on the coal to produce a smoke as an inhalant for those medicines whose virtues were best conveyed in smoke. This was a bit tricky, however, as care had to be taken that the patient did not tip the cone and get a hot coal on his nose. If freshly taken, damp birch bark was used to make the cone, there was a better chance that the coal would not ignite the birch bark before the patient had a chance to benefit from the healing smoke. It was a tricky thing, but it was used when a patient was considered too fragile to be taken into a sweat lodge for the administration of the healing smoke.

A large birch bark cone was also used in the moose hunt when the hunter wanted to lure moose by imitating the amorous moose mating call. A lovesick moose can be lured to the hunter by an imitation of his light of love. All in all, birch bark cones had many and varied uses in the traditional Anishinaabe world.

Grandfather Birch surrounds the traditional Anishinaabe from the moment of his or her birth. A newborn babe, one even too small to strap into a dikinaagan, is placed on a birch bark tray and laced into a *waapijipizon,* a moss bag.[16] The birch bark tray is made of two equal-sized pieces of bark that are laced together with their white, outside of the bark on the inside of the tray, and the orange, outer bark on the outside of the tray. The natural curve of the bark of one piece will counter the curve of the bark on the other piece, making for a stronger tray that will keep its shape. When the child grows a little he or she can be strapped into his or her dikinaagan that is made of Grandmother Cedar.

Because it is a waterproof material, birch bark was the preferred covering for the roof of the *waaginogaan,* the traditional dome-shaped wigwam that was the home of all of the tribes of the Great Lakes area. Pieces of birch bark are stitched together with wadab or wiigob, and the seam smeared with melted conifer sap to which charcoal had been add to ensure a dry roof. When the band moved to different seasonal camps, it was a simple matter to take the birch bark mats off the roof, roll them, and carry them to the next site. They were so light in weight that one person could easily carry the whole roof of their home on their back.

Another added attraction of having a birch bark roof was that it would never be struck by lightning, for the thunderbirds will

[16] This teaching comes from Annie Wilson, traditionally reared Anishinaabe elder of Manitou Rapids First Nation Reserve, through the Masters of Indigenous Thought program of Seven Generations Education Institute, Fort Frances, Ontario. Annie Wilson was called by Queen Elizabeth "a living treasure." [I just put that in because I never before knew a person my queen thought was wonderful!]

not strike a birch tree or an article covered with birch bark. Kee always told the story of how this aspect of birch was first discovered by Naanabozho and told to the People:

"Naanabozho and the Thunderbirds"

Gichi-mewinzha, once in the long ago time, Naanabozho was sitting outside of his lodge feeling very downhearted. He had a comfortable home, a hardworking wife, and good hunting, but he still felt the lack of something. As he sat he gave the matter a lot of thought and finally decided that what he lacked was fame. If only his name was well known and spoken with reverence by the Anishinaabeg, then he felt he could be content. But how was that to be accomplished? The thoughts occupied his mind for some time, until he decided he could not figure it out alone. What he needed was advice. So he put on his moccasins and set out for the village of the Anishinaabeg. The adults of the village all called to him, but they had no time in their daily routines to stop and talk to him. He walked on somewhat dejectedly until he found the village children playing a game down by the lake. He caught one little boy by the hand and asked him to sit down for a moment to give him advice. The boy was somewhat surprised that the Great Naanabozho was in need of his advice, but he dutifully sat down on the ground to listen.

"Boy," said Naanabozho, "As you know, I am Naanabozho, son of the West Wind Spirit and an Anishinaabe woman, and I am a very important person. My problem is how do I get the People to honor me? What is it that the people think is impressive in a man?"

The little boy put his head in his hand and thought and thought on the question. "People think a man is a great man who is a mighty hunter. They always talk about the hunters of old who made a lot of meat and who called everybody to a big feast."

"Howa!" said Naanabozho, "A great hunter, eh? I can do that. Nothing is easier for me. Soon I shall have so much game and call so great a feast that the People will be telling stories of my hunting for generations." He jumped up and happily set out on the trail of game. He hunted for hours, but, except for one little squirrel that somehow managed to dodge his arrows and escape, he saw no game at all.

"Huh," Naanabozho grumbled. "This hunting is tiring and more difficult than it seems. Still I really want the honor not the

exercise of hunting. But, I know a faster and better way to get a
lot of game. I am after all the Great Naanabozho, son of the West
Wind Spirit and an Anishinaabe woman." So he faced the West
and threw out his hands and said, "Oh Great Spirit of the West
Wind. It is I, your own son, Naanabozho. Please send me game
that the Anishinaabeg may know that I am a great person."

As soon as he had spoken the wind started to rise in the West.
The clouds started to fly across the sky, and the waves on the
lake began to pound on the shore. The trees were almost bent
over double by the force of the West Wind. And out of the sky
flew a huge moose, followed by a half dozen rabbits and hares,
twenty and more raccoons, weasels, and wolverines, and dozens
of deer. Huge bears flew through the air and landed on the pile
of game, and then the really interesting animals started to arrive.
Huge animals with long noses and others with great long necks,
striped animals and spotted animals and animals of every shape
and color. Common ones and ones so odd no one had ever seen
their like before. Within minutes there was a huge pile of animals
right outside the Anishinaabeg village right at the feet of Mighty
Naanabozho.

"Howa!" cried Naanabozho, "What a wonderful bag of game!
Surely this will impress the Anishinaabeg, and they will say
'Naanabozho is the greatest hunter that ever lived!' Come out my
brothers. Come see all of the fine game I have brought to your
village. Come feast with Mighty Naanabozho."

The people slowly and cautiously peered out of their homes
at the huge mountain of carcasses that were piled right outside of
their village. Slowly they came forward and looked in awe at the
mountain of meat and all of the strange and wondrous and weird
animals that lay there. They saw the animals they recognized, and
on top of them, they saw the strange and foreign ones as well.

A murmur ran through the crowd. And then low, whispered
talk, and then angry voices saying "What is this, Naanabozho?
What have you done? What are these strange and horrible looking
animals? What are we supposed to do with this mountain of meat
and these horrible, striped and spotted and odd-colored hides?
We will have to move the village when the sun starts to turn this
meat."

The Anishinaabeg became very angry, so a very confused
Naanabozho decide to give this all more thought. He walked away
and sat down by the lake again to think.

The whole village gathered all their possessions, and piled
them in the canoes on the beach, preparing to leave behind

the village that lay in the shadow of the mountain of meat that was starting to smell as the sun touched it. They walked by Naanabozho, muttering rude things and giving him dark looks. Only the little boy who had given him the advice smiled a little and waved his hand as he passed.

"Boy?" said Naanabozho, "Stop a minute. If a mountain of meat does not impress the People, what does?"

The little boy thought and then said, "Well, maybe it isn't just the feast of meat that the people like. Maybe it is the stories that are told after the people eat. Maybe that is the part they like."

"What kind of stories?" asked Naanabozho.

"Well," said the boy, "stories about the great deeds that men do. You know? Stories about great animals that were overcome and conquered by great hunters."

"Great animals, eh? Well, if that is the case, why were the People not impressed by the great beasts I have had brought here? There are very big animals in that pile. Some that people have never seen before."

"Yes," said the boy, "There are some very strange animals, you are right, but they are ones no one had ever seen before, and they are ones no one had ever heard stories about."

"Oh," said Naanabozho. "So the animals have to be ones the people know about and ones that have great stories told about them. Well, what is the biggest animal, the most famous one you know about?"

"*Name*, the Great Sturgeon,"[17] said the boy without hesitation. "He is the greatest. Many stories are told about him. He is the Guardian of the Great Lakes."

"*Name*, eh? Good! I, Naanabozho, son of the West Wind Spirit and an Anishinaabe woman, shall hunt *Name* and gain great fame by killing him. The People will be talking about this for a long, long time. I shall be honored and famous."

Happily, Naanabozho set off for the lodge of his Nookomis, the daughter of the Moon, the ancient *mindimooyenh*, old lady, who had raised him after the death of his own mother. He greeted his grandmother and threw himself down beside her fire.

"*Nookoo*, my grandma," he said, "I am hunting *Name*, the Guardian of the Great Lakes. How does one go about such a great deed?"

"Forget it!" said his grandmother. "*Name* has too great a power."

17 *Name*: the final "e" on this word is pronounced as one would say the "a" in the English word *able*. It is not a silent "e." Also, that final "e" is the part of the word that is emphasized.

"Nothing is too hard for the Great Naanabozho, son of the West . . ."

"I know! I know!" said his grandmother wearily.

"Nookoo," said Naanabozho, "Please help me. You are so very wise. You know how even this difficult thing can be done. Help me! I want to be famous and have people tell great stories about me, too."

"Well," said his grandmother, softening as she always did when he pleaded. "The only way to kill *Name* is to shoot him in the heart with an arrow fletched with the feathers of a Thunderbird."

"A Thunderbird, eh? Well, I am off to get the feathers. I will be famous before long."

And off Naanabozho went to find the Thunderbirds. He traveled for days into the West until he came to the high mountains on top of which the Thunderbirds nested. He sat down at the base of a high cliff and looked up at the Thunderbird nest that was almost in the clouds. Now, how was he going to get up that cliff? It was almost straight up, and it looked like a very long, hard, tiring climb. Surely he could think of some easier way. So Naanabozho turned himself into a rabbit and sat in the clearing, looking up at the nest. Before long a great shadow flew over him. A Thunderbird swooped down and snatched him up in its claws and flew him up to the nest. It dropped him down into the nest where the baby Thunderbirds had just hatched out of their eggs.

"What have you done?" the mother Thunderbird asked her mate. "Why did you bring this rabbit up here? Don't you know Naanabozho is in the area? We have to be very careful with our precious babies."

"Do not worry, wife," said the father Thunderbird. "It is just a little rabbit, and the children are very hungry. They will take no harm. Come, let us go and find them some more supper. One little rabbit won't satisfy our beautiful children long." So the two Thunderbirds flew off looking for more game.

Naanabozho immediately changed himself back into himself and killed the baby Thunderbirds. He gathered two handfuls of their feathers, and jumped out of the nest. He floated to the ground by means of the Thunderbird feathers that he held. As soon as he reached the ground, the mother Thunderbird screamed for she knew her children were no more. The two Thunder Beings swooped down on Naanabozho, the lightning bolts shooting out of their eyes as they screamed their crashing, thunder cries. Naanabozho ran and dodged, and ran some more. The Thunderers were right behind him. Their bolts whizzed by his head, setting fire to the trees on either side of him. He ran until he thought his side would split open, and then he saw a hollow log. He dove into the log and lay there gasping for breath as the Thunderbirds sent their thunderbolts crashing around him. But then the crashing stopped.

The Thunderbirds alighted in a tree on the side of the clearing, and Naanabozho heard the father Thunderbird say, "Well, Naanabozho. You have escaped us. You have found the only place we will not strike. You are hiding in a king-child. This is our own child, and we will not strike it with our power."

Naanabozho lay in the hollow log until he heard the Thunderbirds take wing and fly back to their empty nest. He peeked out cautiously, and then he crawled out of the log, dusting the rotted wood off him with the beautiful feathers.

"Howa!" said Naanabozho, "This tree that has sheltered me is the Thunderbirds' own child! This tree will be very useful to my nephews the Anishinaabeg. If they stand under this tree in a storm, the Thunderers will not hurt them. If they use its bark to cover their lodges, they will be safe even in the worst storms. This will be a very useful tree to my relatives."

To mark the tree so that the Anishinaabeg would always be able to find it, Naanabozho set pictures of the baby Thunderbirds in the bark. The pictures would also serve to remind the Thunder Beings of their children, so that they would never strike either the tree nor anything covered with its bark.

Then Naanabozho went off home, clutching his Thunderbird feathers, to kill *Name* and gain fame. Mii' iw. Miigwech.

Keewaydinoquay said she once told a class how birch is never struck by lightning, only to have a man insist that he had seen a birch that had been struck by lightning and split completely in two. He offered to show Kee, so that weekend they hiked miles back into the bush until they came to a place with a huge, downed tree lying across the clearing. The tree had been struck by lightning, as was evident by the charred edges of the split trunk where the sap had boiled and split the tree neatly into two halves. The only trouble was the tree was not a paper birch. It was a poplar. Kee always got a good laugh with that story!

Birch has another virtue to share with the Anishinaabeg. Birch is a great fire starter. Because of the resins in the bark, birch makes an excellent torch. It was the preferred choice for making a torch with which to attract fish to be speared at night. Early explorers in Wisconsin described the sight of dozens of canoes with lighted birch bark torches on their bows as the Anishinaabeg speared the spawning *ogaawag,* walleyes. They called the lake where they saw the sight Lac du Flambeau, Lake of the Torches.[18]

Birch has helped Anishinaabe light his way, cook his suppers, and warm his home since gichi-mewinzha. A roll of birch bark around a piece of dried cedar bark is still carried in the pocket of careful campers who want to be sure to start their fires under any weather conditions. Birch bark, even if pulled off a floating log, will catch and burn hot enough to start wood on fire. That cannot be said for paper, which burns at a much lower temperature and will often not be hot enough to catch even small twigs. But Grandfather Birch will not let one down in this way.

Grandfather Birch can also be a lifesaving source of food in time of trouble. The inner bark of birch is edible. That taken from a large tree is said to be sweeter than that taken from a smaller birch, but they both have starch and sugars in them. In times of famine Anishinaabeg ate both the inner barks of Grandfather Birch and Grandmother Cedar, but that of birch tastes better because it has less tannin. The inner bark can be eaten raw as it is stripped off the tree, and Crees in the North eat it on portages as a quick "pick-me-up." The inner bark can also be split into strips and dropped into boiling water and cooked as one would cook spaghetti. Or the inner bark can be dried, pulverized with a rock, and used as a flour.

The sap of Grandfather Birch has even more sugar than the inner bark. North of where the maples grow, the sap is traditionally boiled down into syrup and eaten with bannock. The birch sap starts to flow just when the maple sap stops flowing. A family in Alaska still taps birch trees in the spring, boils it down, and sells it as Alaska Birch Syrup.[19] Birch sap is about one half as sweet as maple sap, but it comes out of the tree considerably faster, so it is easier to gather. There is even a soft drink produced now that uses birch sap as the flavoring.

Both the inner bark and the sap have saved many lives. People lost in the woods have only to cut a hole in a birch tree, put a reed in the oozing hole and lay down under the tree to sleep, with

18 Waaswaaganing is the Ojibwe name for Lac du Flambeau, and it has the same meaning as the French and English names.

19 A daughter of the family went to school with my daughter Annmarie at the University of Alaska Fairbanks. The address of the company is Alaska Birch Syrup, P.O. Box 29, Ester, Alaska 99725.

the reed-straw in their mouth. By morning they will have gotten enough energy to continue on. There is a teaching story about this that Keewaydinoquay always told when she lectured about Grandfather Birch:

"The Runner and the Birch Sap"

Many years ago, when the Anishinaabeg were still fighting the Iroquois, a village of the People were all out picking blueberries. It had been a great growing season, and everyone, from the youngest to the oldest elders, was needed to gather the berries that would be dried to last them through the coming winter. As the group labored in the summer sun, a runner suddenly came gasping into the clearing. He bent over, caught his breath, and managed to tell them that a whole war party of Iroquois had been sighted by their relatives in the next village and was headed in their direction.

The elders all gathered together and a hurried discussion began about how they were to meet this dangerous situation. It was decided that they could not face so large a war party on their own. They would need the assistance of both the village that had sent the message and also the assistance of the village of their clan that was a day's travel and more to the west.

The strongest young man of the group was chosen as the messenger. Since there was no time to be spared, it was decided that they would have to send the man off immediately if he was to get to their kin in time to bring them aid before the enemy arrived. There was no time to return to the village to get him the supplies he would need for the trip. The adults all took off their moccasins and made a bundle of them for the young man to carry so that when he ran through his own he would not have to run in his bare feet. But they had no dried food with them to send with the young man to sustain him on his journey. They just had to send him without provisions.

The young man took leave of his family and, with the blessings of his elders, he started as fast as he could to bring word of the coming enemy and to bring the village aid. He ran and he ran and he ran all through the day, stopping only as long as it took to change moccasins as he ran through pair after pair. By nightfall he was exhausted. He fell down on the ground and caught his breath and worried how he was ever to run on in the morning with no supper that night and no food in the morning to give him the energy he needed. As he lay on the ground he heard the lapping of the waves on the lake that was nearby. So, the young man got up and walked to the shore and smiled when he saw the reeds growing close by. He broke off a reed and looked around the shoreline until he found Nimishoomis-wiigwaas, Grandfather Birch, a white birch tree. With his knife he made a slash in the bark and placed the reed in the tree's wound. Then he lay down to sleep under the birch with the other end of the hollow reed in his mouth. As he slept, drop by drop the sap of the birch tree ran down the reed into his mouth. By morning, when he awoke, enough of the sap had dripped into his mouth that he had the energy he needed to continue on his journey. He arrived after much effort at the village of his clan, warned them of the attack, and was able to go back with the warriors in time to save his family from the war party.

Nimishoomis-wiigwaas had truly saved the runner and his people by the gift of his sap. The young man had been saved and cared for by his relative.

Mii' iw. Miigwech.

————————

Birch even helps the Anishinaabeg when its wood has rotted. The dried, rotted wood of birch is added to the rotted wood of white spruce and the cones of jack pine to make a smoky fire used to tan deer and moose hides. The rotted birchwood gives the hides a rich, reddish color. The rotted wood of birch is also used to make a slow, smoky fire used to cure meat and dry fish (Leighton 1985, 32–33).

In the days of the Gete-Anishinaabeg, Grandfather Birch surrounded a person in life and in death. Some Anishinaabeg rolled their dead in birch bark before placing them in their graves. Other Anishinaabeg used sheets of birch along with woven mats of Grandmother Cedar to line the grave. The spirit houses that were made to cover new graves were made of cedar and birch as well. To mark graves the People often braided young, standing birch trees. Birch is a short-living tree, so the family might have to return periodically to make sure that the original marker trees were still standing and to plant and braid new ones as necessary to be able to locate the graves of their kin. Such marker trees might be carved with the dead person's clan symbol carved upside down for further identification. People also braided marker trees as indications of trails. Those too had to be renewed as one set of trees aged or were blown over in storms.

Along with the very real technological virtues that Grandfather Birch has to share with us, it also has many medicinal virtues as well. The budding ends of young twigs taste of wintergreen. It is the same taste as the little, green woodland plant called wintergreen (*Gaultheria procumbens*), because both plants have the same chemical in them, methyl calculate. Paper birch has this chemical in a lesser amount than the Black and Yellow Birch, but they all three have been used by the Anishinaabeg for the healing they have to offer.

The fresh twig tips of Grandfather Birch are used to treat stomach disorders and to relieve cramps. It is also the birch oil in Bengay that gives that commercial product its good smell and that makes the skin feel cooled and refreshed when one spreads it on. Birch oil has been very helpful in making salves to treat rheumatism.

Any part of the birch is aromatic, a stimulant, and a diuretic, increasing the flow of urine. A tea of the foliage and young twigs is used to treat diarrhea, disorders of the digestive track, rheumatism, and stones in the kidneys and bladder. A medicinal syrup can be made in the spring. To kill worms, a tea of leaves or bark, one teaspoon to one cup of boiling water, is given three to five times daily. Eczema is treated with a strong decoction of leaves, twigs, and/or bark as a skin wash, along with birch-leaf tea drunk daily.

Kee's mother, Sarah Good Cook, MinoSoahnIkwe, kept a container of birch charcoal in a box above her wood stove. It was chewed to relieve gas and indigestion.

Birch does not only grow in this area. It is a circumboreal plant, growing all across Europe and Asia as well as North America. Grandfather Birch has been used in traditional Russian medicine in much the same way as it is used by the Anishinaabeg. Birch twigs are put into vodka and used to treat colds and liver and gall bladder complaints. Birch charcoal is used to treat poisoning by both the Anishinaabeg and by the traditional healers of Siberia.

In his highly readable book *Stalking the Healthful Herb,* the late Euell Gibbons said of the active ingredient in the birch tree:

> . . . the essential oil of Wintergreen is 99 percent methyl salicylate. It was not until the latter half of the seventeenth century that

scientific medicine discovered the importance of the salicylates as antipyretics, antirheumatics, diaphoretics, and analgesics, useful in allaying aches and pains, thus confirming the empirical findings that the herbalists had discovered centuries before. When the American Indians and those badly maligned "old wives" were giving strong Wintergreen tea for fevers, headaches, rheumatism, and other aches and pains, they were far in advance of the medical science of their day. (Gibbons 1966b, 93)

There is also medicinal value in a fungus that grows on birch trees. Keewaydinoquay called the fungus "Shaga."[20] It is a dirty black wart, the interior of which was kept and used for a tonic to purify blood. For violent complaints of the stomach it was also used. It was one of the last things used for cancer, when operations were not possible, or for tuberculosis of the bone or stomach. Russians use it the same way for similar conditions.[21] To make Kee's medicinal recipe, one part shaga is added to four parts water. The water is added warm, but not boiled. It is allowed to stand for twenty-four hours, strained, and administered a little at a time, as the patient can take it without being ill.

I believe this same fungus is used by the Anishinaabeg in the Rainy Lake area of Ontario. They called it Zagataagan, and they used it as a cleansing smudge by burning it on a shell or asinaagan.

The *Peterson Field Guide to Medicinal Plants and Herbs of Eastern and Central North America* says that, of the birches, Sweet or Black Birch has an essential oil that was formerly produced in Appalachia but is now produced synthetically; and that it is dangerous, "easily absorbed through skin," and has killed people. Of the Paper or White Birch it says:

> Betulinic acid from many species, including birches, is a promis-
> ing anticancer compound (against melanomas); also anti-
> inflammatory and antiviral. Betulin, contained in bark, has
> anticancer, antiviral, and anti-inflammatory activity. Chagga
> (*Inonotus*), a black fungus on white birch, has a folk reputation
> against skin and internal cancers. It is said to take up betulin
> from birches. (Foster and Duke 2000, 331)

What should be remembered when taking traditional medicines is that the modern way of utilizing the healing of plants is very different from our traditional methods. The essential oil of a plant is used in modern medicine, and it is the part of the plant that

20 This is the way Kee spelled this word. It does not appear to be an Ojibwe word. The *Peterson Field Guide* uses a similar word, "Chagga" (331).

21 Kee was impressed with Russian uses for birch, as they were so similar to Ojibwe ones. She gave lectures on their similarities.

is usually used in scientific studies, but it is a very concentrated version of the plant's medicine. Where we use the plant material itself, either in a tea or a decoction, or the smoke of the burning plant material, or in a tincture made in alcohol, we are using the oil in a much diluted form. The essential oil of the plant is using the oil in very concentrated form that is divorced from the rest of the chemicals that are present in the growing plant itself. Most any chemical that is effective as a medicine may well be a poison if used in too great a concentration or for too long a time. Two aspirin will cure one's headache, but a handful will make one's stomach bleed and possibly kill a person. One must use common sense with medicine as with any other aspect of life if one is to live long. Water taken in enough quantity will kill, too.

My Elder Sister: Nimisenh

Ingiigido'aag
"She Speaks for Us"
"She Stands at Prayer for Us"
Wadab
Aninaandag
"She Points Out"
Balsam fir
Abies balsamea

Another of the plants that stand in familial relationship to the Anishinaabeg is the balsam fir. It has several names among the People, and each name is helpful in remembering the virtues that this tree has to share with us.

She is called *Nimisenh,* My Elder Sister. Just as the oldest girl child in a family will often adopt the role of "Little Mother," caring for and tending the younger siblings, so Nimisenh cares for the Anishinaabeg. She has medicines to ease our aches and scrapes and burns.

Like all green plants, Nimisenh has vitamin C. One can make a great healing tea from this tree's foliage. To make a cup, snip a small branchlet of the new growth at the end of the branch, 3 to 4 inches long. Pour boiled, and slightly cooled, water over the needles. Allow the tea to steep, covered, for 1 minute but no longer. If one leaves the plant material in the water for too long, the turpentines will be released and the resulting tea will taste like a cup of turpentine. The tea should taste like limeade. It is a light, pleasing tea, strong in vitamin C and therefore a good tea to take in the wintertime or when one has a cold.

The chief of the healing virtues Nimisenh has to share with the Anishinaabe is a very healing remedy for burns. The sap of the tree is a wonderful, healing agent, a great first-aid treatment for first- to third-degree burns.

The bark of young and middle-aged balsams has a very characteristic series of horizontal pitch blisters that are full of a golden, yellow, very sticky, sap-like oleoresin.[22] To harvest this

22 Older balsams have a rougher surface to the bark on their trunks, with fine irregular scales.

My Elder Sister: Nimisenh,
Balsam fir (*Abies balsamea*)

oleoresin, one must prick the blisters on the bark of the trunk
with a needle or pin, and push the liquid resin from the other side
toward the pinprick hole. A golden drop will be squirted out of
the hole. Catch the drops in a small glass bottle. Be sure to seal the
blister with your finger to avoid leaving the tree open to insect or
disease infestation through the opening in its bark. It would be
a poor "thank you" to the tree to take healing for oneself and kill
the tree. That would not be maintaining the balance. One gathers
the oleoresin drop by drop from the resin blisters on the trunk. Be
sure to take along a jar of alcohol when going to harvest the resin
because alcohol will clean the very sticky stuff off of the skin. If
one forgets the alcohol, one will have to run one's fingers through
sand or fine, dry, powdered clay to cut down on the sticky effect.
Hand sanitizers are also effective in cutting the stickiness on one's
hands. It is also a good idea to braid one's hair before starting to
harvest balsam resin; otherwise one might find oneself stuck in a
tree like Absalom.[23]

A jar of balsam sap will keep well on one's medicine chest or
shelf for years, but it is best to take the top off the bottle as often
as one can remember to, and to wipe the jar with alcohol to keep

23 Absalom was the long-haired,
vain son of King David in the
Bible who, while rising in rebellion
against his father, was caught by
his long hair in the branches of a
tree, where his enemies found and
slew him. (II Samuel 18:10.)

the cap from becoming securely stuck. If the sap hardens, and one cannot get the top off the jar, it can be reliquified by placing the bottle in boiling water, the way one reliquifies hardened honey.

Balsam sap is easiest to harvest from March through September, when the sap is running in the tree. It is, of course, much slower running in the winter, but it can even be harvested from a cut Christmas tree in December. One of our ethnobotany students at the University wanted a bottle of balsam sap for his end-of-term display, which stood in place of a final exam for the course. He was in the city, with no access to growing balsams, so he went to a Christmas tree lot and asked if he could squeeze their trees. At first the tree lot owners just looked at him very warily and said, "No!" But when the student pointed out that it would make their lots smell wonderful, the owners said, "Do it!" He got his bottle of sap and an "A" for both effort and originality.

The sap will heal burns of any degree of intensity. And it will heal them without scars. It should be poured onto the burn immediately. The sap will form a natural, artificial skin, its own airtight bandage, while the skin grows back underneath.

The sap is antiseptic and analgesic. It will keep the burn from becoming infected, and it will remove the hurt from even a very painful burn, one minute after it is poured on. One time Kee was on her island alone, and she burned her arm and hand on the cabin's wood stove. She grabbed the balsam sap bottle, but the top was glued on too tightly for her to manage it with her burned hand. It was so painful a burn that she was afraid that she might pass out. Then she thought, "How stupid! There are dozens of balsams right out the cabin door." So she stumbled out the door in the dark and found the trees by feel and smell and squeezed the sap right out of the blisters right onto her burn. Within seconds the pain was gone, and she did not faint.

If the sap is applied and allowed to stay on the burn until it falls off on its own, in a week or two, the new skin will grow in without scar tissue forming. One time, on Minis-kitigaan, one of Kee's apprentices was making Indian fry bread on the wood stove. She was being silly and trying to show off her cooking skill to a boy she fancied. With a gay flip of the wrist, she tossed a piece of dough into the hot oil and spattered the oil all over her upper chest and arms. She was wearing a halter-top and most of her skin was exposed. Kee grabbed her and poured on the balsam sap. The girl cried from the pain as well as from the thought that she would look funny for a week.

She said, "I'll be all black and dirty, and he won't like me."

Kee said, "Honey, if I don't do this, no man will look at you again."

The girl survived the pain, and the embarrassment, too. The sap is so sticky that it quickly gets covered with dirt and fuzz and looks dreadful. It is, however, possible to dust the sap with talcum powder, before it picks up too much fuzz and that improves the look of the bandage. When Kee married the girl to another man a few years later, the girl went to her wedding fair and pink and unscarred, thanks to Nimisenh.

Another time on the Island, an Anglican priest and his family were visiting Kee. His kids decided to clean out the fire pit, but, being kids, they took the grill off and leaned it against the rocks, forgot what they were doing, and went off to do something else. Their father came by immediately after they were out of sight and decided to finish the job himself. He grabbed the grill with both hands, and it fell over his forearms. It had been red hot, but it was covered with a fine ash, so the priest thought it was cold. He was very badly burned, with the checker pattern of the grill extending up to his elbows. Kee said she could only think of the fact that this man, being a pastor, would have to spend his life throwing back the sleeves of his robes, raising his arms with the horrid checkered scars, and saying "Let us pray." So she poured on the balsam sap. The priest healed beautifully, and he and his whole family spent the rest of the summer gathering sap. Anytime someone asked, "Hey, where is the minister's family?" the answer was always, "Oh, they are out squeezing balsams." The priest wanted a jar of the sap for each of the households of his extended family and for every household of his congregation.

The only trick to using balsam sap on burns is that one must leave it on until it falls off on its own. By that time, it will look awful, but it will be airtight and it will keep air and infection and dirt away from the burn. The new skin will come in completely smooth.

This sap is also very helpful and healing on shoe blisters. It makes a great first aid when one is out hiking and develops blisters in one's shoes. It has gotten many an Anishinaabe back from the hunt.

The sap is also very fragrant. It is nice just for its smell. It makes a good healing agent to add to other skin ointments as well.

The sap has a commercial value. It is sold as a product called "Canada Balsam" to scientists, to permanently seal microscope slides.[24] It will seal the cover on a slide without trapping air bubbles which can be very annoying under a microscope. Little Cree kids in the north were paid to go around squeezing the pitch blisters and catching the drops for this market.

Another Anishinaabe name that balsam fir has is "She Points Out." This name was probably derived from the fact that balsams always have a head. It is the perfect Christmas tree shape, and it grows that way without being trimmed, too. If, in a hard winter with deep snow or in a high wind, the balsam should lose her "head", the topmost surviving branch will come up to become the top of the tree. That is the reason that, even though it makes the best Christmas tree because of its wonderful smell, the fact that it holds its needles if fresh and leaves only soft, easily swept-up needles when they fall on the carpet, it is also so hard to find a balsam with a perfectly straight trunk. The tree looks beautiful, but it will have a bent trunk that makes it hard to get into a tree stand. The fact that balsams regrow their tops by the substitution of the top branches, however, makes it a very nice tree to grow on one's front lawn. If it should be topped in a storm, it will not just stay topless the way a spruce in a similar situation will.

Kee also called balsam *Ingiigido'aag,* which she translated as "She Speaks for Us" or "She Stands at Prayer for Us."[25] This is her most ancient name, the one by which she is called in the oldest stories. This name is significant because it indicates the spiritual value that balsams have to share with Anishinaabeg.

Have you ever been out in a stand of balsam right after a rain or just at dawn or sundown? Have you ever been hit by a blast of beautiful fragrance that balsams release whenever the temperature changes? This wonderful release of smell is even evident in a six-month-old, dead balsam standing in one's living room covered with twinkling electric lights. When someone opens the outside door and lets in a blast of cold air, one can suddenly smell the "Christmasy" smell again. This release of scent, this present of incense, is said to be prayer. It is almost a Pan-Indian idea that prayer should be accompanied by incense, that the prayers of the People are borne upward, outward to the Spirit World on the wings of the smoke of burning incense. That is the reason for the use of kinnikinnick and asemaa in either an *opwaagan,* pipe, or asinaagan. Rising smoke carries the prayer, the thought, into the Spirit World.

Balsam prays for us constantly, and one can use her as a prayer aid in times of need. MidéOgema told the story of a fisherman

24 Kee discussed "Canada Balsam" in her class lectures. For more information on this product, see Smith 1978, 17.

25 A more literal translation might be "She makes me speak." See Glossary for more information.

of his village who had a large family to feed. The fisherman had been unsuccessful fishing for several days when suddenly he had a huge fish on the line, enough to feed his whole family. The man was very grateful and ordinarily would have stopped work to give thanks, but if he dropped the line to reach for his kinnikinnick to put down as an offering or even if he had thrown up his hands to say "Thank you, Great Spirit for this fish to feed my children," he would have lost the fish. So he just shouted, "Say thanks for me, Nimisenh." He knew that somewhere at that very moment a balsam fir would release a bit of incense to carry his prayer of thanksgiving, leaving him free to land his children's supper. When we do not have enough time in our hectic lives to say our own prayers, balsam fir will do it for us. "She Stands at Prayer for Us" with her arms outstretched and releasing incense to take our prayers to the Manidoog.

The beautiful smell of balsam is a welcome addition to kinnikinnick, if the mixture is to be burned in an asinaagan and not in a pipe. The resins in all of the conifers, although they smell delightful, will produce a sticky, tarry residue when burned that may clog up a pipe or the little air passages in one's lungs, or at least they will be biting to the tongue and break one's concentration.

There was a time when the smell of balsam smoke was considered a great perfume. There are stories in which a lover would stand over a balsam smudge to perfume his clothes before going to see his light of love.

The balsam is a conifer and one of the trees called in the vernacular, Evergreens. This is a poor classification, however, because many plants are "evergreen" that are not trees, and there are trees that are conifers but not "evergreen." There are several ways to know a balsam and to distinguish it from the spruce and the yew, two other native plants that people tend to confuse with the balsam. The needles of balsam are flat, not round like the spruce needles. The needles spiral around the branch, although they may appear to be growing only on two sides of the branch. The needles are soft, not sharp like the spruce nor rubbery like those of the yew. On the underside of the needles one can see two white lines running down the length of the needle. When the needles are bruised or broken, the characteristic balsam smell, what most people call the "Christmas tree smell" is released. Most spruces smell like tomcats, and yews have very little smell at all. Only the balsam has the little pitch blisters on their trunks that run horizontal to the ground.

The cones of the balsam are the only ones of the conifers that sit straight up on the branches. One usually sees the glistening, purple cones only in May, as the squirrels love them and sit and eat them like corn-on-the-cob, leaving only the little stick-like center stems of the cones sitting straight up on the branches. It rather looks like a tree covered with toothpicks or an old-fashioned Christmas tree with little candles clipped to the branches. Perhaps that is the reason people started putting lights on trees at Christmas time, because they had seen the remnants of the balsam cones after the squirrels had eaten their fill. There are both male and female cones on this tree. The female cones come first, followed by the male. Children love to flick the male cones with a finger to watch the clouds of yellow pollen released into the air.

If the tree is free to grow as it likes, and if it has ample space and sunlight, it will be a perfect cone shape, always in whorls of branches around its trunk. Without being tended and clipped into shape, it will grow into a perfectly geometric form.

There are several craft applications to which balsam can be applied. The sap and needles of the balsam can be added to soap for fragrance, if added sparingly. They should be added just at the end of the cooking stage, to avoid driving off the essential oils with heat. The needles of balsam are also delightful additions to potpourri, dried in dry potpourri and fresh in wet potpourri. Dream pillows, where fresh balsam needles are added to cattail down in a pillow ticking, will smell beautiful and possibly bring one a dream of the north woods. A dream pillow with a strong inhalant will often help to clear the head of a cold sufferer.[26]

26 Cedar foliage, juniper wood, sweet fern, or mint leaves are also commonly added to dream pillows.

The balsam foliage and the springy branches are a traditional camp bed. Generations of campers have arranged layers of balsam branches and then laid sleeping mats, bedrolls, or sleeping bags over the boughs for a bed both soft and unbelievably fragrant.

Among the Crees of northern Quebec through Alberta, the traditional floor of the log-and-tarp winter hunting-camp shelter is balsam branches. The branches are pushed into the ground with the natural bow of the wood pointing down. The branches are overlapped to produce a springy floor that keeps the family off of the frozen ground.

The wood of the balsam fir is "... light, pale brown, frequently streaked with yellow, weak, soft, coarse grained and quickly perishable" (Smith 1978, 16). The wood is not particularly valuable. It is not good for paper nor for building as it rots easily. After the original forest was cut in the Midwest, balsam was not replanted. Now it is mostly a cold-weather tree, growing around the Great

Lakes down to southern Wisconsin and Michigan. It is, however, a great tree to plant! Balsam has so many virtues to share with the People that the fact that it is no longer considered valuable by the dominant society as a sale commodity is not necessarily a bad thing.

The rootlets of the balsam fir give it another name by which it has been known among the Anishinaabeg. In reference to these rootlets it is commonly called *Ojiibik*, root, or Wadab. The rootlets are uniform in size, easily gathered, and will split evenly. They are used for binding canoes or for sewing large, tough baskets made of birch bark. They are used where a very strong binding is required.

Nimisenh, "Elder Sister"; "She Who Points Out"; Ingiigido'aag, "She Speaks for Us" or "She Who Stands at Prayer for Us," is a blessed plant. She has so many virtues to share with Anishinaabeg that we should be grateful more often. *Chi-Miigwech,* thank you very much, Nimisenh!

3

Conifers

"Why Some Trees Keep Their Leaves When Others Do Not"

Gichi-mewinzha, gii-oshki-niiging akiing, there was a little *bineshiinh,* bird, who had a serious problem. *Gii-niibing,* when it was summer, in the last storms of the season, the little bineshiinh had been blown from the branch on which he had taken shelter and slammed against the trunk of a tree. He huddled in pain and fear through the night and was most happy to see the sun rising the next morning. He heaved a great sigh of relief and tried to stretch his wings to fly off to find his family, but his wing would not work. It hung at his side, and he could not stretch it out. The little bineshiinh sat for some time pondering his problem and then decided to make the best of things until his wing was strong again. He found that he could still hop very well so he could get around enough to find his meals and cool drinks of water in the stream. By day he sat on a low branch and watched his family and friends as they took short, then long, then longer flights around the clearing, preparing for their coming trip to the Southland. The little bineshiinh tried not to worry, and he sang his best songs to cheer his family and himself.

But *ani-dagwaagig,* fall came. The days were shorter and colder. His family and friends stayed as long as they dared, but in the end they had to call to the little bineshiinh, wishing him well, and promising to see him *wii-ani-ziigwang,* when it was spring again. They took to the air, and soon the little bineshiinh was alone. For a time he felt very sad and almost too frightened to do anything. He had never been alone before. He tried not to think about the long, hard winter that was to come. His kind had always left the Northland at this time of year and did not return until the warm breezes came again.

After a while, though, the little bineshiinh said to himself, "Well, I am alone now for a time. But I can still sing a cheery song, and I can still hop about, and I can still take care of myself. My family would not want me to lose heart." So the little bineshiinh tucked his broken wing up close to his body, and he went about his daily, busy, little life as best he could. After a while he found that it was really not so bad. He found ways of doing the things he had done before when he had the use of both his wings. It might take him longer to find his supper and a place to sleep, but if he tried he found he could do rather well in the cool days *dagwaagig,* during fall.

But then *ani-biboon,* winter came. The days grew even shorter, and the sun seemed far away. The great cold-blower *Giiwedin,* the North Wind, roared down upon the land, and the first snows of winter swirled about the little bineshiinh as he hopped about on his daily journeys. Giiwedin blew and blew, and the little bineshiinh huffed his feathers up so that he would not be cold. As he sat puffed up against the cold, he decided it was time to ask the other beings about him for aid. He hopped across the clearing to the base of a *wiigwaasi-mitig,* birch tree.

"O beautiful Wiigwaasi-mitig," said the little bineshiinh, "I have a broken wing, and I could not go with my family when they left for the Southland. Could I shelter on your beautiful, white limbs and hide myself in your leaves so that I will not be cold when Giiwedin blows?"

"No," said the wiigwaasi-mitig, with a disdainful toss of his leaves. "We in this forest have our own winter birds whom we must foster this time of year. I, for one, do my part, but I am not interested in taking in any other bineshiinyag who should have flown away by now. Be off with you!"

Humph, thought the little bineshiinh. The wiigwaasi-mitig does not seem very friendly. Perhaps he just has such weak branches that he is afraid that the weight of another bineshiinh may be too much when Giiwedin starts to blow again. I will just go ask *mitigomizh,* the oak tree, for help. He has such strong wood, surely he will be able to help me.

The little bineshiinh hopped over to the mitigomizh and asked that he might be allowed to hide in the leaves, close to the trunk of the mighty mitigomizh. But the mitigomizh said, "Winter is a long time. You would get hungry and eat all of my acorns if I allowed you to shelter here. It is all I can do to feed the *ajidamoog,* gray squirrels, and the *misajidamoog,* red squirrels, and the *agongosag,* chipmunks. Be off with you!"

Well, thought the little bineshiinh, perhaps the Mitigomizh is a little crowded at that. Maybe the *bagaanaakomizh,* butternut tree, will help me. So he hopped over to the bagaanaakomizh and asked if he might shelter in her until wii-ani-ziigwang.

But the bagaanaakomizh answered in a huff, "Isn't it bad enough that the Anishinaabeg and the *makwag,* bears, paw through my branches, stealing my nuts? Must I be bothered by another beggar as well? Off with you! Hop south if you cannot fly. Just leave me alone."

Well, thought the little bineshiinh, I suppose it must be very tiring to have people always bothering one for one's tasty nuts. Maybe the *oziisigobimizh,* willow, will help me.

But the oziisigobimizh just waved her long leaves at the bineshiinh and said, "Oziisigobimizhiig do not talk to strangers, and we have never met. It is possible that some lesser tree might not mind a strange bird hopping on her branches, but I certainly do. Go away!"

The little bineshiinh just hung his head and then hid it under his one good wing. Such a lack of hospitality! The disrespect and humiliation hurt even more than the pain of his broken wing. He almost looked forward to the coming of Giiwedin, when he knew he would just get drowsy and slip into the last long sleep if he could not find shelter. In his pain he almost thought it might be better.

But, no, he thought, my family expects me to be brave. If no one can help me, I can help myself. I could just start hopping and maybe I will get to the Southland before Giiwedin blows again.

As the little bineshiinh started to hop toward the South, he heard a friendly voice call, "Little Brother, Little Brother. Come over here. You may live in my branches all during biboon if you choose. I have lots of room. If your wing is too sore for you to follow your kind to the Southland, it is time for the trees to offer their assistance." The little bineshiinh hopped gratefully into the low branches of the friendly *gaawaandag,* spruce tree, and huddled close within her warm, close foliage.

"Indeed," said the deep, booming voice of the great tall *zhing-waak,* white pine tree, "and I can help by sheltering both you and Gaawaandag when the cold winds blow."

"And I can offer my cones for your food," said the *giizhik,* cedar tree.

Safe in the branches of his new friends, the little bineshiinh settled down to wait out biboon. As Giiwedin came down upon the forest glade, the little bineshiinh was snug and sheltered again.

Giiwedin raged over the forest. He heaped snow into deep piles and then arranged them and rearranged them to suit his fancy. As he blew, Giiwedin asked Gichi-manidoo if he could have all of the leaves of the trees as he passed.

"No," said Gichi-manidoo, "You may have the leaves of the wiigwaasi-mitig, the mitigomizh, the bagaanaakomizh, and the oziisigobimizh, and the other trees who would not help my brave little bineshiinh with the broken wing, but you may not have the leaves of the gaawaandag, who offered him a warm branch, the zhingwaak, who offered him shelter, nor the leaves of the giizhik, who offered him food. They shall keep their leaves when you blow over the land."

And so it was then, and so it is now. Mii' iw Miigwech.

"Naanabozho and Paul Bunyan"[1]

[1] This is my retelling of a story told in the 1950s to a group of researchers, working on a grant from the University of Minnesota Fund for Regional Writing, who were trying to determine the status of the oral tradition among the Minnesota Ojibwe. They determined that mostly the elders in the Ojibwe communities kept the tradition. They said their youngest storyteller had been born in 1903. Coleman, Bernard, Ellen Frogner, and Estelle Eich, *Ojibwa Myths and Legends* (Minneapolis: Ross and Haines, 1962), 99.

A hundred years ago, Naanabozho was walking along the St. Croix River in Minnesota when he heard a great cry of distress from the northwest. He heard the *binewag*, partridges, drumming out the distress call on the hard ground. Then Naanabozho heard the *maangwag*, loons, take up the call as their long, long, haunting voices echoed across the lakes. As Naanabozho started to run toward the call he heard the *makwag*, bears, all stomping and huffing. Then the *bizhiwag*, lynx, and the *gidagaa-bizhiwag*, bobcat, started to scream in their highest, most frightened voices. The *zhiishiibag*, ducks, were quacking hysterically, and the *nikag*, Canada geese, were honking their deepest, most terrified calls. As Naanabozho ran he heard the cries of his relatives the Anishinaabeg, too. He ran and he ran until he had covered the two hundred miles from the St. Croix to the deep Northwoods in record time.

As he ran through the woods the cries and honks and quacks and screams and huffs and drumming changed to "Naanabozho is coming! Naanabozho is coming!"

It was a very tired Naanabozho who stumbled into the camp of his relatives the Anishinaabeg, where he was quickly told that the loggers with their great champion Paul Bunyan were clear-cutting the pines. Naanabozho stopped only long enough to reassure his relatives that he would try his best to help before he rushed on toward the sound of the crashing trees.

He found Paul Bunyan swinging his ax and cutting down a whole row of three hundred year old *zhingwaakwag*, white pines, and *apakwanagemagoog*, red pines, with one swing. The giant trees crashed to the ground before Paul Bunyan's ax as if they were so much grass being felled by a gardener swinging a knife.

Naanabozho called out to Paul Bunyan, "Hey, fella. Stop that! Creator gave the trees to my relatives the Anishinaabeg, and their four-legged and winged and creeping Elder Brothers, too. This is their home. They need these trees. Without them, nothing will be able to live in this land."

Well, Paul Bunyan hardly paused in his swing to listen to Naanabozho, so pretty soon the fight started. Naanabozho and Paul Bunyan argued and roared, wrestled and fought each other for three long days and even longer nights. Pretty soon it sounded like *wese'an,* there was a tornado! All of the loggers and all of the Anishinaabeg and all of the birds and animals hid, trembling at the din they made.

The Anishinaabeg say that Naanabozho must have won that battle, or there would not be one tree left standing in the north woods today.

Pines
Pinus

~~~~~~

Like the translation for an Anishinaabe name that Kee used for Pines, "He is tied up," pines have bunches of needles that are tied together in bundles. The native pines of Wisconsin and the Great Lakes states are:

> White Pine, *Pinus strobus*
> Red Pine, *Pinus resinosa*
> Jack Pine, *Pinus banksiana*

Another common, although not indigenous, pine of this area is:

> Scotch Pine, *Pinus sylvestris*

Zhingwaak
White Pine
Pinus strobus

~~~~~~

Keewaydinoquay always said the white pine was like a fine lady. She said Zhingwaak was the most *refined* of the pine family. Every aspect of her being is refined and genteel. When Kee spoke of the white pine she would "become" the white pine. With her body language and her gestures suddenly there would be a stately princess of a woman or a tree right in front of one's eyes. She would make swaying, graceful movements with her arms and hands to make her students "see" the grace of the white pine as it stood on a hill with its branches extended in a picturesque pose. She did "white pine" so well that every single time I have seen a white pine since, I have seen Kee.

Zhingwaak's needles are the most delicate of all of the pines, slender, soft, and delicate. They are always tied together in bunches with five needles to a bunch. A good way to remember that is that there are five needles in a bunch, and there are five letters in the English word "white." The needles are 2½ to 5 inches in length, bright green when new but darker with age. Each

Zhingwaak: White Pine
(*Pinus strobus*)

needle has a faint, lighter-colored strip down the center of it that gives the overall effect of a slight bluish cast to the foliage of the tree (*Trees of North America*, 15).

Zhingwaak's bark is the dress of a fine lady as well. It is tight and gray and very smooth; nothing garish or uncouth about her. She looks as if she is dressed in old, fine, gray silk.

She has long drooping cones, 4 to 8 inches in length. They are tapered and narrow with loose, flexible scales. The seeds in the cones are brown and ¼ inch in length. They are the preferred food of the red squirrel, who will often cache large piles of the green cones for the winter (Smith 1978, 6).

The form of a zhingwaak is graceful. She stands against the horizon rather like a pine in a Chinese painting, with flowing, horizontal, separated branches.

Her sap is clear and strong. It is so thin it does not dry in clumps as the sap of other pines do. It runs down the white pine's smooth bark and dries, leaving long white streaks against the trunk. Her cones, her shape, her sap, her needles. Everything about the white pine is genteel and refined.

As with all truly fine ladies, her value is inestimable. The white pine was the prime lumber tree of the early lumber days. The early history of the United States is intricately connected to that of the white pine. It was the first really important industry in colonial times. The wood of the white pine was very coveted by the British Crown for their navy. Many a sailing vessel had full-sized white pines standing on their decks as masts. It was the white pine that made Britain the Mistress of the Seas and built the British Empire, and the struggle for control of the lumbering business had a great deal to do with the tensions that resulted in the American Revolution. In the Midwest, Wisconsin and Michigan and Minnesota were covered to the edge of the Great Plains with huge stands of white pine so dense that it was said a squirrel could have run from Lake Erie to the prairies in Minnesota on the tops of white pines without once having to come to ground. Nowadays, white pines are considered mature when they are 80 to 120 feet tall, with diameters of 3 to 4 feet, but in the old days there were reports of white pines 150 to 200 feet tall and 5 to 7 feet in diameter, some four hundred years old (Smith 1978, 6).

Apakwanagemag
"He Scalps Himself"
"He Flakes Himself Off"
Red Pine
Pinus resinosa

Keewaydinoquay's name for Red Pine was "He Flakes Himself Off" or, more colorfully, "He Scalps Himself." This was in reference to the fact that the red pine's bark has a very distinctive growing style, where large flakes of the bark are shed from its trunk as the tree ages. The tree has a very untidy appearance, and it does give one the feeling that it is "scalping" itself.

The red pine is also called "Norway pine," but that is a poor name because the tree is native to North America and does not grow naturally in Norway. It may have gotten that name either because it grows around Norway, Maine or because an early European colonist confused it with Scotch pine, which does grow in Norway (Smith 1978, 7).

The red pine is a great, robust tree. Everything about it is oversized and grand. Where white pine is like a fine lady, red pine is like as strapping, young, masculine giant.

Apakwanagemag: Red Pine
(*Pinus resinosa*)

Its needles are the longest of the conifers in this region. They are usually 5 to 6 inches in length, dark green in color, sharp, and are tied together two to a bundle, with a very obvious, dry brown sheath at the bottom of the bunch. If one bends one of the needles in half, it will snap. The needles are thinner and more brittle than the Austrian pine, with which red pine is often confused. The needles are almost twice as long as those of the Scotch pine (*Trees of North America*, 4).

The cones of red pine are about 2 inches long and egg-shaped in appearance. They do not have sharp edges. They produce light brown seeds that are ¼ to ½ inch in length (Smith 1978, 7).

The wood of the red pine is "heavier, harder, and more resinous than White Pine making it a very desirable tree to the lumbering industry" (Smith 1978, 7). It is a quick-growing tree that produces large plants in twenty to forty years. The trunks are very strong and tall with very little tapering at the top. Mature trees are between 60 and 100 feet high with trunks of 2 to 3 feet in diameter. In a forest situation the lower branches will die off, leaving a tall, straight pole with branches starting halfway up, approximately. The branches grow straight out at a 90-degree angle from the trunk in whorls. One whorl is produced a year; therefore, it is possible to read a tree's age by counting the whorls or the branch scars on the trunk. The tree may grow one or two feet a year.

The bark of the red pine has a very distinctive characteristic. The tree gets its common English name from the dark-red to orange-red color of its bark. As the tree ages, the bark gets quite thick and flakes off the trunk in large plates, leaving the distinctive red bark exposed. This bark is so tough that it can actually protect the tree in a forest fire where all of the Reds may remain standing when other timber and brush is burned around it (Smith 1978, 7).

Okikaandag
"He Is Crippled with Arthritis"
Jack Pine
Pinus banksiana

The species part of the scientific name is *banksiana*. The jack pine was renamed with this species name to honor a great botanist named Banks. Kee said she thought it was a good thing that people who spent their whole lives studying plants should be honored for their efforts, but she preferred the older scientific name: *Pinus divaricata*. She said that it was a better name because one of the tree's most distinguishing characteristics is that it has two short needles in a bunch, ¾ to 1½ inches long, that appear to be slightly sprung. The old scientific name means "Jump-apart Pine," referring to the fact that the needles appear to be jumping away from each other.

Kee also liked the Anishinaabe name. She preferred to call this tree "okikaandag," which she translated as, "He is crippled with arthritis." She thought that an excellent name because that is just what this little tree looks like. If it is growing in its natural state, not on a tree plantation of the lumber industry where it may be laid out in neat rows, it is a small, twisted, pathetic looking, little thing that reminds one of a little, crippled up, arthritic old person. Everything about it looks crippled. Its trunk and branches will be misshaped. Its needles are "sprung apart." Even its cones are tight and hard and twisted. They sit up on the branches, but they are reticulated or reflexive, meaning they bend back over toward the branch and toward the trunk. The cones are asymmetrical, always off-center and bigger on one side than the other.

Wakikaandag: Jack Pine
(*Pinus banksiana*)

In the early lumber days, the jack pine was considered a waste tree that was cleared only to make way for the more important red and white pines. Later it was purposely removed because it is an indicator of poor soil, and was therefore removed to improve the salability of the land. However, it has come into its own with the advent of the pulp paper industry. It is grown on tree farms, tree plantations, where it is given room and better soil than it usually gets in the wild. It can grow rapidly to be a straight tree, valuable to industry because it can be harvested in as little as ten years.

The first time Kee saw a stand of jack pines grown on a tree plantation she got very excited. She was driving with a friend and she screamed, "Stop! Stop the car! What is that tree?" She jumped out of the car and ran up to one of the trees and examined it minutely. She discovered that it was just an old jack pine that had been given such a nice growing condition that its trunk was straight and not all twisted as it would have been in the wild. She was truly amazed!

In its natural state, the Jack is usually seen growing in light, dry, sandy soil. It is a northern tree in Michigan and Wisconsin and well up into northern Canada. It is a "pioneer" tree after forest fires because it has cones that only open under intense heat. In the midst of a fire, the hard little cones pop open and scatter their seeds, which quickly grow in the burned-over area. It often produces pure stands of overcrowded, skinny, spindly, stunted, "Crippled with Arthritis"–looking trees.

As slow as the lumber industry was to appreciate the jack pine, there are several other life-forms that consider the jack pine a wonderful creation. Chief among the jack pine's admirers is the Kirtland's Warbler, *Dendroica kirtlandii.* It is a species-specific bird to the jack pine, meaning that it will only live on a jack pine. It will only nest under its branches, and it will only eat the tiny seeds inside of the tough little jack pine cones. Kee said the Anishinaabemowin name for this little bird translates as, "Fire Seed Eater." It is a pretty little bird, black, gray, and white with a strip of orange. It is a very endangered little bird, too, whose numbers since the early 1970s have stayed around 206 singing males, all of them in a sixty-mile area of Michigan's lower peninsula. It has been on the Endangered Species list since the Endangered Species Act of 1973, and it is a federal crime to hurt this wee bird (Benyus 1989, 255).

Some years ago, the jack pines had diminished so drastically that there were only two places left in Lower Michigan where the "Fire-Seed Eaters" could nest. A great deal of pressure from both local bird lovers and even international bird lovers was put on the Michigan state legislature to save the birds. When public pressure became intense enough, it was decided to burn over a small area of jack pines to pop the seeds and increase the birds' habitat. Because the DNR was afraid they could not handle the situation, state troopers and the National Guard surrounded the area to be burned. But, the wind changed! The nice little contained burn escaped and became a forest fire that burned thousands of acres of prime resort and cabin country. The fire worked! The jack pines flourished, and the Kirtland's Warblers are happy in their new, expanded habitat, but the state of Michigan may never get out of debt to the resort and cabin owners and their heirs.[2]

Because the jack pine grows in poor soil, there are usually only mosses and lichens that grow underneath it. Several endangered species of plants, however, also call it home. The bird-foot violet (*Viola pedata*) is an example of one of the endangered species sheltered by the jack pines.

The wood of the jack pine is very soft, light, and not at all strong. In the pulp industry it is chiefly used for heavy craft-weight

2 Kee included this story in her lectures on the jack pine. When telling it she would laugh at the arrogance of humans thinking they could control such powerful forces.

paper and for hardboard. It is, however, very beautiful for use as an interior wallboard, where its many knots and its color are an advantage. It is far too soft for exterior lumber or for flooring (Smith 1978, 8).

Scotch Pine
Pinus sylvestris

~~~~~~

The Scotch pine is not an indigenous tree of North America, but it is a very common one now in the Great Lakes States. It is an import from Europe where it grows all over Northern Europe and where it is called "Scots' pine."

When the Scottish people were forced out of the Highlands of Scotland by their English overlords in the attempt to break the power of the Clans and make room for English sheep, the people took the seeds of the Scotch pine with them. It became a patriotic thing to do to pop a cone or two into one's pocket to take a piece of 'home' along on the exile. Those Scots brought the seeds to North America where the tree and the people, too, flourished. The tree took off. It spread so extensively over the Northern U. S. and Canada that it is now well established in the wilds. We now have far more Scotch pine than they ever had in Scotland.[3]

Some years back, Kee went to Scotland on a speaking tour. Some local people, knowing her love of plants, said, "Oh, you must come to see a very rare tree that has a great history with us." They took her on a long car ride to a forest preserve and showed her a stand of Scotch pine. Since the deforestation of the Highlands, the Scotch pine is a very special, carefully preserved tree, no longer a common sight at all. Kee laughed and told them how Scotch pine grows wild all over her home state of Michigan. The locals were very much amazed! Most Scotch pine are planted today either as ornamentals or as Christmas trees. Eighty-five percent of the Christmas trees sold in Michigan are Scotch pine (Smith 1978, 9).

Scotch pine, when not grown and harvested young as Christmas trees, can grow to 50 or 70 feet in height and 1 to 2 feet in diameter. Large Scotch pines are easily identified by the characteristic bright orange bark that typically covers the trunk, starting halfway up.

The needles come two to a sheath and are usually 1½ to 3 inches long. They are sharp and pointed and twisted on the ends. The little twist that the needles have at the end are what makes

3 Kee always included this piece of history in her lectures on Scotch pine. It meant a great deal to her because these trees came with their people.

Scotch Pine (*Pinus sylvestris*)

them so hard to get out of one's carpet when it is time to take down a Scotch pine Christmas tree. A balsam fir's needles do not have that twist and that is only one of the reasons the balsam makes a far better choice for a Christmas tree than the Scotch pine.

In the wild there are three ways to tell the difference between young jack pines and Scotch pines. Both have two needles to a sheath, but those of Scotch pine are longer. The Scotch cones are not reticulated like those of the jack pine. The needles of the Scotch have a little twist at the ends that the jacks pines lack, those little "Have-to-get-out-the-pliers-to-get-them-out-of-the-rug" twists.

One might also need to tell the difference between mature red pines and mature Scotch pines. The reds have brown-red bark on their trunks, which is definitely red under flaked off sections. The Scotch pines have brownish-orange bark with startling orange on the upper half of the trunk.

Medicinal Virtues of the Pines

In herbalism there is no room for a mistake; therefore it is essential that a person be able to identify the pines. Once one knows that one has a pine, one can proceed to use the virtues that the pine family has to share with humankind. All of the pines can be used. There will be differences in strength and texture of the product produced, but in effect, one can substitute one pine for another.

In the days of the Gete-Anishinaabeg, there were two health practices that were very widespread among different peoples and were most common, everyday health care: footbaths and inhalants.

Footbaths

When a friend or family member or even a visitor came to someone's lodge from the daily work or after a journey, before they were offered food and drink the person was offered a footbath and massage. It was not considered out-of-place or odd for a woman to clean and massage the feet of a man she had never before met. It was considered part of a housewife's common courtesy.

There was a very good reason for this. Footgear was at best minimal, and healthy feet could be of the utmost importance to a person's survival. Hunting and food gathering on foot could require long miles of walking over rough terrain.

Not everyone was a skilled maker of moccasins and other footgear. It was a specialty, although most every adult, male and female, was expected to be able to rough out a pair of moccasins if the need arose. Still, a lot depended on the individual's sewing skills as well as the hides available for the job.

Moose hide is excellent for the bottoms of moccasins. When it is properly smoked, it is quite waterproof, which is essential for winter use in frigid conditions. Buffalo hide was much prized in the Great Lakes area because of its toughness and durability. After the extinction of the forest buffalo, hides from the Plains were an important trade item in this area.

In foot care, fine fragrances and liniments made from pine sap were widely used. A warm footbath with an infusion of pine needles is both healing and an effective, soothing, deodorizing experience.

A most effective medicine, "Wildcat Liniment," is made from pine sap, and directions for making it are in the Recipes section. This recipe was given to Kee by her mother, Sarah Good Cook, MinoSoahnIkwe, who sold it for years to the lumberjacks around her northern Michigan home. Kee said that her mother was a very proper, Edwardian lady who refused to say that the lumberjacks needed the liniment to heal cuts and bruises sustained in weekly Saturday-night recreational fights. She said that the Jacks just fell down a lot and hurt themselves while felling trees.

The recipe calls for white-pine sap. That is the nicest to use, producing a finely textured, extremely fragrant product. However, the pitch of any pine, domestic or from other geographic areas, may be substituted in this recipe. Ponderosa pine, a western, domestic species, produces a very strong, dark-colored liniment.[4]

White-pine sap is very thin, refined, and genteel, as are all of the other features of the tree. It is quite common to see the bark of a white pine marked with the white streaks of dripping pine sap. Gathering the sap from growing white pines is not an easy task. Usually one scrapes a drop here and there, a very time-consuming and frustrating job. However, if one finds a freshly cut white pine, it is possible to collect a large supply of the sap quickly. A cut pine may pump out sap from its stump for a full year or more, depending on the growing situation and the vitality of the tree. A lightning-struck white pine may pump sap for two full years. Kee had such a tree on the island, from which she used to gather a considerable amount of sap, enough to make very large batches of Wildcat Liniment, enough for the extended Miniss Kitigan Drum[5] "family" and also a number of Kee's older, arthritic friends.

I was once in the Kettle Moraine State Forest, in southeastern Wisconsin, in a large stand of white pine on a clear, warm February day. The pines had just been pruned of their lower branches, and their wounds were fresh. It was just the kind of weather that makes the sap pour out of the maples: cold nights and warm days. As I walked through the grove I could see the sap pulsing out of the branch wounds, almost as if the trees had hearts that were pumping their life's blood rhythmically. I could *hear* the sap pumping out of the trees. And would you believe it? I did not have kinnikinnick for an offering nor a bottle to catch the sap, so I had to walk away from enough white-pine sap to have made liniments for years. I have regretted it ever since!

One fall I was in Memphis, helping my daughter Pukwanis

4 One of Kee's former ethnobotany students once sent her a large batch of ponderosa pine sap that he had gathered on a trip out West. We made a great batch of Wildcat out of that gift. Old students always loved to gift the Old One. She was a teacher one did not forget. That ponderosa sap made a very strong batch of Wildcat that was very gritty in texture.

5 The Miniss Kitigan Drum is an organization, registered with the federal government as a church, that Keewaydinoquay and her students founded while she was studying in Michigan. There are branches of the group in Milwaukee, Wisconsin, and Ann Arbor, Michigan.

move into her new apartment. After we got her settled, she took me to the Memphis Zoo for the afternoon. While walking around enjoying the beautiful zoo I found a white pine with a freshly trimmed branch that had pumped out about a gallon of fresh sap. It had accumulated in a puddle at the base of the trunk. Boy, did I want that sap! There were groundspeople everywhere, and I just was not certain how they would react to a person scooping up the sap from one of their ornamentals. Also, the lawns were heavily covered with chemicals to kill weeds. There were signs to that effect all around the grounds. The contamination and the guards were a deterrent, but, irrationally, I still wish I could have somehow gotten my hands on that puddle of sap. It was a beautiful sight!

Red pines present a much easier opportunity for gathering sap for liniment. Red pine's scientific name, *Pinus resinosa,* bears witness to the fact that it is a very sappy, resinous tree. It practically oozes sap! Insects and ants chew holes in the bark, aggravating the tree, which then pumps out sap to seal its wounds. It is possible to break long nuggets of dried sap off a red pine. Globs of sap will often catch and accumulate under the big, loose platelets of bark on the red pine's trunk.

The carpenter ants that chew into red pines produce another usable by-product. One often finds piles of very fine sawdust that accumulates at the foot of a red pine that is being attacked by ants. While chewing the tree, the ants add formic acid to the sawdust with their saliva. This mixture is wonderfully soft and fragrant. It can be used to stuff a dream pillow, or it can be used to make incense.

The sap of any of the other conifers (with the exception of yew,[6] which is poisonous) can be used to make Wildcat Liniment. Balsam fir sap collected from the blisters of the bark of young to middle-aged trees can be used and is most fragrant. Spruce sap is also usable, but it is not nearly as pleasant to smell. Combination batches of pine and other conifer saps can also be used. Pine sap is simply the most fragrant and produces the nicest product.

Inhalants from Pines

The use of inhalants to treat congestion due to various respiratory complaints, flu and colds, etc., was and remains a common Anishinaabe health practice. It has long been felt that the resins of the pine family are especially helpful in opening clogged nasal and bronchial passages.

6 The yew, *Taxus Canadensis,* is a native plant, but European and Asian yews are also widely planted as ornamentals. They are also poisonous.

There are several common methods of administering these resins to an affected individual, used in early days and today. One method is to make use of a birch bark cone, sewn with sinew or wadab. The cone has to be large enough to fit over the patient's nose and mouth. A hot stone or piece of charcoal from the fire is placed in the end with the resin or chopped foliage of one of the pines on top of it. The cone is placed over the patient's face with care being taken to hold the cone down so that the hot charcoal or stone and melting resins do not fall on the patient's face. The healing vapors are inhaled.

Another means of administrating the inhalant is to pour boiling water over either the resin or the chopped foliage of the pine in a large makak or bowl. The patient is seated beside the bowl and a hide or blanket or towel or raincoat is placed over the makak and the patient's head. In a particularly severe case, or when the patient has lung congestion, the whole person might be hooded over so that the steam and vapors can rise over the person's front and back.

A third way inhalants are used is in the sweat lodge. The sweat lodge is an almost Pan-Indian healing and purification institution which makes an excellent vehicle to transmit the resins of the pines to the patient. A sweat lodge erected to treat such a patient will usually have a layer of pine, balsam, or cedar foliage between the sapling frame and the blanket, hide, or tarpaulin covering. The floor is commonly strewn with boughs while resin or foliage might be laid on the hot rocks as they are brought into the lodge. The resulting sweat will be certain to open the congested passages and to help the body sweat out the contaminants and, hopefully, the disease as well.

After using any of the above administrations of the resins of the pines as inhalants, the utmost care has to be taken of the patient. Such a person should be thoroughly dried and put snugly to bed, usually with an infusion of Joe Pye (*Eutrochium maculatum* and *Eutrochium purpureum*) and boneset (*Eupatorium perfoliatum*), yarrow (*Achillea millefolium*) or catnip (*Nepeta cataria*), and/or pine foliage given them to drink as a tea.

In a less serious case, or when the sinuses alone are affected, the inhalant might well be administered in salve form. Wildcat Liniment rubbed into the face around the infected sinuses area is most effective in causing the congestion to be released. In the Recipes section are directions given to me by Keewaydinoquay for the use of Wildcat Liniment to relieve sinus congestion and pain, as well as several recipes for using the pines as decongestants.

Zesegaandag
Wadab
"He Cuts Himself Down"
Spruce
Black Spruce
Picea mariana

Mina'ig
Gaawaandag
White Spruce
Picea glauca

~~~~~~

The black and the white spruce are the only spruces native to the
Great Lakes area. There are, of course, several other spruces here
now, notably the Norway and blue spruces that are often seen on
people's front lawns. The spruces make good city trees because
they can contend with poor soil and pollution.

The white spruce is a pretty tree and is often planted as an
ornamental. Its needles are a bluish-green to dark green in color,
and the tree is often covered with a whitish bloom that increases
the blue tinge. The black spruce, on the other hand, is rarely
planted as an ornamental. It is usually a tall, skinny tree with an
irregular shape, and often it has many dead, but attached, lower
branches. The lower branches die off naturally, but they stay on
the tree, giving it a very scraggy, sickly appearance. Not exactly a
look one would desire for a tree on one's front lawn.

On all of the spruces, the needles come directly out of the
branch and are not held together in clumps like those of the
pines. The needles grow all around the branch giving the branch
a "bottle brush" appearance. When one touches a spruce, all of
the needles are sharp, unlike the blunt needles of a balsam fir.
The needles of the spruces are four-sided, and they roll when one
pushes them between one's thumb and forefinger, unlike the
balsam or hemlock needles, which are flat and do not roll. A black
spruce has little needles, ¼ to ½ inch in length, while those of
white spruce are a little larger at ½ to ¾ inch.

Gaawaandag: Spruce (*Picea mariana* and *Picea glauca*)

There is a difference in smell between the black and white spruces. The white spruce is also called the "skunk" or "cat" spruce, because its needles when crushed have a definitely unpleasant smell. The poor white spruce has a tendency to smell like an old, incontinent tomcat who is intent on marking his territory. The black spruce's smell is much more pleasant. Its crushed needles smell like pitch or a newly tarred road, not the unpleasant, overpowering smell of the white spruce.

The cones of the spruces always hang down off the branches. The white spruce has two-inch cones with long, limber, rounded scales. The black spruce's cones are smaller, ½ to 1 inch in length, oval when closed and almost round when open. They have ridged, grayish-brown scales that are ragged on the edges.

The wood of all of the spruces is not strong. It is soft and rots easily. It is too full of resin to make a good firewood. However, it is valuable as a starter wood. Place a piece of spruce or balsam fir under an oak log to start a fire quickly. Commercially, the wood of both trees is used almost exclusively for the making of high-grade paper (Smith 1978, 13).

Kee translated one Anishinaabemowin name for this tree as "He Cuts Himself Down," and the weakness of the spruce wood is the reason it bears this name. This tree rots readily and falls, or the tops of standing trees blow off or are snapped under heavy snows. It is not a sturdy tree.

Despite the fact that it is not strong, the spruce can be a long-living tree. Under harsh conditions, such as the nutrient-poor bogs, it has been known to grow to be only 3 or 4 inches in diameter in a hundred years. It is usually a small to medium-sized tree, 40 to 50 feet in height, and only 12 inches in diameter at maturity. If it has nicer growing conditions it may grow to 100 feet tall and even live for upwards of two hundred years (Smith 1978, 13).

From a distance, all spruce branches appear to slope down. That is its typical appearance. It will, however, grow toward the light, as any sensible plant will.

The natural habitat of the black spruce is the glaciated, swampy areas of Michigan and Wisconsin, extending well up into Canada even the Arctic. It is a muskeg plant and loves wet, acidy soil. It often grows in poorly drained pockets of the forest and in sphagnum swamps, where it shares what few nutrients are available with tamaracks and Labrador tea.

The white spruce will grow in swampland along with black spruce and tamarack, but it prefers sandier soil. It grows into the far north in Canada, right up into the Arctic, where it is a small bush in the "Land of the Little Sticks" north of the tree line. White spruce has an unusual feature to its needles that keeps them from freezing even in sixty-below, freezing weather. The liquid within the cells of the white spruce flows out of their cells to the area between the cells where it can freeze solid without damaging the cell walls. This is what keeps the trees from exploding as the temperatures drop (Bates 1995, 50).

The Virtues of Spruce

One of the principal virtues that spruce has to share with the People is its rootlets. Another of the spruce's names is wadab, referring to the binding material made from the rootlets of this tree.[7] The rootlets of black spruce are very abundant. Because black spruce is typically growing in swamps or very sandy soil, the rootlets are close to the surface and easily gathered. They are often quite long. It is easy to find a piece long enough to bind a whole canoe. Wadab was the preferred binding for canoes and large makakoon. For emergency "rope" needs, such as binding firewood to carry home or tying up a bundle of herbs, one has only to pull

7 Balsam fir is also called "wadab" for the same reason.

up spruce roots. One chooses an adult tree growing in sandy soil or a swamp, and one digs up a long rootlet. If one strips the bark off the rootlet before the resins harden, it is easier. One can often do the stripping with the thumb and fingernail. If one has more to strip than one wishes to do with a fingernail, drive a split stake into the ground and pull the root through the slit, stripping off the root bark. Next, one splits the rootlet in half. Cut it down two or three inches, being careful to cut it very evenly. Then one can split the rootlet by hand by simply pulling the two haves apart. Spruce roots are very even, with little tapering. One will have two half-round bindings, of a lovely, yellowish-orange color, that are strong and pliable. It can be used at once or rolled like rope and dried for future use. Soaked overnight, it will come back to a very usable pliability.

Another of the virtues that spruce has to share with the Anishinaabe is its resins. They are very strong, and they protect the tree well from molds and animal and insect attacks. Spruce resin is used to make turpentine. The sap is extremely sticky and makes a fine adhesive. It is used to patch holes in canoes or to fill holes and prevent drips in the roof of wigwams.

Another of spruce's gifts to us is her foliage. The foliage of spruce is packed with vitamin C. All of the conifers, as well as all green, growing plants, have a lot of vitamin C, but the spruce foliage releases the vitamin faster and in a larger quantity. It would be the vehicle of choice if a person were actually sick with vitamin C deficiency.

Even though they did not know how to measure it, nor was it labeled with an alphabet letter, the *effect* of vitamin C was well known in pre-Contact days. There is a teaching story, which Kee often told in her classes, that is said to have been an actual occurrence, about the effects of lack of vitamin C in the days when the Anishinaabeg warriors were battling the Bwaan, the Dakota:

"The Ancient Warrior"

There was once a very old man. He had been a great and fearless warrior in his younger days, and he had counted many coup against the Bwaan, the enemy. He had sustained many, many war wounds in defending the People. But he had long since outlived all of the contemporaries of his younger days. When he told the young men of his old battles, sad to say, they laughed.

With the arrogance of youth, they would not believe anyone as old as Ancient Warrior could ever have been young and brave as they.

He showed them his scars, and they said, "Oh, they don't look so bad. You probably just fell over a root in the forest." Their laughter hurt the Ancient Warrior more than the wounds that had made the scars.

He went to the *mashkikiiwinini,* the medicine man, and said, "How can I make the young men believe me? It is not right that they should laugh. There is no respect in that! Also, I knew their fathers and grandfathers. I fought side-by-side with them, and I could tell these young warriors so much that they should know about the bravery of their ancestors. I feel so bad when they laugh. It is almost as if the pain and death of my boyhood friends was all in vain. They and I should be remembered with honor. They died for the People. I could show these young men where their own grandfathers fought and where they died and where they are buried. It is not right. It should not be forgotten."

"Show them your wounds," said the mashkikiiwinini.

"I have, but they say, 'Oh, those little white lines? They are nothing.'"

"No. I mean show them your wounds themselves, not just the scars."

The Ancient Warrior was confused. "How can I do that? They healed before your father was born."

"How badly do you want this honor? There is a way to show the young men your wounds themselves, but, if we do it, I will not be able to save you. You will die."

The Ancient Warrior said without hesitation, "I would do anything. I would die that my honor and the honor of my boyhood friends could be restored to the People."

"Very well," sighed the mashkikiiwinini. "Here is what you must do: do not eat any green, growing thing. Eat no fruit nor leaf. Just eat meat. And in a while your old scars will reopen. The wounds of your battles will be there for all the People to see."

The Ancient Warrior thanked the mashkikiiwinini, and with determination he followed his instruction. All winter he ate only meat. As his wounds popped open one by one, he told the astonished young men how he had received that blow. He lived long enough to relate all of his stories to the no longer laughing, but very attentive, young warriors. He restored his own honor and the honor of his old friends, and he died and was buried with love and respect. Mii' iw Miigwech.

———

There is a story from the history of the early years of the exploration of North America by the Europeans that describes a miraculous cure for the same disease, scurvy. Kee also told this story when teaching about spruce. In 1535 Jacques Cartier's ship was frozen into the St. Lawrence River, below the present site of Montreal, and forced to winter over in a hastily built stockade fort with his 110 sailors. They had not expected the winter to strike as hard and as early as it did because at the same degree of latitude in Europe they would not have encountered such cold weather. The crew subsisted through the winter on dried shipboard staples and the occasional meal of game that they could barter from the local Iroquois tribe. Relations were strained between the Iroquois and Cartier's men, because the Iroquois were insulted that the Europeans had traded with their enemies, the Huron, the previous summer. By midwinter Cartier's men started to get sick. Within weeks all of the company were suffering bleeding gums and reopening wounds. Twenty-five died and many more of the company were deathly ill. Cartier took great pains to not let the Iroquois know that his men were sick, because he was afraid they would attack if they knew how weak the Europeans really were. But one day Cartier saw a man named Dom Agaya, with whom he had traded. Dom Agaya had been ill two weeks before, with swollen joints and bleeding gums like the Frenchmen, but that day Cartier saw him hale and hearty. Cartier asked Dom Agaya how he had been cured, and the Iroquois obligingly sent two women off into the bush to bring Cartier the boughs of a tree. He even told Cartier how to prepare and administer the medicine. As directed, Cartier cooked up a decoction of the foliage and bark of the tree and gave it to his sick sailors as a tea, while poulticing their wounds with the same plant material. Not only did no more of the Europeans die, but within six days they had all regained their strength.

The tree that Dom Agaya gave Cartier was called in the Iroquois language "Annedde." Since none of the Europeans kept a sample of the tree to take home to show their own botanists, and since no one bothered to keep accurate notes on the exact appearance of the tree, there has been almost five hundred years of "mystery" about what tree it actually was that cured Cartier and his crew of scurvy (Bown 2003, 27–31; Weatherford 1988, 182–83).

Some scholars have said Annedde was white pine, and others have opted for another pine or hemlock or balsam fir. In reality it could have been any of the above. Any of them would have done the same thing, but spruce would have been the fastest and the best, as it has the property of releasing the most vitamin C of any of the trees in consideration as the historic "Annedde." If one should ever find oneself, like Cartier, in a situation where one has to cure oneself or others of a vitamin C deficiency (for that is what scurvy is), use spruce. Simmer the inner bark of a standing, living spruce and the chopped foliage of the tree in water to cover for 15 to 30 minutes. Try to keep the decoction from boiling, as that will reduce the vitamin C. Strain and drink as a tea. At the same time, apply the boiled bark and chopped foliage that was filtered out of the liquid to any sores. It is the cure! But it would be wiser, less painful, and certainly tastier to just make and drink a light tea made of balsam fir daily to prevent scurvy. It is always better to prevent an illness than to have to seek a cure later.

Mashkiigwaatig

Mashkiig-mitig
Mashkikii-mitig
Tamarack
Larix laricina

The common name for this tree in English, tamarack, is said to come from an American Indian language,[8] but Kee insisted that it was also a Hebrew word. The Hebrew name Tamara means "Medicine Woman."

The tamarack is a larch, and there are larches found all the way around the world in northern climes. Kee taught that people living with the European larch and the Siberian larch use those trees in their folk medicines to treat the same ills that the Anishinaabe use the tamarack to treat.

8 In her lectures on tamarack Kee said that this was an American Indian word. The *Oxford English Dictionary* says this name comes from "a native Indian name in Canada." For more information, see http://dictionary.oed.com.

Mashkiig-mitig: Tamarack (*Larix laricina*)

The tamarack is the only northern temperate conifer that is deciduous; that is, it loses its needles in the fall the way broader-leafed trees do. It is not an "evergreen," and because of its existence, Kee often argued, conifers in general should not be called "evergreens." In the fall the soft, ¾- to 1¼-inch, bluish-green needles turn a buff color. Then they turn almost-golden yellow. Then they fall off! Many a person has panicked during the first fall in a new home when the beautiful, green "evergreen" on the front lawn suddenly turns yellow and is surely dying. If the inexperienced owner does not cut the tree down, spring will bring a new crop of green needles and relief to the homeowner.

Unlike the pines, the needles of tamarack are not tied together in sheaths or bunches. They always grow out of little spurs or bumps along the branch that are called "short shoots." These bumps with needles growing out of them are arranged alternately along the branch. There can be ten or more needles per clump.

The wood of the tamarack is strong, hard, and takes a long time to rot in the soil. For this reason it has been much used for posts and poles, as well as for mine timbers and in the pulp and lumber industries (Smith 1978, 11).

The presence of a tamarack on a property will tell a knowledgeable home purchaser an important piece of information. If the tree is a very old one and was not purposely transplanted there by a former owner, and the tree does not transplant easily, it is an indication that the land on which the tree is standing was once a swamp. Tamarack seeds will not germinate unless they fall into a swamp. So, if the tree grew there on its own volition, then the house was built on land reclaimed from wetlands or from a swamp. This fact can be an important one to know if one intends to have a basement or a garden or even a stable foundation. A person might have a dry basement in such a house, but it would not do to use it for storage, as things left in it will readily mold. Since the area was a swamp, the water will be sulfurous, brown, and smelly. It will stain porcelain fixtures; therefore it will be necessary to put in brown-colored tubs, sinks, and toilets, or one will have to learn to like deep orange-brown stains on one's white bathroom fixtures. The foundation of one's "tamarack" house would be a problem, too. One would probably have to put the house on a slab, as the basement would always be unsatisfactory. And the slab would have to be of fitted fieldstone, for the acid soil would readily rot one made of cement.

Tamarack is a swamp tree by preference. Its seeds will not germinate unless they fall into the acid water of a bog, sphagnum swamp, muskeg, or onto land that once was one of those. It needs soil low in nitrogen.

The muskegs of glaciated areas were formed at the end of the last Ice Age. Retreating glaciers left or covered huge chunks of ice with silt on top of them. The ice melted and formed very deep ponds. As such ponds aged they became swamps. At the bottom of many of these swamps, Kee said, especially in the far north, there may well still be pieces of ice left over from the mountains of ice that were their parent glaciers.

A tamarack swamp would be a good place to dig a wine cellar or perhaps an icehouse. One would have to put in cedar shelves because cedar does not easily rot. It would keep items cool all summer, but it would also be a readily molding environment, so one would not use it to store dried food, etc.

Although it would not be a good place for a human to have a home, a tamarack swamp is the best of homes for many small animals. Because they grow in a swamp, tamarack root systems are a mass of roots very close to the surface. They do not have to grow deep to find water. Because their roots are so close to the surface, tamaracks will often blow over in a gale, leaving a large, massive root system upright. These roots become the haven of many types of swamp animals. The bog lemmings are especially fond of them, and they love to make their burrows under the roots. Rabbits and snowshoe hares often use the roots as an escape route when coyotes or foxes pursue them. They will dodge into the little openings where the larger animals dare not go. If a person really needed a hare, they would do well to seek one in a tamarack swamp.

The roots present a barrier for larger animals as well as for humans. Do not take a short cut through a tamarack swamp, even in the winter time when traveling on snowshoes. The roots of tamarack cut like a knife, and such cuts are broad ones that do not heal readily.

In the old days, when there were many medicine people, the name of this tree in the Anishinaabe language was a debate topic. Keewaydinoquay remembered listening to her grandfather MidéOgema and his ancient cronies discussing for hours if this tree was "mashkiig-mitig, swamp, muskeg tree" or if it was "mash-kikii-mitig, medicine tree." Of course there was also the possibility, and it was also discussed on those long-ago winter evenings, that the name of the medicine people might have been taken originally from the "swamp tree." Whichever way it was, tamarack remains a "swamp, medicine tree."

The Medicinal Virtues of Tamarack

Tamarack has the medicinal virtue of being a diuretic; it will cause an increase in the amount of urine produced. That is useful in flushing out a person's system. Tamarack is also a laxative. An infusion of the inner bark of tamarack is a gentle laxative. It is not as effective nor as quick as burdock (*Arctium minus*), but it will work nonetheless. Tamarack is also an alterative; it will help to cure a patient's illness by gradually restoring health to the whole body. For this reason it makes a good tonic for toning the whole system.

Tamarack also is beneficial for a hardened condition of the liver and spleen. When a person's personality changes, the mental condition may be a result of a sluggish, underfunctioning liver and/or spleen. This medicine from the tamarack was traditionally used to treat postpartum melancholia and for jaundice, when the whites of the eyes have a yellowish cast, or in viral infections like mononucleosis, where the spleen and liver are affected. To treat these conditions an infusion is made of the inner bark of tamarack. The bark is easy to take off of a living tree or one that has just recently blown over in a swamp. The outer bark is thin and separates easily from the inner cambium layer. It is best to use the bark fresh, but it will also work dried. *Do not use the bark of a dead tree.* One uses 1 teaspoon of inner bark to 1 cup boiling water. Steep, covered, for 30 minutes (although it would not hurt if it was steeped for a longer time). It is drunk as a tea. Since this medicine has to be taken from a living tree, Kee used little trees that were too crowded or recently blown-over larger trees whenever possible, to avoid killing a tree.

Tamarack also has a medicine to treat an ulcerated or fetid sore or puncture wound. One can use this even if one does not know what caused the ulcer or sore in the first place. The sore is washed out with a decoction of the inner bark of tamarack. Comfrey, *Symphytum officianale,* is added to the decoction. If that does not work to clear up the sore quickly, make the inner bark of tamarack into a poultice and apply it four times daily to the sore. At the same time the patient should be given a tea, an infusion of the tamarack bark. This method was once regularly used to treat severe puncture wounds, thorns deeply imbedded, bedsores, and even gunshot wounds.

Tamarack also has the ability to clear lungs badly infected with chronic abscesses, even gangrene of the lungs. One breathes the steam off of the decoction of the inner bark plus the new twigs of tamarack. The steam is an antibiotic and an antiseptic. It will bring up the catarrh, the thick, chunky mucus, and even the diseased lung tissue. It will look very bad indeed, but it will clear the lungs. Tamarack was used for the most severe of conditions.

Tamarack has a gout medicine, too, which Kee learned from Nodjimahkwe. Cherries are the best medicine for gout, eaten or drunk as a juice to ease an attack; but when cherries were not available a decoction was made of inner bark of tamarack, mint, foliage of juniper, and horseradish. It was boiled for 10 minutes and not strained. A person would eat as much of it as he could. It would bring down the inflammation of the joints. Even though Kee was suspicious of using juniper for food, because of its possible poisonous properties, she would use it in this recipe. She said that this was the only recipe Nodjimahkwe ever gave her that contained juniper.

Tamarack is also used to treat arthritis. The traditional treatment of arthritis among the Anishinaabeg is a tea made of the needles of tamarack and willow. The needles were used fresh as long as they were available. Use equal parts tamarack needles and willow bark, with mint oil to improve the taste. For winter use today, the needles can be frozen, or a tincture can be made of tamarack needles, willow leaves and inner bark, and vodka. See the Recipes section for a rough recipe for making a tincture for use with arthritis. Tamarack and willow will help by reducing the inflammation in the joints. Drink as a tea, made with either the fresh or frozen foliage or from the tincture, and use a poultice of cooked tamarack needles and willow leaves and inner bark on the affected joints.

Tamarack had so many uses as a medicine that Keewaydino-quay said that Nodjimahkwe had said, "If you are in doubt as to what medicine to use, use tamarack." Use it as a tea or use it as a poultice. Tamarack can substitute for any other conifer in a medicine recipe. One can even, for instance, use its sap for Wildcat Liniment, although the sap is weaker than that of the other conifers. It is very hard to overdose with tamarack.

All of the parts of a tamarack are medicinal: roots, bark of trunk, twigs, inner bark or inner roots or foliage. To make a poultice of the inner bark, blender it, pound it, or cook it to a soft consistency.

The sap of a tamarack is the tastiest of the saps of the conifers. It is the preferred one for use as a natural chewing gum.

Gaagaagiwanzh
"Porcupine, His Tree"
Eastern Hemlock
Tsuga canadensis

~~~~~~

Kee called this tree "Porcupine, His Tree," which she said was
an English translation of one of the Ojibwe names for this tree.
Porcupines love hemlocks for their acid, salty taste. If one was
looking for a porcupine, one would do well to look in a hemlock.
There are several reasons to go seeking a porcupine. In Canada
as a child I was told in school that if I was ever lost in the woods
I should look for a porcupine, kill it by hitting it on the head
with a branch, and then throw it into a fire to burn off the quills
and cook the meat. I have never been lost in the woods, but I
did remember the advice these past fifty-five years or so. In the
Gete-Anishinaabeg time, people sought porcupines for their
quills, to use to decorate birch bark makakoon and to sew onto
leather in the time before the people routinely traded for beads.
Kee's mother, Sarah Good Cook, MinoSoahnIkwe, always kept
her porcupine fat for fine baking like birthday cakes, because,
she said, it was clear and did not add an extra animal taste to the
baked goods. These are all good reasons for one to go looking for
a porcupine.

Hemlock prefers to grow in cool, moist hardwood forests
in the northern Great Lakes states and into Canada. It grows in
shade and is often found with white pine, maple, beech, yellow
birch, balsam, basswood, and elm.

Hemlocks grow very slowly, taking 150 to 200 years to reach
maturity. Six-hundred-year-old, 150-foot hemlocks fell to the
lumbermen in the early logging days. Until the advent of the pulp
lumbering industry, hemlocks were often felled and left to rot,
simply to make way for the more valuable pines. Nowadays, with
price increases, a lot more hemlock is being used (Smith 1978, 15).

Hemlocks grow to 60 or 80 feet high, and 2 to 3 feet in
diameter. They have massive trunks and ragged outlines. Their
crowns bend away from the prevailing winds, and this gives the

Gaagaagiwanzh: Eastern Hemlock (*Tsuga canadensis*)

hemlocks the appearance of a flag. One can even use this tendency of the hemlock as a natural compass out in the wild if one sees a hemlock standing on a hill. If one knows that the prevailing wind comes from the north, the hemlock will give one direction (*Trees of North America*, 11).

The bark of the hemlock is smooth and purplish-gray-brown when the tree is young. As the tree ages the bark becomes red-brown to deep cinnamon-colored and deeply cracked into flakes.

The needles of the hemlock are very short, ½ to ⅔ of an inch flat, with a rounded end. The needles appear to lie on two sides of the twig the way the balsam needles do, but they really spiral along the branch. They are a shiny, dark yellow-green color on top and light green marked with two white lines underneath. If one twists the foliage one gets a silvery look. The hemlock needles are the shortest of the needles of the conifers. They are fatter and softer than those of balsam fir. The hemlock needles are attached to the twig by a tiny petiole; therefore the tree looses its needles readily. An easy way to identify a young hemlock is to shake it. If the needles fall from even a green, growing tree when one shakes it, it is a hemlock. For this reason it makes the very worst choice for a Christmas tree. It is capable of losing every single needle the very night one brings it into one's living room.

One time in Kee's youth she was in a cafe in the North when some loudmouthed white hunters came in, badmouthing Indian women at the tops of their voices. She left in a huff before she told them off (Kee was always a lady), and when she stepped outside she saw their car in the parking lot. Like many hunters they had decided to cut a free Christmas tree to take home from their hunting trip. She smiled when she saw the tree they had picked. They had a little hemlock tied to their roof. She somehow felt better knowing those nasty people would not find that tree a satisfactory choice. She would chuckle about that tree she had seen on those nasty hunters' car even fifty years after the incident.

Hemlock does not make a good Christmas tree, but it does have a virtue to share with mankind. The bark is high in tannins. It will impart a beautiful, orange-red, chestnut to mahogany color to leather as it tans and preserves it. To tan a skin with hemlock, one should locate a fallen tree in the autumn, one that is well rotted. The heartwood of hemlock rots out first, often leaving a large quantity of red sawdust. The ants love to eat hemlock, and they chew the wood into a very fine and powdery texture. Return to that tree once the winter sets in, but before the snow gets too deep, to take the decayed wood. By coming for the rotted wood after the winter as come, one will not have to contend with the insects for the prize. The rotted heartwood of hemlock is added to the water used to soak the skin during the tanning process.

The bark of hemlock causes pregnant sheep and goats to abort. Therefore, pregnant women should not drink a tea made of any part of this tree. The tea would not be fatal to the mother, but it would be so to the fetus.

The hemlock is such a strongly acid tree that almost nothing will grow underneath it. The deer may use it as a deer down. They love to lie on the carpet of 8– to 12–inch-deep needle beds that one finds under older hemlocks. However, it would be a poor place to go looking for a deer if one was hunting, because one would not find prime deer there. The deer go there to be cured of skin sores, worms, and insect infestations. The hide of a deer taken under a hemlock might not be of very high quality. It might be all full of holes.

The cones of the hemlock are very decorative. They are little (¾ of an inch long) but sturdy, and a pretty purplish-brown. They are a little larger than a tamarack's cones. Kee used them a great deal in crafts and to decorate baskets.

The Eastern hemlock of our forests is not the plant that killed Socrates. That plant, the European Hemlock, *Conium maculatum*, is a bush that is rarely more than five feet tall.[9] It has lacy, soft leaves, not needles. It also has a very stinky smell when one crushes one of its leaves (Bremness, 243). People have transplanted those poison hemlocks to North America, but they are not our beautiful, lofty, tree-sized conifer, Gaagaagiwanzh.

9 This is a good example of why it is important not to rely on English common names of plants for identification purposes.

Juniper

~~~~~~

There are three kinds of juniper native to the Great Lakes Area:

Ground juniper
Juniperus horizontalis

~~~~~~

This is a very low plant. It rarely rises more than 6 feet off the ground. As a ground cover it is very decorative and effective for holding the soil in place, but it is difficult to transplant, making it unsuitable for commercial sales.

In the snow, ground juniper creates a mini-greenhouse for the plants that grow under it. It is a good place, in sandy, poor soil, to look for elkhorn lichens, which can be used as a starvation food for humans.

Gaagaagiwaandag
Bush or Common Juniper
Juniperus communis

~~~~~~

This juniper never grows to tree size. Its maximum height is 4 to 5 feet, and then it bushes out to the sides.

The chief virtue bush juniper possesses it does not share with humankind. Bears and deer seem to "use" it more than we do. They use it for a playpen for their young. Baby cubs and newborn fawns are often left in clumps of bush juniper by their mothers for short periods of time. The babies will not stray as the foliage is quite sharp, and it deters the casual wandering baby things are prone to. At the same time it protects the babes from attacks by predators.

Gaagaagiwaandag: Juniper
(*Juniperus communis*)

Miskwaawaak

Red Juniper
Tree Juniper
Red "Cedar"
Eastern Red Cedar
Pasture Juniper
Pencil "Cedar"
Baton Rouge/Red Stick[10]
Juniperus virginiana

10 Called Red Stick by the French in Louisiana because the smooth, red, inner bark is often exposed to view. They named the city of Baton Rouge for this tree that grew all around that area (Smith 1978, 18).

The tree-size juniper is the tree that in this area is called red cedar. That, of course, is a very poor name, because it is by no means a cedar. One can always tell the difference between junipers and cedars because juniper foliage is razor sharp, and Grandmother Cedar has the softest of needles. This is easy to remember because "Grandmother would never hurt you."

The foliage of juniper is of two kinds. On younger trees and on the new growth of older trees one finds very sharp, awl-shaped needles. As the tree ages it grows needles comprised of very short ($\frac{1}{16}$ of an inch long), overlapping scales. Both kinds of needles are found on the tree at the same time (Wilson, 16). It produces a well-armored tree that is more than able to defend itself from animals. Only little birds nest in the junipers, and they use the protection of the sharp foliage to keep their eggs and young safe.

Juniper has two great enemies. Because its bark peels off into narrow shreds the tree is unusually susceptible to fires. Even minor grass fires that would pass by most other mature trees will catch a juniper because of its flaky, stringy bark that will quickly wick the fire up into the tree itself. The other enemy of the juniper is the cedar-apple rust that spends half of its life on junipers and half on apple trees. The rust will kill both trees, and before it kills an apple tree will damage the fruit for years. Because of that it is best not to plant both apple trees and junipers on the same property. Unfortunately, however, the rust can spread by means of its spores from an infected juniper tree to an apple tree up to two miles away (Smith 1978, 18).

Historically, from early colonial times, the juniper's wood was widely used for making pencils. This demand became so great that most of the timber of junipers in the Great Lakes States is no longer available commercially. Now most juniper wood is produced in the South. Juniper's wood is that from which "cedar" chests and "cedar" closets are made. The beautiful, soft, fragrant, red wood deters moths and keeps woolens from being damaged by insects. "Cedar chests" are really "juniper chests" (Smith 1978, 18).

Juniper trees grow to about 40 feet in height and 1 foot in diameter in Wisconsin now, but in earlier days there were 100-foot ones that were four feet in diameter. Junipers can live for two- to three-hundred years (Smith 1978, 18).

Non–Native style herbals and European American folk medicine utilizes the blue-colored cones, often incorrectly called "berries," for treating many different ailments and in cooking as a spice, but Kee always taught that junipers were simply too dangerous to be used as either medicine or in cooking. She said Nodjimahkwe had not given her food recipes using juniper, and when she read all of the uses that Europeans made of juniper she had thought it odd that Nodjimahkwe had omitted it from her instruction. There was a time when Kee made a lot of her money making and selling Indian crafts. In those days, she said, she always went looking under junipers if she needed bird feathers, because she often found dead birds under them. She said that she thought it strange and wondered why little birds who looked completely uninjured would be lying dead there. At that time, she said, she thought it was the fact that little birds can hide in junipers, where bigger predators could not reach them, and that the little birds might go there when they were sick. But then she had a chance encounter on her island which settled the matter in her own mind. Kee was out gathering plants one day, when she lived alone on her island, and she found a young man doing research. She invited him back to her camp, and over supper he told her about his work. He was a botanist employed by a well-known gin company, and he was testing junipers growing in different locations and growing conditions. Distillers use the cones of junipers to give gin its characteristic flavor. But the company had been sued and had had to quietly buy off the families of several people who had died suddenly after drinking their product. The company and the botanist suspected that the cones of juniper have arsenic within them that can be strong enough under particular growing conditions to be fatal. Because of meeting that botanist and because of the dead birds she had often found, Kee was always leery of using juniper and taught her students and apprentices to avoid it.[11] She thought that was the reason Nodjimahkwe had not taught her to use them.

I once had a very favorite juniper. It was my pet, if a tree can be called a pet. It grew on the neighbors' property, right off of our driveway, when we lived on the Southside of Milwaukee. I loved that juniper because it was the home of literally hundreds of birds. I would sit on my back doorstep by the hour and watch the little birds fly into and out of that tree. At least a dozen birds must have nested in that tree every spring. In the evenings I would wash my supper dishes, listening to a cardinal who loved to sit on the topmost branch of that juniper to sing his good night song as the sun went down. He was a very important part of my life, that little bird. When the neighbors cut down the juniper, I wept for the birds whose home they had taken away. And my friend the cardinal had to move to a telephone pole to continue his nightly serenade. Humans so seldom think of the other beings who live on this planet with us.

[11] There is one exception. See the recipe for gout medicine in the section on tamarack.

4

Three Food Plants

"Naanabozho and the Dancing Men"

~~~~~~

One time Naanabozho was walking along down by the shore, near to where a stream came down from the hill and emptied into the lake. As he walked along he heard a great whooping sound, and he saw a large crowd of men standing on the shore.

The men were all naked except for one feather which they each wore on their heads, pointed straight up. The feathers had been scraped so that there was only a tuft of fluff on the top of the shafts.

"Naanabozho, *Boozhoo,* Hello" the men called, "We are preparing a great dance. We expect to dance for eight days."

"Howa!" called Naanabozho. "My little brothers, this is just what I am traveling along hoping to find, a place to dance. I shall come and try with all of my might to dance with you."

"You would be welcome, Naanabozho, but perhaps you should not do it. We intend to dance all eight days and all eight nights as well. Perhaps it would make you too tired to dance for so long a time."

Naanabozho laughed and said, "Ahow, my little brothers. Never mind. I shall certainly dance with you."

"We are concerned about you, Naanabozho. If you dance you will be tired."

Naanabozho took off all of his clothes and trimmed a feather and put it upright on top of his head. Then when the men rose to their feet, he joined them in their dance. Naanabozho danced most enthusiastically, trying in every manner to keep up with the dancing men. For four straight days and four nights they danced and danced with Naanabozho whooping and whirling and dancing with the rest.

On the morning of the fifth day, Naanabozho began to feel rather tired. It was all he could do to keep dancing through the night and into the sixth day, and then through the sixth night into the seventh day. As the seventh day turned to night, Naanabozho was very, very tired. He so wanted to sit down and to eat and to sleep. But he could not. He had said he would dance the

Eight Day Dance, and so he kept on lifting each tired foot and whooping a little now and then. As the night grew longer, tears flowed down his cheeks, and it was all he could do to keep his feet moving up and down to the beat of the men's dance. Just as the first glimmer of light touched the eastern shore, Naanabozho slumped to the ground exhausted. He could not dance even one step more. He lay on the ground and cried, and he feared he could hear the others laughing at him.

He closed his eyes and drifted into a long, long sleep. When he awoke, he looked around him, and then he too started to laugh. The wind had died down as the sun came up over the lake. In the light of the morning Naanabozho could see that he was sleeping in a large stand of cattails. He was truly surprised! He had been dancing with the cattails whom he had mistaken for dancing men.

He put his head down and closed his eyes and slept for two days, then he crawled out of the swamp and down to the shore as he continued on his way.

Apakweshkway

Apakway
"Defender of the Shoreline"
Cattail
Common Cattail
Typha latifolia
Narrow-leafed Cattail
Typha angustifolia

~~~~~~

The shoreline of many of our Northern lakes is lined with
lush stands of cattails. Keewaydinoquay always called the plant
"Defender of the Shoreline," which she said was a translation of
one of the Anishinaabemowin names for this plant. She liked that
Anishinaabe name because it described one of the chief virtues
that the plant has to share with the People. Note I said "virtue,"
not "inconvenience." Many a cottage owner curses the cattails that
line his shoreline, never giving a thought to the fact that a shore
lined with cattails is protected from wave erosion. The "Defenders
of the Shoreline" stand like warriors against the water that would
otherwise eat at the land. As land animals, humankind should
be more grateful to those plants who hold the land in place for
us. And this plant has many other virtues to share with us, too.
At any time of the year it has a food for the hungry. The leaves of
the cattail in the summer and fall are ready to provide weaving
materials. Even in the dead of winter the cattail has a very valuable
product to share that will help keep out the cold.

Every stage of the growth of cattails is a different food for
those knowledgeable enough to take what is offered to them. The
only caution that should be given is that one must be sure that
the water in which the cattails are growing is not polluted. Plants
cannot get up and move when poison is in the soil or water in
which they are standing. They have to pull up into themselves
whatever is available to them. The cattails are especially good
at absorbing poisons. The U.S. Department of Agriculture uses
them to clean badly polluted water. They even have the ability
to pull heavy metals out of water and are being used to clean

Apakweshkway: Cattail (*Typha latifolia* and *Typha angustifolia*)

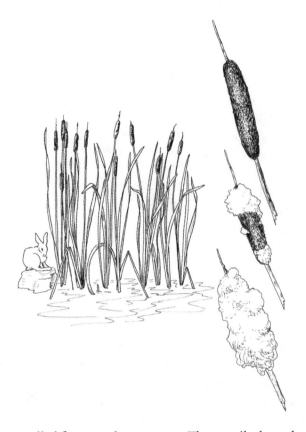

1 Kee always included a description of how cattails clean up pollution in her lectures. For those wishing to read more about this, see Economic Research Service, USDA, 33.

water expelled from nuclear reactors. The cattails draw the heavy minerals out of the water and hold the pollutants within their own cells. The only problem is one must then dispose of radioactive cattails, but the water is then reusable.[1] Because the cattail is so good at catching and holding pollution, one must be very sure one is taking cattails from clean water if one wants to use them for food or for any of numerous crafts.

Kee always told her classes that if they had nothing better to do with their time they might consider gathering cattail rhizomes, the underwater, underground stems of the cattail plant, which are commonly called roots, and processing them into flour. She used to laugh that every book on foraging for wild foods recommended the rhizome of cattail as a source of readily available flour, but Kee always said it was far too much work for far too little reward. She thought a starving person would waste more of their available energy harvesting and processing the flour than they could get from the food so produced. (She warned her students not to ever get themselves into the position of having to test her hypothesis, as it might be a lethal experiment.) Once, when she was a graduate student studying ethnobotany in Michigan, she took three weeks to make enough flour to make three loaves of bread. She said that just as she was taking the loaves out of the oven her professors came to visit, thought the bread smelled wonderful, sat down, ate all three loaves, and left. She said she had not bothered with the flour of the cattail root since then.

Kee did remember, however, as a child helping her family gather the roots[2] of the cattail. They would go out on a warm day in August and wade around in the shallows, breaking off the upper parts of the cattails and digging the roots out with racks and with their own toes. It was a messy job, but one that a child could think was fun.[3] Her family then washed the roots, scraping the outer skin off the roots immediately after harvesting them when the outer skin is easy to remove.[4] They would cut the roots into slices to hasten the drying process, so that the roots would dry before they molded. Then they strung the slices on string and hung them over the wood stove to dry. Later, after the growing season, the roots could be ground up to be used as flour. As an adult, however, Kee did not recommend the use of cattail roots as an emergency source of flour.

Gibbons offers a way to get the starch out of the roots without having to dry and grind them that would speed up the process of using them as an emergency food. One washes and peels the roots, then crushes them in clean water, filtering out the fibers and allowing the cloudy wash water to settle for half an hour until the starch settles to the bottom of the container. One pours off the excess water and puts in more water, stirring up the starch again. One allows the starch to settle out two or three times and then pours off the excess water and uses the starch in its wet stage. He did not try to dry it, but says the taste is improved using it half and half with wheat flour. He said drop biscuits made with the starch were rather tasty (Gibbons 1962, 57–58).[5]

But there are other foods in the cattail that are worthwhile and easier to use. In the early spring, just after the cattails have begun to grow, they have a green bloom-spike that is covered with a papery outer husk. One cuts those spikes and peels the paperlike husk off, as one would husk corn. The inner bloom-spike can be boiled in water and eaten covered in melted butter. One picks the spike up in one's fingers and nibbles the buds off the spike the way one eats corn-on-the-cob.

After the green spike stage, the cattail develops its pollen. That was a food that Kee loved. She remembered as a girl looking

[2] When she told this story, Kee said she and her family were gathering the "roots" of the cattail plant. I don't know if she meant the actual roots or the rhizomes, although both are found under the water and under the ground at the bottom of the plant.

[3] In the modern world, one would have to be more cautious. Fishermen often snag their lines on cattails, breaking the lines and leaving hooks on or under the plants. Encourage children to wear old tennis shoes when they wade out into the cattail roots so that they will not get the hooks in their feet.

[4] The outer layer of the root becomes harder to remove when the root dries, so one should remover it as soon as one has pulled the roots.

[5] Gibbons also cites research by a Cornell University scientist who studied cattails during World War I as emergency food: P. W. Claasen, "A Possible New Source of Food Supply", *Scientific Monthly* (August 1919).

6 She said that in later times she used plastic bags for this job, pulling the bag over the spike before shaking the pollen loose; that way she caught more of the pollen than she had been able to do as a child shaking the pollen over a bowl.

forward to the golden-yellow pollen of the cattail because her mother would make her golden pancakes. It was Kee's job to harvest the pollen by shaking the flower stalks over a bowl and catching the pollen as it fell.[6] Then it was her job to find tern nests and take eggs for the recipe. Her family used tern eggs because the terns would just lay another clutch of eggs if they lost the first, and the terns always seemed to be laying their eggs just when the cattail pollen was ready. Her mother mixed half pollen with half wheat flour, added tern eggs and a little oil, and fried the mixture in a frying pan. She said it made the most beautiful, golden yellow pancake that had a delightful flavor.

Kee said that her family always used the pollen the day they harvested it. Since the pollen season is only a few days, a week at most, she could only have the golden pancakes for a very short time. As an adult she tried to dry the pollen for later use but had never had success. It always molded before it dried.

After the time when pollen is available one can then harvest the inner part of the young growing plant. When the leaves are about two or three feet tall, grab the upper part and break it off at the root. Peel the outer leaves off at the bottom the way one peels a banana. Inside is a light-colored part about one foot long. This is the part that they eat in Russia, calling it "Cossack Asparagus."[7] It is good either raw in a salad or cooked. Kee liked it parboiled in a little water then serve with a cheese sauce or baked in a pan next to a nice roast of beef or venison.

7 Kee felt that it was important to point out in her lectures that cattails grow all around the world in the Northern Hemisphere. She stressed that they were not brought here by the Pilgrims or any later European settlers, either. Cattails are simply a circumboreal plant.

After the tops of the cattails turns brown, the tastiest food of the cattail is gone for the year, but, at any time until the leaves dry in the fall, one can cut the leaves at the root level and use the clear and starchy, gunky, mucilaginous stuff that is between the leaves as food. One can just suck the stuff out of the cut off leaves for an instant energy jolt, or one can put it in a soup or stew as a thickener. It is not a nasty taste, just a blah one. It would come in handy if there was little else to eat.

When taking the cattails to eat, one must always be conscious that humans are not the only ones who depend on the cattails for food. The beavers and the muskrats and the geese also eat the roots, and they use the leaves to build their homes and nests, too. Good neighbors do not eat up all of the food supplies and leave nothing for the others who live around them.

In the days of the Gete-Anishinaabeg, people also used the cattail leaves to cover their lodges. The mature leaves were gathered in the late summer, when they had their full growth. They were then woven into mats to cover the outside of the traditional wiigiwaam.

When Kee was living on her island, Minis-kitigaan, in the middle of Lake Michigan, one of her apprentices wanted to cover her wigwam in a traditional manner, not with the plastic tarps that the rest of the camp used. So she arrived on the island one summer with huge bundles of cut cattails. She strung lines up in camp, outside of the lodge were the food was stored, and spent hours stringing the cattails up to dry in preparation for weaving them into mats. She got distracted by the camp activities, something that used to be very easy to do, and never finished the job. All summer long the cattails hung there, drying, and serving as a curtain in front of the lodge. The odd thing was the flies used to congregate on the hanging cattails. Whenever one brushed against the hanging cattails a whole cloud of flies would fly up. They would fly up and around and settle back down on the cattails. As a consequence, there were very few flies inside of the food storage lodge.

When the hanging cattails started to attract and contain the flies in camp, Kee remembered a similar situation. As a child she would sleep in her co-grandmother's wigwam on Minis-kitigaan in the summertime. She said her grandmother had woven cattails into screens that she put around the outside of the lodge. They were little cattail screens, framed with cedar strips, and they were all around the wigwam on the ground and up about 18 inches. Kee said it made the wigwam very cool to sleep in because the night breezes could blow through the holes so easily, yet she did not remember ever being bothered by flying insects when she slept in her grandmother's lodge. She thought that there must be something in the cattails that either attracted the flies or just made it so that the flies did not want to fly through the cattails to get into the lodge.

If one wants to weave a fly-stopping screen for a lodge or one's window, one weaves the cattails while they are still fresh, before they dry. One should weave the leaves as tightly as one can, even overlapping them. Then one dries the woven mat under weight. I managed it by putting newspaper over the woven mat and stacking encyclopedias on top. In a few days the mat was dried and flat. As the leaves dry they shrink, so the resulting mat will have little holes between the leaves, just perfect for a screen that will discourage the insects from coming into one's home.

If one wants to make large mats to cover the outside of a

wigwam, all the way around, instead of smaller mats just to use as screening, cut the leaves and hang them to dry in the shade. Once the leaves are dry and have had their initial shrinking, one can then re-soak them to a pliable stage for weaving. If one does that, the resulting product will not shrink as much as it would if it were woven with green leaves, and the resulting product will be tighter than it would have been if the leaves were used fresh.

Leaves dried in the sun will be brown, and those in the shade will stay green. One can, of course, dry them both ways and use the different colors to weave patterns into the finished product. In the old days a weaver might even use one of several dyes to get even more colors into the leaves. One dries the leaves, then re-soaks them to make them pliable, and then they are boiled in dyestuff until they soak up the desired color.

I went to the Milwaukee Public Museum one time, to watch museum staff members who were supposedly making a traditional cattail mat to cover a wigwam. They were doing the work outside of the museum in a courtyard, but on the day they had chosen for the display it rained and rained. I arrived late, only to find that the staff had given up the idea and had gone back inside, off to their other duties. I stood in the rain and looked at a frame with hanging cattails, that the staff had started to weave in and out with string. As I stood there a little, old, Indian lady hobbled up with her daughter, and we stood together and looked at the frame in the rain.

The little old mindimooyenh sniffed a little laugh. I turned to her, saw the disdain on her face as she looked at the museum's display, so I said, "Do you know, Grandmother? Are they doing it correctly?"

"No!" she said, "It is wrong. This will be a very poor mat that will break too easily. It will not last very long on their wigwam."

I asked, "Have you done this work before?"

"Oh, yes," she said, "We always made such mats when I was a girl. But this one is wrong. They should have alternated the bottom and the top of the leaves, hanging one leaf by the top and the next by the bottom. That way the mat will be strong. I wouldn't want to sleep in this wigwam." Then she laughed and turned and walked away. I had no asemaa with me at the time. I have since wished I could have thanked the little mindimooyenh properly for her teaching that day in the rain.

The dried leaves of the cattail are a weaving material that has been used for a wide variety of crafts. Numerous children's toys

were/are also traditionally made from cattails. The dolls called
"No Face" dolls are easy to make from them and have undoubtedly entertained many an Anishinaabe child. Kee used to encourage the children of her acquaintance to make hoops of red osier
or willow, the interior of which were laced with sinew or twine in
a dream-catcher pattern, leaving several large holes. A dried cattail
flower stalk with its intact brown-cigar head was the javelin that
the child tried to throw through the rolling hoop to score various
points for the different holes hit. It is an ancient Anishinaabe
game designed to teach hunting skills. Another traditional toy
that is made with cattail leaves are miniature duck decoys that are
folded out of a single cattail leaf. The ducks are made in groups
of five[8] and floated in a bowl of water. When they are moved by
the breath of the child or the wind they move most realistically,
bobbing around like ducklings. There is a cave in northwestern
Utah where duck decoys made out of bundled and sculpted cattail
leaves were found that are at least three thousand years old. The
decoys were sculpted to resemble ducks, then either covered
with a real duck's feathers or painted to make them more lifelike
(*America's Fascinating* 1978, 24). The technique of sculpting
hunting decoys of cattails is therefore proved to be a very ancient
one among the People.

At one time craftsmen and women used the dried cattail leaves
to make many useful products. Kee taught me how a quick and
easy basket can be made using red osier for the frame and cattail
leaves as the weavers. I have also seen chair seats woven of dried
cattail leaves and rounded by spinning against the weaver's leg as
they were woven. Cattails have another great gift to share with the
Anishinaabeg. They are the source of a marvelous insulation that
will keep out even the cold of our Northern winters. Once the fall
comes and the leaves dry out in the autumn winds, it is time to
pick the tops of the cattails. One waits until after the first frost so
that the majority of the bugs will have been killed. If one does not
get to them in the fall one can still gather the tops all through the
winter.

Go out to the swamp and snap off the brown, cigar-shaped
heads that stick up on top of the leaves. It is easier to do if one has
a knife, but if the stalks are very dry, as they will be once the snow
comes, they can even be snapped off with a flip of the wrist.

Once one has one's cattail tops gathered, one has to take off
the fuzzy part. One puts one's hand on the stalk at the bottom
of the brown, cigar-shaped flower stalk, and with the other hand,

8 I have wondered why we make
these toys five at a time. I do not
know of an Aadizookaan of our area
that addresses that, but I do know
a Western Coyote story about a
time when Coyote fooled the Five
Mallard Sisters. It is a wickedly
funny story. Perhaps that story was
living among the Anishinaabe at
one time, too.

one pushes along the stalk, toward the sharp pointy end, using the opposite thumb and forefinger. As one pushes along, the brown head will break up into a cloud of fluffy, white, incredibly soft material. Do this job out-of-doors if possible, as it is a rather messy job to do in one's living room. It is also a good idea to do the work with one's hands, with the cattails inside of a plastic garbage bag, so that the fuzz does not fly away in the wind or cover one's winter coat. After pushing off the fuzz, the hard center stalk with its sharp spike remains in one's hand. Take this spike out of the bag and dispose of it so that only fluff is left in the bag.

This fluff is a marvelous insulation material. When Kee was a child, her bed in the winter was a bearskin underneath and a cattail quilt above. She said the quilt was a big bag that had cattail fluff inside of two pieces of cloth. It was just a big bag, without the fancy quilting that people do on quilts nowadays. There was a little pocket at the bottom for her feet. She said it was marvelously warm even in the coldest weather. All one had to do was shake it once a day to fluff up the cattail fuzz on the inside.

When I was taking Kee's ethnobotany class at the university for the first time, I made a cattail quilt for part of my final project. I had gathered the cattails, fluffed the fuzz off the stalks, and sewn the fluff into a quilt top that I had made with rubbings of autumn leaves. I thought it was rather pretty. It had taken me many hours of work, and as I was just finishing the quilting, I pushed the needle up through the cloth, and out came my needle with a larva impaled on it. I was furious! It had been a lot of work, and here I had the quilt all but finished, but it was full of worms! I threw it into the freezer, and put the larva in a jar, and the next day I took both of them to the ethnobotany lab. I tossed it at my teaching assistant instructor and demanded to know what I should do with the "buggy" thing. Luckily, there was a botanist in the lab that day who took the larva and looked at it under a microscope. He assured me that it was the larva of a little, white moth that lives in cattails. He said it was not the kind that eats woolen clothing, just the kind that eats cattails, so I should not worry about them hatching in my home. But, he said all I really had to do was throw the quilt into the dryer and cook it for a while to kill the bugs that may have hatched in the fluff.

So now to use cattail fluff, I gather the brown heads after the frost. I fluff the heads and put the fluff into a pillowcase, tied very tight, and then I put it inside another pillowcase.[9] Then I put it into the dryer set on high for about an hour. That will cook

9 I put the fluff inside of two securely tied pillowcases so that the fluff will not break out inside of my dryer. I suspect it would be a mess to have it all floating around in there uncontained, to say nothing of the fact that it might be a fire hazard. One woman I know "zaps" cattail fuzz in her microwave to kill anything that might be in it. I have never tried that but it should work, too.

anything that might be in the fluff. Then I set the pillowcase beside the dryer for two or three days, then I cook it again. Sometimes I do that three times, depending on how soon I want to use the fuzz. The waiting period is to allow any other larva to hatch out of their chrysalis before I cook it again, as the heat will kill the already hatched bugs, but it might not get the unhatched ones.

Kee laughed when I told her about how upset I had been about the "buggy" quilt. She said in the old days she doubted a little, white moth would have worried anyone. Also, she said that most people would go screaming into the night if they knew what was living in their feather pillows. After that I started routinely, several times a year, taking the pillows off my bed and throwing them into the dryer a few times, too.

Huron Smith, a botanist working for the Milwaukee Public Museum in the 1920s and early 1930s, wrote that the women of the Lac du Flambeau Ojibwe boiled the tops of the cattail plants after gathering them in the fall, before they dried them and fluffed them for insulation. The boiling was said to kill any bugs that were in the cattail fluff (Smith 1923, 423). I am sure that it would work, but one would have to be very careful to dry the heads well after the boiling to assure they would not mold prior to or after use. According to Smith, the Lac du Flambeau called the cattails "bebaamiseng," "It flies around." They remembered that it was used as a war medicine that was said to blind one's enemy if thrown in his face (Smith 1923, 390). Perhaps one would be wise to wear one's glasses or a pair of goggles when fluffing cattails just in case.

In the old days cattail fluff was used for bedding and for winter clothing as well. It traps a lot of air, and that is why it makes for very warm garments. In one ethnobotany class, when I was teaching assistant, I remember Kee being delighted when a student made a beautiful child's quilted hat for her display at the end of term. It was made of green velvet, and she had quilted the cattail fluff into little star-shaped pockets. It was one of the prettiest baby bonnets I ever saw, and it would have kept a baby's head toasty in the coldest weather. Kee said this was what was always done in the days of the Gete-Anishinaabeg.

When using cattail fuzz, one would have to quilt the material so that the fuzz cannot move around too much. If the fluff settles down one would have cold spots in the garment or bed covering, unless one could just shake it the way Kee shook her childhood bed covering before she went to bed at night. The quilting can be minimized, however, if one uses a woodland plant called Cleavers (*Galium aparine*) inside of the ticking to keep the cattail fluff from shifting. Cleavers are covered with tiny prickers that catch and hold the fluff, or wool or feathers if those are one's insulating materials, in place.

In the old days the People used cattail heads to insulate the winter wigwam. A winter wigwam is made with two walls, a snug, waterproof bark covering on the outside and another on the inside. In the space between the two walls one put in cattail heads. When they fluffed out on their own as they dried, they created an insulation that would keep the family warm all through the coldest winter. Insulation is not an idea invented in the 1970s, during the oil crisis, obviously!

When Kee was a girl, her mother hired some men to take down an old shed that was attached to their home cabin. The shed had been built more than fifty years before by her grandfather and her great-uncle. She said that the room had been used by her family as summer kitchen and an extra sleeping place because it was always very warm in the wintertime. It was being removed because they wanted to enlarge their cabin. Kee said that the workmen called the family out to see what they had found when they took down the inner wall. There were two walls, and the space between them was stuffed with cattail heads that had fluffed out on their own and insulated the building. Kee's father said that it was just the way his family had built their winter wigwams in the old days. The contractor made Kee's mother swear she would not tell anyone about the cattails because he said it would cost him business if people knew they could keep their houses warm just using something that grew for free in the ditches.

In her lectures, Kee talked about another use of cattails that the American government found and made use of during World War II. The German U-boats had made travel to Southeast Asia somewhat hazardous, to say the least, and the United States needed the kapok that grows there to make life preservers for the Navy. They discovered that cattail down, dried and stuffed very tightly into a cloth cover, made a very acceptable substitute for kapok.[10] Many an Anishinaabe sailor went off to war safe inside the cattails from home. This is an example of how these elder brothers of mankind can actually aid us physically and spiritually. In this example, the cattails are actually going to war with their younger brothers. Plants actually want to help us.

10 Kee included this story about cattails in her class lectures. For information see Allen and Melinda in the Bibliography.

Mashkiigobag

Labrador Tea
Swamp Tea
Hudson Bay Tea
Rhododendron groenlandicum

My father, George Shomperlen, did not go to World War II. He was working at the time at the Aldermac in Northern Quebec as a foreman in a mine. Because of his work in a wartime industry he was not drafted but continued at his job, which was deemed vital to the war effort.[11] Because he was working in the Far North, my mom and two eldest sisters also lived in the bush with him for those years. One of my family's most vivid memories of the War involved a plant called Labrador tea, or as it is called in Canada, swamp tea, rebel tea, or Hudson Bay tea.

Most all imported goods into Canada at the time were strictly rationed, and Asian black tea was no exception. Since tea is a product of South East Asia, the war in the Pacific seriously cut down the availability of tea throughout North America and Europe. Very little tea made it into my parents' part of northern Quebec. The coupons that enabled a person to purchase tea were as closely guarded as the meat coupons, possibly more so to my family, who had been passionate tea drinkers like many Canadians of the time.

Mom said that as soon as the community would get their allotted shipment of tea, people would line up to cash in their coupons. The first pot of tea brewed with the family's allotment was very much anticipated and drunk with great ceremony. Then the rest of the tea was very carefully sewn into little muslin bags a spoonful at a time. My mom learned to make the little bags from the nuns in the community who sewed all of their tea into such bags so that they could use and reuse the same leaves several times in an effort to make the most of such a valuable and scarce commodity. They would use the tea leaves once, then they would pin the wet bags to dry on a clothesline strung over the woodstove. Once the tea bags were dry they would use and reuse

[11] He was, however, a corporal in the Canadian Army Reserve. He said he spent the war drilling his men up and down in the snow. He and his men were sure they could have stopped the German attack across the Arctic which the people of the time actually expected.

Mashkiigobag: Labrador Tea
(*Rhododendron groenlandicum*)

12 Tea in those days was always sold in loose-leaf form. Tea bags were not sold, or if they were my family was not aware of them. My mother thought that the idea of tea bags was invented by the nuns and their hand-sewn tea bags. The very idea of a tea bag was a joke. I remember an old minister who used to say, "Making tea with a tea bag was like taking a bath with your socks on."

them as much as four times.[12] The tea kept getting weaker, but it was better than no tea at all. Even the judicious reuse of tea would only stretch it so far. When the time came to admit that the leaves were completely used up, they had to look around for substitutes.

To a real tea drinker, herbal teas usually just do not satisfy. Somehow they just do not have the kick of real tea, and they will seldom stand up to the addition of milk and sugar that real tea drinkers require. But there was one local plant that came very close to the real thing. That was swamp tea. My mom said she would give the little Cree children of the neighborhood a quarter, and they would happily go out in the muskeg and bring her back a bag of swamp tea. Mom said that it was swamp tea that got my family, and most everyone else in the community, through World War II.

She also said that on the day when the war finally ended everyone in their community ran into their kitchens and made a big pot of their hoarded Asian black teas and drank it all day. They had just assumed that with the War ended, of course, the shipping lanes would be open again to the East, and "real" tea was sure to be on the first ships into port. But Mom said that there was not one drop of "real" tea in the community for six months. Everyone had celebrated and drunk all of their hoarded allotments. The little Cree kids made a killing picking and selling swamp tea to the parched tea drinkers.

Swamp tea got my family and many other Canadian families through the wartime shortages of tea. It is a shrub that grows in the bogs, muskegs, and the wet woodlands from Alaska in the west, across the Canadian Arctic, around the Canadian Shield to Labrador, from one ocean coast to the other. It also grows across much of the northern United States. Swamp tea is a perennial bush that usually grows from one to two feet high, although it can reach four feet in height in a favorable spot. It is an evergreen plant that holds its leaves throughout the winter. The twigs and branches of the plant are covered with little hairs, and the one- to two-inch narrow leaves are rolled under on the edges, dark green and leathery on the top and very fuzzy on the underside. On new leaves the wool on the underside will be a dirty, off-white color, but as the leaves age the wool becomes rust brown. The rusty color is the tannin, the chemical that is also in tea and that gives tea its characteristic taste and astringency.

One makes a cup of swamp tea in exactly the way one would make a cup of black tea. One pours a cup of boiling water over a teaspoon of dried leaves or several leaves of the fresh plant into a warmed teapot. One steeps the tea for a few minutes depending on how strong one wants the drink to be, then one filters the leaves out of the tea while pouring it into one's cup. Milk and sugar or lemon and honey may be added to one's personal taste.

Of all of the available woodland teas, and in our land there are many plants that can be used to make tea, only swamp tea is really capable of making a cup of liquid that even comes close to black tea. It makes a tea that has a strong taste, but one that actually satisfies, too. It is flavorful and aromatic, with an almost fruity taste that is reminiscent of jasmine or oolong teas, yet it is a taste that within a few days can actually be a replacement for black tea. If I ever have to live through a time as my parents did, when one simply could not buy black tea, I would make a concentrated effort to change my tea habit over as quickly as possible to swamp tea. I would give my tea coupons away and start drinking swamp tea with milk at every opportunity. I anticipate that within a week, two at most, swamp tea would just be tea to me. Once I had acculturated my taste buds to swamp tea it would no longer be a hardship to drink it at all. Switching back and forth between black tea and swamp tea would be more difficult, however; I think I would just go "cold turkey" and make the complete shift as quickly as possible. There is no shortage of swamp tea on our continent.

My parents told me that they did not drink swamp tea only when they could not buy black. They had been very familiar with it before the war, too, and often drank it by preference. My dad said that when they were first married and living in northern Manitoba they would often go for picnics in their canoe. They would take along matches, their fishing poles, a frying pan and some grease to cook the fish, and a tin can with a wire attached to it as a handle. They would catch their supper and cook it in the frying pan on an island in the lake and make tea in their tin can with water out of the lake and swamp tea, which was always available. Their idea of a luxurious picnic was one where they bothered to take along cups; otherwise, they would just drink their tea out of the same tin can in which they had boiled the water.[13]

Swamp tea is a fairly common plant in the northern bogs and swamps in the Great Lakes states. When picking it one must only be aware that there are two other plants in the swamp that one must not confuse with swamp tea. They are bog laurel, *Kalmia polifolia*, and bog rosemary, *Andromeda polifolia*, both of which are poisonous.

Bog laurel has a general similarity to swamp tea, but it has opposite leaves where Labrador tea has alternate leaves. John Bates, in his highly readable *Trailside Botany*, suggests that one can remember bog laurel's different leaf orientation if one remembers the little rhyme: "Laurel and Hardy had opposite personalities / And Bog Laurel has opposite leaves" (Bates 1995, 173).

Bog rosemary, which is also poisonous, has an alternate leaf that looks like swamp tea, too, but the undersides of the bog rosemary leaves are a bright bluish white. They never have brown or cinnamon colored fuzz on the undersides of the leaves the way the swamp tea does (Bates 1995, 176).

There are two factors that are the real keys to knowing one has a swamp tea, and neither the problematic bog laurel nor the bog rosemary. First, it is the smell. Nothing else smells like swamp tea. Its spicy, tea-smell is a good identifying factor. Secondly, neither of the problem plants have leaves that are fuzzy and brown underneath. Smell the plant and check for the brown fuzz to know if it is real swamp tea.

13 The last time I spent a summer vacation with my parents in northern Wisconsin, at Radues, a resort on Pickerel Lake, my family and I were camping near the cabin in which my father, mother, and sister were staying. One evening they came out to have supper with us at our campsite, and we served them fresh-caught bass and swamp tea cooked in an old camping pot that looked like a tin can with a wire handle. I remember how tears came into my dad's eyes when he saw the pot and told me about the picnics of their younger years. Sometimes the smell of a campfire and the tastes of the foods of one's youth are as good as a swig from the proverbial Fountain of Youth or a trip in a time machine.

Giizisoojiibik

"Sun Tuber, Root of the Sun"
Ashkibwaa
Jerusalem Artichoke
Helianthus tuberosus

The common name of this plant, "Jerusalem Artichoke," is a particularly poor name. This is a native plant that does not come from Jerusalem, and it is by no means an artichoke. It was gifted with the "Jerusalem" part of the common name because the name for a sunflower in Italian is *girasole* and the Spanish is *girasol*. When the plant was first introduced into Europe the word got corrupted into "Jerusalem" (Gibbons 1962, 25; Coffey 1993, 265). It is anybody's guess why the Europeans started to call a plant whose tuberous root is the food part an "artichoke."

But the scientific name for the plant is right on. It means the same thing as the Anishinaabe name that Kee liked: "Giizisoojiibik: Sun tubers or roots of the sun."

Keewaydinoquay taught that sun tubers have a very long history with the People. She said that if archeologists and anthropologists want to find a site of a pre-Contact Anishinaabe village, this is one of the plants they should look for. The People always liked to have a stand of sun tubers close by, and the patch will go right on growing, year after year, untended. Kee said she used it as a young girl to locate a place where she could go to search for arrowheads. I planted a patch of them when I moved into my home eighteen years ago, and they come up dutifully every year for me. The only help I give them is a little straw out of the duck house as a fertilizer now and then, and a little water if our August is so dry that they look wilted. With no more care than that they keep producing bushel baskets of food for my family every year.

The sun tubers are a type of sunflower, the only one of the genus that has tuberous roots. All the rest of the sunflowers have fibrous roots. In grocery stores in the fall one can now usually buy two different kinds of sun tubers, although they are called "sun

Giizisoojiibik: Jerusalem
Artichoke (*Helianthus
tuberosus*)

14 Kee did not like that name
because she thought it an insult to
the plant to say it "choked" people.

chokes";[14] ones with a light yellow skin and ones with a reddish
skin. Kee said the reddish ones are the ones indigenous to our
area.

Sun tubers are very impressive plants. They grow in a patch all
together, and they can get to be ten feet high in a summer. They
do not bloom in our area until late in the fall, just before the frost.
And their flowers are not the big, impressive ones that the rest
of the sunflowers produce. They are much smaller, usually two
or three inches across, with a yellow center that is dome-shaped,
not brown like the rest of the genus. Also, they do not produce
the wonderful edible seeds that the rest of the sunflowers have
to share with us. They hide their food underground. Right at the
base of the stalk, one digs down to find numerous tubers that can
be three to five inches long and either rounded like a potato or
slightly elongated.

The time to go harvesting the sun tubers is after the first frost
of fall. That is when the plant has gone through its whole life
cycle, and it will do no harm to the continuation of the patch to
dig up the roots. When one harvests the tubers one will inevitably

cut a few in half with the shovel or find a few of the smaller ones among the rest that are hardly worth the effort to clean and eat. Those are the ones I return to the soil in the same spot so that the sun tubers will grow for me again next year. Sun tubers have eyes just as potatoes do, and if one cuts the tuber into sections, each individual eye is capable of producing a new plant in the spring.

The best time to gather the tubers is after the frost but before the snows come. It is a lot less work to gather before the ground gets frozen stiff! However, if one forgets and does not gather them then, they will be perfectly edible all winter until the ground thaws in the spring. The dry stalks of the plants are clearly visible in even our deepest snows, sticking up to remind one where the emergency food supply is located should the need arise.[15] I have eaten tubers that have spent the winter in the garden, but by March or so they have a sharper taste that is not as pleasant as fall-dug ones. Still, they would be better than going to bed hungry!

Dig up the tubers, wash off the soil, pat them dry, and store them in a cool place. In the crisper in my refrigerator they will keep for a month at least, sometimes two or three. One can also keep them all winter in a bucket of sand in the basement, or in a cold frame outside if they are protected from freezing by layers of sand or sphagnum moss and straw.

One time in her younger days, Kee was the sole supporter of five elders. She used to grow and dig the sun tubers in the fall, wash them, dry them, and deliver them to the elders in buckets of sand. She said no one ever said "No, thank you" to the gift and that those elders ate them all winter.

Kee said that sun tubers are an excellent food for elderly Anishinaabeg because they have a marvelous virtue to share with us. They taste and feel and satisfy like carbohydrates, but they are high in inulin, which is a low-starch carbohydrate. That is very good for diabetics and others who have to have a low-starch diet. Since so many of our Anishinaabe elders are either diabetics or borderline diabetics, the sun tubers are an excellent food for them.

Sun tubers are very tasty eaten raw. Just scrub them and slice them and nibble them as a snack. They also make great crunchy additions to salads or relishes. Kee especially liked them cut thin and added last to stir-fry dishes. She thought them an excellent and inexpensive substitute for water chestnuts. They are also nice cut thin and served in a sandwich, either alone or with other sandwich ingredients.

15 For some reason it just makes me feel safer if I know that if I ever could not buy food I would not starve while that stand of sun tubers is outside of my back door.

The tubers can also be cooked any way one would cook a potato. However, if one boils and mashes them they are a little wetter than a potato, and that bothers some people. See the Recipes section for sun tuber cooking instructions. Kee especially liked the Chiffon Pie that one of her aunties used to make with them.

5

Four Traditional Plants in the Anishinaabeg Culture

"The Shut-eye Dance and the Creation of Red Osier, Bittersweet, and Lichens"

One day Naanabozho was walking along down by the shore of a lake. It was getting towards suppertime, and he was feeling more than a little hungry. As he looked out over the lakeshore he saw a great number of zhiishiibag of all kinds, quacking, swimming in the reeds, and bobbing for fish and tender greens in the shallows.

"Howa!" said Naanabozho to himself. "If I could get a number of those plump fellows they would make a fine supper. But they are so far out in the water. If I swim out to them, they will surely fly. No, I must make them come to me."

So he walked back from the shore into a swampy area. He bent over and quickly grabbed handfuls of sphagnum moss and stuffed the moss into his blanket. Then he slung the blanket over his back and walked back down and along the shoreline. He staggered as if there was a great weight on his back. The ducks, who are very curious fellows, stopped their various pursuits to watch him. Finally one little fellow, *Ininishibens,* a mallard duckling, could contain his curiosity no longer and cried out, "Naanabozho, what is it you have on your back? What is such a great weight that you must stumble as you carry it?"

"Oh," said Naanabozho, "it is just my bag of songs. I have many, many of them, and they are heavy to carry."

"Songs, eh?" said Ininishibens. "What kind of songs?"

"Oh, all kinds. But especially my most secret one, 'The Shut-eye Dance.'"

"We have never heard of that dance. Show it to us," called the other zhiishiibag on the lake who had been listening.

"Sure," said Naanabozho, "I could do that, but it takes a lot of preparation, and I would need help if I was going to do it."

"We will help," said the zhiishiibag and the other waterfowl who had been swimming nearby. Soon great numbers of them swam to shore and offered to help Naanabozho with his preparations for the dance.

"First," he said, "we need a large lodge, up there on the top of the dune, where we can dance. We will go into that lodge so no one else can see our ceremony."

"Good, good," said the zhiishiibag, because they were very pleased with the idea of a secret ceremony just for ducks and geese and the other swimming birds. It would make them very important people indeed to have their own secret medicine dance. They had not seen such a thing before, but they had always known they were a very special people who deserved their very own dance and their own song and their own medicine. So they all joined in to build the lodge. The biggest *nikag,* Canada geese, helped to bend the saplings down to make the structure for the lodge, while the littlest zhiishiibag swam gaily out to the reed beds to uproot many, many reeds with which to cover the sides of the lodge. The *zii'amoog,* the wood ducks, flew up into the birch trees and used their sharp claws to strip the bark for the roof.

With all of the ducks and geese, loons, and other waterbirds of the lake helping, Naanabozho did not have to do any of the work himself. He sat under a tree and directed the work. "Good," he'd call to the group of nikag who had bent down the saplings for the frame. "Now bind them together with wadab, and wiigob. Fine, fine. That will do nicely. Now, you *ininishibag,* mallards, pull up some more reeds and cattails. We must line the walls well, so that no one can see what we do when we dance our medicine dance. Good, little Zii'amoog, that *wiigwaas,* birch bark, is just right to cover the roof."

The birds worked all busily, and by the time the sun was about to set they had a beautiful, long, sturdy wiigiwaam standing on the shore.

"Fine, fine," said Naanabozho. "Lets all go in and start our dance. Here, I will stand in the middle, and you all stand around the outside of the ring. I will sing with this Grandfather Drum, and you all dance around me, each using their own clan's step. Good! Good! Now everyone sing along with this Grandfather Drum and me. Sing loudly, little brothers and sisters! Dance and dance! Flap your wings and throw back your heads and sing! But most important, close your eyes. This is a very secret dance. No one must see it. You must dance with your eyes shut tight. If you open them up your eyes will get red! Now sing, sing, sing!"

Soon the whole crowd of ducks and geese, loons, mergansers, and all of the other waterbirds were dancing in a circle around Naanabozho. They all kept their eyes tightly shut, and they all sang at the top of their voices, quacking and honking and calling until one could scarcely hear the Grandfather Drum nor Naanabozho as he sang:

Do not look,
Or your eyes
Will always be red.

On the dance went with its wonderful din, and it might have gone on a lot longer, but one little *aajigade,* coot, opened one eye and saw Naanabozho grabbing one duck after another as they danced past him. He grabbed them and snapped their necks and tossed them into a pile beside his feet so quickly he barely missed a beat with the drum. With all of the ducks and geese and others singing so loudly, no one could hear the victims' cries, nor the snap of their necks.

"Fly, brothers! Fly!" The little aajigade screamed in his shrill, little high-pitched voice. "Naanabozho is killing us!"

The cry was picked up one by one by all of the dancing birds, and the dance erupted into a mad dash for the door flap. Out of the door they burst, some running, some jumping into the air, in a general panic. The air was full of a cloud of loose feathers and flapping wings and the screams of the ducks: "Fly! Fly, Brothers! He is killing us!"

As the little aajigade who had given the alarm dashed for the door, Naanabozho gave him a swift kick in the rump. The kick flattened out his tail and left his legs as they are today. And his eyes turned bright red, his payment for giving the alarm and for violating the Shut-eye Dance.

When all of the ducks and geese had escaped from the dance lodge, Naanabozho looked around at the pile of birds he had managed to kill with his trick, "Howa!" he said with pleasure, "These fat fellows will make me a fine supper. I think I shall bake them. That will certainly make them a tasty meal"

He gathered the geese and ducks and carried them down to the shore where he prepared a large fire. When the fire was burned down to glowing hot coals, he dug down in the sand around the fire pit and placed the bodies of the birds in the hot sand, with only their feet sticking up above the ground.

Naanabozho was yawning as he worked, and he decided to take a little nap while his dinner was cooking, but he was worried about how he was to guard his supper while he slept. "Surely I must have a guard to watch that no one comes and steals my supper while I sleep," He said. "My Bottom I shall set to watching my supper."

So Naanabozho addressed his Bottom and told it that it must wake him if thieves threatened to steal his supper. His Bottom replied and agreed to keep a good lookout for thieves.

Naanabozho turned his back to the fire on the shore and lifted his Bottom into the air so that it could have a good view of the lake as it guarded his supper.

Naanabozho soon fell into a deep sleep, but his faithful Bottom watched the lake. Soon around a distant point, the Bottom spied a group of men paddling a canoe in Naanabozho's direction.

"Wake up! Wake up, Naanabozho!" the Bottom cried, "Men are coming. Perhaps they will steal your supper."

Naanabozho lazily opened one eye and then another and looked out over the lake. But as he did so, the paddling men happened to be rounding a point of land and were no longer visible from Naanabozho's sleeping place. "Foolish Bottom," he murmured, "I do not see anyone coming. Don't wake me up again unless there are really people coming to steal my supper." And he turned over and was soon snoring again.

The faithful Bottom took up the watch, and as the men in their canoe started to get closer, it cried out again, "Naanabozho, wake up! Men are coming! Perhaps they will steal your supper."

Naanabozho woke with a start and looked out over the lake. Once again he failed to see the approaching canoe because it happened at that time to be around a point of land right off the shore. Naanabozho was angry now.

"You liar!" He screamed at his Bottom, "If you cannot be a better lookout than that, at least stop waking me up." Then he turned over and went back to a deep sleep.

Meanwhile out on the lake, the men in the canoe had seen the smoke of Naanabozho's fire, and as they rounded the point they could see him sleeping with his Bottom up in the air. "Oh, look," they said to each other. "There is Naanabozho asleep by his fire. Let's sneak in there, and see if we can play a trick on him, we might even get a good supper."

So the men beached their canoe and crept up to the fire. They saw the feet of the ducks and geese where Naanabozho had buried them in the sand to cook. Smiling to each other, the men dug up Naanabozho's dinner and, breaking off the legs, set them back in the sand. They thought it a good joke as they took the meat and hopped back in their canoe and paddled away gleefully.

After a time Naanabozho woke up and stretched and said, "Howa, that was a good nap. Now I shall have my goose dinner." He pulled up on the feet of one of the geese he had buried in the sand, only to have the legs come loose. "Oh, I have overslept," he said, "And my dinner is cooked too long." Then he grasped another set of legs, only to have them come up too, then he grabbed a stick and poked around in the sand looking for his dinner. "I have been robbed!" Naanabozho wailed. "Someone has come while I slept and stolen away my fine meal, and it was all your fault, my Bottom. You did not wake me when the thieves came. I will show you what it means to betray the Great Naanabozho, son of the West Wind Spirit and an Anishinaabe woman!"

Naanabozho heaped more wood and soon had a roaring fire with great, leaping flames. Then he stood over the fire and burned his Bottom to teach it a lesson. His Bottom screamed, "Chii, Chii, Chii," but Naanabozho, just gritted his teeth and kept his Bottom in the flames.

After a long time, Naanabozho, stepped out of the fire and said, "There, Bottom! That will teach you to do what the Great Naanabozho tells you to do in the future." But it was a very sore and stiff Naanabozho who waddled off down the beach, his legs as wide apart as any of the dancing ducks whom he had tricked.

As he walked he noticed that the bushes on either side of the path were bright red where he had brushed against them, for he was leaving a trail of blood from his burned Bottom. "Miskwaa-biimizh, red osier," said Naanabozho when he saw the red bushes. "As long as the world and the sky shall last, my nephews the Anishinaabeg shall use you in their kinnikinnick."

Then he walked and waddled a little further down the path until he came to a little hill. He was so sore; he sat down and slid down the rise on his burned Bottom. When he looked back he saw pieces of his flesh had scraped loose from his Bottom and were sticking to the rocks and the dry ground. "Howa, my nephews can cook those for food," said Naanabozho as he pointed at the lichens.

As Naanabozho went further down the path, he heard something right behind him. He looked around and saw his intestines dragging along behind. He broke off a bunch of them and threw them up into a birch tree. "My nephews can use that for food when the winter is very hard and they have no game," he said as he pointed to the bittersweet.

Then Naanabozho waddled off down the path, continuing his journey. He scratched his Bottom from time to time and smiled about what a good trick he had played on his unfaithful backside. That would teach it to do what he told it to do in the future.

Mii' iw. Miigwech.

The Cornus Family

Miskwaabiimizh
Miskoobimizh
"Bend and Stay Plant"
Red Osier
Cornus sericea

Zhakaagomin
Zhaashaagomin
Zhaashaagominens
Bunchberry
Cornus canadensis

~~~~~~~~~~~~~~~~~~~~~~~~~~~~~~~~~~~~~~

These are two very different-looking plants that are grouped together by scientific genus, and that Keewaydinoquay always taught together as well. Red osier, which is misleadingly called dogwood,[1] is a woody shrub that can grow to ten feet tall and that likes wet, marshy land, while bunchberry is a little woodland plant that rarely grows higher than eight inches. These two plants may be cousins, but they have very different growing habits and different virtues to share with Anishinaabeg.

The scientific name *Cornus* is the Latin word for "horn." It refers to the hardness of the wood of the larger tree and shrub-sized members of the genus. These plants get called "dogwood" because a similar plant in Europe was called "dagge," which is an Old English name for a dagger (Niering 1979, 478). The wood of the red osier is so very hard when it dries that a person could conceivably make a weapon of it. In Virgil's *Aeneid,* Book 5, there is a passage that proves the *Cornus* of Europe was used even in ancient times as a weapon:

> Now the boys ride in, before the eyes of their fathers,
> In perfect dressing, a brilliant sight on their bridled horses—
> Sicilians and Trojans greet them with murmurs of admiration.
> They wear on their hair ceremonial garlands, well trimmed,
> And each of them carries a couple of steel-tipped cornel-wood
>   lances. (Quoted in Coffey, 139)

[1] Kee did not call it dogwood, because she thought it just misled people who expected the plant to have the beautiful flowers that southern dogwoods have. She was always leery of common names that were misleading.

Miskwaabiimizh: Red Osier
(*Cornus sericea*)

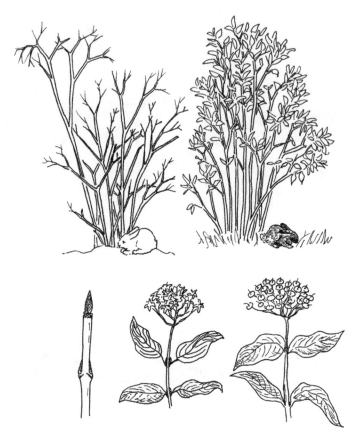

The smallest member of the genus in our area, the bunchberry,
likes cool and wet woods, or it may be found growing at the
edge of swamps. It is a pretty little plant with white flowers, a set
of four petals with a fuzzy, yellow-green center, surrounded by
a whorl of leaves. The flowers are so white that the plant is even
visible in the dark of night.

In the summer the flowers of the bunchberry are replaced by
a clump of bright red berries that hang on through July, August,
September, and may even be on the plant in October. Once the
frost hits the leaves and turns them bright red, the leaves are the
same color as the berries. The berries are edible, but they have a
rather insipid taste and a large stone. They can be munched on
raw as a trailside snack or cooked into an acceptable pudding,
jam, or jelly if a stronger flavor like mint or apple is added
and if the stones are sieved out. The berries do provide a good
nutritional boost and are often very abundant, so they should
be remembered if a person is in need and no other berries are
present.

Zhakaagomin, Zhaashaagomin,
Zhaashaagominens: Bunchberry
(*Cornus canadensis*)

Although they are rarely prized by humans except as an
emergency food or one good for stretching more favorable
berries, the bunchberry is food for others here on Turtle Island.
Another of the common names of the bunchberry is crackberry
or crackerberry, which comes from the old name for a crow, a
"crack"[2] (Coffey 1993, 139). It might have been assumed at one
time that crows ate the bunchberries, or, perhaps because crows
have always been considered a pest bird, the plant may have been
given the name as a derision or insult. In the spring, leaves of
this plant are the nurseries of the caterpillars of the spring azure
butterfly (Tekiela 2000, 243). Those little caterpillars, at least, find
the bunchberry very much to their taste.

Keewaydinoquay did not teach me a medicinal use for bunchberry, but Peterson's *Field Guide to Eastern/Central Medicinal
Plants and Herbs* claims several (Foster and Duke 2000, 17).

Red osier is a much taller plant than the little bunchberry,
growing from two to ten feet high. It has the ability to cover large
areas because it sends down roots from its lowest branches, if the
branches should touch the soil. These rooted branches, which
are called stolons, will grow into new plants that are really clones
of the parent plant. This ability to root itself is celebrated in the

2 This name may have derived from
the sound that crows make.

red osier's earlier scientific species name of *stolonifera,* meaning "bearing stolons." By reaching out and rooting itself in a different place the red osier is capable of "traveling" over large areas of wetland (Stokes 1989, 168).

The most impressive feature of the red osier, and the one that makes it easy to identify, is its signature bright-red bark. In the wintertime, against a backdrop of snow, the stems of the red osier are easy to identify, even if one is traveling at 55 miles per hour on the highway. The red color is evident in the fall, after the first frosts, right up until the bushes leaf out in the spring, when the flame-red stems usually turn green (although some of the older branches may retain a deep mahogany color near the ground).

The red osier's flowers are not nearly as visually impressive as the stems of the plant, but they have a useful virtue to share with the People. When dried, the flowers produce a very pleasant tea which has an effect on the body similar to that of chamomile tea: it produces calming thought and relaxation.

The bark of the red osier and all of the other members of the *Cornus* genus, with the exception of bunchberry, can be used as a substitute for quinine. It will relieve cramps on the base of the foot even when the reason for the cramps is unknown. It also will strengthen the interior walls of the lower intestine. A decoction of the bark is good for elders or younger people who have a weakness in their intestines. It will increase the circulation and clean out any pockets of festering material trapped in the intestines that give a person constant gas or a grumbling stomach. One should know, however, that this medicine does not taste good, and when cleaning out the lower intestine it may give one diarrhea. The related *Cornus florida,* flowering dogwood, is said to have been used for these kinds of problems, too (Foster and Duke 2000, 304–5). The name for red osier that Kee liked and used most often was "Bend and Stay Plant." This name celebrates one of the chief virtues this plant has historically had to share with Anishinaabeg. If one bends this plant and ties it until it is dried, it will retain the shape permanently. Because it is a dense wood, it makes a very strong bend that will withstand considerable pressure. Because of this, Bend and Stay Plant can be used to make hooks to hang meat or weapons or household goods in the lodge. It can even be used to form the frame of a wigwam, if very long osiers are used. Once dried, such a lodge will stand for many years and be capable of holding up under very deep and heavy snows. It is also a very good plant to use for baskets, not pretty, little, touristy baskets but those that a person might use to carry potatoes back from the field.

This plant can be harvested any season of the year, but it is easiest to gather in the wintertime. The bright red of the outer bark will dry to a rich mahogany color. Gathering in the winter also eliminates the necessity of stripping leaves from the stalks before weaving; this keeps the bark from being torn, too.

The interior of the branches has a pith that is easy to remove or burn out with a hot wire. A coathanger, straightened and heated in the campfire, is a good tool to remove the pith. With the interior of the branch removed it can then be cut into beads or peashooters or straws that will dry with a deep red coloration. The hollow stems also make quick, attractive pipestems. They are especially useful for making corncob pipes for smoking those medicinal plants whose virtues are best administered in their smoke. Such medicinals are smoked in quick, disposable pipes so that they will always be fresh and clean and will not harbor or spread disease.

Humankind is only one species that loves the red osier. Many types of wildlife depend on it to get them through the fall and winter. The young twigs serve as winter browse for deer and moose, rabbits and hares, and chipmunks. The berries of the red osier are a dull white or steely gray color. They ripen in August but often stay on the plant into the winter snows. They are a great favorite of many birds, including cardinals, grackles, starlings, evening grosbeaks, and cedar waxwings (Stokes 1989, 170). Kee used to laugh when she would tell about watching the cedar waxwings eating the fermented berries at the end of hot summer days on her island. She said they would swarm over the berries, eating one and spitting it out, then chowing down on others until they were positively drunk and swaying on the branches. She said she could almost hear them chuckling.

In many of the books one reads on herbs utilized by the American Indian tribes one finds references to the inner bark of red osier being used in kinnikinnick. This is a claim that Keeway-dinoquay did not teach her students. She firmly believed that it was an Indian joke propagated on gullible European botanists, published as fact by them, and read by Indians who then believed that their own ancestors had used the bark in this fashion. Kee said the inner bark of red osier is a very harsh smoke that people used to secret into the kinnikinnick of a person they thought needed to be taken down a peg. She said that if a guy was acting a little too macho and uppity, someone might sneak a little of the inner bark into his kinnikinnick just before he was to stand up in front of a big gathering to smoke his pipe. She said if he drew in a whole lungful of the smoke he would then probably be bent over double coughing for a considerable time. She said she thought that it might also have been remembered as an ingredient in kinnikinnick because it is so easy to recognize, as the red bark does stand out very well against the snow. She said that perhaps this is the reason people keep printing and reprinting the idea that osier bark is kinnikinnick.

Personally I only partly believe Kee's take on red osier in kinnikinnick. The origin story of the plant credits Naanabozho as saying that "Oh, red willows[3] shall the people call them till the end of the world! The people, when they smoke, shall use them for a mixture (in their tobacco)" (Jones 1974, 111, 113). I have seen other Ojibwe elders talk about and use the inner bark of red osier to make kinnikinnick. My daughter's late grandfather-in-law, George McGeshick Sr., from the Sokaogon Mole Lake Band of Ojibwe, taught a group of young people to do this at a language camp where we were working in December of 2003. He recommended using a potato peeler to take off the outer bark and then peel off the inner bark.

I also think, as Kee taught me, that the People have asemaa mixed up in their thoughts with Whiteman's tobacco. The real Anishinaabe asemaa was *Nicotiana rustica.* Today people smoke *Nicotiana tabacum.* This is a much milder plant that produces a smoother, less biting smoke. Real asemaa, *Nicotiana rustica,* was a far harsher smoke and was said to even produce hallucinations. It has a higher nicotine level than *N. tabacum* and is today used commercially in nicotine-based pesticides (King 1998, 176). Some Indian people still grow their own *Nicotiana rustica,* and one can occasionally buy it at powwows. But I think that when the People started to smoke Whiteman tobacco, *N. tabacum,* they probably missed the harsh, biting smoke of the real asemaa, and the inner bark of red osier might have started to be added to ceremonial tobacco to make up the difference.

3 Red osier gets called "red willow" colloquially because the stems are used in basketry the way willow is used.

Gookooko'oo-miinan

Baakwaanaatig
Baakwaan
Staghorn Sumac
Rhus hirta

～～～～～～～～～～～～～～～～～～～～～～～～～

When I was a girl growing up in Canada, I learned a poem in school, William Wilfred Campbell's "Indian Summer." We learned a lot of poetry in those days. It was supposed to be a way to increase memory and was much used as a teaching method with grade-school-aged children. I am sure that I benefited from the technique, and even if it did not increase my personal ability to remember, it did leave me with a lifelong phrase or two that come back to me in dreams and whenever I see a stand of sumac in the fall:

Indian Summer

Along the line of smoky hills
The crimson forest stands,
And all the day the blue-jay calls
Throughout the autumn lands.

Now by the brook the maple leans
With all his glory spread,
And all the sumachs on the hills
Have turned their green to red.

Now by great marshes wrapt in mist,
Or past some river's mouth,
Throughout the long, still autumn day
Wild birds are flying south.

The sight of a stand of frost touched, flame-colored sumac in the fall is one of the great compensations for me for the loss of the summer.

For some strange reason people who do not know sumac always immediately worry about "poison sumac." In the lower parts of Wisconsin and Michigan, but much less in the northern

Baakwaanaatig: Staghorn Sumac
(*Rhus hirta*)

parts of those two states, we do have a poison sumac, but it would be very difficult to confuse it with the staghorn sumac. Poison sumac grows in swamps and bogs, while the staghorn grows in dry, sandy places on hills, in old fields, or along roadsides. Poison sumac has smooth, hairless twigs and buds, while the staghorn sumac is covered with a light, downy fuzz, which gives it the common name of "staghorn" because it is reminiscent of the fuzz that covers a stag's new antlers in the spring. Poison sumac has dirty-white-colored berries in spreading and drooping loose stalks, while the staghorn has dark, wine-red berries that grow in a tight clump at the end of branches. It would be difficult to confuse the two plants. Poison sumac might give the person who touches it dermatitis similar to that of poison ivy, but both problems can be avoided with the use of the sap of jewelweed, which always seems to be growing near both poison sumac and poison ivy. It is as if Creator placed the plants together so that the remedy will be within reach to eliminate of the pain of the disease.

The "eye candy" that staghorn sumac becomes in the fall is only one of the virtues it has to share with the People. At the same time as the leaves turn, the staghorn sumac also has clusters of berries that grow on the top of the plant, on the ends of the branches. One should pick the berry clusters during fine, dry days, not after a period of rain, for two reasons. First, they dry very easily if one picks them dry, avoiding mold that may render them useless. Dried, they can be kept and used all winter. Second, the acid that the berries contain is very water-soluble, and it may be considerably reduced if the berries have been exposed to the long, drenching rains of autumn. Therefore, take the berries on a warm, sunny afternoon after a dry spell.

The berries thus gathered make a really nice lemonade-type drink that most people find pleasant and refreshing.[4] The only trick is getting to the berries before the ants and other insects have had a chance to find them. One could float the clumps in water to remove the insects but that will reduce some of the flavor as well. Personally I just take "non-buggy" berries for use as a drink, and I keep the insect-infested ones for use in dyes.

To make the drink one crushes a clump or two of the berries and either pours boiling water over them, or puts them in cool water and sets the jar in the sun, the way one makes sun tea. However, because the whole of the staghorn sumac is covered with tiny hairs, it is necessary to filter the solution before one drinks it, because the tiny hairs will irritate one's throat. I use a double thickness of cheesecloth to filter out the hairs, but a coffee filter would work, too.

The resulting drink is good either hot, like a tea, or cold, like lemonade. Sweetened with honey, the tea is very soothing on a scratchy, sore throat as well. If using the boiling water method, allow the water to cool a few degrees before pouring it over the berries, to retain more of the vitamin C.

There is another medicine in the staghorn sumac that Anishinaabeg have used traditionally. The blossoms that appear on the plant in spring are dried and used to make a tea that in times past was used to lessen the pain of stomachaches. Kee always said, though, that when a chemical is in one part of a plant it often is in the whole plant. It is usually less in the upper part of a plant and concentrated in the root. So if there is a medicine in the blossoms it is also probably in the leaves as well.

The sumac has several virtues that it shares for artistic purposes, too. If one carves the fresh wood, it will exude a moist substance that will shellac the finished product. Pipestems carved of living, standing sumac will, within days or a month at most,

4 See Recipes section for other food uses of sumac.

have a beautiful glossy finish. Then the pipestem is cut from the plant. A hole can be easily bored in the middle of the stem with a sharp, long stick, or it can be very easily burned out. One takes a wire coathanger, straightens it, heats it in a fire, and uses it to burn out the interior pulp of the stem.

The pulp in the interior of the sumac stem makes a wonderful, strong dye. I once used it to dye porcupine quills a brilliant yellow. I also, at the same time, used a commercial dye to dye another batch of quills yellow. Then I left both the sumac and the commercially-dyed quills side-by-side on a windowsill that got light most of the day. After about six months the sumac quills were still bright yellow, but the commercially-dyed quills were a very pale, cream color. Obviously the sumac has a much more lasting dye.

My husband, Bob, is an artist, and he makes sculptures out of handmade paper. He and his artistic partner were sitting at my kitchen table one day bemoaning the fact that their favorite dye, cambian yellow, would no longer be available because the one mine in the world that produced the mineral that made the dye was going out of business. The entire vein of the ore had been worked out. The mine had been in business for hundreds of years, and it had produced all of that particular shade of yellow that was used in various fine oil paints and dyes.

I laughed at them. I said, "Look at your hands." They had just spent the afternoon cutting and stacking a large stand of sumac that had been growing around the studio in which they made their paper. Their hands were dyed beautiful shades of yellow from their contact with the sumac they had been cutting.

I said, "Why bemoan a fancy French pigment when you have an endless supply of the same color? There is so much of it that you consider it a weed and root it out while it is growing all around your workshop."

I showed them the porcupine quills that I had dyed with sumac pith and had tested against the commercially available dyestuff for a whole winter. They looked at the color, then they looked at each other, and then they both ran out the door, jumped in the car, and raced back to their studio to get the sumac they had just cut and stacked by the road for the garbage truck. They got back in time to save the sumac, which was suddenly a valuable art commodity and no longer garbage. They pithed the stems and used the pulp to make an absolutely beautiful batch of cambian yellow cotton-rag paper.

There are numerous other artistic applications of sumac. The pith of the stems will also make a long-lasting paint if it is mixed with oil or grease. The pith will also dye wool yellow, either alone or mixed with the inner bark of the sumac stalk. All parts of the sumac except for the roots can be used for dyes. The leaves and bark make interesting yellows. The berries will make a lovely deep gray that can be deepened further by adding rusty iron nails or cooking the dye in a rusty iron kettle or by adding commercial iron mordant. The leaves are very rich in tannins, and they can be used fresh or dried as a mordant to make vegetable fibers, like cotton and linens, retain colors of other dyes, too. Some people use sumac straight as dye. Other people mix the sumac with the roots of bloodroot (*Sanguinaria candadensis*) and/or the roots of ozaawijiibik, goldthread (*Coptis trifolia*), but since those two plants are such fine medicinals, I just use the sumac straight. It is so plentiful in our area that a person should be able to gather all they would conceivably need, because the sumac will happily regrow in the same patch even if one cuts a number of its stalks, since it spreads readily by root suckers.

When gathering sumac berries for tea or art and when cutting stalks for the wood or pith for dyes, one must remember the others who love the sumac, too. The berries are very valuable to birds because they hang on the plants well into the snows. Many birds, such as grouse, mourning doves, crows, bluebirds, flickers, catbirds, robins, phoebes, and thrushes, eat them. The young growth is a favorite winter food of rabbits and hares and deer and moose (Bates 1995, 57). Leave a little on the table for the rest of the family!

Aasaakamig

Sphagnum Moss
Sphagnum spp.

~~~~~~

In the days of the Gete-Anishinaabeg, as soon as a babe was born
it was blessed with Sacred Cedar Oil, bathed in warm water, dried
with soft cloth or a rabbit skin, and tied into its *waapijipizon*,
moss bag. The child was safe and snug as it had been in its
mother's womb and would immediately go to sleep. Being born
must be an exhausting experience!

The waapijipizon has cradled our ancestors down through
the years, since the great ice sheets of the glaciers covered this
land. The moss that has been and is used in the moss bag is
sphagnum. It is a moss that science says pioneers the land after the
ice withdraws. When the great mountains of ice retreated about
twelve thousand years ago here in Wisconsin, great chunks calved
off those ice mountains and were left behind on the land. The ice
chunks, covered as they were in the debris of sand and rock and
soil and grit that covers a glacier, stayed behind as the climate
warmed. Slowly those ice pieces melted and filled the scooped out
kettles that the weight of the ice chunk had formed on the land.
When the water from the melted ice filled the resulting crater,
the future home of the sphagnum moss was formed. Sphagnum,
along with other Arctic plants like Labrador tea, bog rosemary,
and leatherleaf, came down from the North with the glacier ice
and stayed behind after the ice withdrew. Over the centuries,
sphagnum crept out over the water of the glacier-formed kettle
lakes and filled them in with countless generations of growth
and decayed plant material. Sphagnum moss in this manner
pioneered the land scoured clean by the ice sheets and in time
laid down the great bog areas and peat fields of northern Canada
and the northern parts of the United States, especially Wisconsin
and Minnesota, as well as significant stretches of northern Europe,
Scotland, the Scandinavian lands, and all across Russia and
Siberia, too. The little Ice Age traveler, sphagnum, in our own
inner glacier age is estimated to cover a full 1 percent of the total

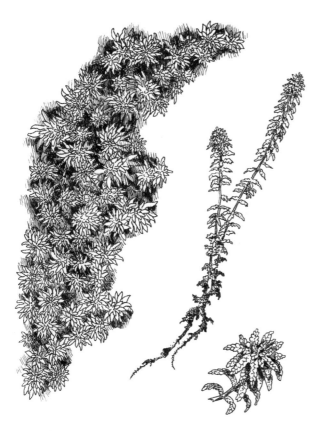

Aasaakamig: Sphagnum Moss
(*Sphagnum spp.*)

surface area of Our Mother the Earth, and that is a considerable area for one life-form to cover.

Sphagnum moss has been a very important part of the lives of our ancestors because of its amazing ability to hold water. A piece of dried sphagnum will soak up and retain twenty-five times its own weight in water. And it can then be squeezed out, and it will do the same thing again and again. The structure of sphagnum is such that the little capillaries within it that suck up and retain the moisture will continue to operate even after the moss is dead and dried out. This ability has made sphagnum invaluable to our people as a diapering material, as a dressing for severe, bleeding wounds, and for use as a sanitary product for women's periods.

To use this plant for any of the above purposes, one goes out into the swamp- or bogland, in the muskegs of the north or into the marshy lands around our northern lakes, and gathers the moss, any time of the year that it is not frozen into solid chunks. Take along a bag to put the moss in, or take a tarp on which to put the moss while gathering it. Do not put the newly gathered moss on the ground because there is a fungus in some swamps that will cause an illness called sporotrichosis in humans. It is not on the sphagnum. It is in the soil. The sphagnum is safe to use if it does not come in contact with the dirt on the ground around the sphagnum bog. One should clean the moss as soon as one gathers it, gently pulling the little plants apart from the clumps in which they grow, taking care to injure them as little as possible. One takes out any twigs or branches that have fallen into the moss and around which the moss may have grown. Then one lays the fluffed moss to dry, either in the trees, on a woven screen of branches or cattails, or on layers of spruce branches that have been cut and laid down in a dry area in the sun. In a few days, depending on the weather, the moss will have dried completely. One can speed the drying process by turning the moss over once a day or so and by taking it into shelter at night to keep it from being exposed to rain or dew. Once the moss is completely dry, it can be stored for months or even years. This was a job that was typically done by a woman or her family in the summertime if she was pregnant and was expecting to give birth later in the year, when the snow would be covering the moss fields. And once a family had gathered a bag of dried sphagnum moss, they were ready to welcome a newborn with a lot of the diapering material that would be necessary throughout the child's infancy, because that same sphagnum could be used and reused as needed. Unless a piece was badly soiled and a person just did not want to go to the bother of cleaning it, the soiled sphagnum could be just tossed into a stream to rinse clean, then redried in the sun to sanitize it and to make it ready to be reused in the moss bag, or any of the other uses for which our people found for this plant.

Kee said the use of sphagnum moss as diapering material for infants must have been widely known, as it seemed to be used anyplace where sphagnum is available to the People. She noted that the Lapps of northern Scandinavia and the various tribal peoples of Siberia and the Inuit of Greenland and Iceland also used this plant for the same purpose as did our Anishinaabe ancestors. The European "language of flowers," which was a Victorian English adaptation of much earlier oral traditions, says that sphagnum moss means "Maternal Love." It fits![5]

Sphagnum moss was also the material of choice for use as sanitary napkins in pre-Kotex days.[6] It was gathered and cleaned and dried in the same manner as the moss dried for infant diapering material, then it was left in the Moon House for use by the family's girls in their menses. When Keewaydinoquay was a girl, many women of Minis-kitigaan whose Moontime had come still

5 It actually is like a form-fitting Pampers diaper on a toddler's bottom.

6 Actually, the very first disposable menstrual pads on the market were made of sphagnum, too. Then some nutcase decided to make the product "look cleaner," and they started to soak the sphagnum in bleach. The resulting product actually killed women and gave sphagnum a bad name. In reality, it was the bleach that was the problem, not the sphagnum. I remember Kee crying as she lectured on this history. She described it as "the death of our sisters," and said we must not forget it.

jumped into their canoes and paddled over to Women's Island, a high island that is very close to Minis-kitigaan in the Beaver Chain of islands in the middle of Lake Michigan. They stayed there for the full week to ten days of their monthly cycles. Kee said she often envied the girls whose families still followed the ancient custom of female isolation. Kee's own mother was bound and determined that Kee would be raised in the new, modern ways, especially in regard to menses isolation, which the Christian church was attempting to stamp out as an undesirable, primitive, pagan custom. Kee said she envied the girls of her acquaintance who got a week's vacation from work every month. She said she often walked her girlfriends down to the shore and waved them off as they paddled to Woman's Island. Kee did not believe that a woman was somehow dirty in her Moontime. She did not teach that at all! She believed that, if anything, a woman at such a time is more powerful, not contaminated. She did not hold with the twentieth-century revival of Indian ways that, she always said, had confused Anishinaabeg customs and Judeo-Christian ideas of female contamination during menses. Kee saw nothing wrong with a woman participating in ceremonies or even her touching children or drums or sacred objects, which readapations of ancient ideas said was problematic. She just thought it was a neat idea that a girl could get off work once a month just by having her period. Kee thought that in the old days it probably was the only time a woman was spared from her family obligations[7] and really had a chance just to be herself and pursue her own thoughts and interests. She said she knew women who made beautiful homes for themselves to use as Moon Houses, filling them with their favorite crafts and personal treasures. Kee thought it a shame that what had been a custom that strengthened women had been twisted to be used to keep women from full participation in their own communities, their own homes, as well as in their religion.

The use of sphagnum moss as sanitary products actually kept women from joining the Christian church in the early missionary days. If a woman became a Christian, she was given a bag of rags, and was told to use those instead of sphagnum. Kee said the idea of using cloth for such a purpose actually kept women out of the church for two reasons. First, the idea of using cloth for such a purpose must have seemed almost sacrilegious to women who had to spend long, hard labor producing textile material. The manufacture of cloth was very laborious when a person had to pick the plants and process them into thread and then weave the

7 In the old days, a woman's sisters or her mother or her female friends would just take over the woman's family obligations at such times. They would watch the children and cook the meals and keep the woman's family cared for in her absence. In their Moontimes, the favor was returned in kind.

thread into cloth, in the days before one could trade an animal skin for a bolt of cotton. The memory of how hard it was to make cloth and how precious the finished product was as a result was still a vivid one to the women of Kee's youth. Even a rag was too precious to use for a purpose that could be filled by an easily obtained and processed plant.[8] Second, washing a used cloth is just a lot more unpleasant work than tossing a used piece of sphagnum into, or leaving it to rinse on its own, in a convenient stream.[9]

Kee said the Church was opposed to the use of all plants in Native culture because of the fact that our people gathered natural materials with prayer, and the Christians taught that such prayers were examples of pagan superstition and idol worship. Kee said the Christians just did not understand that all that was necessary in our ways was to be grateful for the gifts Creator gave us. She always said one could say any prayer one liked over the plants when one picked them. One could say, "Thank you, Mother Mary, for this gift," or any other prayer that fit into one's concept of religion or reality. She said all that really was important was just to say "Thank you" and to be grateful.

Aasaakamig also has a natural antibiotic in it that protects baby's tender skin and prevents diaper rash. A British doctor first scientifically studied the antibiotic in sphagnum after World War I. The doctor had been treating the wounded from the trenches of Normandy in that war when the supplies all but ran out. When the bandaging materials were in short supply, the decision was made to only treat the men whose wounds made it likely that they would recover. The badly wounded boys were being put aside without treatment. There were two Anishinaabe guys in the doctor's unit who were working as ambulance drivers, bringing the wounded soldiers in from the front. The decision to just put the badly wounded aside to die really bothered the Anishinaabe drivers. They asked the doctor if it would be all right if they went down into the swamp to get some sphagnum moss to dry and use to plug the wounds of the badly wounded soldiers who were to be left without treatment.

They said, "Hey, these guys are going to die anyway, but they are just so terrified watching themselves bleed to death. They cry, and they call for their mothers. They are soldiers, and they deserve a better death. Couldn't we just use the moss that our folks use back home?"

8 People tend to forget that art forms like quiltmaking grew out of the need to reuse a product that took so much time to make in the old days. I think of it a lot when I am in a clothing store and watching women buy cloth to cut up and re-sew into quilts. Their own grandmothers who made the very quilts they so admire did the work out of necessity, not as a pleasant, leisure-time craft. And they reused old cloth. They did not buy new material and cut it up into little squares to re-sew it back into a big piece of material. How the world changes!

9 My own mother, Mollie Shomperlen, said her mother had proved her love for her daughters by doing the washing of their monthly rags herself instead of requiring her daughters to scrub them themselves. Waubee, my Cree, Bear Clan maternal grandmother, Mrs. John Blain of The Pas, Manitoba, raised three of her daughters, Mom, Aunty Bea, and Aunty Chrisy. With four sets of such rags to wash by hand every month I bet she longed for the days when one could just grab a hunk of sphagnum moss to fill that need instead.

The doctor, assuming that the wounded soldiers were doomed anyway, agreed that the two Anishinaabe guys could use their traditional medicine to bind up the wounds. He did not expect it to help, so he was very surprised when a good number of the soldiers who had had their wounds stuffed with sphagnum moss not only survived but did not develop infections, either. After the war the doctor spent years studying the chemical properties of sphagnum until he concluded that the moss actually does have an antibiotic in it that keeps infection from developing.

The above story of how sphagnum helped the wounded in the First World War was told to me by Keewaydinoquay thirty-some-odd years ago, when she was teaching ethnobotany at the university. I liked the story, probably because of the part about the Indian guys using a traditional medicine that was then scientifically studied and acknowledged by non–Native style doctors.

I have attempted to verify the story with the methods taught me by non-native academic tradition. I have searched libraries and recently even the Internet for some glimmer of the "truth" as to whether the story portrays actual historic truths. I have found references to the use of sphagnum as surgical dressing during the "War to End All Wars" that spawned a huge, volunteer-run industry in Canada and the British Isles to keep the wounded on the European battlefields from bleeding to death unnecessarily.[10] It is estimated that upward of one million people, mostly women's groups and church groups, made up the totally volunteer workforce to harvest the sphagnum and process it into surgical dressings for the war effort. I even found a detailed account of how one actually goes about turning raw sphagnum into a surgical dressing in a 1930s-era herbal.[11] But I did not find the story that Keewaydinoquay told me.

At first not finding the story bothered me. "I have spent far too long in non-native schools!" I thought. Part of my mind said, "If you cannot verify a fact, it is not a fact." But my Anishinaabe mind and training soon resolved the problem for me. The story Kee told me is "true" because it contains traditional usage knowledge and it enables the mind to retain that knowledge for years of no-usage. It was the story that enabled me to retain the knowledge for years despite the fact that I did not have to use the plant or the technology in all of that time. Because of the story I retained the knowledge of the traditional use of sphagnum down through the years, even though I did not have to use it to diaper my own wee daughters or to plug the bleeding wounds of any gutshot warriors

10 A full account of the World War I sphagnum industry is given in Natalie Riegler, "Sphagnum Moss in World War I: The Making of Surgical Dressings by Volunteers in Toronto, Canada, 1917-1918," *Canadian Bulletin of Medical History/Bulletin canadien d'histoire de la médecine* 6 (1989): 27-43.

11 Mrs. M Grieve, *A Modern Herbal.* available at http://www.botanical.com. If you ever have to do it yourself, this is the procedure: Pick sphagnum, being sure to put down your kinnikinnick and asemaa first. Do not let it touch the ground. Pull the wet fresh moss apart gently, taking out any plants or twigs or bugs in the stuff. Dry it in the sun. Pack it very loosely into muslin cotton bags, loosely because the moss will expand with the discharge from the wounds.

during a shortage of cloth and professional emergency care. It was the story that retained the knowledge for me all of those years.

My Indian mind says that it does not matter if non-natives have not written down and retained and transmitted the story the way our oral tradition has done. That would probably have been impossible for them anyway. This amounts to a different worldview.[12]

12 Non-native logic seems to say that something does not actually exist unless a White male knows about it. The Inca mountain city of Machu Picchu, 7,000 feet up in the Andes of south-central Peru, was there long before the conquest of the Inca Empire by the Spanish but is said to have been "discovered" in 1911 by the American–European Hiram Bingham. Bingham "found" the "lost city" because he heard about some old ruins from native people in the area, and then a ten-year-old native lead him to the site. But even though the people knew where the city was and a child led him to the site, Bingham is still the "discoverer of Machu Picchu." For more information see the Carnegie Museums of Pittsburgh website: www.carnegiemuseums.org/cmg/ bk_issue/2003/sepoct/feature1 .html. Quilter also describes local people knowing about Machu Picchu before Bingham "discovered" it (18). As I once read in a letter to the editor, "does nothing truly exist unless a white male knows it?" (Kellly, 10). The idea is so very "Zen"!

"Naanabozho and the Squeaky-Voice Plant"

~~~~~~

Gichi-mewinzha, gii-oshki-niiging akiing, a very long time ago, when the Earth was new, Naanabozho became very angry. This sort of thing happened to Naanabozho often, unfortunately, and he tore around the countryside, laying waste to everything he touched. He grabbed great, tall trees and ripped them out of the ground. He strained and strained and pulled up huge boulders and threw them as far as one could see. He even grabbed rivers and yanked them out of their river beds and threw them out over the countryside. He left big holes in some places and heaved up mountains in others. Then, as fast as the fit had come upon him, he stopped. All of his frantic energy that came with his anger melted away like a spring snow. And he fell on the ground and instantly was deep, deep into sleep. How long he slept he never knew. It might have been an hour. It might have been a decade.

This time, when he finally awoke, he heaved a great sigh and tried to sit up. He could not sit up. He could not move at all, for he was held down to the ground by what felt like a thousand, tiny ropes. He squirmed and fought with all of his might, but he was held fast. He could move his head only enough to see that there were roots and runners of a tiny, green, woodland plant that had crisscrossed over his body and were holding him tightly to the ground.

Then, he heard a tiny, squeaky little voice singing in his ear:

What I used to be.
Oh, woe is me!
I was taller than
The tallest tree!
Oh, woe is me!

Naanabozho screamed, "Who are you? Why do you hold me captive? Don't you know I am the Great Naanabozho, son of the West Wind Spirit and an Anishinaabe woman? Let me go! Do you hear me? Let me go!"

He screamed and fought, and then, exhausted again, he lay still and listened to the little squeaky voice as it said, "Oh, Naanabozho. You must listen to me. I hold you captive until you hear me and understand what I must tell you. I was once as proud as you. And I thought I had every right to be proud. I was the tallest tree in the forest. I was so beautiful. In my pride I would not share with creation as Creator had told all of us to do in the Beginning Time. I was too proud. I would not let the little birds nest in my branches. I would shake them down and send their eggs or their children crashing to their deaths on the hard forest floor. I would not allow the animals to climb up my trunk, and if they tried to burrow among my roots to make their homes, I would fill their burrows with rootlets and choke them as they slept. If other plants tried to grow under me, I would shade them from the sun until they died. If the birds flew over me and defecated on my leaves, I would even spit poison at them that they might not dull my smooth, glistening branches. I was so very, very proud! But then Creator, who sees everything, had enough of my arrogance.

Creator said to me, 'This is not the way I told all of my creations to behave toward one another. I told you to share everything and to see to it that all of creation survived. Until you learn this lesson, until you learn to share with the others I have placed here with you, you will not be the biggest tree in the forest. You will look very different. You will become a tiny little plant on the forest floor, but you will still look like a tree. When others see you, they will be reminded of the necessity to share with the rest of creation. They will remember the time when you were too proud and lost your place as the tallest tree and became the little plant that runs along the forest floor.'

"So, Naanabozho, listen to me! Do not be so very proud. You may come to regret your arrogance as I do."

"Huh!" said Naanabozho, with a short, snarly laugh. "Do you mean that I might wake up some day to find I have been transformed into one of the Little People? Ha!"

"Well," said the little voice, "it did happen to me just like that, but there is also something else I can share with you, besides the example of my punishment. You should not let yourself get so crazy. You should not go so mad you rip up trees and boulders and throw around hills and rivers. You should not do it because then you get so tired you fall down into too deep a sleep. Sometime or other someone might come upon you in that state, someone who is not as kind and meek as I have become. That someone might do more harm to you than simply tying you to the ground. You would be at that someone's mercy."

Naanabozho listened and thought a moment about what the little voice had said. The thought of being helpless and at an unknown enemy's mercy was not an idea that he liked. In fact it made him shiver! "Well," he grumbled, "what can I do about it?"

The little plant voice said, "I and my kind have a medicine that will help you. Follow our roots and dig up the little green discs that grow there. They will keep you from going so wild that you must crash down onto the forest floor to sleep all unprotected."

After that time, Naanabozho was careful to carry with him on his long journeys the little green discs that the Squeaky-Voice Plant had told him about. He chewed them whenever he felt the need to rush around and do crazy things, for he feared being helpless and at the mercy of whomever came upon him sleeping and defenseless. Mii' iw. Miigwech.

Naanabozho's Squeaky-Voice Plant

Lycopodiaceae spp.

For some strange reason, some of these plants get called "club mosses" in books and even by botanists who should know better. They are not mosses. They do not grow, nor reproduce, like mosses. They do not have the medicinal qualities of mosses, nor do they fill the ecological niche that mosses fill. They simply are not mosses. They get called "club" mosses because someone thought the fruiting heads of the plants look like little clubs, but even that is weird. *Lycopodiaceae* family members that grow in the Great Lakes states are all taller than mosses. Some of the *Lycopodiaceae* can grow to a height of ten feet. They have different internal structures than the mosses, too. They have a rudimentary vascular system, unlike the mosses, which have none, and therefore the Lycopodium can survive when only one part of its tissue is touching a water source, because they have the ability to take water up into their tissues. Kee always urged her students to get used to calling them by a scientific name or a native name like "Naanabozho's Squeaky-Voice Plant," which she used as a name for all the plants described in this section, to keep from perpetuating a foolish name that just did not fit the plants in question. She thought that the name of "club moss" kept people from really looking at a whole group of plants and just categorizing them as "little green things" instead of an interesting and different species of beings. The only real use I have for the name "club moss" is that one has to know it to find the plants in plant books.

In the 1980s, when Kee was teaching at the University of Wisconsin–Milwaukee, a number of Naanabozho's Squeaky-Voice Plants in Wisconsin and Michigan were endangered, and there was a fine on the books that could be, but seldom was, charged per plant picked.[13] Unfortunately, the law was not applied very often, and Naanabozho's Squeaky-Voice Plant has been stripped from much of its former range. One of the reasons why it needs protection is because of its odd reproductive systems. It actually has both sexual and asexual forms of reproducing its own kind. In one phase of its life cycle it reproduces sexually, with separate male and female plants mating by means of male cells actively seeking the female cells where they grow under the decaying leaves and rich humus of the hardwood forests they prefer. Once a fertilized zygote is produced it takes seventeen years before the

13 Various species of *Lycopodiaceae* are still endangered, all around the Great Lakes region. It is important to check the USDA's website (http://www.usda.gov) to check if a species of the *Lycopodiaceae,* or any other plant, is endangered in the area before one picks it.

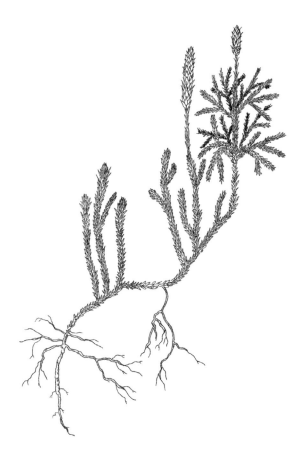

"Naanabozho's Squeaky-Voice Plant": Lycopodium (*Lycopodium spp.*)

plant is ready to reproduce by means of spores above the ground level. In their asexual form, Naanabozho's Squeaky-Voice Plant sends out runners and sends up clone plants where they find a likely spot. By this means they can "run" over huge areas of woodland, with the parent plant that was produced by a wind blown, sexually produced spore dying down as it exhausts its available nutrients and leaving its cloned "children" carrying on in another spot. Such a complicated reproductive life makes Naanabozho's Squeaky-Voice Plants endangered if they are over-harvested in an area.[14] Also, these plants can be very long-lived beings, some of whom may be 1,200 years old (Bates 1995, 208). The plant family of Naanabozho's Squeaky-Voice Plant is a very ancient one that may stretch back 300 million years (Kavasch 1977, 74).

Like all living things, the different types of this particular being all look different. If one looks carefully one will see that plants look different from each other; that animals look different, and people look different. All of Naanabozho's Squeaky-Voice Plants look different, too. In North America there about twenty

14 Kee loved to describe what she called the "Love Life of the Lycopodium." She did it so well that she actually kept her young adult classes *listening,* and that is not an easy task when one is teaching the sexual and asexual reproductive habits of a bunch of little, green plants!

different species, with about 100 worldwide, but the most common ones in the Great Lakes Area are:

1) Mitakamig-giizhikaandag, Running Cedar, Ground Cedar, Christmas Club Moss, or Ground Pine. *Diphasiastrum complanatu*. Mitakamig-giizhikaandag is a species that runs along the forest floor, preferring moist hardwood forests and sunny, exposed roadside areas. The foliage does resemble that of the cedar tree, with flattened needles covering spreading branches. It is lovely pale green in color.

2) Zhingonaakwaan, Gaagaagiwaandagoons, Princess Pine or Tree Club Moss. *Lycopodium dendroideum*. Zhingonaakwaan really does resemble a tiny, miniature tree, with branches that circle up to a perfect little Christmas-tree form. It has tiny needles growing on a branching, tree-shaped plant. It creeps along on underground running stems, with little clone plants that spring up every six to twelve feet or so. One plant can spread over huge areas of woodland.

3) Miishiwiiganens, Wolf Claw or Stag Horn Moss. *Lycopodium clavatum*. Miishiwiiganens has a branching upright stem six to twelve inches apart on its running ground stem, and it sends up a spore-head that looked to someone like a wolf's claw.

There has not really been much scientific research on Naanabozho's Squeaky-Voice Plants, because they have only a few commercial uses nowadays. But one commercial use that it does have almost led to the plants' total annihilation. It was used widely by the floral industry for making Christmas wreaths and decorations and for putting in bridal bouquets. The florists liked these plants because they have the ability to hold their green color and their living, pliable texture for a very long time after they are picked. They will even hold their shape and coloration when used as an underwater decoration in a fish aquarium, where they are anchored with a weight and used to approximate green, growing seaweed.

Many Indian people were utilized by the floral industry to strip the north woods of great stands of Naanabozho's Squeaky-Voice Plants. Kee's mother was taken, as a child, out to the islands of the Beaver Chain in Lake Michigan with groups of other Indian children and set to pulling up the plants. The florists paid the children per bundle of the greens and even offered prizes for the child who could pull up the longest single plant. As an old woman, Kee's mom felt remorse because she felt she personally had been responsible for denuding large areas of her own family's former territory of this plant. Many, many Indian people were so utilized for the taking of this plant before federal and state laws were passed to make the taking of the endangered plants illegal. But, because the laws have few teeth and are seldom employed, the "harvest" continues, with Indian folk now being encouraged to pull the "greens," as they are called.

And, in reality, it is perhaps hard to understand when one sees acres and acres of woodland covered with the running stems of Naanabozho's Squeaky-Voice Plants (*Lycopodium* or *Diphasiastrum*) that the plant could really be endangered if one was to take it. We had an ethnobotany student who turned up for her final display for the semester, which we held in lieu of a final exam, with four absolutely beautiful Christmas wreaths made out of these plants. Kee had a very hard time convincing the woman that she just could not put the wreaths out on public display. She told her that they were in a university building and so professional botanists were bound to attend the display as it was a very popular event. Kee pointed out that the woman and probably the program, too, could have been fined per plant for the taking of an endangered species.

The woman said, "That's impossible. It grows all over back home."

Although in some places Naanabozho's Squeaky-Voice Plant is still very prevalent, the law is to protect the plant from the kind of abuse it received in Wisconsin after World War II, when huge numbers of areas were absolutely stripped of the plant by the floral industry's efforts.

In reality it is just a bad idea to uproot these plants, even if one does it for the best of intentions. Many people who are unfamiliar with them dig the kind called "Princess Pine" when they are up north on their summer holidays. These people often bring them home and gaily plant them on their front lawns, expecting them to grow into towering, majestic pine trees. Of course, they are not pine trees and just will never grow more than six inches to ten inches tall, no matter what loving care they are given. The little, transplanted "trees" die, and if the person is really dumb, they might just dig up another one next summer to try again. Naanabozho's Squeaky-Voice Plants just need the forest environment that they choose in the wild, and they simply do not take to suburban front lawns readily.

15 These green, dime-sized discs are actually gametophytes, the egg and sperm producing parts of the plant. Kee always referred to them as "lozenges," and these discs do look like round throat lozenges.

If they are allowed to stay in their forest home, Naanabozho's Squeaky-Voice Plants have several virtues to share with us. The Anishinaabeg in days past used them as an emergency food source. The little, green, dime-sized discs[15] that are spoken of in the Naanabozho story of the "Squeaky-Voice Plant" were dug up and eaten as a starvation food. It was called "Slow Down Plant" when it was so used. Kee thought that it actually had the ability to slow down the metabolism of a person and would help a person survive in such extreme circumstances.

Kee always said that if she had another life she would gather the green lozenges and have scientific tests run on them. She said she thought they might have chemicals in them that would slow a person's body down and that might be of help in cases of nervous disorders like ADHD or in some types of madness. She thought her people had suspected this, as witnessed by the Naanabozho story of the "Squeaky-Voice Plant." The Peterson *Medicinal Plants Guide* says, "A related Chinese species in the Clubmoss family is being researched as a potential treatment for Alzheimer's disease" (Foster and Duke 2000, 344). Our legends are repositories of great wisdom!

Another virtue that Naanabozho's Squeaky-Voice Plants have to share with humankind is the combustibility of their spores. If one goes into a forest in the fall (in Wisconsin it is usually October when this happens), one often finds the plants' fertile stems ripe and releasing clouds of spores at the least touch or in the wind. In times past these spores were taken and sold for use in fireworks and in flash powder for early photography. The Waaba-noowin, the traditional "Eastern medicine" religious sect of the Anishinaabeg, make impressive use of the spores of Naanabozho's Squeaky-Voice Plant in their fire rituals. Our own *mashkikiiwinin-iwag*, medicine men, and *mashkikiiwikwewag*, medicine women, use these spores, too. When one is treating a patient, it is essential that the patient trust the doctor. If a person actually believes that the doctor has "power" to heal them of their problems, half of the battle for the cure is achieved. Kee said that in times past such "impressing of the patient" was helped by the doctor's use of the spores of this plant. One gathers the spore and, very carefully and with sleight of hand, drops the spores into the fire. The fire will suddenly flare up and make a very impressive display. It is sure to convince even the most reluctant of patients that the doctor knows a thing or two.

But one must be very careful with such a display. Kee was once in a lecture hall when the professor thought he would show his students the combustibility of these spores. He had his teaching assistant light a Bunsen burner, and the professor casually tossed a handful of the spores at the flame. The resulting tower of fire reached the ceiling of the auditorium and scorched the tiles. And it stayed burning as long as the spores were in the air and as they were sucked up into the fans at the top of the room. Kee said the departments fought for years as to which one of them was responsible for fixing the damage caused by that very impressive display. It is obviously something one should attempt outside and away from trees, structures, and anything else one does not want to see burned.

The spores of Naanabozho's Squeaky-Voice Plant have another great virtue to share. They coat the skin and are much used to protect skin from friction. In the time of the Gete-Anishinaabeg, people used it like talcum powder to keep their cloths or footwear from chafing their skin. If a person was setting out on a very long foot journey they would take these spores along in a bag to use as needed to keep their thighs from chafing or to put in their moccasins to prevent blisters. It was also used in diapering babies to keep the child's skin dry. If one coats one's hand with these spores and plunges the hand into water, the skin will not get wet. Kee always included in her lectures the fact that the spores have been used in surgeons' gloves to keep the skin dry, so that it will not become sore and irritated.

6

Medicinal Plants

Waabanooganzh

Waabanoowashk
Ajidamoowaanow
"Plant of Light"
"Giver of Knowledge"
Yarrow
Achillea millefolium

Yarrow is a perennial that has a very wide distribution across
North America as well as Europe and Asia. It will grow in most
any kind of soil in fields, yards, or meadows. It loves sun. It stands
10 to 24 inches high and has a dull white, or occasionally a
grayish pink, flat-topped flower head. The leaves of yarrow look
like feathers, and their multiple, almost fernlike, divisions are the
reason its species name is *millefolium,* meaning "thousand leafed."

Yarrow is sometimes confused by beginning students with
Queen Anne's lace, also called wild carrot[1] (*Daucus carrota*), but
Queen Ann's lace does not have the rosette pattern of growth in
the spring that yarrow has, and yarrow does not have the long,
taproot that is characteristic of Queen Ann's lace. And no other
plant smells like yarrow. This is one plant it is best to positively
identify by its smell. It is a memorable smell that will always
assure one that it is really yarrow.

Yarrow and mankind have a very long history together. Before
men were *Homo sapiens,* they already had a knowledge of yarrow.
There is a grave in Iraq, dating to 60,000 years ago, of a Nean-
derthal who was laid to rest by his people on a bed of medicinal
flowers. One of those flowers, identifiable because of the pollens
in the grave, was yarrow (*America's Fascinating* 1978, 51).

The ancient Greeks were well acquainted with yarrow, too.
The genus name of *Achillea* is in commemoration of the tradition
that Achilles, the great Greek hero of the Trojan War, who is said
to have learned the use of this plant from his foster father, the
centaur Chiron, used yarrow to staunch the wounds of his men
at the siege of Troy. It is also said that the arrow that hit Achilles

[1] Wild carrot and garden-variety carrot are the same plant, with only varietal differences. Most herbals say that wild carrot is the ancestor of the garden variety, but Euell Gibbons believed it was the other way around. He thought that Queen Anne's Lace was an escaped garden carrot that after a very few genera-tions reverted to an ancestral form, with a white and woodier taproot. Kee never taught her students to use Queen Anne's Lace nor wild parsnip for either food or medicine because there have been cases of fatal poisoning where people have picked and eaten water hemlock thinking them either wild carrot or wild parsnip plants. There was a very sad case of whitewater-rapid rafters on a western river who ate water hemlock by mistake. A number of them died. I remember the local Indian tribe felt so bad that they came to the funerals and hung eagle feathers on the graves so that the dead would have the help of warrior spirits on their four-day journey to the Other Side.

Waabanooganzh: Yarrow
(*Achillea millefolium*)

2 Kee included this story in her
class lectures. Hyam and Pankhurst
also mention the association with
Achilles (4).

in the heel, his only vulnerable spot, and killed him was made of
yarrow, too.[2]

Many herbals and scientists insist that yarrow is an imported
European plant, brought to the Americas by the first settlers, but
this plant at least can be defended as a true indigenous plant
because of its association with the Waabanoo. The Jesuit Fathers
in their letters home to their superiors, letters now called the
Jesuit Records, recorded in 1535 meeting the Waabanoo, an Algon-
quin group on the East Coast. It was already an ancient sect when
the Jesuits met them. Kee remembered watching Waabanoo ceremonies when she was a child. She said that the Waabanoo, those
who practice the Waabanoowin religion, hold *Waabanooganzh,*
yarrow, as their sacred medicine. According to what Kee saw,
the Waabanoo made/make great use of fire in their ceremonies.
They carried live coals, swung around burning brands, walked
across glowing coal beds, and jumped through flaming hoops, all
with the aid of yarrow. They would all but strip the land of the
plant before their big ceremonies. They would make a big vat by
digging a hole in the ground and lining the hole with skins, birch

bark, or, later, tarps, then they would make huge batches of yarrow infusion to pour into the vat. The participants would soak in the infusion all day in preparation for the nighttime ceremonies. The yarrow protected their skin so that the fire did not burn them.

As a young girl Keewaydinoquay was fascinated by the Waabanoo. They had a burial ground near her people's village. They buried their dead on poles, like the Plains peoples, but they put the scaffolds over swamps so that when the poles finally fell the dead would be returned to Mother Earth through the swamp. Once a year they would return to the burial grounds, bringing their dead to leave them on the platforms, and they had their big fire ceremonies at night.

One time Kee crept to the edge of the Waabanoo burial ground and stayed hidden all afternoon watching the preparations for the ceremonies, and then she watched the fires at night. She loved their swinging songs and their pretty little drums, all of which were very different from her family's own Midewiwin ceremonies. She described the difference between the Waabanoo-win and Midewiwin as similar to the differences that one would find in Christianity between a traveling tent-show revival and a High Anglican Mass. She was sure, thinking about it years later, that the Waabanoo must have known she was there watching, and that they probably got a kick out of the idea that MidéOgema's[3] granddaughter had come to their ceremony. She stayed hidden and watched the people soaking in the yarrow infusion and the participants coming out of the bath at night to juggle burning sticks and walk one by one across a long bed of glowing coals.

3 MidéOgema's name means "Leader of the Midewiwin."

Yarrow toughens the skin. Fire and sword swallowers in the circus use it the way the Waabanoo did, too. Kee's mother used to soak her hands in a yarrow and alum infusion before she wove baskets. She helped to feed her family by weaving baskets to sell to tourists. But someone told her that the use of plants, yarrow in particular, was an un-Christian practice. After that she stopped using the yarrow infusion, and she would weave until her hands bled onto the black ash strips. Then she would put on gloves and weave some more.

Wherever yarrow grows, in the Old World as well as in the New, it has been credited with spiritual value. To the Anishinaabeg, yarrow is said to scare off evil. It is hung or tied along with sweetgrass and cedar on doors and/or windows. The yarrow is to scare off the bad. The sweetgrass is to encourage and attract the good. And the cedar is to balance the two. One must be very careful never to drive out one evil and leave a void, for a greater evil may take advantage and rush in to fill that void. It is always seen as important to maintain the balance. In a case where a person is very worried about evil attacking them, for instance in a Bear Walk or in a haunting situation, dried yarrow is pounded and mixed with sand. The mixture is then poured across doorways and window sills or around the entire foundation of a home or around the entire perimeter of a property. It is said that evil will not cross a line of yarrow.[4]

Yarrow has many, many medicinal values to share with Anishinaabeg, too. Any strong medicine can do harm. Yarrow is strong! One can overdose on yarrow. Three or four cups of very strong yarrow tea may give one vertigo and could numb one's body. When it is taken very strong yarrow is a depressant. It could cause an abortion, but usually the woman would get nauseated and vomit before that would happen. It is best, though, not to take yarrow when pregnant, and children should not be given yarrow. Catnip should be used for children.

Yarrow is an astringent. It makes tissues shrink and will thereby stop bleeding. The scientific genus name of *Achillea* and its English common names of woundwort, soldier's woundwort, knight's milfoil, sanguinary, and nosebleed all bear witness to this property. Yarrow is an excellent first-aid plant for use as a field dressing. It stops the flow of blood from a wound. The fresh leaves themselves, packed into a wound, will stop the bleeding by shrinking the blood vessels. An infusion of yarrow poured over a wound will stop blood flow, too. The infusion is also very good for treating skin rashes. A small roll of the green foliage of yarrow, gently pushed into the nose, will stop a nosebleed.

Yarrow is also a diaphoretic; it will promote sweating. Therefore, it is very good to break a bad cold and fever. But, the patient must be put to bed and kept warm and dry after being treated with yarrow. Kee once broke the fever of a teenage boy, only to have him get much worse the next day. After Kee had given him the yarrow tea and left, the boy decided he was feeling so much better that there was no reason he should miss the big football game. Then he went off to the big dance following the game and danced and danced and got all sweaty, both from the yarrow tea and from the exertion. The next morning he had pneumonia. After being treated with yarrow a patient must stay in bed, and his or her bed linens and pajamas must be kept dry, too, for the patient may sweat so much that a change is necessary before the person sleeps or the situation could get much worst.

4 Edward Benton-Banai, the Anishinaabe author of *The Mishomis Book,* told my master's class at Seven Generations Education Institute that if the devil is here in North America now it should be remembered that the devil did not come from here. In the old days we did not have the concept of a devil. Our ways speak of balance and imbalance, never of incarnate evil.

As a cold medicine yarrow can be mixed with mint and catnip. It can be drunk as a tea or pulverized and put into gelatin capsules. As a cold remedy, it must be remembered that yarrow will break the fever, but it will raise that fever before it brings it down. Therefore, do not use yarrow to break a fever or treat a cold or flu in a child, to avoid Reye's syndrome or to avoid having the fever go too high before it begins to come back down.

Yarrow is also an analgesic; it will stop pain. Chew thirteen leaves of yarrow and even the pain of an ulcerated tooth will be relieved. One can use fresh or dried yarrow for this pain relief. If a strong infusion of yarrow tea is given, it will relieve painful headaches, menstrual pain, etc. The fresh leaves placed on a wound will numb the area, too.

Yarrow is an antiseptic; it will destroy microorganisms that cause infection. It may even be an antibiotic, as it will clear up infected wounds.

When Kee was a young apprentice, she was with Nodji-mahkwe at a sugar camp one March. A man brought a boy to Nodjimahkwe with a badly infected old wound on his leg. Nodji-mahkwe did not have all of her supplies with her because she was away from home, so she sent Kee out to find yarrow under the snow. She told Kee to look for the new growth of yarrow leaves at the base of the dried stalks of last year's plants that she would find above the snow. The yarrow was used to poultice the wound to draw out the infection, and the child was cured. The father was roundly chastised for allowing his son to go so long untreated as well.

Yarrow infusion is an excellent wash for skin rashes. It is somewhat stronger than jewelweed, so jewelweed should be used first in treatment, especially on children's skin problems. A combination tincture of jewelweed and yarrow is an effective treatment for ringworm or other fungal infections.

Kee taught that there is a Midewiwin teaching which says that every plant has one chief virtue to share with the rest of Creation. She said that yarrow's chief virtue is that it has the ability to cure severe acne cases, the kind where large areas are covered with pus-filled pimples, and often leave the skin scarred and pockmarked. The first time she told me that this was yarrow's chief virtue, I wondered how curing acne could be more important than the other wonderful things yarrow can do. One has to think about the times in which the Gete-Anishinaabeg lived. Before the discovery of penicillin, people died quickly from infections brought on by open sores.

One would use this treatment if a simple tincture or infusion wash with yarrow did not cure the problem. Fresh yarrow is necessary for this acne treatment, therefore it is available from April through the summer and fall until the frost. Kee had not tried the process with frozen yarrow so she did not know if it would work. A person might try to extend the treatment time by refrigerating the yarrow at the end of the fall.

One of Kee's teenage relatives had a friend, an Irish boy with a florid complexion who was all covered with pimples. Kee offered both her relative and his friend "an old Indian cure" for the pimples, but only the friend would try it. Kee had him gather large amounts of yarrow. She took the green yarrow and blended it to a mushy applesauce consistency. If one does not have a blender, one can cook the plant material in a little water until it is the same mushy state. If the yarrow mask does not have enough elasticity to stick to the skin, add a little glycerin to the mixture. She spread it as a paste over the infected areas on the boy's face and back. She had him sit down with his feet up, listening to soft, soothing music, for 30 minutes a day while sipping yarrow tea. At bedtime she had him drink another cup of yarrow tea from a bowl, so that the steam would come up around his face. Kee said she was not sure if it was the internal treatment or the steam of the tea that was beneficial. The treatment was to be continued for thirty days, although the benefits were apparent well before that time limit. With an adult a blood purifier would have been used before the beginning of the yarrow treatment. It would help to clear the toxins from the body. Burdock—new leaves and a small piece of root—drunk as a tea would accomplish that body cleansing. The Irish boy to whom Kee gave the full treatment had perfectly clear skin without scars. Her own relative, who refused the treatment, had scars, the kind that are hard to shave around and in.

Yarrow is also a relaxant. Kee once had a neighbor who was an abused wife. She would sit in Kee's kitchen by the hour and tell her all about her fights with her husband. Kee would give her yarrow tea to calm her down so that she could send her home better able to handle the situation. After the woman left her husband and started to put her life back together, she came to see Kee to thank her for her help. She said. "Thank you for everything, but I just have to tell you. You make the worst tea in the world." She had not realized that she probably owed her life to the yarrow tea, despite its bitter, medicinal taste. Yarrow tea calms nerves. It is a relaxant that is just right if one is having trouble falling asleep.

It will not give one a hangover in the morning. It is not the tea to drink just before a big test, however.

The human ills that can be helped by yarrow are numerous. Nodjimahkwe told Kee, "When you are in doubt of how to treat a problem, use yarrow. Use it as a salve or a tea or a wash or a poultice, whatever is necessary. Then proceed to look for a further cure if necessary." It should be remembered by anyone wishing to use yarrow that it is a serious medicine, and that it should be used on adults and not children.

The Anishinaabeg also use yarrow in cooking. Yarrow tea has a strong taste. To counteract the taste, try mixing it with mint, lemon, or ginger root to taste.[5] Personally I think only ginger really works to offset the yarrow taste. It is probably best to just get used to the medicinal taste of yarrow and drink it straight. No one likes the taste of aspirin, but few of us stop using it because of its taste. Kee always thought medicine should taste like medicine, not like candy. She said a person should know they are using medicine.

Anishinaabeg also use yarrow as a spice. When it is cooked, the bitter properties of yarrow are lost. Kee made a wonderful bean recipe called Sagamoety that she had of her paternal co-grand-mother, MinissingOhdanikwe. It had three kinds of beans, two kinds of corn, and yarrow as a spice. To one gallon of the food one adds one handful of green yarrow. See the Recipes section for more information. A student in Kee's ethnobotany class made an excellent potato stew/soup for his ethnobotany display that stood for the final grade in the class at the end of term. He used seven sprigs of yarrow to flavor an ordinary potato soup recipe. He got an "A."

It is not only humankind that loves the yarrow. Bees relish its pollen. The common sulphur butterfly, a little butterfly with black-rimmed, yellow wings, is often found flitting about a stand of yarrow in the summer sun. Others also value things that delight us.

[5] Under no circumstances mix Yarrow and Coca-Cola. The resulting nauseating mixture is memorable, but not something one would try a second time. I speak from experience.

Nookaadiziiganzh

Mullein
Verbascum thapsus

~~~~~~

Keewaydinoquay taught her students to call mullein by the
Anishinaabe name of Nookaadiziiganzh. I do not remember that
she ever gave us a translation of the name, but the word may have
to do with being "soft" or "meek and mild." The leaves of mullein
are totally covered in tiny hairs that make the plant incredibly
soft to the touch and to the eye. My own little children called it
"Teddy Bear Plant."

Everything about mullein is meek and mild. It is a very pale
shade of green. It stands out against the other greens of the fields
where it grows because of its gray-blue-green shade. In some light
it is so very different that it is actually ghostly and glowing. It has
a very mild taste, too. It is a plant that loves disturbed ground.
One often finds it on roadsides where the soil has been recently
turned, and it is one of the first plants to reclaim the soil when a
whole area of woodland has been clear-cut, where the flora has
been stripped from the land.

Kee also loved the scientific name for mullein, *Verbascum
thapsus*. She said it was as thick and hairy as the plant itself. She
often joked that it would make a great swearword, as it filled the
mouth and could be spat out with great feeling. I can still hear
how she would roll the name around in her mouth and spit it
out with spirit. "Verrrrr-bassss-cum thaaaaps-us," she would hiss.
It always got a good laugh from her classes, but it really made it
hard for us to forget the scientific name, too.

Mullein has had a whole host of common names. In England
alone it is called "Velvet Dock . . . flannel leaf, beggar's blanket,
Adam's flannel, velvet plant, feltwort, bullock's lungwort, clown's
lungwort, Cuddy's lungs, tinder plant, rag paper, candlewick
plant, witch's candle, hag's taper, torches, Aaron's rod, Jacob's staff,
shepherds club, and Quaker rouge" (Gibbons 1966b, 224).

Several of the common names for mullein attest to the fact
that it has been used as a fire plant. The dried second-year flower

Nookaadiziiganzh: Mullein
(*Verbascum thapsus*)

stalk was said to have been soaked in tallow, oil, or grease and used as a torch by ancient peoples, hence "torches" and "tinder plant." The leaves of the mullein have also been used as candle-wicks, where a strip of the dried stalk or a sliver of the dried leaf was soaked in oil and laid on the top of an oil source to serve as a lamp, hence "candlewick plant." Because anything that was used by pre-Christian peoples was deemed suspect by the church, it was also associated with the occult, hence "witch's candle" and "hag's gaper." Euell Gibbons writes:

> In ancient England it was believed that those who 'trafficked' with the devil used dried mullein stalks, dipped in tallow, to light the orgies of their 'witches' sabbaths. In other areas mullein was thought to drive away evil spirits, and in southern Europe, mullein torches were formerly burned at funerals. In India, some considered mullein a sure safeguard against evil spirits and black magic. Even the ancient Greeks considered mullein a powerful agency against evil spirits, and it was this herb that Ulysses carried to protect himself against the wiles of Circe. (Gibbons 1966b, 229)

In her teaching Kee always told her classes the fun common names that the plants had acquired in their long association with humankind. She said they were often helpful in remembering what virtues the plant had shared with different peoples. She always said it did not matter what one called a plant as long as one did not use a derogatory name because that would insult the plant. She was always solicitous to the honor of her friends.

Mullein is one of a large group of plants that are easy to spot in the early spring as they grow in rosettes, perfect swirls of leaves low to the ground. They start up even when the ice is still on the ground. They are very resistant to frost. Rosette plants can even photosynthesize under the snow and right up to and through the early frosts. To the Gete-Anishinaabeg, these plants that grow in a circle, the sacred shape, were seen as plants of great strength that had great virtues to share with humankind.[6] Rosette plants are everywhere. Most have a heavy root that stores a great deal of energy, enabling the plant to come to flower quickly. Some even flower twice in one growing season. All of the rosette plants are strong medicinals, which, of course, one must be careful in using because they are highly effective.

Mullein comes up as a rosette in the first year of its growth. It is a biannual plant that takes two years to go through its life cycle. For that reason, the Anishinaabe mashkikiiwinini or the mashkikiiwikwe must be sure to take this plant in its second year, after it has had a chance to set seed and insure the survival of its kind in the place it has chosen. If it is absolutely necessary to take the first-year plant, it is best to take the outermost leaves of the circle, leaving the inner leaves. If one does this, the plant should be able to get through the winter and grow its flower stalk in the next summer. It is a poor exchange to take the whole plant the first year and deny the plant its maturity and continuance. That is not the way to maintain the balance and to get the plant to send its spirit along for the full healing of the person. Incurring spiritual debt is taken very seriously by the Anishinaabe herbalist, who is as worried about her own health and ability to live Anishinaabe-bimaadiziwin as she is about her patient's health. In our culture, health and long life are the direct results of how we treat other living beings in this cycle. Our elder brothers, the plants, the animals, and the Aadizookaanag, are very powerful. They have the ability to help us but also to hinder us if we do not treat them with respect by only taking their lives when it is absolutely necessary and after making an offering. If we do not

6 This statement should not be understood to suggest that the Anishinaabeg believe/believed in the "Doctrine of Signatures." That is simply not true. Please see chapter one's section, "How Do We Know This," for more details.

treat them with this respect we will incur a debt that will have to be repaid with our health or our lives or the health or lives of those dear to us. When we take something from the natural world we are not taking something from inanimate objects. We are taking something from very powerful beings.

Mullein has several strong medicinal virtues to share. Its leaves are a specific for bronchial conditions. One uses mullein for bronchitis; deep, thick coughs; bronchial pneumonia; and chest colds. Mullein also has an oil that will stop internal bleeding.

To make a cough medicine to treat bronchial conditions, put dried mullein leaves, crumbled, into a thick-bottomed pot. Have a kettle of water boiled and ready to add to the leaves. Add enough water to cover the leaves. The dried material will soak up a lot of water. Just keep adding the boiling water from the kettle to keep a little water under the plant material. Heat the pot until the water under the leaves is brown. One must keep stirring the pot to keep the mixture from burning. Once the water under the leaves is brown, add more water to cover the leaves and turn the heat down so that the mixture will simmer. Put a top on the pot and simmer for 30 minutes, stirring occasionally, and adding water to keep the mixture from sticking and burning. Take off burner. Filter through cloth to get out the bulk of the leaves. Put mixture back on the heat and add honey or brown sugar to the liquid. Stir to melt and mix. Take off heat. Add the juice of a lemon. The proportions of this recipe are about 1 quart of liquid to 3 tablespoons of lemon juice. Sweeten to taste, but honey soothes the throat, so making the mixture sweet actually helps the cure. Filter mixture once more; a coffee filter will work well to get out any little hairs that may still be in the mixture. The hairs will irritate the throat and sore tissues, so they must be removed before the mixture is used. The liquid can be bottled and kept under refrigeration for about a week. One can smell it if it begins to turn, and any remaining liquid should then be replaced by a fresh batch.

This bronchial medicine is taken in about a half-cup dose, two or three times daily, until the cough goes away. One can drink it cold, but it is more effective if one heats it by adding boiling water to a cup with the measured dose in it. This is a pleasant-tasting cold medicine that will not make a person sick if he or she takes too much. The worst it would probably do is give a person diarrhea if one took a lot at one time.

Mullein is also administrated as an inhalant to treat asthma, bronchitis, smoker's cough, emphysema, and other lung conditions. It is either burned or taken in steam. To use mullein as an inhalant by burning, one can crumble dried mullein leaves and make the material into a cigarette. Anyone who can roll their own tobacco cigarettes can roll a mullein one, too. Or the material can be smoked in a pipe. Pipes used for medicine should be clean. This is where a disposable corncob pipe comes in handy. Kee's mother was too much of a lady to smoke a pipe, so she put mullein in her frying pan on the stove and inhaled the vapors. By this method she was able to get the benefit of the smoke while retaining her ladylike demeanor.

Dried mullein can also be taken in steam as an inhalant. The dried, crumbled leaf can be added to boiling water, and the steam carefully inhaled. It is best, however, to take the water off the stove and to pour it over the leaves in a separate pan so that the patient is not breathing in live steam. A person can also put the oil of mullein into the hot water steam. When steaming with mullein one creates a mini–sweat lodge. Drink a cup of yarrow tea after the sweat and go to bed. It should clear one's head and chest very well.

Mullein has another major virtue to share with the Anishinaabeg. It has an oil that is effective against internal bleeding. It is healing to broken inner parts of the body, hemorrhoids, postoperative bleeding, bleeding ulcers, post-childbirth bleeding, etc. It will reach parts of the body one could not get at otherwise. One drinks the oil or, in the case of hemorrhoids, one also applies the oil manually to the parts affected.

To extract the oil one should pick the little yellow flowers of the second-year mullein plant. The flowers are on a tall seedstalk. Float the flowers in a wide-mouthed glass jar of pure water. If one is in the city it is best to use bottled distilled water for this job. Put the top on the jar and place it in the window in the sun. The oil will accumulate on the top of the water, ⅛ to ¼ of an inch, overnight. Take the floating oil off the top of the water with an eyedropper or remove the water with a bottom-stoppered jar. One can get three batches of oil from the same flowers, but it is best to take the oil every day. This oil will keep very well in the refrigerator for use over the winter months, but it is best to renew the supply every year. It should be administered to the patient by the tablespoonful, as much as it takes to stop the bleeding. If it is being used for bleeding hemorrhoids, one also applies the oil anally.

Kee had a family member who had many operations for hemorrhoids. She had a great deal of scar tissue. She was bleeding again and was in need of another operation, but her doctor was reluctant to do it because he was not sure it would work with all of the scar tissue she had accumulated. Kee offered her this cure, and it worked very well for her. After that she was out every summer popping mullein flowers into canning jars and setting them up in her kitchen windows.

This oil will not hurt a person. Kee's husband once mistook a jar of the oil in the refrigerator and made a salad dressing with it. Kee said the salad tasted great, but it had taken her a very long time to get the oil so she was not very pleased. It did, however, teach her to keep her medicinals well labeled.

Mullein has numerous other virtues to share with Anishinaabeg. The dried leaves are an excellent addition to kinnikinnick. All of the little hairs on the leaves trap air, and this really helps with the ignition of the material. Mullein is also used to wean smokers off of tobacco when it is smoked in a pipe or in a roll-it-yourself cigarette. When breaking the dried mullein up to roll it into a cigarette or to put in kinnikinnick, if one finds one's skin irritated, use jewelweed tincture to wipe away the tiny, irritating hairs and soothe any skin rash that develops. Or, better yet, wear long sleeves when doing such work, and launder the shirt afterwards. It is always better to prevent a problem than to have to seek a cure later.

Mullein is filled with ways to help someone in the woods who is in need. The leaves of fresh mullein make great and quick emergency pads for sore feet. When one is on a hike and does not think he or she can make it home because of pain in his or her feet, that person should find a mullein plant and slip a few leaves into his or her shoes. "Dr. Scholl's" be darned. When one is out on a hike on a hot day and one has used up one's water supply, mullein is a great thirst quencher. Find a second-year mullein plant. Feel down the flower stalk as one does with asparagus to feel where the soft stalk begins to get harder. Snap the stalk off the plant at that point and peel the stalk as one would peel a banana. The interior of the stalk is a juicy, edible pulp. It is bright green in color, rather the color of a honeydew melon. The taste is sweet with a slight bitter aftertaste that is by no means unpleasant. It will ease a thirst. It is a readily available source of pure, safe water for those in need. Mullein also makes a handy field heating pad. Heated in a frying pan or on a flat rock beside the fire, the fresh leaf will hold a considerable amount of heat for quite a while. It can ease a child's earache or a leg muscle sore from too long a hike. If on such a hike, a person or their child gets a smudged or dusty face, the mullein can help, too. The fresh leaves make a handy woodland face wipe. It is a strong and soft washcloth, readily available to help as a quick pick-me-up tissue. Kee always said the soft leaves of the fresh mullein plant are also the best outdoor, emergency toilet paper. It is a strong leaf that will not break. It is absorbent and tough, yet soft ... sounds rather like Charmin, does it not? However, mullein is also called "Quaker's rouge" because the Quaker girls who were denied makeup by their religion used to rub their cheeks with mullein to give them a healthy, reddish glow. So, personally, if I have to use mullein for an emergency toilet paper, I will have the jewelweed tincture in my other hand.

Mullein is also a good illustration of why it is not a good idea to take medicinal plants found growing along the highway. It is a great temptation for one can always see the tall, second-year plants standing along the road. Personally, I know I can identify them even at 55 miles per hour, and every single time I want them. But if one just looks under the leaf of a mullein plant growing along a highway, one will see a sticky, black gunk caught in the hairs of the plant. People are less likely to pick roadside plants after seeing the underside of such a mullein plant. It makes it easier to pass them by in the future. And it is not just the gunk one can see on a plant that one has to be conscious of when choosing a medicinal.

Plants cannot get up and move, with only one exception that I know.[7] Because they cannot move, they are forced to take up whatever is in the soil where they are growing. If good things are in the soil, they soak up good things. If poisons are in the soil, they have to take up the poisons. Plants growing along roadsides are growing in lead that years of leaded motor fuels left there. In the mullein plant exposure to lead has caused a mutation where one plant may have two or more tops. Some such affected mulleins look like candelabras with branched flower stalks on the second year plants. While we were working at the University of Wisconsin–Milwaukee, the botany department was running tests on mutated mulleins, and they concluded that the mutation was the result of lead exposure from gasoline additives. Kee would never take a mutated mullein for use either as medicine or to add to her kinnikinnick. She thought a medicine person should destroy such

[7] Slime molds do move on their own, but there is some disagreement as to whether or not they really are plants. Kee always said they were a wonderful reminder that we humans do not know everything there is to know.

plants, preferably before they came to setting seed. Take only those mulleins that have a single, unbranched, second-year flower stalk.

One must always when taking plants from the wild be conscious that humankind are not the only ones with whom the plants share the virtues that they were given to share with the rest of creation. Kee loved to watch the whole cloud of butterflies and moths that can be seen at sunrise and sunset rising off a field of mullein. The golden flowers are visited by hummingbirds as well as by honeybees. The little brown seeds produced in capsules on the flower stalk by the second year plant are relished by gold-finches (Hendstrom 1984, 156). Lots of folk love the mullein!

"The South Wind and the Maiden of the Golden Hair"[8]

8 Kee told an outline of this story in her classes. I cannot remember if she ever told the whole story to me. This version is a compilation of Kee's outline and Henry R. Schoolcraft's "Shaawondasee" (79–80).

Gichi-mewinzha, gii-oshki-niiging akiing, a very long time ago, when the earth was new, ten Anishinaabeg warrior brothers fought a great battle with a famous, huge, monstrous and dangerous bear who wore a marvelous necklace of shells. Mudjekewis[9] and his nine brothers overcame the great Manidoo Mishi-makwa with the help of their Guardians and with cunning and bravery. They succeeded in killing the monstrous bear who had threatened their people, and, in so doing, they obtained the wondrous necklace that he wore. As reward for their bravery in obtaining the necklace that brought great happiness to the Anishinaabeg, the ten brothers became Manidoog themselves. The nine eldest went off to the Spirit World to undertake their new duties, and the youngest Mudjekewis was given control of the winds of the Earth. To acknowledge his new responsibilities he was given the name of Kabeyun, Father of the Winds.[10]

9 The spelling of this name is from Schoolcraft.

10 The spelling of this name and its translation is from Schoolcraft.

Kabeyun himself undertook the job of directing Ningaa-bii'an, the West Wind, the wind that blows from the Gates of Espingishmuk, the place of our Landing, the blood-red land of the Ancestral Spirits.[11] To his son Giiwedin he gave the North Wind and instructed him to blow winter down on the land of dreams and healing, the black of night, the dark of the year. The East Wind he gave to his son Waaban, that he might blow from the white land of the rising sun, bringing the spring of infancy and new beginnings, inspiration and light to the earth.[12] To his son Shaawondasee he gave the South Wind, on which the warm breezes of the South Land blow summer's warmth and the green of new growth, adult life, and creativity onto the earth.[13]

11 The spelling of Epingishmuk comes from Schoolcraft, but the translation of the name and description of the place comes from Kee.

12 Schoolcraft has Wabun. See glossary for more information.

13 The spelling of this name is from Schoolcraft. See glossary for more information.

Kabeyan's son Naanabozho was given nothing until, after a long journey and great struggle, Naanabozho found and fought his father the West Wind, to avenge the death of his mother the Anishinaabekwe. Once reconciled to his father, Naanabozho was given the Northwest Wind to manage jointly with his elder brother Giiwedin. Naanabozho's nephews, the Anishinaabeg, say that when the Northwest Wind is playful and pleasant their Great

Uncle Naanabozho is controlling it, but when it turns colder and harsher it is being controlled by Giiwedin. All of these things happened in the beginning of our world when all things were put to right and assigned their proper places in the order and balance of life.

Shaawondasee was a mild fellow. He grew fat and happy lying in the warm and gentle South Lands. He lay with his face ever toward the north, that he might watch his brothers and how they blew upon Anishinaabewaki. One day as he lay watching his family, Shaawondasee saw a beautiful maiden standing alone in a grassy meadow. The maiden was tall and straight, slim and graceful. Her hair was as golden as the light of the sun, so he called her Wezaawaaskwaneg, "Golden Light." Shaawondasee sighed when he saw her, and his sigh caused the maiden to dance. Each day the South Wind looked for his new *Niinimoshenh*, little cousin, little sweetheart, as he lay in the South Land with his face toward the north. Each morning as the sun arose, Shaawondasee would look for his beautiful, golden-haired maiden, for watching her filled his heart with love. One morning, as he looked for her eagerly, Shaawondasee saw that overnight she had grown old. Her beautiful golden hair was now a mass of white.

Shaawondasee was shocked and grieved. He thought, "A Mindimooyenh, an old lady! Oh, my beautiful maiden! My brother Giiwedin the North Wind, the Cold Blower, must have touched Niinimoshenh, my beloved, with his breath and made her old."

In his sorrow Shaawondasee sighed a great sigh that blew the white hair of the maiden up and off in a swirl of white. As he watched his beloved's hair blowing away, Shaawondasee laughed a great laugh for he realized his Wezaawaaskwaneg, "Golden Light," who in her age is called Mindimooyenh, "Old Lady," was a meadow flower, the dandelion (*Taraxacum officinale*).

Doodooshaaboojiibik
Mindimooyenh
Wezaawaaskwaneg
"Little Suns"
Dandelion
Taraxacum officinale

Dandelions have always been my favorite flower. It is the one flower I personally want on my grave. I have asked my children to visit my grave after the dandelions have gone to seed and to kick a few of the white seed heads if they want to plant flowers in my memory. I really am not kidding. I just love dandelions. I know of no prettier flower. The sight of a full field or lawn covered with gold in the bright sunlight is as aesthetically pleasing as any sight I have ever seen.

People say, "Ya, but they go to seed." Well, that is true, dandelions do go to seed, but so do tulips and daffodils. They look just as scraggy after their flowering. I truly believe that the hatred of dandelions is just the hatred of the natural world. People spend fortunes and pollute a lot of ground water all in an attempt to kill this beautiful little plant. Then they plant exotic bulbs in the spot and struggle to get them to grow. Perhaps the dandelion is despised because it is free.

The scientific name for the dandelion is *Taraxacum officinale.* The genus, the first part of the name, comes from the Greek word *taraxos,* meaning "disorder," and *akos,* meaning "remedy" (Grieves 1931, 250). The species name, the second part, means that at one time it was on the official lists from which a physician can write prescriptions. So the scientific name for this plant means the "Official Remedy of Disorders," and that is a very good name for this plant because it has been a strong medicinal for the Anishinaabeg and for many, many other peoples as well, all over the world, all across the Northern temperate zones of the planet, across Turtle Island and Europe and Asia, too.

The English common name "dandelion" is a corruption of the French "dent-de-lion" meaning "the teeth of the lion," because someone thought the leaves of the plant look like the canine teeth of a lion (Grieves 1931, 249). The old medieval herbals sometimes really intensified this supposed similarity by drawing viscious-looking illustrations of the leaves and of open-mouthed

Doodooshaaboojiibik:
Dandelion (*Taraxacum
officinale*)

lions. But it cannot be denied that this little plant really does "put
the bite" on many of the problems that beset the People.

In the times of the Gete-Anishinaabeg, the end of winter was
a time of hardship. Since so much of the People's diet in winter
consisted of dried foods and whatever game was still available,
diseases that we now know are caused by vitamin deficiencies
were very prevalent. For such disorders, the dandelion has very
effective medicine. The green-growing parts of the plant are
rich in vitamins A, E, B1–thiamine, and C. The roots store a lot
of calcium, protein, phosphorus, iron, riboflavin, niacin, and
potassium (Crowhurst 1972, 53), but Kee taught that the chief
virtue that the dandelion has to share with Anishinaabeg is the
fact that it is the only natural source of body-assimilatable copper.
The human body does not need very much copper. It is one of the
trace elements that, although we do not need much, we cannot
entirely do without, either. And dandelion has it for us. If a person
just ate three or four helpings of dandelion greens or flowers in a

whole year's time, they would get enough of the mineral to keep them healthy. Kee told me to dry either the flower petals of the dandelion or the leaves and to pulverize them and sprinkle them across a stew or soup for my family a few times a year to be sure that they received all of the copper that they needed.

When using dandelion flowers for cooking be very, very sure to take all of the greens off of the heads when picking the flowers. One has to use one's thumbnail to scoop out the part of the stem that is at the bottom, where the stem goes into the green leaves at the base of the flower. If even a tiny bit of stem gets into the plant material, the resulting food will be bitter.

In the old days, if a person was suffering from lack of vitamins come *Onaabani-giizis*, "The Hard Crust on the Snow Moon," or in *Iskigamizige-giizis*, "The Maple Sap Boiling Moon," at the end of a hard winter, the mashkikiiwikwe would dig up dandelion roots and pulverize them and pour just-boiled and slightly cooled water over the roots. The plant material was allowed to steep, covered, for 10 minutes or so; then it was filtered and given to the patient as a tea, three or four times a day. This treatment was sure to act as a "spring tonic" on a person suffering from poor diet and get them back to feeling chipper in a very short time.

The spring tonic approach to curing vitamin deficiency is not as tasty as utilizing dandelions as a food source early in the year. One can get all of the vitamins and minerals in the plants by just adjusting one's cooking habits to include a good dose of dandelions as soon as they start to grow in the spring. Nowadays we have fresh fruits and vegetables available to us year-round, but who knows whether we always will be so privileged. It pays to keep the knowledge against the time when we or our descendants may need it.

Dandelions have a food to share with Anishinaabeg at any time of the year. In the early spring, when the leaves are first up and before the flowers form, one can eat the leaves of dandelions raw. They have a pleasant, if slightly nippy, bitter taste that will enliven a "blah" lettuce salad, rather the way radishes do. If the leaves are a little too bitter for one's taste (and they do get more bitter as the season progresses, until they are all but inedible once the flower develops), one can cook them in one or two changes of boiling water to remove the bitter taste. The resulting potherb is both a healthy and a tasty addition to the diet and really very good with a dab of butter or salad dressing or a few shakes of parmesan cheese. One can extend the time in which leaves are edible by covering them and allowing the plant to blanch, the way celery is blanched, to make it white and bland-tasting. One can cut off the top of an older plant or just cover the older leaves with mulch or a piece of black plastic or with an overturned bucket to keep the sun off of the leaves. Since dandelions have a good, strong taproot, the plants will just put up more and tenderer leaves even if they are denied the sun for a week or more. Some people even dig roots up in the fall and put them in sand in a basement to harvest the blanched, mild-tasting, but nutritious leaves all winter long.

The flowers that follow so readily in the spring and continue into the summer (and may even come back again in the cool of the fall) are really good, too. My family likes dandelion flowers dipped in egg and cornmeal and fried in butter. The complete recipe is offered in the Recipes section under the name "Little Suns," which was Kee's title for dandelions cooked this way. One can pick the yellow petals off of the bitter stems and green leaves and scatter them over a mixed salad or over a bowl of mashed potatoes or cooked rice or over the top of a soup or stew to create an interesting and pretty dish. One can extend the time in which dandelion flowers are available by picking the flowers when they are in full bloom and spreading them to dry on a cookie sheet or a cooking rack. Once the flowers are dry, one then pulls the yellow petals off of the green part of the flower and stores the petals in a jar for later use. I have included recipes for using either the fresh or the dried petals in baking dishes in the Recipes section, too.

Once the flowering is over for the season, the roots of the dandelion are ready for harvesting. If one wants the biggest roots, dig the plants that had the biggest flowers. It is easiest to dig the long taproot after a rain or when one is weeding a flower or vegetable garden that has had its soil tilled recently. Kee always hated using the roots of any plant, probably because as the child of gardeners and the apprentice of a medicine woman she had spent too many hours scrubbing and cleaning roots of various food and medicinal plants. But she was rather fond of dandelion and chicory root coffees, and so she did teach about the process of turning dandelion roots into a coffee-like drink. One digs and cleans all of the dirt off of dandelion roots. One scrubs the roots with a good, stiff vegetable brush or one uses a potato peeler to get off the skin. Then one dries the roots very well in a very slow oven overnight or in the hot sun for several days or on rocks beside a fire. It is the key to making a palatable coffee to dry the roots very slowly. Roots dried too quickly are much too bitter to make a tasty drink. One knows when the roots are properly dry when one breaks one in half: it will snap when it is really dry, and it will be dark brown all of the way through. The roots can be cooled and put in sealed jars for later use, or brewed into a coffee-like drink immediately. One breaks the roots into pieces and grinds them in a coffee grinder, then perks them in a percolator the same way one makes coffee, but, because dandelion roots are strong, only about 1 teaspoon of the root is necessary to make one cup of the dandelion-root coffee. I have never been a coffee drinker, but Kee, who was, assured me that one could easily get used to dandelion coffee if one had no access to coffee beans. She actually preferred a drink made by mixing dandelion roots with similarly processed and dried chicory roots to the one made with dandelion roots alone.

There is another use of dandelion root that Kee taught me about but that I have not yet tried. She said one could make a pretty magenta, purplish-pink, dye from the crushed roots of mature dandelion roots. One digs the roots, washes them well, cuts them up very fine, smashes them with a rock, or grinds them in a meat grinder. Then one covers the crushed roots with water. Rain water works well, as it is softer than tap water. Then one simmers the plant material for several hours and allows it to sit in the pot at the back of the stove until morning. One filters out the liquid, then one puts pre-wetted wool in the bath to simmer gently for one half hour or longer. The resulting color is said to be rather pretty and can be made more permanent by soaking the material to be dyed in alum before adding to the dye bath.

Keewaydinoquay taught me several medicinal virtues dandelion has to share with the People. She said it was helpful as a blood purifier and was often given after a long illness or in cases of severe acne and eczema. In such cases a person was usually given a dried-leaf infusion, 1 teaspoon dried leaf to 1 cup boiling water, covered and steeped for 10 to 15 minutes with cover on pot. The resulting tea would be filtered and sweetened with honey and given once or twice or three times a day, depending on the severity of the case and on how well the patient took it. Dandelions can be a laxative, and they also increase the flow of urine, which helps in some cases where the system has to be cleaned out.

Dandelions are a powerful liver treatment as well. They were traditionally used to treat jaundice. A tea of the dried leaf, rather weaker than the tea described above made from roots, is used for small children. A decoction of the root is used in an older person with jaundice if they do not respond to the tea of the leaf.

Dandelions are also used to treat arthritis. A leaf tea of the kind described above, 1 teaspoon dried leaf to 1 cup boiling water, sweetened with honey or maple sugar to make it palatable, is given to a person with arthritis to reduce the swelling of joints. The affected joints are wrapped in a poultice of chopped dandelion leaves and flowers covered with boiling water and simmered to break down the plant material until it is very soft. The material is slightly cooled and applied to the swollen joints warm and covered with cloth. This kind of poultice helps to reduce the swelling if applied several times daily while the patient is sipping dandelion tea.

Another of the virtues that the dandelion has to share with the People, and a virtue that should not be disregarded just because the plant also gives us so much for our physical comfort both as a food and as physical medicine, is the fact that dandelion are just so much fun. They are a beautiful flower in all stages of their growth. The perfectly formed, little, golden flowers soon give way to an equally beautiful, delicate white seed head that when blown upon by wind or child explodes into a cloud of tiny, fairy-winged parachutes. As children we used to pick the mindimooyenyag, the "old ladies," and blow upon their hair. Some of the kids said that one should count how many puffs it took to completely blow all of the seeds off of the head, and that would tell one what time it was. If one had to blow twice it was two o'clock, three times and it was three o'clock. Some said if one blew on a seed head and there were any seeds left on the plant that was the number of children one could expect in later years. We also believed that a wish made on a dandelion would be granted if one could blow off all of the seeds with one breath. We used to say that if one whispered a secret one wanted another person to know, but instead of telling the person one whispered it to a dandelion, then blew off all of the seeds with one blow, the other person would hear one's words. We picked the stems, and nipped off the flowers, and pushed the small upper part of the stalk into the wider lower part to form a circle. This circle became a link in a chain when we pushed another stem through the first circle and continued to make a chain long enough for a necklace. This project always got our fingers wonderfully stained with juice, and for some reason that was part of the fun of the game. I went through the summers of my childhood with wonderfully grimy fingers. And dandelions were always a flower that no one scolded a child for picking, even out of a neighbor's garden or lawn. A person could bring a big handful to his or her mom and make her smile. To this day I always pick a big handful of the first dandelions of the season. I bring them into the house and put them in the finest crystal vase that I own, and I put them on my dining-room table.

Ginebigowashk

Omakakiibag
Mashkiigobag
Native Plantain
Plantago rugelii

"Whiteman's Footprint"
Common Plantain
Plantago major

English or Narrow-leaf Plantain
Plantago lanceolata

~~~~~~

Two Anishinaabe names for plantain that Kee often used were "Whiteman's Footprint" and "Whiteman's Footstep," and she cited the commonly held belief that plantain was an imported plant to explain these names. In fact, there are both native and imported species of plantain on Turtle Island today. Two of these, *Plantago rugelii* and *Plantago major,* look very similar, often grow together, and can be used to treat the same ailments.[14] *Plantago rugelii* is the indigenous one. The other is truly the "Whiteman's Footprint." In this chapter, either plant can be used when we talk about "plantain."

Plantain is a common "weed" in suburban lawns and in every available crack in the sidewalks of cities. Both varieties cited here have roundish or egg-shaped leaves and flowers that grow all down the tall flower stalk. They both have leaves that grow up out of the rosette shape that Keewaydinoquay said was an indication to Anishinaabeg that the plants were strong medicine with good, deep roots that helped them to come up early in the spring.

In the early springtime, just after the last of the ice has melted, the plantains will be one of the first plants to appear and re-green the world. Its familiar rosette-shaped leaves appear with the first of the green grass shoots. If one picks them at that time, well before they send up their characteristic seed heads, they make a nice addition to a spring salad or, chopped, they add texture, vitamins, and flavor to a vegetable soup or stew. As a potherb they

14 There are slight differences between these two plants, and anyone interested in learning how to distinguish between the two can find more information at http://wisplants.uwsp.edu/namesearch.html.

Omakakiibag: Plantain
(*Plantago major* and *Plantago lanceolata*)

are nice steamed or cooked in boiling water for about 10 minutes and served with butter. But they have to be eaten very early in the year because they very quickly get stringy and too tough to be used as food. One could, however, in dire food times cut off the leaves and force the plant to re-grow a new crop of leaves later in the season. See the Recipes section for more plantain recipes.

The seeds produced on the seed head have been a traditional food for caged pet birds and are also much relished by their free cousins as well. Throughout the summer and fall, and even into the winter until they are well covered with the winter snows, the seeds hang on the flower stalks and provide food for a variety of birds and small mammals.

There are two other amusements that we played as children using plantains. The first game is "Finding the Fairy Fiddle." One takes a leaf from the broad-leafed plantain and cuts the stem half through with one's thumbnail, just where the leaf joins the leaf stem. Then one gently pulls the leaf and the stalk apart, taking care not to break the fibers of the leaf that are said to be the strings of the fairies' fiddle. Some people can make a sound by blowing through the strings. The other game we played with plantains was to make headbands with the broad leaves, using sharp, dried twigs as skewers to pin each leaf to the next one until one had enough to fasten into a type of leaf crown.

Keewaydinoquay taught me to use a poultice of plantain leaf, either species, for isolating the sting and the poison of an insect bite. One just takes a leaf of the plantain, chews it up, and puts it on any painful bite. It works wonders!

I was once driving a stick-shift car back into town from an herb-gathering trip in the country. It was a warm summer day, and I was driving with the window open. A bee flew in the window and stung me on my arm in the inside bend of my elbow. Before I got the car pulled over on the country road, my arm had started to swell up, and I could hardly bend the elbow. I really did not know if I would be able to drive with the arm in that condition, since it was a stick-shift car, and I needed both arms and hands to drive. So I got out of the car and looked up and down the ditch until I found a plantain. I chewed up a leaf, trying not to think about the lead in the soil, and spat the leaf into my elbow. I picked a few more leaves and bound them to my elbow with a piece of string that I had in my plant-picking backpack. Within three minutes the pain of the sting was considerably reduced, and the swelling had gone down enough for me to bend my arm. I took a few extra plantain leaves along just to be certain I would have enough to get home on, and I managed to drive. I have been very fond of plantains ever since.

One time I was working in Kee's ethnobotany office at the university with her when a former student, from the semester before, came into the room and said, "A present for you, Grandmother," tossed two huge bags of Florida oranges and grapefruit on her desk, and turned and walked out. Kee and I looked at each other, then Kee said, "Go and stop him! Bring him back! There has been a healing."

So I chased the student down the hall and got him to come back to see Kee. He told us that he had liked Kee's class, and at the winter break he had gone home to visit his parents who lived in Florida. At breakfast one morning, he told his mom all about the neat class he had taken given by this old Indian lady and how she had taught him to use all kinds of weeds as medicines. His mom asked for an example and the one he had told her about was plantain. He told her how Kee had told him to put it on insect bites. The same morning the mother went off to her usual Ladies' Garden Club, where the ladies had sat in lawn chairs and listened to a speaker. While she was sitting there, a bug bit her on her ankle. It hurt so much she thought she was going to faint, but she remembered what her son had just told her about plantain. She reached down, picked a leaf of a plantain that was growing by her chair, chewed it up, and held the chewed leaf with another plantain leaf as a bandage against her leg while she listened to the rest of the lecture. Then she went home and went to bed because she just was not feeling very good. She said the plantain had made her leg feel so much better that before she went to bed she chewed up another leaf and put it on the bite under a bandage. That afternoon she was still not feeling well so she went to the clinic near her house.

She told her doctor how she felt, and he said, "You weren't, by any chance, at the Garden Club today with Mrs. Jones and Mrs. Smith were you?"

The mother said, "Yes, we always sit together."

The doctor asked, "You didn't get bit by something did you?"

She said "Yes" and showed him her leg and told him how her son had told her about this old Indian cure for insect bites, how she had chewed up a leaf and put it on the bite when it happened.

The doctor said, "I am sorry to tell you this, but the two ladies you were sitting with are both dead. They were both my patients. They were bitten by spiders at the Garden Club, and I am afraid they have both died."

The doctor put the boy's mother in the hospital to run some tests on her, but he made her show him the plant that she had used before the ambulance came to take her away. She found a plantain in the yard outside of the clinic and gave it to him, and went off to the hospital. They determined that a deadly spider had bitten her but that the poison had been contained around the bite area and had not gotten into her system.

Because of his mother's cure, the boy was grateful and so he brought the oranges and grapefruit back to school to thank Kee. The story delighted her more than the fruit, and she used it every time after that that she taught about plantain. Plantain has the virtue to share with us of localizing poison.

Oginii-waabigwaniin, Roses (*Rosa*)
Oginiig
Rose Hips

Wild Roses in Anishinaabewaki
Oginiiminagaawanzh
Prickly Wild Rose
Rosa acicularis

Smooth Rose
Rosa blanda

Wild Rose
Rosa virginiana

Bizhikiwigin
Wild Prairie Rose
Rosa arkansana

Everybody loves the Roses.[15] We have four different roses that are indigenous to the Great Lakes area and a whole host of imported roses that have been brought here by other peoples. But they are all of them a delight! The Gete-Anishinaabeg loved the roses as much as do the people living today, and the rose had and has many virtues to share with us.

Roses are commonly added to kinnikinnick so that their beautiful fragrance may bear our prayers into the Realm of the Manidoog, the Spirit World. It is an ancient concept that what is most pleasing to mortals must be most pleasing to Those Who Care For Us as well. And so we give the most beautiful gifts we can to show our appreciation and respect for the Powers that maintain our lives. And roses are a part of the respect that the Anishinaabeg offer to Spirit in return for the beauty of our lives.

In the story of "The Year the Roses Died," we are told that for all of creation to continue as Creator wanted it to in the Beginning when Creator created all that is, we must all do our part to keep the whole in harmony and in balance. We forget that to our peril! The sight and the smell of a rose are here to remind

15 Juliet: "That which we call a rose/By any other name would smell as sweet." *Romeo and Juliet* 2.2.43–44.

us of the harmony inherent in our world. The thorns are there to keep us mindful of greed that endangers the balance and thereby endangers the whole of creation.

In a physical sense, roses have one truly great virtue to share with people, too. They are the best source of vitamin C that we have. They have ounce-for-ounce and pound-for-pound far more vitamin C than either oranges or tomatoes or any of the other fruits or vegetables that we use. Gibbons says that one cup of cleaned and seeded rose hips have as much vitamin C as ten to twelve dozen oranges (Gibbons 1966b, 168).

To utilize the gift of vitamin C that they have to share with us, one takes the rose hips, the seed capsule that grows under the blossom and remains on the stem after the flower is finished. For this purpose one can use any of the wild roses or any of the domestic roses as long as they have not been sprayed with poisons. The vitamin content of the rose hips is greatest right after the first frost of the fall, when the rose hips have turned a bright red color. That is the time to gather enough of them to see your family through the winter.

There are several ways to process the rose hips so that one can use them with one's family, but the initial preparation of the material is the same. First, one cuts off the stem end of the hip and the blossom end, too, with a sharp knife. Then one has to take the seeds out of the rose hips. Both of these jobs are easiest to do as soon as one gathers. The seeds are bitter, and by removing them one is improving the taste of the finished product. The seeds have very little vitamin C in them, although they do have vitamin E. If one wanted to use the seeds as a source of vitamin E one could grind them after removing them from the rose hip and mix them with a grease or oil base for use on the skin. A new, clean nail makes a good tool for the job of removing the seeds from the newly gathered rose hips. Use the sharp point to pierce the side of the rose hip and to make a slice down the length, then turn the nail around and use the head to scoop out the seeds. Once one has all of the seeds out, one is ready to dry the rose hips for future use or ready to process them into a readily usable vitamin dosage.

Dried rose hips make a lovely tasting, astringent tea that is good all by itself or is often added to other herbal teas to increase taste and vitamin content. Commercial herbal teas often include rose hips, but because it is labor-intensive work to remove the seeds they are often left in, which can give store-bought herbal teas a biting and a bitter taste. Some people actually like the taste of "bitters," but for the rest of us the bitter taste distracts from the sweetish-sour taste of rose-hip tea. That bitterness can be avoided if one processes rose hips oneself for one's own herbal teas. Such a tea is not only delightful, it is also an excellent source of vitamin C.

Keewaydinoquay said that when she started to get back into the use of Anishinaabe medicinals she used a lot of rose hips to keep her children healthy during the wintertime. She had not used the knowledge she had been given by Nodjimahkwe much before her children became school-aged because her husband did not like the "silly, old, Indian stuff." To keep peace in the family, Kee had kept her household as European as she knew how. But when she was left to raise the children on her own, she found her income just would not stretch to things like store-bought vitamin pills. She started to use a lot of the knowledge that Nodjimahkwe had given her just to keep her family healthy.

After that her family did maintain rather good health, and the people around them started to notice that her children stayed well and in school even when most of the rest of the community had colds and flu all winter. Kee said that the talk[16] started to bother her children, and they started to resent the fact that they had to drink teas while their friends got to take vitamins in cute, animal-shaped, chewable tablets. As kids will, they began to whine and say, "The other kids don't have to drink rose-hip tea. If you loved us you'd buy us children's vitamins, too." Kee said she tried to tell them how she had to save money to take care of all of the other family needs, and she suggested that they buy the vitamin pills with their own allowances. Of course, the kids balked at that, too, and they refused the rose-hip tea and started to get colds like their friends.

Because she could not afford to stay home with sick children, Kee started to make rose-hip jam. The kids ate it at first, and then they started to want the store-bought strawberry jam that came in cute little jars. So, Kee started to make a conserve that her own mother had made for her when she was a child that had rose hips, and nuts, and raisins in it. It was pretty and it tasted really good, so the children in the neighborhood started to want it, too. That turned things around in Kee's household. Once the neighborhood children started to stop by after school for a piece of toast with a tablespoon of rose-hip conserve on it, that method of getting

16 The Indians in the community said, "Oh, she is just using the plant knowledge Nodjimahkwe taught her." So the Whites said, "Oh, a witch, eh?"

one's vitamins suddenly became acceptable to Kee's children as well.

It is a possible to make a very modern-looking and easy to use vitamin from rose hips if one runs into the kind of family problems that Kee had raising her children. One can use dried rose hips, smash them into a powder, or put them in a blender until they are pulverized, and put the powder into gelatin capsules. Or one can mix the chopped or powdered, dried rose hips with apple pectin and maple sugar and form the mixture into little tablets. If one rolls such homemade tablets in powdered sugar, one will reduce the stickiness and keep them from sticking together when they are stored in the fridge. These tablets have a nice sweet-sour taste quite like Sweet Tart candies, and children do love the taste.

One can also make a very child-appealing vitamin pill by taking dried rose hips, crushing them, and mixing them: ⅓ rose hips; ⅓ Knox gelatin, softened in a little boiling water, or flavored Jell-O if preferred; and ⅓ honey. Mix the three ingredients. If one is going to store the tablets for future use, put in a few drops of glycerin as a preservative. Roll the mixture into a small rope[17] and cut off ¼-inch tablets. Or drop them in small teaspoon amounts onto a foil-wrapped cookie sheet to set up like gumdrops. They can be rolled in powdered sugar to keep them from sticking together in a covered container in the fridge.[18]

One can make one's own rose-hip tea by just crushing a dried rose hip into a cup and adding boiling water, or one can add dried rose hips to any other herbs or even to commercial black tea. If one allows the water to cool a moment or two after boiling in the kettle, a lot more of the vitamin C will be retained in the resulting tea, and the tea will taste better, too. Black tea or green tea is said to be scorched if one applies the boiling water to the tea without allowing the minute or two for the water to cool. A real tea drinker can tell the difference in taste. If one really wants to feel modern, one can even purchase empty paper tea-bag covers that one can fill with one's own rose teas. It is a sight easier than sewing a teaspoon of tea into a little square of muslin or cheesecloth, the original method of making tea bags.

One can make a very effective and healthful rose tonic and cough syrup. To do this, mix ground rose hips with warm water to cover in a covered bowl or cup. Allow to sit for 30 minutes. Filter out the rose hips. To the liquid add honey, lemon extract, a few drops of rose oil, lemon juice to taste, and 3 tablespoons vodka. The vodka helps to preserve the cough mixture, and it also helps

17 Roll it with your hands against the table the way you rolled clay or Play-dough or Plasticene to make a snake or a coil pot when you were a child. We used to have great fun making rose-hip pills in the ethnobotany lab. Adults love playing with their food, especially when they are getting university credit for doing it.

18 Old-time pharmacists used to use Lycopodium spores for this purpose.

to relax the throat. Taken a tablespoonful at a time, this mixture is very useful in treating colds.

If one is not into processing one's vitamins, one could use the ancient Anishinaabe method that my own daughter Pukwanis used the winter she spent studying at the University of Alaska Fairbanks. The groundspeople of the university had surrounded the buildings with native plants that both looked good and were edible. Pukwanis and her friends, including several moose, just snacked on the rose hips out of hand while walking between classes. Because of the long days of summer sunlight, the roses in Alaska grew rose hips as big as small apples.

Rose petals also have another wonderful virtue to share with Anishinaabeg. Most commercially grown roses, unfortunately, have been sprayed with poisons to keep down the various rose pests and diseases, so it is best not to eat them. One can however, use them in one's kinnikinnick. Just enjoy the cut roses in the bouquet until they start to droop. Then take off the flower petals and spread them to dry in a shallow basket where air can get around the petals to help them to dry without molding. Once the petals are dry, add them to kinnikinnick to be burned on an asinaagan, a stone dish, or smoked in a pipe. They are a beautiful addition to the smoke.

Rose petals gathered from one's own garden, where one knows they have not been sprayed with rose spray, or rose petals gathered in a clean place in the wild, are a delightful addition to cooking. The only caution necessary in using rose petals in cooking is that the little white part at the base of each petal is bitter-tasting and should be removed. One takes a rose between one's thumb and forefinger and cuts off the white portion of the petals of the whole rose all at once. Several recipes for the use of rose petals in cooking are offered in the Recipes section.

Dried rose petals or rosebuds also are a nice addition to potpourris. They add visual appeal to a dish of dried herbs, but they will add little smell, so it is best to add a few drops of rose oil if one wants the full rose experience.

Eupatoriums

Bagizowin
Joe Pye
Gravelroot
Eupatorium purpureum

Meskwaanakwak-bagizowin
Spotted Joe Pye
Eupatorium maculatum

Ogaakananiibiish
"Shield and Lance Plant"
Boneset
Eupatorium perfoliatum and *Ageratina altissima*

19 Kee always told this story when she lectured on Joe Pye. To her this was a very important part of this plant's history. However, the racial identity of Joe Pye has recently been challenged, notably in Foster and Duke, where Joe Pye is contemptuously called ". . . a nine-teenth-century Caucasian 'Indian theme promoter'" (185). Anything good has to have come from Europe or it is simply stolen and identified as originally European. Why is that? Why can't European North Americans just start thinking of this place as a good place. Maybe it is vestiges of a "we are here just to make a killing, then we will be going home again" mentality. Maybe that is really what is at the core of the rape of this continent: people who just do not feel a part of this place even after a half-dozen generations here. Kee thought the answer was to embrace the Indian wannabes and just adopt away a whole generation of Whites. Sometimes they make our strongest allies or they marry into our families and give birth to our strongest mixed-blood warriors. Remember Quanta Parker?

The Eupatoriums were a family of plants that Keewaydinoquay always taught together. These plants are grouped together by European science and also by Anishinaabe plant knowledge as well. The European scientific system groups these plants together because they have similar physical structure; specifically, they have florets in terminal clusters (Mathews, *Wild Flowers,* 470). The Anishinaabe system groups these plants together by usage.

In the European tradition, the genus was named in memory of Mithridates Eupator, king of Parthia from 120 to 63 B.C., who was a great enemy of the expanding Roman Empire. He was said to have discovered and used plants of this family for a variety of cures (Coffey 1993, 259).

In the Anishinaabe tradition, two plants of this genus, Joe Pye and boneset, were used by an Eastern Algonquian, Abenaki, medicine man from the area around Stockbridge, New York.[19] Zhopai, a name that was anglicized as Joe Pye, used them to cure typhoid fever. When a typhoid epidemic struck the Indians and the nearby white community, this medicine man had great success with treating his own people using a combination of those two plants. A White blacksmith from the neighboring town, who had been a friend of the Indians, repairing their plows and harnesses, etc., came to Joe Pye and begged him to cure his two young sons who were about to die of the fever. He said, "You can see I am an older man. I probably will have no more children. I will give you anything I have, including my farm, if you will save their lives."

Joe Pye declined the farm and agreed to help the children because he believed the blacksmith had done a lot for his people in the past. He treated the boys with two plants of the Eupatorium family, Joe Pye and boneset, and the children lived. But that decision to help the White blacksmith cost Joe Pye his family and his people. The Stockbridge Indians were being forcibly removed to Wisconsin to make room for more European settlers. That removal, understandably, caused a good deal of resentment among the Indians who were being deported and divested of their land. They were taken to Wisconsin in the dead of winter and deposited on land that belonged to the Menominee. It was just lucky for them that the Menominee pitied them and allowed them to live and even gave them a part of Menominee land to live on. The band is still in Wisconsin, where it is called the Stockbridge Munsee.[20]

His own people left Joe Pye behind in New York State when they were forced out because they said, "If you like these Whites so much you can just stay with them."

As his family was leaving, the old man gave his grandchildren a bag to carry with them. They said, "Oh, Grandfather, we have too much to carry as it is. We can't take anymore."

But Joe Pye said, "It is very light and won't take much to carry it." The bag was full of the seeds of the Joe Pye, which the grandfather asked them to scatter on their journey, whenever they went through a wet or swampy area that the plants would like. He said, "When I follow you, I will just look for this plant. Then I will know you passed this way."

Of course, he and they knew he would never be able to follow them in this life, but his grandchildren took the seeds, sowing them on the journey, and it is true that the growth of the Joe Pye stretches all the way from Stockbridge, Massachusetts, right to Wisconsin where the People were taken. Joe Pye may not have been able to follow, but his plant is still here for his people to use as he used it.

Keewaydinoquay drew a poster of Joe Pye that we always gave as a handout when she taught this unit. She called Joe Pye the "First American Martyr to the Concept of Professional Ethics." She loved the idea that the plant that a medicine man had used for healing was called by his name. She always thought it a good idea that healers should be so honored.

20 For those interested in Stockbridge Munsee history, see Lowe 2001, 113-24. The story about Joe Pye is not included in this text.

Joe Pye's plant is a very showy, tall swamp plant. It always grows where it can keep its feet in water, at the edge of a swamp or in a wet meadow. The flowers are on the tops of the stalks in a cluster, and they can be any color from light pink to a deep purplish shade. They can grow up to six or even eight feet tall if they have a nice situation.

Keewaydinoquay usually called this plant Joe Pye to honor Zhopai,[21] but she also liked the English common name of gravel-root, because it acknowledges the chief virtue that this plant has to share with us. Gravelroot has the ability to break down and expel stones that form in a human body. It will dissolve kidney and bladder and gallstones, too. Kee always said it was not necessary to have an operation to have these stones removed if one has access to Joe Pye and the knowledge to use it. One can take the plant as an infusion or a decoction or even in capsule form. The chemical that has the ability to dissolve and remove the stones is in the whole plant, but it is less concentrated in the stems, foliage, and flowers and more concentrated in the root; therefore one decides which part of the plant to use in a particular situation according to the distress of the patient. If possible, one uses a tea of the foliage first and saves the root decoction for a more serious or stubborn case. She said that the root decoction will expel the stones so forcefully that one can actually hear the stones hitting the bed pan of the patient or the porcelain of the toilet. She said she had heard it as forceful as gunfire. In a situation that severe, one would have to warn the patient that the expulsion of the stones would be very painful, and there might even be blood; but, after the initial treatment, this blessed plant has the ability to prevent the problem from happening to the person again. A tea infusion of the foliage and flowers could be drunk daily at first, then every other day or even once weekly after awhile, as a preventative that would keep the person from ever having to experience the intense pain of the stones again.

Kee said that after one treats the condition, one then has to find out why it was that he or she had developed stones in the first place, as it is not a usual condition for the human body. One should look at his or her diet. From where was the excess calcium coming? Was the person eating too much dairy? Dairy products combined with grease can create the problem. Or was the person eating too little acid? Acid breaks down calcium and keeps it from developing into stones. That glass of orange juice in the morning has more value to the diet than just vitamin C. Was the person

21 Zhopai is Kee's spelling.

drinking water that was too hard? To ascertain this one looks in one's teakettle. Is it caked with calcium buildup? In severe cases, bottled water that came from an area of softer water might be safer. Kee always maintained that prevention was better than a cure.

The other great gift Joe Pye has to share with us is when it is used in combination with the other Eupatorium cousin, boneset, a plant that Nodjimahkwe called "Shield and Lance Plant." The plant is called that because the leaves appear to be pierced by the stalk. What appears to be one leaf grows out from both sides of the stalk for all the world as if it had been thrust through by a lance. This growth pattern makes it very easy to positively identify this plant and keeps one from confusing it with other white and off-white flowers.

Keewaydinoquay said that the boneset's chief virtue is that it is a specific for the periosteum tissue[22] around the outside of a bone. When a bone is broken, this tissue may be cut. For the bone to regrow properly, this tissue has to be mended, and this plant helps the body do that.

When my husband broke his leg, while I was working for Kee, she gave him a quart jar of dried boneset and equisetum that she told him to drink as a tea three times a day.[23] He drank the stuff, although it has a particularly strong taste. My husband actually liked the taste of the tea because, when he was a drinking man, he had always preferred gin and bitters and he claimed the boneset and equisetum tea was very reminiscent of that drink. I tasted it once and resolved to be very careful of my own bones to avoid the necessity of drinking the stuff myself.

I really noticed that the odor went through my husband rather dramatically. When he went in to his doctor a week after the accident, to finally have the leg put into a cast,[24] his doctor had a hard time actually finding the break on the new x-ray.

He said, "What have you been doing since I saw you last week?"

Bob said, "I sat in a reclining chair with my leg up as you told me to do, and I drank a tea that my wife's grandmother told me to drink." The doctor would not have had to ask if he had been familiar with boneset, because a person could not help smelling the plant as soon as my husband entered a room. But, smell or not, it is a blessed plant, and my Bob has two strong legs now on which he has walked thousands of miles since that accident.

Keewaydinoquay also credited boneset with having mended her leg when she broke it the winter she spent alone on Minis-kitigaan. She had been forced to set the leg herself, and she

22 The term I have in my notes for this tissue is "sclerotic tissue," but my doctor son-in-law says that the sclerotic is the scar tissue that forms on the periosteum tissue when a bone is broken.

23 Kee gave Bob equisetum that she had picked herself, so she was sure of its safety, but in a similar situation I would probably use boneset mixed with dried stinging nettles. Nettles are a wonderful source of calcium. Nettles are readily available and impossible to mistake for a problematic plant, although care must be taken when harvesting nettles if one is to avoid their sting. Use gloves, and hang the nettles to dry so that their problematic sting will be gone. Do not touch them with naked skin.

24 For the full story of why it took a week to set Bob's broken leg, see the section on Equisetum.

said she drank all of the dried boneset she had stored in her cabin. As soon as she could hobble about using a tree limb for a crutch, she all but stripped the island of boneset plants. After that she spent the rest of her life trying to reseed her island with boneset, to repay the debt she had incurred to the plant in her need. Her friends and former students would send her envelopes of boneset seed, which she would then take out to her island to scatter in places she thought boneset would like. She was a woman who repaid her debts.

Nodjimahkwe used shield and lance plant for all broken bones. She would both have the patient drink the tea and she would also poultice the area with the plant for a time before she put the bone in a cast. She always taught Kee to use a plant externally as well as internally whenever possible. She said such external application often helped immeasurably in the actual cure.

European herbals often say that this plant is called boneset because it helps in a severe fever, dengue, called in the South "bonebreak fever." In such a fever a person shakes and thrashes so much that they are said to be in danger of breaking their bones.

Our Anishinaabe people also give this plant for a fever that often comes after a person breaks a bone or in connection with severe influenzas and typhoid. Both boneset and Joe Pye are diaphoretics, and will help a person sweat out a fever. For that cure one mixes dried boneset half and half with Joe Pye, to be taken as a tea, an infusion, or a decoction for a more serious case or dried, pulverized, and put into a capsule if the person gags on the taste and refuses the cure in liquid form.

There is another Eupatorium cousin that Keewaydinoquay always taught about in this unit of her ethnobotany classes. But this cousin is the black sheep of the family. It is *Eupatorium rugosum*, which has the English common name of white snake-root. Kee, of course, refused to call it white snakeroot, not because it was an insult to the plant, but because it would be an insult to the poor snakes to associate them with this plant.

This plant will poison any mammal who eats it, and they may well die of it, too. The only way to get the poison out of the system is in mother's milk. Only a lactating female would survive, but the poison will be excreted in the milk, and the baby who drinks that milk will die. A male or a non-lactating female would not live. Because this is true of any mammal, human beings are in danger from this poisoning through cow's milk if the cow has eaten this plant. In human beings such poisoning is called milk sickness. The mother of Abraham Lincoln died of it when he was seven years old.[25] This was a deadly and misunderstood illness until Dr. Anna Pierce identified its cause in 1830. Actually, the credit should go to a native medicine woman, whom Pierce identifies only as "Aunt Shawnee," as Pierce says that this woman showed her "white snake root" and explained its connection to milk sickness (Duffy 1990, quoted in Coffey 1993, 239).

Louis Pasteur's little sister died of milk sickness, too, and that was the reason he became so interested in finding means of making milk a safer product. Pasteurization does not remove the poison of *Eupatorium rugosum,* but it does help make our milk supply safer from the poison of this plant because, in the pasteurization process, the milk of many cows is put all together. If one cow has eaten the plant, a full dose will not be in a glass of milk one buys in the store. That is one of the reasons it is unsafe to drink unpasteurized milk from a small farm, as many people were doing in the 1970s and 1980s, when Kee was teaching. She always warned her classes about this danger.

Kee said that, before she came to Wisconsin to teach, she had thought that this was one plant that Wisconsin, being the "Dairy State," would have long since eradicated. She actually made provision for a farm family in Michigan to pick and send her samples of *Eupatorium rugosum* so that she could show her students here what the plant looked like. But it grows all over our state. It is a very common "weed" and is even in city gardens and planted in flower beds as an ornamental. Kee could always find a plant to show her students, usually on quick trip across the campus or on a city street as she walked to class.

One of Kee's Anishinaabe students was going to buy a farm to use to raise horses. After hearing Kee's lecture on *Eupatorium rugosum* he went to the people who were in the process of selling him their farm and told them his teacher had told him about this plant and asked them did they know anything about it.

They said, "Oh, ya, that is the reason we have that double fence around that area in the back of the barn."

The student said, "But you knew I wanted to raise horses on that land. Why didn't you tell me that plant was growing there?"

They said, "Well, we didn't think you would buy the land if you knew that plant was growing there." They were right! He did not!

[25] For more information on the history of milk sickness see Relda E. Niederhofer's article cited in the Bibliography.

Omakakiibag
Yellow or Brown Jewelweed, Touch-me-not
Spotted Jewelweed or Spotted Touch-me-not
Impatiens capensis

Pale Jewelweed or Pale Touch-me-not
Impatiens pallida

Animikiibag
Doodamakiibag
Maji-aniibiish
Poison Ivy
Toxicodendron radicans
[formerly *Rhus radicans* or *Rhus toxicodendron*][26]

26 U.S. Forest Service website.

It is an ancient Midewiwin teaching that for every problem humankind may have in this life there is a plant that can help. We may not know the answer to every one of our discomforts and problems, but, in the Beginning Time, Creator foresaw our future needs and built the answer into the fabric of the world. We may not know at this time what it is, but the answer exists. We may have forgotten it, but the answer exists. We may not know it yet, but the answer exists. Some plant somewhere can help with any problem a human can have in this life. A very good example of that ancient teaching is embodied in the relationship between the plants we call poison ivy and the ones called jewelweed or touch-me-not. The problem created by the one is answered and relieved by the other.

Everyone who goes into the woods or the wilds or even into the neighborhood parks on this continent needs to know about poison ivy. Few people grow old enough to read a book such as this without having been shown this plant or at least have heard about this plant from a parent, a Scout leader, or a teacher. The well-known saying "Leaflets three, let it be" is probably the best-known plant identification rhyme in existence; but people should also be taught "Leaflets five, let it survive," because people often mistake the harmless Virginia creeper, *Parthenocissus quinquefolia* for poison ivy (Crockett 1977, 61). Kee said that teaching people to know the plant by observation of its growth pattern is a far better way to keep them from getting a poison ivy rash than to just frighten them away from the natural world.

Keewaydinoquay also said that there was a real need for a plant book that made distinctions for the general public about poisonous plants. She said if one opened any poison-plant book on the market one would find poison ivy and poison sumac and poison oak listed. All of those plants will give one a rash, but unless one actually eats them or breathes in their smoke, they are not likely to kill a person. There is a big difference in a plant that will give a person a rash for a few days or weeks at most and a plant that will kill one dead the way *Eupatorium rugosum* or water hemlock, *Cicuta maculata,* will. We need a plant book that makes such distinctions on toxicity and a lot more research on poisonous plants in general.

The smoke of burning poison ivy is a great danger to forest firefighters. The poisonous resins of the plant can become volatile and airborne in thick, sooty smoke, enough to give a person a rash if that smoke touches them. It can, if breathed in, give a person the rash internally, which can be fatal. There is a vaccine on the market to keep a person from contracting poison ivy, but the drug companies have not as yet made more than is needed every year to vaccinate forest firefighters, so the general public cannot buy the vaccine.

NEVER burn poison ivy in your yard! While wearing gloves and long sleeves, pull up the plant before it flowers and bears fruit, and put it in a bag; then put the bag in the garbage to be taken off to a landfill where it can be buried under a ton of garbage and earth. Composting the leaves is not a good idea, either, as one might just be assuring it a nice home to grow in next season. But whatever you do, do not burn it!

However, that being stated upfront, poison ivy and its cousins are really just an annoyance that can be handled either by minimizing the risk of contracting the rash or by helping to alleviate the symptoms after the fact. The solution is jewelweed.

If one is walking in the woods and suddenly realizes that he or she has been walking through a healthy stand of poison ivy, here is what to do. Look around. Many, many times one will find a stand of jewelweed growing very near the spot where one has encountered the poison ivy. It is almost as if it has been placed right there for a person to use to get rid of the possibility of

Omakakiibag: Impatiens
capensis (*Impatiens pallida*)

contracting the rash. It is a visual example of the ancient Midewiwin teaching described at the beginning of this chapter. Grab
a handful of the jewelweed, hopefully after putting down kinnikinnick or asemaa and asking the plant to send its spirit along to
help you in your time of need. Crush the stems of the jewelweed
plant and use them as a wipe to wash down your legs and feet or
your hands or any other exposed part of your flesh. The stems of
the jewelweed are succulent and full of a golden liquid that will
just wash away the oil of the poison ivy.

If one does not see jewelweed growing nearby, wash the
exposed skin with hot, soapy water. We used to use a good strong
soap for this. Fels Naphtha was a soap that most homes had
around in former times for laundry, but it works wonders on
getting the poison ivy oils off of one's skin, too.

It is a good idea for a person to get out of his or her clothes as
soon as possible. Wash them by themselves in hot, soapy water in
a clothes washer to get rid of the oils that could reinfect a person
if he or she comes in contact with them later. Many people have
forgotten about the original patch of poison ivy, or even not

Animikiibag: Poison Ivy
(*Toxicodendron radicans*)

known that they had walked through such a patch, and given themselves the rash when they picked up their dirty socks on the floor of the bathroom after their shower. Those pesky oils! People have gotten a rash after touching clothes that were infected with poison ivy a whole year before.

If one's dog has walked through the same patch of poison ivy, grab more jewelweed and wipe him all over with it; then give him a bath, preferably while wearing gloves, as soon as possible. I knew a young, newly married couple who had their dog in bed with them after he had come in from a walk in the woods where he must have encountered poison ivy. The oils on his fur got onto their bed sheets. That couple developed the rash in some extremely painful spots!

If all of the cautions above have not helped and one develops the rash anyway, jewelweed can help with that as well. One can crush fresh jewelweed and dab the juice on the rash, or one can bind the crushed plant material against the sores with a light bandage. If one does not have access to fresh jewelweed one can keep and use the juice in one of two ways. First, one can extract the juice or crush the plant material and make it into an infusion by pouring boiling water over it; then one freezes the juice or infusion into ice cubes and stores them in a plastic bag in the freezer. Some people find this cure very soothing on a poison ivy rash.

Second, one could make and keep the medicine in the jewelweed by the means taught to me by Keewaydinoquay. One picks a quantity of jewelweed, the whole plant except for the root, in late August or early September, when the plant has had a chance to flower and produce viable seed. One knows when it is ready to pick when the seed pods on the plant pop and fly apart when one brushes against them. If one takes the plant at that time, one is actually helping the jewelweed in that area because one will be scattering the seed for the next season's growth while taking the plants. Otherwise, the plants will have to hope a deer or a rabbit or some other person brushes against it to release the seeds.

Take the plants home and smash them up. This is a time when a nice, smooth rock comes in handy. If rocks are just too "primitive" for a person, use a hand or a potato masher or a hammer, but pulverize the fibers of the stalk as much as possible. Put the crushed plant into a clear plastic bag and tie it shut. Hang the bag in the sun for the rest of the day. I always hang it on a diagonal to the ground so that there is a corner of the bag for the juice to accumulate. Take the bag in at night when the sun is no longer on it, as it will only drip when the sun is warming the bag. Pour or siphon off the golden yellow juice that has accumulated at the bottom of the bag. Measure the liquid and put it into a clean jar with an equal amount of rubbing alcohol. The next morning, hang the bag and the plant material back in the sun for the day. One can usually do this for three days running. One knows when it is finished when the juice is no longer the clear, sweet-smelling jewelweed juice that it was at the beginning. When it begins to get cloudy or smells "off," take the material out and place it in a clean spot out-of-doors. Do not forget to say "Thank you" for the medicine when doing this. Then one filters the jewelweed liquid that has been mixed with alcohol through cheesecloth or a coffee filter to remove any solids or sediments at the bottom of the jar. Allow the filtered liquid to sit for a night on the kitchen counter. In the morning, a fine white sediment may have accumulated at the bottom of the jar. Use a meat baster or an eye dropper or pipette to remove the clear liquid on the top, being careful not to take the cloudy sediment at the bottom. One might want to do this, allowing the liquid to settle and then removing the clear, for a few more days, just to be sure that the liquid is as clear as possible. This will help the medicine keep longer, as molds will not start to grow as quickly if the sediment is removed. Label the bottle with contents and date it. It is very easy to accumulate odd bottles of liquids around the house if one does not make a habit of labeling the medicines as soon as one makes them.

This liquid made from jewelweed is very helpful for poison ivy, poison sumac, poison oak, and stinging-nettle rashes. It is also soothing and healing on other kinds of allergic rashes, too. It is an antifungal medicine that will help to clear up athlete's foot, ringworm, or similar fungal infections. This is a medicine that usually will not hurt and often helps very much.

One will want to renew one's supply of the jewelweed tincture once a year if possible, but I have found that it still works if one has to keep it longer than that due to a bad growing season or because one has just missed the harvest time for one reason or another. But, for maximum strength, it is a good medicinal to renew as often as possible.

Some folk-medicine systems tell a person to drink jewelweed infusion as a tea to keep oneself from developing poison ivy, but that was not a part of Keewaydinoquay's Anishinaabe teachings. I had it in my notes, and underlined, too: "Do Not Ever Drink jewelweed!" I remember asking Kee about that, because some books even say that jewelweed can be used as a potherb and emergency food.

I said, "Is it just because the medicine we make uses rubbing alcohol? Couldn't a person use vodka and make it safe to use internally?"

She told me she did not know why, but that was what Nodji-mahkwe had told her. Kee said, "Don't think about it. Just don't drink it."

But, of course, I continued to worry about it until I found the Peterson guide entry on Western Jewelweed, *Impatiens noli-tangere* or *Impatiens occidentalis,* which is said to be a "closely related to and used interchangeably with the more eastern Common Jewelweed (I.capensis) . . . WARNING: Do not use internally. It is potentially toxic, especially when fresh." (Foster and Hobbs, *A Field Guide to Western Medicinal Plants and Herbs* [Boston: Houghton Mifflin Co., 2002], 118). So, do use this medicine on the skin, just do not drink it.

My eldest daughter, Makoons, has asked me what we did before we had plastic bags to make the jewelweed medicine. I asked the same question of Keewaydinoquay when she taught me, and I bet she asked Nodjimahkwe the same question eighty years ago, too. Kee told me they made this medicine in canning jars in the 1920s. I do not know what Nodjimahkwe told Keewaydino-quay when she asked this question about the pre–canning jar days.

What is necessary is to heat the plant material very gently so that the liquid will seep out of the stems. A canning jar would work as well as the plastic bag method, and so would a covered makak placed in the sun. In the old days, when our people did not have alcohol, such medicines were routinely made and preserved with vinegar. We made vinegar from apples and from sumac for this purpose and for use in cooking, but people undoubtedly adopted store-bought items as soon as they had access to them, as the making of home products like homemade vinegar was time-consuming. I suspect that the medicine in jewelweed was one that the Gete-Anishinaabeg utilized in its fresh condition most times, as one would hardly need the cure when the season for poison ivy was over for the year, and when the next season of poison ivy leaves were lurking, the fresh jewelweed would be up again and available. The medicine for use on fungal infections such as athlete's foot or ringworm could as easily have been made using animal fat, and bear grease was widely used for such skin preparations. The fat would have done a great deal to have pre-served the plant material, and it would have been a good vehicle for holding the plant material and its chemicals against the skin.

If I ever had to make this particular medicine without modern plastic bags and meat basters, coffee filters, and rubbing alcohol, I think I would experiment using a vinegar-based liquid or a fat-based one using whatever fat was available, either vegetable or animal. It is the plant that is the cure. All we have to do is adapt the method of preserving and utilizing the healing that was placed in the plant for us to use. One adapts to the times and the situation if one has the fundamental teaching that tells one what plant to use for what problem. As Kee would have said, "Blessed be the plants."

Poison ivy and its cousin plants are an annoyance to humans and many people are prone to the philosophy of "if it hurts us we should just eradicate it." But, although we do not usually appreciate poison ivy, that does not mean that it is not a very valuable plant to our Elder Brothers. Many animals and birds love poison ivy. I knew a hunter who swore that he always waited for deer near parts of the woods where he knew there was poison ivy. He claimed deer eat it, and it was as good a lure for them as a stack of apples. And many songbirds, including robins and cedar wax-wings, seem to relish the white berries of poison ivy, which they will actually swarm to get at. And one must admit that there really are few plants as pretty as a poison ivy that has been touched by the frost and has changed to its beautiful orange and flame-red autumn colors. We may not know why Creator did and does any of the things Creator did and does, but Creator is always right!

The Monarda Family
"Baby-Saver Plant"
Wild Bergamot
Monarda fistulosa

Aamoogaawanzh
Bee Balm
Oswego Tea
Monarda didyma

~~~~~~

The Monarda family is absolutely beautiful. The two plants of this family that Keewaydinoquay gave me the knowledge of are two of the most beautiful flowers imaginable, capable of rivaling or surpassing in beauty any other flower, domestic or wild. Baby-Saver Plant, or wild bergamot, has a delicate purple to violet–colored flower, while the bee balm's flower is fire-engine red. Both plants have their bright, showy flowers at the top of their stems. They are the delight of bees and butterflies and beetles, and the red bee balm is a particular favorite of hummingbirds.

Keewaydinoquay encouraged her students to call these two plants by their scientific names, *Monarda fistulosa* and *Monarda didyma,* to avoid confusion, because she said the common names were just too common. Many plants are called "bee balm," and wild bergamot is not a bergamot. Bergamot is *Citrus aurantium bergamia,* a small Mediterranean citrus tree from which oil of bergamot is produced (Coffey 1993, 205). Someone just thought the *Monarda fistulosa* smelled like the oil of bergamot, and that is how it got the common name.

If one is going to call them by common names, Kee preferred "Oswego Tea" for *Monarda didyma,* because it is acknowledgment of the native people of New York State who used this tea traditionally as a beverage and taught its use to colonial settlers. Kee always preferred to acknowledge any Indian association with particular plants because they were given to our ancestors here on Turtle Island. For *Monarda fistulosa,* Kee preferred the name "Baby-Saver Plant," because that name acknowledges the primary virtue this plant has had to share with the Anishinaabeg.

"Baby-Saver Plant": Wild
Bergamot (*Monarda fistulosa*)

The scientific name Monarda is in acknowledgment of the
physician and botanist Nicholas Monardes, a Spaniard and court
physician of Philip II who published the first book in Europe
on the plants of the "new found world." His book, *Joyfull Newes
out of the newe founde Worlde,* was translated and published in
English in 1577 (Coffey 1993, 204). Kee always thought it was
good to acknowledge the people who spent their lives studying
plants. I remember her wistfully saying she had been looking for
a new plant all of her life, but in vain. The person who finds a
plant new to science usually has the honor of naming the plant,
or they have the plant named after them. I would have liked to see
a scientific name of Something-genus keewayinoquayana or even
Keewaydinoquay something-species.

The Monardas are mints, but they are classed in a genus
together and called "Horse Mints." When a plant name or plant
family name has the word "horse" in it, it usually does not mean
that it is a particular favorite of horses, nor does it mean that
people use it for a horse medicine. It means that the plants in
question are large or that they are of a coarse growth pattern.

Aamoogaawanzh: Bee Balm
(*Monarda didyma*)

Monardas are called "Horse Mints" because they are much larger
than the other mints and often have thicker, coarser, hairy leaves
and stems.

Both Oswego Tea and Baby-Saver Plant have very distinctive
flavors and strong tastes. Baby-Saver is said to resemble the taste
of true bergamot, which is the flavoring in the fine English
blended drink Earl Grey tea, in which true bergamot oil is used to
flavor Asian black tea. The flavor to a true tea drinker is different,
however, and perhaps our Baby-Saver Plant mixed with black tea
would be best described as "Mr. Grey" instead of Earl Grey, being,
after all, a distinctly North American, not a British, drink. To use
either of the plants for a recreational tea, one can use any of the
upper foliage or the flower. They make very tasty teas that are
mild stimulants. Since they are rather strong-tasting compared to
other herbal teas, they can be made to substitute for Asian teas,
as they often were by colonial Europeans as well as Anishinaabeg
in times when it was difficult to obtain Asian tea. Oswego Tea is
one of several native plants that were used by those colonists who

refused the British tax on Asian tea, the unfortunate movement that resulted in the Boston Tea Party and the war that followed.

Both plants have long histories of being used in medicines.[27] Their strong flavors have been used successfully to mask more unpleasant herbal medicinals and also to enliven blah-tasting ones. Keewaydinoquay taught her University classes to use *Monarda didyma*, Oswego Tea, as a recreational drink and to keep the *Monarda fistulosa*, wild bergamot, for medicine. *Monarda fistulosa*'s principle gift that it has to share with the People is its help for colicky babies. In her classes Kee told her students to make a light-tasting tea of *Monarda fistulosa* to soothe children with infantile colic, where, for no apparent reason, a young baby starts to cry every day at about 4:00 P.M. for an hour or so at a time. Such children scream and scream and, typically, will not be comforted. They scream and turn bright red and bring their little legs up to their bellies and clench their tiny fists, and they cry. The behavior often starts soon after birth and may continue until a child is three or even four months old. It can be a very trying time for both the new babe and the new parents as well. A bottle of warm Baby-Saver tea will often calm such children very effectively. This tea has probably saved a lot of children over the years. Infant colic is not a fatal condition in itself, unless it drives the parents to madness, which has happened.

27 *Monarda fistulosa* has been an officially recognized drug by both the Anishinaabeg and by the United States Dispensatory, from 1882 to 1950, and the National Formulary since 1950 (Hart 1976, 138).

Ozaawijiibik

Giizisoomashkiki
Goldthread
Mouth Root
Canker Root
Coptis groenlandica
Coptis trifolia
[Both scientific names are applicable.]

~~~~~~

When I was the teaching assistant for Keewaydinoquay's ethnobotany class, *nindaanisag,* my daughters, were young children. My youngest, Pukwanis, was a toddler. One fall she became very ill with flu, and she was slow recovering. At the end of that illness she developed a severe case of mouth sores, canker sores, on the inner sides of her lips and throughout her mouth, and down her throat, too. Because her mouth was sore, she refused food for several days running, a very unusual condition for Pukwanis. I had a tough time even getting her to drink water, and I offered her any of her favorite drinks. After a few days of that, she was noticeably thin, and her cheeks were sunken in. Her pediatrician was really no help at all. He just concluded that she would eat when she was hungry enough.

I mentioned the above to Kee while working with her in the office one afternoon. She was appalled that a little child's doctor would be so callous when the child was getting noticeably thin. She reached into her desk drawer and pulled out a jar of golden, dried plant material and filled an envelope with it. She instructed me to make an infusion of about 1 tablespoon of the plant and to get Pukwanis to hold it in her mouth. She then sent me home and told me to see to her namesake before I came back to work again.

I always did exactly what the Old One told me to do. I had never known her to be wrong. So I jumped on the next bus that went south to my home, and cooked up the infusion by pouring boiling water over the root and allowing it to sit until the liquid was as golden as the root had been. While I waited for the infusion to cool, I cooked my family's supper. I remember, for

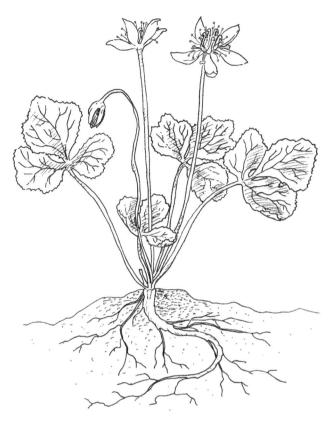

Ozaawijiibik: Goldthread
(*Coptis groenlandica*)

some odd reason, that I made mashed potatoes, Polish sausage, and corn. When the infusion was cooled, and after I had filtered out the roots, I took a small glass of the liquid to Pukwanis. I told her I wanted her to take it in her mouth and swish it around before she drank it. Being she was a trusting babe, she did as I asked, but tears filled her eyes, and she spat the liquid out almost immediately. But then she jumped up and ran into the kitchen where I had laid the supper out on the table. She sat down and ate the first meal she had had in a week, with two portions of mashed potatoes.

I have very seldom in my life seen so instantaneous a healing. My principle problem, of getting her to eat, was solved, but the sores remained, and Pukwanis was leery of the infusion after that. She flatly refused to open her mouth if I had a glass of it in my hand. So, I resorted to mommy-stratagem. I got an atomizer bottle, the kind used to mist hair, and I put the liquid in it. Because it was a novelty, Pukwanis allowed me to mist her mouth, gums, and the sores several times a day after that. It must have minimized the bad taste because she allowed the application. After only a day of spraying her mouth with the tea, the sores were noticeably better, and they were gone within three days.

The plant that Kee had given us was goldthread. It is a little wet woodland plant that is happiest growing around and in sphagnum moss and in bogs and cedar swamps, although one can also sometimes find it in wet woods. Its three-part leaves grow up from the ground on a single thread-thin leafstalk. Goldthread is a tiny plant, and tall ones are no more than six inches high. The leaves remind me of a wild strawberry or large, ragged-leafed clovers. When I think I have found goldthread I dig down to find the roots. If I have the right plant, the roots are a surefire identification because they are a very vivid gold.

Goldthread is a very small plant, and the roots, the only part of the plant that one uses, are almost as thin as a hair, so it does take a while to gather and clean them. In the nineteenth century goldthread was a much-abused plant when it was a popular one sold in drugstores. The Shakers, a Christian sect that lived in religious communes in the east, are said to have paid "very well" for the roots of goldthread. There is an account of families gathering whole wagonloads of the plants and roots to sell to them (Coffey 1993, 15–16). I have gathered goldthread many times, and I cannot even imagine how much goldthread it would take to fill a wagon with the dried plant. I bet those families all but stripped the swamps of the plant to have gotten that much, and since it is such a tiny plant, they must have netted about two bucks for the summer's work as well. Unbelievable! This beautiful, bountiful land has suffered so much under colonists' "care"!

Besides being a help to people with sores like the ones Pukwanis had in her mouth, goldthread is also used for teething babies, ones with thrush, and for tooth problems of older people. Keewaydinoquay had trouble with her teeth all the time I knew her. She swore by goldthread for taking down the inflammation and pain of even abscessed teeth. That was the reason she had the goldthread in her desk drawer to send home with me for my daughter. She often had a piece of it in her mouth.

I had occasion to use goldthread myself for infected teeth. I found that if I kept a piece of the root, about an inch or two in length, in my mouth between my cheek and the gum beside an abscessed tooth, it really helped both with the pain and with the swelling until I could get to my dentist. My dentist was a saint who had been taking care of my teeth for years, and he did not even bat an eye the first time he pulled a piece of goldthread out of my mouth before he started to work on my tooth. He was, however, glad to be told it was a root that our people used to treat such conditions; he told me later that he had at first been afraid it was some kind of a golden worm. Goldthread placed against the gum in such a condition really helps with the pain. I think it is even better for an abscess than cloves. I had used cloves all my life for cavities or when a filling would fall out, but even though cloves will numb a tooth, they will not take down the swelling. Goldthread does do that very well.

Goldthread has another virtue to share with Anishinaabeg. An infusion or a decoction of the root will remove mucus from the body in a rather dramatic way. One has to be careful when giving it to a child, and one would only give a child a light infusion and not a decoction for this purpose, because a child might actually choke when a mucus plug is loosened too quickly. It will clean out sinuses and lungs and all of the area in between rather rapidly. One can drink the decoction or infusion, or put it in a mister and spray it into the nostrils or throat. Be warned, however, that it has a strong taste.

Goldthread can be gathered at any time of the year because it is an evergreen. One could just push back the snow and scoop out a handful of sphagnum that has goldthread growing in it. It is, however, always easier to pick medicinals in the summer sunshine and just keep them dried for winter use, rather than having to take a pick or ax to chip them out of the frozen swamp.

Waawiyebagoon, Violets (*Viola spp.*)

American Dog Violet
Viola conspera

Common Blue Violet
Viola sororia[28]

Canada Violet
Viola canadensis

28 Because of disagreements on classifications, many botanists are now lumping many blue violets under the species *Viola sororia* (Tekiela 2000, 23).

When the snows of winter and those of spring finally melt in my backyard, and this can be rather late in the season as I live in swampland where the cold ground keeps our snow long after it is gone from the rest of the area, my lawn greens up very quickly. The year I was writing this chapter the grass was up and green within a week of the last snow. And immediately thereafter (actually three days later; I timed it), the violets were up, too. The first few violet flowers were very tiny and huddled almost as if for warmth down among their heart-shaped leaves. But within a week the whole host of violets that cover my yard this time of year were up and opened. The lawn, which had been the vivid yellow-green of new grass the day before, was awash with purple-blue. The violets are up! It must be spring!

In the long-ago time of the Gete-Anishinaabeg, the violets were also welcome as they are today. The sudden burst of color of the new grass with the nestled violets must have been as welcome to our ancestors as it is to us. The winter in our climate is so very white and dull gray, with only the deep greens of the conifers to lighten the eye and the spirit. The sudden burst of the spring yellow-green-blue-purples is a tonic to the eye and the soul, now as much as ever it was in the past.

I always try to catch the violets' return somehow. One year I found a needlepoint pattern and tried to capture the purple-blue of the violets in a pair of needlepoint earrings for my daughter Makoons. Another year I found a wool that approximated the violets' color so that I could sit in the backyard among the violets and knit a pair of mitts. I wore those mitts all of the next winter.

Waawiyebagoon: Violets (*Viola spp.*)

They always reminded me of spring, and that made them warmer somehow. When I was writing my master's thesis, "Anishinaabe Gikendaasowin and What I Have Learned from Ducks," during violet season, I sat outside in the grass among the violets and watched my flock of ducks; then I wrote about how they and I relish the brief violet days. This year I am writing this violet chapter as my tribute to the season. The only trouble with trying to capture the violet time the way I have in the past is that it is hard to complete the project due to the distraction of the violets. Violet time is so short that I find myself hastening the craft to be sure I have the time to capture the violets themselves. Violets are very tasty, so tasty in fact that they call me away from my preservation task to eat them while they are still to be had.

After I wrote the above lines, my computer crashed. I could not get into my files nor onto the Internet for a whole week, until my daughter came home and succeeded in fixing the system. It was almost as if I was being given the opportunity to get away from my writing to enjoy the short violet days of spring. So I did just that. I got a handful of kinnikinnick and a measuring cup from the kitchen, and I went out and gathered violets. I made salads for suppers and omelets with violets for breakfasts and a big batch of violet syrup to take into the rest of the year. Violet time is so very short and so very sweet that I wish I could thank my computer for deciding we should both take a break to celebrate the season.

Violets grow over most of the planet's land surfaces, with the exception of the polar regions and the oceans. There are listed approximately 22 genera and 900 different species in the Violaceae or violet family (Niering 1979, 817; Coffey 1993, 73). There are violets growing across Europe and Asia and the Americas and Africa, although the plant we call the African violet (*Saintpaulia ionantha*) is not really a member of the family. There are at least 80 different species in North America alone (Tekiela 2000, 23).

Kee always said no one had told the violets that they were supposed to stay within their various scientific classifications, so they are out in the field merrily crossing and recrossing with each other in happy abandon. One can often find blue and purple and white and different shades, combinations and variations of the above, all growing happily together in the same field. She thought it unlikely that our early Anishinaabeg ancestors really cared about such things and, with only a few exceptions, one can just feel free to utilize the virtues that the violets have to share with us by taking the ones that grow nearby. She did caution, however, against the use of yellow violets for food or medicine as they can be a problem, making some people sick to their stomachs. Since the yellow violets are also much rarer than the common blue or purple-blue ones, she thought they should not be used. She also thought that the bird's-foot violet, which has a leaf that looks like a fan or a splayed bird's foot, were far too endangered and rare to use. She said that there were so many of the other more common violets free for the taking that one should just pass by the more exotic ones.

The violets are so beautiful in fact that a person may feel bad about picking them for pleasure or medicine or food, but one should not worry. One can feel free to take as many violet flowers as one could possibly wish in the spring, because the beautiful flowers have nothing to do with the well-being of the violet plant or the species. Unlike most other flowers, the violets are not beautiful to attract bees and to entice the insects to pollinate the plants. Violets are self-pollinating. In many places, the violets also blossom before the bee season begins, so the nectar in the violet flowers is not there for the bees. The beautiful violet flowers of spring are really just for show. Or perhaps they are just the violets' way of sharing their virtues with the rest of creation, as their ancestors were told to do in the Beginning Time by Creator.

In late summer or in the autumn the violets will bloom again, but the flowers of the late bloom are small and without petals or scent and hidden under the leaves of the plant. Those are the ones that produce the seed, if the violet even bothers to produce seed at all, and they do not do so in many areas. In very warm climates the spring flowers may develop seed, but they usually do not in our climate.

Violets depend on runners to see to the continuance of their species. As soon as the plants have finished with their burst of color in the spring, they send out runners that are capable of taking over large areas very quickly. They put down roots from the running scions, and new plants grow up at a distance from the "parent" clone plant. The really nice thing about this arrangement is that the Anishinaabe medicine person can feel free to take all of the spring violets that she wishes without being afraid that she is harming the balance. The violets are gifting us and, as with any gifting relationship, it is rude to refuse a gift!

Violets are a lovely plant to grow on one's lawn. One has the beauty of their spring flowering and the soft leaves underfoot the rest of the growing season. Violets are very forgiving. They can be mowed and will just come back for more. Actually, mowing the violets just makes them send out more runners and concentrate on moving their kind across the rest of the lawn. Plant a clump of violets and watch them merrily run off. If one does not pour weed killer or grass fertilizers on them, the violets will provide a person's family with years of beauty and tasty food as well.

There are three plants in our area that could be confused with violets by the novice plant gatherer: larkspur (*Delphinium tricorne*), buttercup (*Ranunculus* spp.), and monkshood (*Aconitum* spp.). All three are poisonous, but the monkshood is the most dangerous. There are, however, very conspicuous differences between all of the above and violets, so a person can easily learn which plants to avoid. Buttercups are yellow, so if one does not use the yellow violets one will not end up with a buttercup instead. The larkspur has a stem with multi-flowers and leaves growing off of the stem, unlike the violets that have flowers that grow up on their own stalks from the base of the plant on the ground. The leaves are also on individual stalks coming up from the base. The violets do not have a stem the way larkspur has.

The monkshood has a flower that resembles a violet that has not unfurled. It is in a tight roll. All three of these possible lookalikes to the violets have leaves that are cut and palm-shaped, like a bird's-foot violet. The true violets have heart-shaped leaves, so if one just avoids the ones that have the leaves that resemble the bird's-foot, one will not be in danger of taking a problematic plant. It is easiest and probably safest for a novice to take violets only when they are in bloom, because then one can avoid the lookalikes entirely. Just take the blue, purple, or white-flowering violets, not the yellow, that have heart-shaped leaves, and one can be sure of the identification (Marrone 2004, 328–329).

Violets have several virtues to share with us. As an early spring food, they cannot be easily surpassed in their high vitamin content. They are rich in vitamins A and C. Several recipes are offered in the Recipes section to help people start to utilize violets in their families' diets. It is usually better to get one's vitamins in food form than in supplement form. It is tastier and a surer way than relying on manufactured tablets of dubious contents and questionable age.

Violets have a long medicinal history with people, too, beyond their role as a high-vitamin food source. They have been used by many different peoples to relieve congestion due to colds, bronchitis, and pneumonia, and the coughs that such ailments produce. A handy way to use the decongestants in violets for this purpose is to make a syrup of violets and utilize it throughout the year as a cough medicine. A standard recipe for making Violet Syrup is offered in the Recipes section, too. A person should take the syrup straight, by the teaspoonful, as needed. The same syrup can also be utilized as a very gentle laxative, so one would modify the amount given for a cough if it begins to cause loose stools.

The only part of the violet that one must be careful of using is the root. It contains a chemical that induces vomiting. In a case of poisoning where the person has not swallowed a caustic material and would not therefore be at greater risk if they vomited the material up before it was neutralized, vomiting can sometimes be a good thing. If a vomit is what is desired, the root of the violet will serve the purpose efficiently.

The violets have been sharing their virtues with mankind for a very long time. The common name "violet" comes from the *Viola,* the Latin form of the name Ione. The nymph Io or Ione caught the eye of Zeus, who changed the girl into a heifer to hide her from his jealous wife. The poor girl-cow started to cry because the grass was too harsh for her to eat, so Zeus changed her tears into violets for her to feed upon. Poor Io in cow form, despite her new exotic food, was still not happy, because she was harried by a fly sent by Hera. She ran crying over much of the world, before she found sanctuary and human form again in Egypt. There she married a king and gave birth to Zeus's child. In time Io was worshipped as Isis (Graves 1955, 57–58; Bulfinch 1964, 25–26, http://herbalmusings.com). But before she became a girl again and before she became a goddess, poor Io must have been chased a long way by the fly that Hera sent, and she must have been crying all the way, too, because the violets that came from her tears certainly have a very wide growing area.

The ancient Europeans used many of the virtues that the violets have to share. The Greeks called violets the Flowers of Aphrodite and used them in love potions. The Romans loved violets, too. They scattered the violet flowers and leaves around their dining halls and had parties to welcome the season, at which they drank a sweet wine made from violet flowers, called Violetum. Despite the fact that they enjoyed their violets as alcohol, the Romans also thought that violets had the power to dispel drunkenness. Pliny recommended wearing a garland or wreath of violets to a feast to dispel the effects of too much wine and to prevent the accompanying headaches and dizziness. The Celts used violets in a cosmetic, mixing the flowers with goat milk to beautify the face (Grieves 1931). A recipe for a skin cream using violet leaves mixed with lanolin and cocoa butter is given in the Recipes section.

In later European history the violet even played a role in political intrigue. When Napoleon surrendered to the British after his abdication in 1814, he was shipped off to imprisonment on the Isle of Elba. He told his followers that he would return to them with the violets of spring, so they referred to him in their councils and plots as "Caporal Violette." The secret followers of Napoleon wore a bunch of violets on their coats to make themselves known to each other while they awaited the return of the violets of spring and their own "Corporal Violet," too (Grieves 1931).

A reader of this chapter may be asking themselves why the authoress insists upon telling these weird little historical facts and stories when she is supposedly writing about the Anishinaabe usages of the violet. It is done because it is a traditional way of thinking about the plants. Nodjimahkwe encouraged her apprentices to tell all of the little, fun facts about the particular plants so that the whole history of the plant's association with mankind would be preserved, and Keewaydinoquay continued the practice. It helps a person see the plants as the individuals that they are. It helps one remember, too. The human mind is a wonder. No one really knows how it works. Brain researchers in the late twentieth and early twenty-first centuries are constantly coming up with new and different schematics for how we store and retrieve information. Anishinaabe belief in the use of Story as a teaching method and memory aid may just be part of the puzzle of how our brains really function. So, readers get the stories if they want the plant information from this oshkaabewis!

"Naanabozho and *Name*"[29]

~~~~~~

With the feathers of the baby Thunderbirds, Naanabozho fletched strong, straight arrows. He made them with great care because his greatest task was before him. He would hunt and kill *Name*,[30] the Guardian of the Great Lakes, and thereby he would win for himself great fame. The arrows fletched with the marvelous feathers in hand, Naanabozho walked to the shores of Gichigami, Lake Superior, where he peeled a birch tree and felled a cedar tree and proceeded to make himself a fine canoe. When the canoe was ready he climbed aboard and paddled far out into the waters of the lake.

"Hummnh," said Naanabozho to himself. "How am I to find *Name*, since he has all of this great lake in which to hide? Certainly I must get him to come to me." So Naanabozho hooked bait onto his fishing pole and let the line down into the water as he sang,

> Oh Great *Name*, Great Sturgeon!
> Oh Great *Name*, Great Sturgeon!
> Come swallow me. Here is my decoy.
> Come swallow me. Here is my decoy.

Deep down in the depth of the water, *Name* was roused from his sleep by the words of Naanabozho's song and by the rubbing of the hook against his cheek. *Name* called to Adikameg, Whitefish, and said, "Naanabozho is disturbing me, Adikameg. Please take his bobbing hook in your mouth." Adikameg did as his chief had asked and seized the line with such force that Naanabozho was forced to clutch his pole tightly as he drew the whitefish to the surface of the water.

"Bah!" cried Naanabozho. "You are not what I wished for. You are not *Name*! You are fouling my hook!" And he unhooked the whitefish and tossed him contemptuously back into the water.

Adikameg swam back to *Name*, who asked, "What did Naanabozho say?"

Adikameg said, "He said I was fouling his hook and that he wanted *Name*."

29 The events in this story come right after those in "Naanabozho and the Thunderbirds," which I have included in chapter 2, in the section on Grandfather Birch. Traditionally these stories are either told in order, in a winter storytelling session, or they are told, as Keewaydinoquay told them, when the teachings about the various plants are given.

30 *Name*: the final "e" on this word is pronounced as one would say the "a" in the English word *able*. It is not a silent "e." Also, that final "e" is the part of the word that is emphasized.

Name closed his eyes again and tried to sleep, but Naanabozho's voice came down to him again singing"

Oh Great *Name*, Great Sturgeon!
Oh Great *Name*, Great Sturgeon!
Come swallow me. Here is my decoy.
Come swallow me. Here is my decoy.

And again the hook of Naanabozho's line rubbed against *Name*'s cheek.

"Namegos," *Name* called, "Take this hook in your mouth. Naanabozho is bothering me."

So, Namegos, Lake Trout, took the hook and was pulled up to the surface.

When Naanabozho saw the fine, fat lake trout on his line he screamed, "Get off my line, Namegos. You are fouling it. I am hunting *Name*, not stinking little fish," and he contemptuously threw the Namegos back into the water.

When the hook once again rubbed against *Name*'s cheek he said, "Now Naanabozho has angered me! *Name* he wants and *Name* he shall get!" He grabbed Naanabozho's hook in his mouth, and he ran with it right up toward the light, where he broke the surface of the water with a great leap.

Naanabozho grabbed his line with both hands and held on with all of his strength. There was a thunderous noise, and what looked like an island rose up out of the water right in front of his canoe. Naanabozho held on, but he was suddenly aware that there was a great buzzing noise in his ears and a rushing of water, and suddenly he was in a dark and smelly place. He could see only enough to see that the walls of the place were pressed right up to the sides of his canoe. From a little further into the darkness he heard a little voice saying, "Woe is me! Woe is me!"

Naanabozho squinted his eyes until he could make out the form of a bedraggled little creature sitting on a ledge in the dark place, swaying back and forth with misery. "So, Naanabozho, *Name* has swallowed you too," the little creature said mournfully.

"Aaniin! Little Brother," said Naanabozho, "This seems to be a dreadful place. How did you get here?"

"I was climbing the tall pines that grow along the shore, looking for a nice, ripe cone for my breakfast, when I slipped and fell, and *Name* caught me," said the little voice.

"Well," said Naanabozho, "We must help each other now, Little

Brother. What is that loud noise that I hear? It sounds like a great Grandfather Drum. Has *Name* swallowed a drum and the singers, too?"

"No," said the little animal, "That is *Name*'s heart you hear. It beats like that all of the day and all of the night. It is a very noisy place we are in."

"Heart, eh? "said Naanabozho thinking, "Yes, I can see that great heart beating over there. But it is too close in here for me to draw my bow, or I would soon put a stop to that noise. But I do have my arrows with their marvelous Thunderbird feathers." So, clutching an arrow in both hands, Naanabozho crawled across the bow of his canoe and jabbed the great, beating sack that was *Name*'s heart.

Then was heard the great booming voice of *Name* saying, "Oh, my heart is sore! Truly I am afraid for my heart."

Then smaller voices answered, "You swallowed Naanabozho, and he is a tricky one. You must vomit him out and chew him up properly."

So, down in the great stomach of *Name,* the walls began to tighten and heave as *Name* tried to vomit out Naanabozho.

"Come, Little Brother," cried Naanabozho, "Help me turn my canoe in *Name*'s throat, or he will vomit us out and chew us up." With the little creature's help, Naanabozho wrestled his canoe until it was wedged in the great, dark throat of *Name*.

Then the heaving stopped and there were heard mournful voices saying, "Our chief is dead! It would be hard for us to bring him back to life. We must bury him deep in the depths, for *Name* was a great leader."

Inside of the now-quiet fish, Naanabozho and his brother listened to the water rushing over the outside as the fishes pulled and tugged and managed to tow their chief's body down to the deepest water and cover it with sand.

"Oh, Woe is me! Oh, woe is us! Now how will we get out of *Name*?" the little creature wailed.

"Well," said Naanabozho, "I am not without friends. I shall call my father the West Wind Spirit, and he will send a wind to churn up even the deepest part of Gichigami." So Naanabozho put down his asemaa and called on his father to send a strong west wind. Presently the body of *Name* started to rock as the waves turned over everything at the bottom of the lake. Deep in *Name*'s belly, Naanabozho and his little brother were thrown back and forth and churned about until suddenly the motion stopped.

"Listen," said Naanabozho, "Do you hear that? I think *Name* has washed up on a beach. I think I hear his rough skin rubbing against the sand."

Both Naanabozho and his new little brother strained and strained, trying to get out of the dead fish.

"We can't get up his throat, Little Brother. Can you chew our way out?" So the little creature started to bite and chew on the walls of the fish's stomach, and presently he managed to get open a small hole to the light. The little creature pushed his way through and popped out onto the beach.

"Thank you for your help, Little Brother," Naanabozho called as he watched the little creature shake himself off and run merrily across the hot sand to a stand of pines that were growing on the shore. "From now on, my Anishinaabeg relatives will call you "Ajidamoo, Tail in the Air."[31]

31 Kee used this name and translation when telling this story.

Then Naanabozho pushed his head into the same hole and tried to get out of *Name,* too, but the hole was far too small. He stuck fast with his shoulders caught on *Name*'s ribs, with just his head sticking out of the fish.

As Naanabozho lay there trying to decide what to do next, a bird flew down and alighted on the ridge of *Name*'s spine. It cocked its head to one side and watched the head of Naanabozho. Then it cried out, "Brothers! Brothers! Come see this thing! It looks like a talking head sticking out of the belly of a fish."

One by one a half dozen more birds of the same kind flew down and alighted on the fish's spine, too.

"Aaniin! Little Brothers," said the head, "I am Naanabozho, the son of the West Wind Spirit and an Anishinaabe woman. I am a great hunter. I have killed the Thunderbirds. I have killed *Name,* the Guardian of the Great Lakes. If you will do me a favor, I will reward you very well."

"Oh," said the bird nearest the head of Naanabozho. "He offers a trade." And each bird in turn told the one on his right about the offer, until the message got to the littlest bird of all, who was perched on *Name*'s tail, who asked, "What does he want, and what does he offer?"

"Yes," said the one next to him and all down the line the birds asked, "What do you want, and what do you offer?"

"Well," said Naanabozho, "If you will just peck a little bigger hole in the side of the fish so that I can get out, I will give you marvelous moccasins, all beaded and quilled with bright colors."

"He offers beautiful moccasins," said the birds excitedly one to another down the line on *Name*'s back, "and all we have to do is peck a hole for him to get out."

When the offer got to the littlest bird on the tail, he said, "Moccasins? But we have beautiful, big, webbed feet. What good would moccasins be to us? We would just get sand in them when we walked on the beach, and they'd get wet in the water."

"Yes," said the rest of the bird. "You are right. What else do you offer, Naanabozho? We really have no use for moccasins."

"Well," said Naanabozho wrinkling his forehead, "How about if I gave each of you a beautiful ribbon shirt?"

"Oh," said the birds. "He offers ribbon shirts! We would look so very good in those that all of our females would think us fine fellows." They twittered over the offer until the message got down to the little bird on the tail, who said, "But ribbon shirts would cover up our beautiful feathers, and how would we fly in them?'

"You know, he has a point," said the birds. "We do have beautiful feathers, and it would be a shame to cover them up; also, it might be difficult to fly with a shirt on. What else do you have to offer, Naanabozho?"

Naanabozho was getting a little worried now. He was very uncomfortable, stuck with just his head out of the fish. The sun was warming the dead fish, which was beginning to smell, and the sand and water were getting in his eyes. "Weapons," he said frantically. "I will give you wonderful weapons to bring down your game and to protect you from your enemies."

"Oh, he offers weapons," said the birds. "With weapons we will be a powerful people,"

"But," said the little bird on the tail, "we already have sharp claws and even sharper beaks. Why do we need more weapons? We find all we need to eat, and we do not make war on anyone."

"You are right, Little Brother," said the birds. "We really do not need more weapons. Well, Naanabozho, if that is all you have to offer, we think we will just be going on our way now. Time for supper."

"Wait," cried Naanabozho, "I have something you do not have. I can give you a wonderful name that will make all of the birds envious, and it will make the Anishinaabeg remember you for all time."

"A name! He offers a name!" all of the birds called together. And the little bird on the tail cried the loudest, "A name! Yes, we can use a name. Everyone will think us fine fellows if we have a name." And the little bird was the first to fly up to start pecking the sides of *Name*'s stomach to free Naanabozho. They pecked, and they ripped, and they clawed, and they opened a big enough hole for Naanabozho to crawl out.

As he sat on the sand, trying to wipe the fish oil and fish guts out of his hair, Naanabozho said, "Thank you, Little Brothers. From now on, you shall be called "Gayaashk, the Noble Snatchers."[32]

The waves washed up on the shore and carried the blood of *Name,* the Great Sturgeon, the Guardian of the Great Lakes, up onto the sand. The blood washed over a little plant that was growing there, and it stained its stems with the red of *Name*'s blood. From that time to this Anishinaabeg have gathered the Namebiniganzh[33] and used it for medicine for it carries the strength of the blood of the Great Sturgeon.

Mii'iw. Miigwech!

32 Kee used this name and translation when telling this story.

33 Namebiniganzh, which Kee translated as, "The Plant of the Great Sturgeon," I believe is *Satureja arkansa labella.* Kee said it was a subspecies, and another of Kee's apprentices says it is a *Calamint.* Other members of the mint family are also called by *Name*'s name.

Oombendaan
Dakaasabendaanag
"To Rise Up or Open Up the Interior"
"Opener-upper"
Mints
Lamiaceae
Mentha spp.

Aandegobagoons, Wild Mint
Mentha arvensis

Peppermint
Mentha Piperita

Spearmint
Mentha spicata

Namewashkoons, Mountain Mint
Pycnanthemum virginianum

~~~~~~

Whenever I am in the woods or among the herbs in a garden and I smell mint, I think of Keewaydinoquay. She comes rushing back into my consciousnes and, of a sudden, she is all around me. It is as if I hold the memory of her and the memory of the smell of mint in the exact same cells of my mind. I cannot think of the one without the other. She would have liked that. She was a self-proclaimed "mint addict" or, as she preferred, "a mint freak." She would put mint in anything; tea, coffee, soup, cookies, candies, her bath, potpourris, candles, kinnikinnick, anointing oils, various medicinals, and skin creams. Just about anyplace it was possible to add mint, she did![34] Many Anishinaabe medicine people develop a particular fondness for one plant or group of plants, or as Kee would have said, "Perhaps the plant develops a fondness for that particular person," and they become expert in the use of that particular plant. Kee's plant was mint! It makes sense, of course, because mint is a plant that loves water, and Kee was named for the Northwest Wind on which the Thunderbirds come to bless the Earth with cleansing water. Eya! It all makes sense.

34 . . . with the exception of alcohol. She thought a mint julep was poison. A friend once poured creme de menthe over a fruit salad, and she would not eat it.

Oombendaan: The Mints
(*Mentha spp.*)

Kee used to say that when she was a young student she had been told that the one thing a scholar could count on was that the classification system of plants would never change, but she lived long enough to see the mints classified by two different scientific names and to suspect that sooner or later the family would be split up into the square stemmed and the non–square stemmed, the aromatics or the non-aromatics. In the old books, the family of mint is called Labiatae, but by the 1970s the family was being called Lamiaceae. One has to be aware of that when using older reference materials. But, the change Kee thought a silly one. She said that it was changed at the insistence of female botanists who objected to a group of plants being named for a part of the female genitalia. They pointed out that there was no family of plants named after the corresponding parts of male anatomy, so it was not fair that there should be one called by the female equivalent.[35] But, as Kee would say with a hearty laugh, the new name meant the same thing and that maybe the female botanists might need refresher courses in the ancient languages.

35 Apparently, mature mint seeds seen under a microscope looked to some (probably male) botanists like the exterior part of a female human's private parts. Some scientists should get out of their laboratories more often!

The name that Kee always preferred for the mints was the Anishinaabemowin "Oombendaan," which she translated as "To Rise Up or Open Up" or "The Opener-upper."[36] She loved that name, because one of the really memorable aspects of the mints is their incredible volatile oils. Those of the family that are aromatic, and not all of them are, but the ones that are aromatic, do "open up" all of a person's senses.

For uncountable generations, and throughout the world wherever these plants grew, they were utilized by humankind for their medicinal properties and for their pleasant qualities as well. This huge family of plants has 221 genera and at least 5,600 species (Coffey 1993, 196). And the mints are busily making more species as I type these words. The characteristic that makes a species a species is that the members of that group are not supposed to cross with any other species and stay fertile. But nobody told the mints that, so they just go merrily along, crossing and recrossing and making more and different mints whenever they get the opportunity, and apparently they have had plenty of opportunity. One readily sees the proof of this whenever one foolishly plants two or more different mints in the same garden. The first year one has real peppermint and real spearmint, real apple mint and real pineapple mint and real chocolate mint, but things get interesting the next time the mints come up in the garden. One suddenly has a completely different tasting mint. Some such crossed mints are wonderful, and some are not. But they are all interesting nonetheless. Kee said that at least with the mints one does not have to be very careful about the exact classification, since one will probably just be fooling oneself anyway. None of the mints are poisonous, with the exception of pennyroyal (*Hedeoma pulegiodes*), and pennyroyal just does not smell like a mint.[37] If it smells like a mint, it is safe.

Anishinaabe teachings about plants emphasize utilizing all of a person's senses for identification, not just their eyes. The novice medicine person is encouraged to smell and taste and feel and even listen to the plants that their teacher indicates are safe for them to explore. Kee always had the students in her classes drink mint tea while she gave this lecture.

The mints are a relatively easy family of plants to identify. Many of them have square stems. One can see that under a microscope if one looks at a cross section of the stem, but one can also use the square stem for identification in the field. One takes a piece of the stem and rolls it between one's thumb and forefinger.

36 This is how Kee wrote this word. See Glossary for more information.

37 Foster and Duke say of pennyroyal: "Pulegone, the active insect repellant compound in [pennyroyal] essential oil is absorbed through the skin and converted into a dangerous liver cancer–inducing compound. Ingesting essential oil can be lethal; contact with essential oil (a popular insect repellant) can cause dermatitis. Components of essential oil may be particularly dangerous to epileptics" (213). As little as ½ of an ounce of pennyroyal oil can cause severe, fatal liver damage (*Magic and Medicine* 1986, 251). Kee did not teach her students to use pennyroyal, because it is just too dangerous, but she did make sure we knew what it smelled like so we could avoid it. She also always cautioned us to be very careful with any essential oil. She said that distilling out just the essential oil of a plant, as modern drug companies, modern herbalists, and homeopathic healers do, creates a far more dangerous product than just using the plant in its original form. The essential oil separates the chemicals from the rest of the chemicals in the parent plant and that can be dangerous. The plant itself is always the way to go. It is the way our ancestral mashkikii-wininiwag and mashkikiiwikwewag utilized the Blessed Plants and that is the way it should be.

One can actually feel the four corners of the square stem very distinctly. The flowers of mints are not very showy, and therefore less useful for identification, because they are usually small and either in whorls around the stem or in the joints where the leaves grow out of the stems. The seeds of the mint plants carry the symbol of the Four Directions, the Sacred Four Winds of Our Mother the Earth; they are in clusters of four.[38]

38 Now isn't that a more pleasant way to think about the seeds than the previously mentioned idea?

The entire Oombendaan family is beneficial to the Anishinaabeg. Many of them are aids to digestion. Many of them are tonic and stimulant to other parts of the body. They are a very easy set of plants to move and to grow in one's own garden, or in a pot on a sunny windowsill. There are little joints in the stems, nodes, that will readily root if placed in water or wet soil. One can go for a visit to a neighbor's garden or meadow, find a particularly interesting mint, snap off a six-inch-or-so part of the upper growth of stems and leaves, bring it home, put it in a cup of water, and one will have a new little mint to plant as soon as the clipping has a week or two to produce a root system.

The volatile oils of the mints are possibly the most pleasing aspect of their beings, the aspect that humans and nonhuman persons, too, seem to enjoy the most. There are several ways to enjoy that aspect of these plants. One can use them fresh, dried, or in the form of oils. As food, fresh mint is often the best for salads, or as additions to stir-fries, or in stuffing or sauces, for jams and jellies, and various other types of cooking. To utilize fresh mint after the growing season, many people either take the plant indoors to use as a houseplant during the winter or they chop the fresh mint up, put it in water and freeze it into ice cubes, adding a cube or two to soups or other cooking. The dried plant material is excellent for preserving the mints for winter use, and the dried mint can be utilized in cooking, too, if one bears in mind that the dried material is much more concentrated than the fresh. A good cup of tea might take a whole six- to eight-inch sprig of fresh mint, but a teaspoon or tablespoon of dried mint, depending on the strength of the mint used, will make a whole pot of tea.

The mints are very strong medicinals. They are especially good for digestion. The aromatic ones, like peppermint, spearmint, and the wild mint, *Mentha arvensis,* are carminative, meaning they settle an upset stomach. They are also antiflatulents, meaning they relieve intestinal gas. Mints are also stimulants, and will increase circulation either internally or externally. As a medicine, they seem to work best as a cold infusion. One makes a tea of either fresh or dried mint, allowing the plant material to steep for ten to fifteen minutes, then one cools it before sipping a cup at a time. A nice cup of mint tea will settle most upset stomachs and a lot of headaches, too, although the caution must be added that strong mints can make the valve at the top of the stomach work ineffectively and can actually increase heartburn in people who have acid reflux disease. A cup or two of mint tea in the afternoon or after a fish supper should be fine, just do not use it before bedtime, because that may both keep one awake and increase the acid reflux and the resulting heartburn if one goes to bed on a full stomach.

For medicinal use, the oil of mint is often more convenient to use than the whole plant. Since Keewaydinoquay was cautious in teaching her students to use the essential oil of plants, and because she thought commercial essential oils particularly unpleasant, she preferred to teach them how to make their own plant oils from the whole plants. It is possible to distill the oils of mints with very little equipment. One really does not need a whole drug company's machinery. In our ethnobotany lab at the University of Wisconsin–Milwaukee we had a little still that is sold commercially to make perfumes. We loaned it to students who wanted to distill plants for their final ethnobotany displays or for their own use. Several students took us up on the offer, or they just studied the still itself so that they could make their own version.[39]

If one does not have a real perfume still, it is still possible to make an effective distilled oil with more humble methods. Out on her island in the middle of Lake Michigan, Kee made a still out of an old tea kettle. She put the chopped plant material and water in the kettle, and then she put a tube over the spout and ran the tube through a cold spring to distill the oils. In one's own kitchen it is possible to distill a very useful product using kitchen bowls and pots. In a deep pot[40] place some kind of rack to keep a bowl off of the heating surface. A tuna fish can with both ends removed and holes punched in the sides to release steam will do to keep a heatproof cereal bowl off the bottom of the pot, where the heat may make the bowl crack as the pot is heated. Next, put boiling water and the chopped, fresh plant material into the pot around the bowl on top of its rack. Put the lid on the pot upside down and put ice cubes and cold water in the upturned lid. When the water and plant material in the pot are heated, the volatile oils of the plant will be distilled in the steam. It will hit the cold surface

39 We always hoped that the students had not seen one too many episodes of the TV program *M*A*S*H* and that they restricted their distilling to mint or flower oils. Kee, like many Anishinaabeg, did not approve of the recreational use of alcohol, although she used several distilled liquors in various medicinal compounds for their preserving qualities. The medicinal qualities of some plants are just easier to dissolve in alcohol. She used them the way the monks of the medieval monasteries, hopefully, used brandy.

40 One can use any cooking pot, but do not use galvanized metal as it will make a poisonous product. Kee also disliked aluminum cookware as she suspected that the molecules of aluminum were not stable. She feared that cooking in such a pot could get minute particles of aluminum into one's tissues, and that worried her because of the research that links aluminum to Alzheimer's disease. Kee was always worried about retaining brain cells.

of the ice water–filled top, turn back into a liquid form, and drip down into the cereal bowl inside the pot. There will be water in the resulting liquid, but the oil will be floating on the top where it can be retrieved with an eye dropper or pipette. A very nice distilled mint product can be produced in that way.[41]

If one does not want to go to all the trouble of distilling mint, a very useful product can be made as an infused oil. One takes a clean, boiled and dried canning jar and fills it ⅔ of the way full with chopped mint leaves and stems. Then one covers the plant material with a cooking oil that has little or no taste. Olive oil is a little too strong for this, but one could experiment with canola or a similar salad oil. Kee loved to use apricot-seed oil, but it is rather expensive. Then one puts the top on the jar and sets the jar on the counter or in a sunny window for a couple of weeks. One shakes the jar occasionally to mix the oil and plant material around. Then one filters out the plant material and bottles the oil, being sure to label the bottle with the exact ingredients and the date the oil was made. It is easy to forget such things, especially if one really gets into this kind of medicinal work and accumulates several such bottles of dark plant materials and oils, or in a crisis situation. One always thinks, "Oh, I'll remember that." And then, of course, one can't. Labeling is always a good idea.

An oil that is either distilled or infused by the above methods is ready to use in various medicinal produces or to be used just for fun. Kee always carried a bottle of such oil in her purse. She used it in coffee during the day when she needed a little pick-me-up. She also found it indispensable for surviving long, boring faculty meetings. She would place a drop of the oil on the Third Eye region of her forehead, about ½ an inch above the eyes in the center of the forehead, a little on each temple, and then a drop on the Life Spot on her neck. She always recommended the practice to her students as a good way to get through a long test or a long, trying car trip. The only caution that is necessary is that one must never let any of the oil get into one's eyes. It would not damage the eye, but it is an extremely unpleasant experience for several minutes even if one flushes the eye with warm water.

In making the above oils, Kee usually used a combination of mints. She especially liked a mix of mountain mint, wild mint, peppermint, and spearmint. She found peppermint alone too strong a mint, but she did like it in combinations. Spearmint is a milder mint with the distinct taste which most people just describe as "spearmint gum" taste. Both the mountain and wild mints have distinct, different tastes, too. And the mint-made mints that result from illicit matings in one's garden are always an adventure in taste. One just mixes and blends until one finds a taste one prefers.

For cooking, one can use commercial mint extracts or one can make extracts with very little work. One makes extracts from fresh plant material, chopped, and put into a clean canning jar and covered with an edible alcohol. We always used vodka, as high a proof as we could get, in the ethnobotany lab. Rubbing alcohol, of course, cannot be used for any extract that one will take internally as it will poison a person, make them go blind, or possibly kill them. If one is going to all of the bother of making one's own extracts one might just as well make an extract that one can use both internally and externally. Fill the canning jar with the plant material and use enough alcohol so as to completely cover the plant material.

Whatever the form in which mint is used, either fresh or dried, as an infusion, a decoction, a tincture, or an oil, they are all very helpful to us. And mints are just plain delicious and fun to use.

The love of mint is not a completely human addiction. I have a house cat, Rainbow, our resident alpha male and Chief Gardener, who is as much a mint freak as Kee was. Rainbow has his own garden where he sits for hours at a time, even in the dead of winter when all of his plants are under a foot or two of snow. He sits so sadly in his garden, nosing the snowdrifts and pawing halfheartedly at the frozen ground. But come spring and the first of the new growths, he is elated. He sits like a lawn ornament among his mint plants for hours on end, purring so loud one can often hear him inside of the house. When it is time to come back inside, Rainbow will inevitably first roll over several times in the mints so that he can carry some of the garden vapors back into his workaday life keeping the household running with cat efficiency. When he comes in smelling of the mints, the other cats will crowd around him, licking his head, and purring their appreciation for the scents he has captured for them. The mints seem to just please my cats. They do not react with the drunken, unruly disorder that catnip, another mint, has upon them. They just purr and rub their approval.

A few days after I wrote the above account of Rainbow and his mint garden, he taught me the real reason he rolls in mint. We were having a particularly severe mosquito infestation here in our little home swamp. As soon as one stepped out the door one was clouded with the bloodthirsty little wretches. I had to hang a load of laundry on the clothesline, and, as I stepped out the door, I noticed Rainbow batting at mosquitoes that were biting him on his nose and around his ears. Then he rolled in the mint and stood back up with every indication of relief. His purr was deafening! So I grabbed a handful of the mint leaves and crushed them all over my exposed skin. I even put a bruised sprig into the brim of my hat. Presto! No mosquitoes!

Ingijibinaa

Ogijibinaan
"Very Great, Drawing Out One"
"The Great Drawer-Outer"
Heal-all, Self-heal
Prunella vulgaris

~~~~~~

Heal-all is a little, square-stemmed mint plant that is a great adaptor to its circumstances. Kee used to say that Heal-all was a great example of making the most of whatever life hands a person and an inspiration to living Anishinaabe-bimaadiziwin, life in the fullest sense. If it has a nice place to grow in, a moist and sunny or semishaded place, this plant can grow to be eighteen inches tall, but if it is growing on a suburban front lawn that is dry and regularly mowed, it can be two inches tall. In either extreme it will endeavor to put out its little flower and live a full life. As Kee used to say, "If a little weed can do that, so can people."

Heal-all has a flower that grows on the end of its stem and is some variation of purple, depending on the minerals in the soil. It may be any color from white to pale violet to a deep purple. The flowers are on a cone-shaped spike that looks like a dried flower or a mini–spruce cone. Because the flower is on the plant all through the summer and into the fall, it is useful in locating and identifying the plant, unlike most mint flowers, which are less useful for identification purposes.

Kee always liked the scientific name *Prunella vulgaris*. The species name "vulgaris" just means "common." But Kee liked the sound of "Prunella" and thought it might make a good name for a daughter. It sounded to her rather like a European fairy tale–type name. I can still remember how she would purr the name out "Ppppprrrrruuunn-elllla" when she was teaching about this plant. It made it easy for her students to remember because of her performance.

Kee also liked and always used the Anishinaabemowin name "ingijibinaa" because it encodes the chief virtue that this plant has to share with the People. It is the most effective poultice for

Ingijibinaa: Heal-all (*Prunella vulgaris*)

Kee seldom used roots. She hated to wash the sand and dirt off roots, and she also knew that if you leave the root, the plant will often be able to grow back for you to use it again in the future.

removing foreign objects from flesh. One takes the whole plant, not the root,[42] and puts it in a blender. Or, if one has no blender, one can smash it with a rock or cut it very fine with a sharp knife. Or one can cook it up with a little water until it is the consistency of applesauce. In the field one can just chew up the plant and spit it onto the skin. This poultice is most effective if put on at night and covered with a bandage to keep it in place and moist. By morning it will have drawn out whatever is stuck in a person's skin. It will pull out wood or metal or glass or anything, including infection.

One time on her island, at the summer camp she and her students maintained, Kee had a camper who had been in the Army Medical Corps. He would always refuse Indian medicinals, saying, "You aren't going to put that dirty plant on me!" But one day he was limping very badly. He had insisted upon going around with bare feet, even though Kee had repeatedly asked people to wear shoes. He just thought he had such tough feet that nothing would hurt him. But this time he was limping. Kee convinced him to at least let her try to fix his foot, so she put a poultice of ingijibinaa on his foot and covered it with a plastic bag. By morning it had pulled a long shard of glass out of his foot. In the fall, hunters often went to Kee's island, drank their beer, and smashed the bottles on the rocks for fun. The camper with the medical background was more interested in the herbals after that cure, and he wore his shoes, too.

One time an old fisherman and his wife, who were living on Isle Royale, came to ask Kee's help. He had what they thought was an old boil or carbuncle under his arm that his wife had not been able to cure. Kee looked at the sore and thought she saw something shiny in it, so she poulticed it with ingijibinaa that night. In the morning it had drawn a piece of metal up so that she could get a pair of pliers around it. She pulled out a half of a fishhook. The old guy was very amazed. He said that the only fishhook he had ever had in his flesh had gone into his leg when he was a boy in Denmark. They had cut off the top and left the rest in his leg. And there the other half of the fishhook was, a lifetime later, come festering out under his arm!

Kee said the incident with the fishhook made her think that old stories about women suddenly struck dead might have been due to the practice of craftspeople keeping porcupine quills in their mouths to soften them when they were sewing the quills onto leather. She thought maybe those quills finally worked their way to the person's heart or another vital organ and killed them.[43] When we worked with porcupine quills she insisted that we soak them in a bowl with dishwashing detergent and water. She did not want us to keep them in our mouths. She made us flatten the quills with a spoon, not our teeth as the ancient practice had been. She also worried that there was perhaps a chemical in porcupine quills that caused blindness, because of the old stories about quill workers often going blind as they grew older.

Another time, a young couple came to Kee in real trouble. The girl and her new husband had been trying to fix up the shack they lived in. They had been painting the outside of the house on a scaffold made of an old, splintery plank. It was a hot day, and the girl had only been wearing a bra and panties. She had slipped and slid to the ground on that old plank. When they got to Kee, the girl walked out of the car all bent over with pain. She had numerous huge splinters all between her legs and up into her vaginal area. Kee wanted them to go to a doctor because the woman was in such pain, and she thought that the girl would

43 I had a doctor tell me one time that a foreign object cannot travel around in the body, but I am not sure I believed him. I remembered the old fisherman and the fishhook.

definitely need numerous operations to remove the splinters. But the kids were completely broke and could not get a doctor to help them. So Kee tried. She got the boy picking handfuls of ingijibinaa while she got the girl to bed and gave her a strong yarrow tea to fight the pain. Then she packed the girl with the poultice and covered the area with a wet towel and a plastic bag. By morning the poultice had worked, and the worst of the slivers had either worked their way out completely, or they had worked so far out that they could be pulled with a tweezers. Kee said she kept the girl for several days and kept the poultices fresh and pulled out even more of the slivers. She sent the kids home again quite happy.

Kee had just dozens of those kinds of stories. I also remember her telling about a man in Ann Arbor who came to her because he had a piece of metal so close to his eye that the local doctors had said it was too dangerous for them to pull it out. They wanted him to go to the Mayo Clinic, in Rochester, Minnesota, but the guy was worried about the trip and the expense. Kee told him that she thought the doctors were right and that he should get the best care he could find if he wanted to save his eye. But she agreed to try a poultice if his family would work on getting him to the Mayo Clinic while she did it. She said she really did not expect the results she got. The next morning the entire piece of metal had been pulled right out of his face. She sent him back to his doctor who took over from there.[44]

44 When I think about it, it is no wonder that the doctors in Ann Arbor threatened to bring suit against Kee for practicing medicine without a license. She was showing them up! And with "weeds" no less!

Another time, an old Indian elder from Milwaukee came to visit Kee on her Island. She had been dropped off by a fisherman on the wrong side of the Island and had to walk the several miles through the bush to get to Kee's cabin. When she got there she had a badly infected leg that had blood poisoning lines running up from it. Kee had no way to communicate with the authorities at the time, since she relied on boats coming in to take her messages back to Beaver Island, which was the main island of the chain and the place that had a Coast Guard station and a clinic. She knew a group of her students were due to come to visit her and would probably arrive the next day, but Kee was really worried, because blood poisoning can kill a person rather quickly. So she poulticed the leg with ingijibinaa and prayed that the elder would still be with her in the morning when she could send her to the clinic. But in the morning the leg was much better. The lines were actually gone. Kee sent the elder off to the clinic as soon as the boat arrived, but the woman was back smiling and cleanly bandaged by nightfall. They just gave her a salve and told her she could go. Kee was convinced that the ingijibinaa had actually pulled the blood poisoning right out of the leg.

This cure is one that Kee thought could only be done with the fresh plant. She said she had never tried it with dried or frozen Heal-all because she had always used it fresh. She said when her kids were home and always getting slivers she would gather a bunch of the plant in the fall and chop it up and put it in a canning jar in the fridge. She said it always kept for her until she could gather the fresh plant in the spring. She said her mother had done the same when she was a girl and that her mom had only had an icebox, not a refrigerator. The plant itself is available until November most years, and one can find the new growth even under the snow in March, so one really does not have to keep it many months in the fridge.

I had an occasion to use the dried plant, however, and it worked just fine for me. One time I took my husband's hand in mine, only to have him wince. I looked at his hand, and he had a bump about the size of the end of his thumb in the center of his palm.

I said, "What is that? How long has it been there?"

He admitted that it had been there for months, and he had just been ashamed to show it to me.

I said, "Why?"

He said he had burned it while he had been working at Summerfest, the Milwaukee music festival where they also had craft projects to entertain the children, in the summer past, and he had not wanted me to chide him for being stupid. Also, he had not wanted me to insist that he go to a doctor because he was afraid that the doctor would cut open his hand. Bob is an artist, and his hands are precious to him.

He got a gentle chiding for fearing my chidings, and then I decided to see if I could do anything before I took him to the doctor. I only had dried Heal-all and no access to fresh because we were in the city at the time, and it was night. So I cooked up the dried Heal-all, put a glob on his palm, and covered it with a bandage. The next morning when I took the bandage off there was a whole glob of pus that had been pulled out of the bump, but the bump was still there. So the next evening I put more of the poultice material on his hand. The following morning there was no new pus, but there was something else that was just below his skin. My husband has tough skin on his palm, so I got my leather needle, swabbed it in alcohol, and cleaned the skin, and then I cut the skin over the bump. I stuck in the needle and pulled out a perfectly round glob of hot glue. Bob confessed that he had burned his hand with a hot glue gun, kept it a secret, and that the skin had grown back over the burn. He had not known that a piece of glue was still in his hand because the glue was the same color as his skin. It is one of the strangest things I have ever witnessed. That little plant really works!

Other cultures believe in the power of this plant too, as witnessed by this old French proverb that says, "No one needs a surgeon who keeps Prunelle" (Headstom 1984, 16).

Niibiishikaabijigan
Motherwort
Leonurus cardiaca

~~~~~~

Keewaydinoquay said that motherwort was a circumboreal plant that European botanists loved to insist was an introduced plant to its range in North America, which is almost all of the country east of the Rockies. She said she could not bring herself to blame the Europeans for trying to lay claim to this plant, however, because it was such a strong medicinal.

Motherwort is a very odd member of the mint family. It has the square mint stem, but it is far sturdier and taller than the other mints, with two- to five-foot plants being common. It does not have leaves that look anything like mint leaves. It has down-right odd leaves, with three differently shaped and sized leaves that get smaller and less cut and lobed as they go up the stalk. The basal leaves are scalloped, and have an almost maple shape to them. As the leaves grow higher on the stem they become smaller and less cut-looking. They are dark green in color and quite hairy. The leaves are a way to identify this plant, if one is not familiar with it, because the leaves of all three kinds all have a quilted or crinkled look to them. The flowers, which can be a pinkish or pale purple or a dirty white color, grow in whorls around the stalk, just where the leaves join the stem. Its aroma and taste is anything but "mint-like"; in fact, Kee always described this plant saying, "Mother stinks!"

Despite the fact that motherwort is not a delightful-looking nor a delightful-tasting nor a particularly delightful decorative plant, it has a wonderful medicinal quality to share with the People. The species name cardiaca is proof that more peoples than the Anishinaabeg have known about the fact that this plant is a specific for the muscle of the heart. It is particularly helpful in heart conditions where there is a genetic condition that renders the heart muscle ineffective, such as in children born with holes in the heart, leaking hearts, so called "blue babies," or people said to have weak heart muscles or heart palpitations. Kee thought it

Niibiishikaabijigan, Motherwort
(*Leonurus cardiaca*)

worked best for young people who were still growing. This plant
has the ability to stimulate a heart muscle and actually make the
muscle repair itself.

Kee once had a little girl as a student, when she was teaching
grade school in Michigan years ago. The girl had been a real
favorite of Kee's, because she was a really smart and sweet-natured
kid. The child had been born with a genetic defect to her heart.
Her blood was not being cleansed properly, and it was leaking
back into her system instead of being cleaned. She looked blue,
with noticeably blue lips. The doctors told her family that she
was just too weak for an operation and that she could not hope
to get beyond seventh grade. But years later Kee was invited to the
girl's high school graduation. Motherwort worked for her. Her
parents had asked for Kee's help because they were so deeply in
debt for the child's doctors' bills that she was their last-ditch hope.
Motherwort is a specific for the musculature of the heart, and it
worked for Kee's little student.

Another time, when Kee was a Ph.D student in Michigan, she had a young friend who had such acute angina pain that it was affecting the quality of her life and work. Her doctor could not find a cause, so he sent her to a psychologist instead. Kee suggested that she try motherwort. When the girl went to another university, to work on her doctorate, she moved in with plants. The people helping her move said, "Oh, you like plants, eh? Oh, they are all the same plant. You must really like this plant." The girl had fourteen motherwort plants all growing in pots, with their own grow lights, that traveled around with her as she studied. Before she took motherwort, she would come home from school with pain so severe that she would just lie across her bed, shaking. But, after taking motherwort for only a week, at three cups of infusion a day, she felt a lot better. The pains went away. After the pain subsided she could cut back on the dosage, and she took it as a preventative, a cup a day or even every other day. She had a weakness in the heart muscle. The motherwort really helped her with the resulting angina pain.

To treat such a condition a person usually makes an infusion of the leaves, one heaping teaspoon of the dried plant to one cup boiling water, and drinks a cup two or three times a day, depending on the severity of the problem. The tea is quite awful and bitter, so most people drink it diluted by at least one-half with water. The only trouble with that is one must then drink two cups of the stuff instead of one. Kee, who was admittedly something of a mint freak, would make motherwort tea with a healthy addition of other mints, and she said it did help somewhat to disguise the taste. Kee said she once had a young man say he would rather die than drink the motherwort infusion, and he did, too.

One can make this medicine as a decoction with alcohol as a preservative. In this form it is a little more palatable. One heats water to boiling then one puts in the leaf and stems cut into pieces. One boils it for about five to ten minutes, then one filters out the plant material, cools the liquid, and bottles it with ½ edible alcohol (such as vodka) to ½ decoction. Keep it in the fridge. It is used by putting 10 to 20 drops in a cup of water taken twice daily. As a decoction with alcohol it is usually easier for people to use, and that sometimes keeps them using it long enough for the medicine to work.

If one dries the leaves, powders them, and puts them into gelatin capsules, one can take this plant without gagging. The problem with this is, the medicinal qualities of the plant are best released in either a water infusion or in an alcohol tincture. And since gelatin capsules are a new invention, we have no traditional teachings about using them. Therefore a person would have to very carefully experiment with dosage. This is serious medicine for a very serious condition and is never something undertaken lightly. If a condition is this serious, it would take a lot for me to alter the instruction I received from Kee and my ancestral teachers through her. I would have to be in a completely unsupported position where I had no other medical care, like after an atomic war or similar unforeseeable catastrophic condition. One does not know what tomorrow will bring! I long ago united myself with the ongoing of the People and the ongoing of the Clan of Makwa and the ongoing of our family. So I write this stuff in case one of us needs it someday.

The tea does have an effect on the mental attitude of the patient. Drink a quart of the infusion of the leaves and one will be sedated. One's whole body will feel heavy. Drink a pint of it and the world will suddenly be a beautiful place with no worries.

It is also used to bring on the menses if they are delayed or irregular. That is the reason it has the English common name of "Mother." The "-wort" part is the old Saxon word for a plant, but the Old Saxons seem to have just called plants by a name if they were good medicinals. Most of the plants that have "-wort" in them are strong medicinals known to the people for a very long time. There is an old saying, "Drink Motherwort and live to be a source of continuous astonishment and grief to waiting heirs" (Coon, 158). Eya! Yes! Always grieve those waiting for you to die!

Gichi-namewashk

Gaazhagensibag
"Little Cat Ears"
Catnip
Nepeta cataria

Catnip is another of our native plants that Europeans insist is an import from their homeland. This one, however, Keewaydinoquay was sure had been here long before the traders and settlers arrived. She said her own grandfather MidéOgema told her that he remembered his own grandfather teaching him about the plant and showing him its growth and how to gather it, and then sitting with the old man and drinking it as tea. He said his grandfather said that his own grandfather had done the same for him when he was a boy, and that was long before there were Chi-mookomaanag, "Long Knives," meaning white men, in their area. MidéOgema said that in his grandfather's time the plant was a gift in the Mide Lodge and that he was sure that those old Anishinaabe Mide would not have so honored a plant that was new to their area even if it was the strong medicinal that catnip is. He said other good medicinals that the Indians knew were Chi-mookomaanag plants had not been so honored in the Lodge, therefore, he knew catnip was a plant that had been here before the Chi-mookomaanag arrived. But, whatever. Kee would have just laughed and said that what was important was that we do know the chief virtue that catnip has to share with the People.

The great virtue is that catnip will lower a fever, any fever, in a child or adult, without raising that temperature first. That is something that no other plant or drug, native or non-native, scientifically discovered and approved drug or pill can do. But this little plant can do it. Everything else from aspirin to Tylenol and the newer pain and fever drugs, too—all of them raise a fever at least one degree higher before they lower it. But not catnip.

Reye's syndrome[45] is a disease that only strikes children or young adults who have been given aspirin and have just had B-type influenza or chicken pox. Some studies, inconclusively,

45 Kee always included the information presented here on Reye's syndrome in her lectures. For more information on Reye's syndrome see www.webmd.com.

Gichi-namewashk,
Gaazhagensibag: Catnip (*Nepeta cataria*)

have linked it to baby shots and environmental spraying, too. In Reye's, the mechanism in the body that takes down a fever after the drug has pushed it up is out of whack. The temperature goes up and just keeps going up. The liver is destroyed, and the child dies because their brain swells and is pushed into the skull.

My own children have been raised on catnip tea. When they were little and had childhood ailments or sun fevers or fevers from shots, I always gave them a cup of catnip tea to bring down those fevers.

My eldest daughter taught me to never tell a little child that I was giving them a cup of catnip tea if that child had not had it before he or she was sick. Soon after I first learned about catnip, Makoons had a cold, and I brought her a cup of tea.

She said, "This doesn't taste like tea." My family drinks tea, and Makoons knew that the stuff in that cup was not a good cup of black tea.

I said, "No, Darling. It's a nice cup of catnip tea that will make you feel better."

Well, Makoons started to holler at the top of her vocal cords for her father, screaming, "Daddy! Mommy thinks I'm a cat. She made me a cup of tea out of the cat's catnip mouse."

Her father calmed her down while I took the cup back into the kitchen, put milk and sugar into it so that it looked and probably tasted more like tea, and brought it back to her. This time I told her it was "Princess Tea," and she drank it quite happily. Her fever was safely reduced, and we all got a good night's sleep.

That episode convinced me to make sure my second daughter knew the look and smell and taste of catnip tea well before she was sick next. My mother came from Canada one Christmas and brought the girls a little china tea set to play tea party with their dolls. I was always careful that the "tea" in that tea set was always catnip. For years my daughters both insisted on calling catnip tea "Princess Tea."

Besides reducing fever, which is undoubtedly the virtue catnip has to share with us, catnip tea is also a great relaxant that is quite safe to use as a sleep aid. Many people drink a cup of it anytime they are too keyed up after a hard day to fall asleep easily. It does not put you to sleep. It relaxes one so that you can sleep. And in the morning one will wake without a headache or the sluggish, drugged feeling that sleeping pills can give a person.

And it is a nice-tasting tea once one is used to it. Milk and sugar will not harm the relaxant qualities of the tea, and some people think it improves the taste so that one can sit of an evening and sip it leisurely before going to bed.

To use the tea as a sleep aid one uses the standard 1 teaspoon dried herb to 1 cup boiling water. Steep a full 10 minutes. Strain out herb and drink straight, or with milk and sugar or honey or lemon.

To use the tea as a fever reducer, however, one has to take the size and weight of the person to be treated into consideration. One uses much less for a small child or infant than one does for an adult, with less for a 110-pound woman than one would need for a 300-pound man. One makes the tea by color of the infusion, not by size of the spoon. One gives an infant a light yellow-colored tea. A larger child or small adult would need an amber-colored tea, while a larger person would need an almost black tea color.

This is one herb that most of us prefer to gather ourselves, but it is possible to buy it in herbal outlets, alternative food stores, and food co-ops in major cities. One will find it growing even in parking lots in the city, and it is a great temptation to gather it in such places, but one must resist such a temptation if one intends to use it for anything but a quick gift for a pet cat, who probably will not suffer much from occasional use of even city-grown, and therefore rather contaminated, catnip. Catnip is routinely grown for sale as a cat treat, but that catnip is not regulated at all and is intended for use by animals, so who knows where it comes from. If one intends using it for humans, it is best to either pick it in a clean place in the country, away from roadside lead and other common twenty-first-century contaminants, or from a pot on one's own doorstep or windowsill.

If one buys this or other medicinal herbs, one is really buying it on faith. Kee had a pair of students who, after they married, bought and ran a goat farm. They also raised and sold herbs that grew on their land, but then a chemical fertilizer company opened up not far from them. They noticed that the milk goats born into their flock were developing horn and hoof abnormalities. So they decided that their land, which was downwind from the factory, was being contaminated. They decided that in good conscience they could not continue to pick and sell the herbs that were growing on their land, so they wrote to the herb company, one of the major herb companies at the time in the 1980s, and told them that they could no longer supply the herbs they had sold them in the past because of the possibility of contamination. The drug company wrote back and said, "We know you are a conscientious couple and that you are making every effort to sell us clean herbs. Please continue to send them to us." Kee's students were appalled. They had been using that company for medicinal herbs for their own family for years. Just be warned: Where money is involved it becomes more important than any other consideration! If you want clean medicinals for your family, find or grow them yourself.

Kee also loved using catnip in cooking. She said it was a favorite flavoring herb in French cooking. She especially liked to stuff a fish with catnip before she baked it. She said the aroma and light taste was a great delight and was especially useful for larger fish that otherwise might be strong tasting. She said catnip countered that tendency very effectively. Other recipes call for adding fresh, chopped catnip to butter and using it to rub fish or fowl before cooking.

And of course, one must not forget our furry friends either. Many cats love catnip, but not all of them, as catnip appreciation is "an inherited autosomal dominant gene, absent in about one-third of cats" (Foster and Duke 2000, 83). Some cats appreciate it more than others do. And it is not something to give small kittens who really need little stimulation. Most kittens will not react to it at all, and others will give every indication that it makes them feel ill. I have seen kittens vomit after eating it and others who really looked and acted as if they had headache from sniffing catnip. Keep it for the cat until he is bigger. He will probably enjoy it then.

It is not just our domestic feline friends who love catnip. Larger cats are affected by it too. Lynx and mountain lions have been observed rolling in catnip patches, acting for all the world like a housecat on a "catnip Trip."

Periodically people start saying that if a person smokes catnip it will have the same effect on a human that it does on those lucky cats, but it just is not true.[46] That is fortunate, because if it did affect humans that way it would undoubtedly be illegal, and the Feds would be hot on the trail of every "smiling," happy cat in the country, trying to root out the "evil." And that would make it a lot harder for Anishinaabeg to reduce those fevers that every cold season brings.

A good cold and flu remedy is made with this plant. Dry catnip and powder it with equal parts dried and powdered yarrow and mint. Place the mixture in gelatin capsules and take one of them two or three times a day. Many people feel more "modern" if they can use a capsule, especially if they have to go back to work while the cold is still in full swing. This same mixture of catnip, yarrow, and mint makes a good hot tea for treating these same types of problems, but then a person should really be in bed, because it will cause them to sweat. The sweating will be helpful in breaking the fever and "sweating out" the disease, but the patient will then be in danger of pneumonia if he goes out all wet and sweaty. Such a person belongs in bed with a change of dry linens.

[46] Smoking corn silk doesn't work either. I did live through the Hippie Era of the '60s and '70s. I know whereof I speak! Trust me on this one.

Jill-over-the-ground

Creeping Charlie
Ground Ivy
Glechoma hederacea

~~~~~~

This plant has a thousand names, but none that I can find in Anishinaabemowin. It probably has not been here long enough to acquire a new name among us yet, or maybe it came with such a great array of interesting names that the people here just found one they liked and did not feel the need to give it another. It is called Jill-over-the-ground, Gill-over-the-ground, Gill-Ale, Gill-run, Gill-run over-grass, Lizzie-run-in-the-hedges, Hedge-maids, Haymaids, Robin-run-up-the-hedge, Robin-runaway, Creeping Charlie, Roving-Charlie, Run-away-Jack, Run-away-Nell, Run-away-Robin, Creeping Jenny, Cat's-foot, Cat's-paw. Ale-hoof, Tunhoof, Field Balm, Ground Ivy and many, many, more names to boot (Coffey 1993, 199; Gibbons 1966b, 96). To me and mine it has always been "Jill-over-the-ground," or less formally, "Jill."

This little plant is a vining mint, the only vining mint in our area. Because it looks slightly like an ivy, it is erroneously called "ground ivy." That is a poor name for it, though, because it is simply not an ivy. Jill-over-the-ground has a strange scientific name because it has its own genus. There is really no other mint, nor any other plant for that matter, that is enough like Jill to be classified with it. There is occasionally talk of reclassifying it with catnip, but they have different flowering habits. Catnip has its flowers at the end of its branches or stems, while Jill has hers in the pocket where the leaves meet the stems. Different flowering habits mean a lot to botanists, probably a lot more than they mean to the rest of us.

Jill is a very aromatic mint, but it really does not smell "minty" per se. Some people think it smells and tastes "almost lemony" or more "salty than minty," but I think it just tastes and smells like itself. On a warm day in spring, when the Jill is up and running, the smell of it in my garden is one of the chief delights of the season. It means "spring" to me. I have been known to lie right down

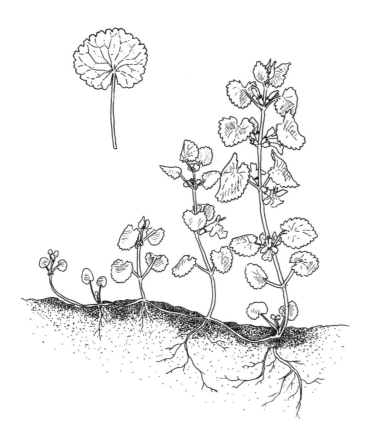

Jill-over-the-ground (*Glechoma hederacea*)

in a patch of Jill and roll in it like my house cat Rainbow, just to gather the smell into my hair and onto my skin, too. Then I pick a sprig or two of the uncrushed plant and take it into my kitchen to make a cup of tea. This is one tea that one should be sure to put a top on the pot or cup of while it is brewing, to retain the volatile oils and therefore both the smell and the taste. I sit and sip a cup of Jill and feel the winter melt out of my bones.

Jill is not just my personal "rite of spring." It has a long history as a spring tonic, probably owing to the fact that it has a large amount of vitamin C, which in the old days everybody needed after the limited diet of dried foods on which people had survived the winter. As a source of vitamin C it should be used fresh, but for just a nice cup of tea it can be used dried. It retains most of its taste and aroma as a dried tea, but, of course, one needs only ¼ as much of the dried foliage as one does the fresh to make the same amount of tea.

This tea is not only a pleasant tea to enjoy for its taste; it is also a good medicinal. It is an antiscorbutic, meaning it will prevent scurvy or rickets because of the high amount of vitamin C in the

47 Most all green plants have some vitamin C, but some have more of the vitamin than others do.

green plant.[47] It is also carminative and an antiflatulent, meaning it will reduce both stomach acid and lower intestinal gas. It is also to a lesser degree a febrifuge, meaning it will lower a temperature, but it will raise it at least one degree higher first, as does every other febrifuge except catnip, so be sure to use it only on an adult's fever, keeping the children on catnip instead. Like all of the mints, it is diaphoretic and will induce sweating.

When using Jill it might be a good idea to keep the following in mind:

> WARNING: Reportedly toxic in horses, causing throat irritation and labored breathing. Also reported in humans. In one case, the fresh leaves were steeped in ½ cup of hot water for ten minutes and then drunk. Within five minutes tea produced swelling of throat and labored breath, and resulted in difficulty sleeping that night. Symptoms abated in 24 hours. (Foster and Duke 2000, 216–71)

I had known that horses have trouble eating Jill, but they usually will not touch it in their paddocks. I had not known it ever had that effect on humans, but I suspect that it was an allergic reaction of that particular individual. One should always be careful the first time one eats or drinks anything strange to one's diet. Food allergies can be very dangerous. But a person can become allergic to anything. I once knew a woman who developed an allergy to her own husband and broke out in a rash whenever he came into the room. A divorce cured her.

In Europe, Jill has a considerable history in the brewing of beers and ales, hence the names of Ale's Hook, Tunhoof, and the various forms of Gill and Jill. The Gill, and its corruption Jill, comes from the French *guiller* meaning "to brew or ferment beer." *Tun* is an Old English word for the barrels in which beer was brewed. In the days before hops were commonly used in northern Europe and England, Jill-over-the-ground was added to beer to clarify and improve the taste of the finished product. Even after hops arrived, Jill was still used by the poorer people for their home brewing needs. Jill apparently has the ability to clarify or cure a beer that has become "skunky" tasting and developed a clouded look. A handful of Jill is said to clear such a brewing mistake and save the batch of beer (Grieves 1931, 442–43; Gibbons 1966a, 96–101).[48]

48 I was never a beer or ale drinker so I did not keep them, but I have seen recipes for beers using Jill. Euell Gibbons, in his *Stalking the Healthful Herbs,* offers a recipe for making a herbal wine using Jill-over-the-ground if a person wanted to give it a try (100-101).

Kee thought Jill made a nice houseplant because it looks lovely draped over the side of a hanging basket. It needs a lot of light in the wintertime, so one should keep it in a sunny southern window or give it a "grow light," although Kee said she knew few people who would put a grow light on a "weed." Such a house-plant is not only a good indoor air purifier in a closely insulated house, but it also is a good source of a vitamin-rich tea all through the off season. I have kept Jill plants over the winter just so that I could crush a leaf or two and dream of spring in the scent.

Aanikawishkoons

Zhiishiibinashk
Meadow Horsetail
Equisetum pretense

Scouring Rush
Field Horsetail
Equisetum arvense

Scouring Rush
Horsetail
Equisetum hyemale

Woodland Horsetail
Equisetum sylvaticum

Marsh Horsetail
Equisetum palustre

~~~~~~

The Equisetum are a group of plants that Keewaydinoquay always taught together. They are called by the colloquial name of horsetail because somewhere along the way someone thought that they looked like a horse's tail, but it is a name that is also in the scientific name for this family of plants. It is an odd connection, however, because the family is one that poisons horses. If they eat it (and they appear to like the taste of the plant so it has to be removed from their pastures), it gives them a disease called "equisetosis."[49] The plants contain chemicals that affect the horse's ability to absorb thiamine, vitamin B1. These plants also get called colloquially "snake grass." That particular name always gave Kee a good laugh. She would say, "They are no more a grass than you are a dog." And she could never figure out why they were called "snake" except as an insult. To get around both of the most common colloquial names, she always taught her students to call the plants "equisetum," and this student learned that lesson so well that she taught it to her daughter, who had no idea that she was using the plant's scientific name until she tried to look the plant family up in books. Because she had not been told they are also

49 Kee mentioned equisetosis in her lectures. For more information on this disease, including a description of how to cure it, see the University of Pennsylvania School of Veterinary Medicine's webpage: http://cal.vet.upenn.edu /projects/poison/agbook/dicentra .htm#Equiset

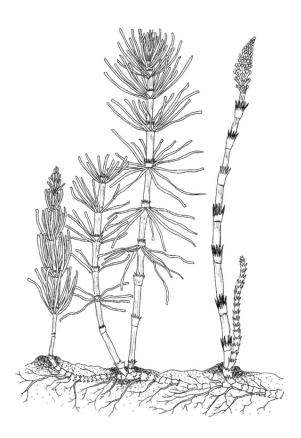

Aanikawishkoonsag: Equisetum (*Equisetum* spp.)

called "horsetails," she had considerable trouble using standard reference books.

This family of plants has the amazing ability to take minerals up into the tissues of their bodies. They have a vascular system and can suck water in which minerals are dissolved up into their tissues. Because the equisetums have space within their tissues, these dissolved minerals can actually reform the crystals of their mineral within the plant's body. If one takes a cross section of an equisetum and looks at it under a microscope, one can see what looks like gems in a little, round crown.

Most of the equisetums in the Great Lakes area take silica up into their fibers. One can see the six-sided quartz crystals of the silica in cross sections. Kee said she had not seen other minerals in the equisetum with her own eyes but she had heard a yarn about equisetum that she firmly believed:

A poor immigrant family went West in the latter part of the nineteenth century seeking a new life. As so often happened with such people, they were cheated by someone in the East who sold them marshy, sandy, unproductive land. The family had no more funds so they were forced to try to make a go of the homestead although their efforts were doomed from the first. The mother of the family finally died after an exhaustive struggle with the land, and the father wanted to give up and return to their ancestral home in defeat, but his sons begged for one more crop. They decided to burn over the back, marshy meadow to clear the land for the crop. They burned the field and went out the next morning to turn the land over with their shovels. To their surprise they saw the whole field was covered with shiny specks of gold that glistened in the sunlight. The equisetum in the field had taken gold flecks in the soil and in the water, taken the mineral up into their tissues. When the plant material was burned away, only the gold remained. The family gathered the gold from their field, and it was enough to buy them a new life on better land.

Kee loved that story and said she always thought about it when she looked through a microscope at equisetum cross sections. She said she did not find gold, but she loved to look for it anyway. She said it made her feel that she was on a treasure hunt.

The silica that most of our equisetums in this area take up into their bodies has made the equisetums very useful to Anishinaabeg and later to the early European settlers. They can be used to scrub metal pots, to get off burned-on food and also to brighten the metal by buffing the surface. It was much used when pewter was a common cookware. It has also historically been useful to sand wood for pipestems, and, later, for fine European- style cabinetry. The next time you go camping and are having trouble cleaning the bean pot that you used to cook your family's supper, grab a handful of equisetum, wrap the stems around in a circle and through to make a knot of the stalks, or form a handful of stems into a little wreath shape. That will clean a pot as quickly as a metal pot scraper that one can buy in a store. The next time you are refinishing a piece of wood furniture, use a similar clump of equisetum to give the wood a beautiful, smooth surface.

Equisetum has a medicinal virtue to share with Anishinaabeg, too. Keewaydinoquay used equisetum's ability to soak up water-soluble calcium to treat broken bones. As mentioned earlier, when my husband, Bob, broke his leg, Kee gave him a quart jar of dried equisetum and dried boneset and told him he had to drink the whole jar as tea, 1 teaspoon to 1 cup of boiling water, three times a day. He did as she told him, although the boneset has a distinctly bitter taste, and his leg healed very quickly. Not knowing he had broken his leg, Bob had walked around on the break for several hours before the secretaries at the school he was working in begged him to go home. By the time we got him to a doctor, his leg was so badly swollen that the doctors could not cast it. They x-rayed his leg, saw the break, and sent him home to elevate the leg for a week before they could put it in a cast. In that time he drank almost the whole jar of Kee's tea. By the next doctor's appointment, his leg had healed so well that the doctor had a very hard time actually seeing the break on a new x-ray. Kee said the calcium that the equisetum had taken up into its tissue was dissolved in the tea water and was helpful to Bob's body in regrowing the bone.

There is controversy in using equisetum as a medicinal because of the possibility that it contains a drug that will affect the body's ability to absorb vitamin B1, thiamine. It is however, used in Anishinaabeg medicine, and in German medicine as well, where it is approved for use in various kidney and bladder complaints (Foster and Duke 2000, 342–43).

Kee knew about the controversy, but she believed the problem came in when various strands of equisetum hyemale crossbred with other equisetums and produced a poisonous plant. She solved that by not using hyemale. She felt confident enough in her ability to tell the different types of equisetums apart, especially in the areas that she was most familiar with in Michigan and on her island, that she was not too worried about poisoning.

If I had to use the equisetum that I pick myself for medicinals, I would just be sure that my patient also took supplementary vitamin B1 as well. Even a horse poisoned by equisetum can be saved with injections of the vitamin if the disease is diagnosed quickly enough (Crockett 1977, 243). Kee had no problem with using modern medicine and research. She always taught us to use the best of both worlds.

There is another use for equisetum that Huron Smith was told by the Pillager Ojibwe. They would gather equisetum and feed it to their domestic ducks (Smith 1923, 400).[50] I know from personal experience raising ducks that the calcium that equisetum in our area take up into their tissues would be very beneficial to ducks. When a duck is laying eggs, especially in a home flock situation where someone keeps stealing her eggs, the poor duck is forced to keep laying eggs week in, week out, month in, month out. If she were in the wild, she could just lay a clutch of eggs and then take a break from laying eggs for a month while she sat on

50 Smith records the Ojibwe name for this plant as Gîji'bînûsk, which he translates as "duck food" or "duck round." We retranscribed this word as zhiishiibinashk; see Ojibwe Plant Name Glossary for more information.

the eggs. But if someone takes her eggs she will just go on laying
an egg a day all through the season. Such heavy laying strains
the poor, wee duck's body, and her need for calcium can become
critical. If she is not fed supplemental calcium her egg sack
may collapse, and that can kill her very quickly. If I cannot buy
supplemental calcium for my flock I will use equisetum, as long
as I can find enough, or I will just wash, dry, and crush eggshells,
sprinkling it on the duck food, refeeding the duck her own eggs
to help her sustain the calcium level her body requires. I have
seen wild mallards eat the infertile eggs in their own nests and the
eggshells of their hatched ducklings as well. I would bet that in
the wild they also eat equisetum if they need it.

Equisetum is one of the most ancient of life-forms on this
planet. In the Carboniferous Period of the Upper Paleozoic Era,
there were giant, tree-sized equisetum that formed huge forests.
Those giant equisetum of ancient times were among the organic
substances that formed the fossil fuels, the great beds of coal that
we use for power (Coon, 131-32). It is a strange thought, but the
electricity that powers the computer on which I type this chapter
on equisetum was first trapped from the rays of the sun by our
tiny equisetum's ancient, giant kin. Our Anishinaabeg ancestors
always maintained that "There is no Death. There is just Change
of Form." Power is power is power. I type on ancient sunshine.

Makwa-miskomin

"Bear His Red Berry"
Kinnikinnick
Bearberry
Arctostaphylos uva-ursi

~~~~~~

Both the scientific name for Bearberry, *Arctostaphylos uva-ursi*, and the Anishinaabe name, Makwa-miskomin, "Bear's Red Berry," betray the fact that this circumboreal plant has a very long history of being connected to Bear.[51] Makwa, black bear, the great doodem animal, has always been associated with medicine, and he is said to be the guardian of those who heal. There are many ideas of why this association between bears and healing began. It has been suggested that bears are so very similar in physical form to man that the ancients thought that what cured a bear would cure humans. A skinned bear's body looks frightfully human! It has even been suggested that humans and bears had a common ancestor in the distant past. Our Anishinaabe Bear Clan stories certainly celebrate a time when bears and men were one family. Anishinaabeg say Makwa is great both in a physical sense and in a spiritual sense. He still comes to us in dreams and visions. This ancient association with power is the reason many medicine people carry some part of Bear about their persons as a reminder of our connection to the power of Makwa.

Nodjimahkwe gave Keewaydinoquay the lifetime assignment to pursue and learn about plants that other peoples called by Bear's name. She said that she herself knew of eighteen plants called Bear but that she suspected there were at least twenty-four called Bear by the Anishinaabeg and many more called Bear by other peoples. She said if one hears a plant called Bear one knows it is a powerful plant that our people have used for a very long time. If elders talk about a bear plant, listen very closely. Stop whatever you are doing and find out all you can about that plant and how it can help people. This same assignment Keewaydino-quay gave to all of her oshkaabewisag, and I have done the same with mine.

51 Kee always included this in her lectures. Hyam and Pankhurst (1995) describe the scientific name as being from "the Greek *arkots*, a bear, and *staphyle*, a bunch of grapes, bears are said to eat the fruit" (36).

Makwa-miskomin: Bearberry
(*Arctostaphylos uva-ursi*)

Bearberry is a low-growing, vining plant that likes to grow near water. It will grow in limestone rubble on the beaches of the Great Lakes, but it will also grow on granite in the western mountains. It likes an area with high humidity. Bearberry is very sensitive to pollution and civilization. In Wisconsin now, one has to look for it north of the Menomonee River.

Bearberry always grows flat on the ground and is never more than nine or ten inches high. It has small, oval-shaped leaves that are glossy with a waxed look. It stays green all winter, even under the snow. A way to know for sure whether or not a plant is bearberry is to see if it has a real, woody stem. The other plants that are easily mistaken for bearberry all have succulent, juicy stems, but bearberry's stems are definitely as woody as a tree.

In the early spring, bearberry has a beautiful flower that is white with a brilliant, startlingly pink border. It looks for all the world like a tiny Japanese paper lantern. All of the members of the Heath family of plants, among them wintergreen and blueberry, have flowers that are of this shape, but bearberry flowers are the ones that are both white and pink.

The berries of bearberry are beautiful, but like many beautiful things, more fun to see than to "own." In the early spring the berries are green, turning orange by early summer and a deep, dull red by fall. But they are not as delicious as they look! They are very dry berries with a huge seed in the middle. They have very little flesh and practically no taste at all. They are edible, and there are accounts of Western Indians eating them after frying the berries in grease and then pounding them into pemmican; but Kee always said the bearberry berries were more trouble than they were worth as food. She also said one would have to have strong teeth to eat them at all.

Although it is called "Bear's Berry," bears do not much relish the berries either. In *MukwahMiskomin* or *KinnicKinnick,* Kee-waydinoquay quotes an old man of her village as saying:

"Look to the Muhkwah," says old Grandfather LoonHeart in the Long-Night-Moon legends of the Anishinaabeg. "In the times of starvation before NamahbiniGissis (Moon-of-the-Suckers-Running-Upstream, mid-February) he goes to the places where the berries called by his name are still fresh in the snow. If he breaks his winter sleeping and you see him chewing starvation berries, then you know he is desperate; it is his very own saving medicine, a good deed done by his long-ago ancestor now returned to his own kind. You will not see him stamping in delight as he does at the bee tree, you will not hear him snorting in anticipation as he does at the fishing rapids, but the food of the red berries and the medicine of the leaves will carry him through his time of need. Each of us will do well to remember. (From the Grandfather LoonHeart series among the oral traditions of the Leelanau Anishinaabeg. Told every winter at Cathead Point Village to the Crane Clan children as long as Wawbeno lived [1897–1952].

One often reads in non-native herbals that a plant is said to be used to cure many illnesses, but this is not an Anishinaabe idea. To the Anishinaabeg, Creator gave a spiritual and a physical virtue to every separate type of being so that they could share that virtue with others to maintain the balance of creation. Every type of animal and every type of plant has one physical thing that it does very well to help the rest. The thing that bearberry can do for us is that it is a wonderful internal antiseptic. It will cure or ward off problems one did not even know he or she had.

Liver and pancreas disorders are great killers of native peoples. There are some native communities where most of the adults have diabetes. Kee believed that Indian folk inherit a weakness in the area of the liver and pancreas that makes them unusually susceptible to these health problems. She said that before the Europeans came and diagnosed people as having diabetes mellitus, the Anishinaabeg knew about the problem. They called it "the trouble with sugar in their water" or "the slow death when ants come to their urine," meaning that the sugar in one's urine attracted ants.

Bearberry made it possible for many people to live long enough to bear and raise children. Nodjimahkwe urged Kee to begin daily usage of bearberry tea as a young woman to ward off the development of diabetes. When I knew Kee as an old woman she was still drinking it daily in a tea mixed with white or yellow sweet clover.[52] She would make a gallon of the tea at a time and refrigerate it. She drank it cold all day long. She said that she could occasionally miss a day or two of using bearberry, but that her body would remind her to keep using it if she skipped the tea for a week or more.

When asked if she thought using bearberry all the time would make it less effective when she really needed it, she replied that she thought any herbal or synthetic medicine could work that way. A body can get used to most anything if it is exposed to it too long, but she still took bearberry daily. She did that because she thought it warded off the onset of full-blown diabetes and inhibited the growth of bacteria that could cause all kinds of problems, too. She said it was usually more effective with herbal or other, modern medicines to use them as a preventative than to have to cure an already existing disease. She said her own teacher had been convinced of that, too.

Nodjimahkwe taught Kee several ways to treat diabetes with bearberry. The simplest was a tea made with half dried bearberry leaves and berries and half dried blueberries and/or leaves, about a tablespoon of the mix to one cup just-boiled and slightly cooled water. Another way to prepare the medicine was to make a tincture in alcohol[53] of bearberry leaves and berries and another tincture of blueberry leaves and berries. One instructs the patient to put 20 to 40 drops of the blueberry tincture and 10 to 20 drops of the bearberry tincture in one cup of boiled but slightly cooled water. The differences in the numbers of drops to a cup of water corresponded to the severity of the person's problem. This mixture was to be drunk three or four times a day. The patient must be warned not to drink more than the prescribed dosage,

52 White Sweet Clover is *Melilotus alba* and Yellow Sweet Clover is *Melilotus officinalis*, although some sources say these are just different color variations of the same species.

53 Kee preferred to use the highest proof vodka that she could buy for her tinctures. When making tinctures one uses the plant materials fresh, not dried. Dried plant material is best and strongest when making teas, also called infusions, or in mixtures that are boiled or simmered in water, which are called decoctions.

however. Nodjimahkwe also used bearberry and quaking aspen, *Populus tremuloides,* as a tea for elderly diabetics.[54]

Bearberry is a highly effective internal disinfectant. It cures infections of the kidneys and bladder, or as Kee would have it, of the "waterworks". She had seen it cure many women of cystitis. In one class on ethnobotany she knew of eight women, who were in the class or had heard about the bearberry cure from students who were in the class, all of whom were cured of cystitis through the use of bearberry. And two of the women had the problem so bad that they were about to undergo operations for it. Kee said a person should drink bearberry tea three or four times daily and use the tea as a douche as well to treat cystitis.

Kee said there are now Indian men who say that bearberry is just a "woman medicine." She said that is just plain nonsense! There are some plants that should be used by women because they tend to help the separation of the sexes by boosting male or female hormones, but bearberry does not do that. She said she knew of Indian men who had refused to use bearberry because of that particular prejudice and had died of their prejudice, too. Bearberry is a plant that has good medicine for both sexes, and has cured many children as well.[55]

Perhaps the virtue that bearberry has had to share with our people that has been the most appreciated for the longest time has been its use as kinnikinnick. See the Recipes section for a more complete instruction on making Anishinaabe kinnikinnick and what plants to add to the bearberry and cedar. All across Turtle Island, from the Arctic to the northern tier of American states, bearberry is picked and dried for use as the burning material that, along with Grandmother Cedar, is essential for the carrying of prayers into the Spirit World. In the areas where these two plants are not immediately available they have been trade items since prehistoric times. The exact ingredients of kinnikinnick differ from one group to another and even from one individual member of a group to another, but the two plants that are necessary to form the bases of the mixture are always cedar and bearberry. The Anishinaabeg say that is because these two plants were created at the same time, to save mankind when they were in need of spirit connection to their Guardians.[56]

Kee used kinnikinnick alone or with asemaa on an asinaagan or in a pipe. If the kinnikinnick is to be used in a pipe, add only a little of the conifers, balsam fir or cedar, as they will make the smoke somewhat bitter. If it is to be burned on a stone, one can

[54] A full description of the diabetic cures Keewaydinoquay learned from her teacher are given in *Mukwah-Miskomin or Kinnikinnick, Gift of Bear.*

[55] Those using bearberry should note the following: "Warning: Contains arbutin, which hydrolyzes to the toxic urinary antiseptic hydroquinone; therefore, use is limited to less than one week in German herbal practice. Leaves are high in tannins (up to 8 percent)" (Foster and Duke 2000, 29–30).

[56] See chapter 2 for the story of the creation of cedar and bearberry.

use as much of the conifers as one wishes. If the kinnikinnick is
to be burned as a fumigant in a sickroom, a lot of cedar would
be added. If the kinnikinnick was to be burned where a person
feared evil or imbalance, a lot of yarrow would be added.

People routinely mix two kinds of kinnikinnick: "Sacred Kinnikinnick" and "Friendly Kinnikinnick." The difference is that the
Sacred Kinnikinnick, because it is going to be used as an incense
to carry one's prayers to the Realm of the Manidoog, will be made
of plants that have been "prayed over." That means that the plants
will have been told while they are growing that they are to be
used to carry prayers. Often people go out in the spring of the year
and find the plants and tell them that they will be coming back
in the fall to take their year's growth to be used for this sacred
purpose. Kee always said if one did that, the plants seemed to
grow particularly lush that year because they knew they were to
be used for a good purpose. When one goes to take the plant one
asks the individual plant to send its spirit along for the purpose of
conveying prayers to the Manidoog.

A Friendly Kinnikinnick differs in that the plants need not
be prayed over early in the year while they are growing, but their
permission must still be asked before they are picked. Any other
method would disrupt the balance and put the picker in debt to
the plant. Friendly Kinnikinnick is the type a person might smoke
with friends, just for fun.

In the days before White Contact the Anishinaabeg had
another need for bearberry. The wood was much used to form
tools when the only metal the People used was soft copper. Bearberry grows very, very slowly and produces an incredibly hard,
tightly grained, dense wood. This is one reason why a person must
be careful in harvesting the foliage of bearberry. The vine takes so
long to grow that a stem one inch in diameter might well be over
a hundred years old. If a person wants the bearberry to continue
to grow in his or her lifetime, that person must be careful to
not damage the stem of the growing plant in his or her favorite
picking place. But in pre-metal times, bearberry was much used
to make tools and to make the handles for tools because it was so
strong. Kee's paternal co-grandmother had a set of gardening tools
that she wore on a belt that looked like a carpenter's belt with the
tools hanging from it. Kee loved that belt with its old tools, and
she always wished she still had it. She said the tools might have
been ancient, but they were a beautiful mahogany color and they

fit the hand perfectly. She said they were a joy to use or to just hold in one's hand.

Bearberry has one more fine medicine for the Anishinaabeg, but it is one that sounds very strange to modern ears. Kee was always reluctant to tell this to classes of university students because they had a tendency to laugh when they heard it. She was sensitive to the honor of a plant and did not wish to be the one to make people laugh at either the plant nor the people who used it for this cure. She said that bearberry had the virtue of enabling an infertile couple to have children, either because the woman did not conceive or because she could not carry the child to full term. The man and his wife would gather the little pink-and-white blossoms of the bearberry in the spring and dry them out of the sun in an open makak, so the flowers would retain their beautiful colors. Then, when the flowers were completely dry, the man, not the woman, would burn the flowers in the family pipe, and he would blow the smoke all over his wife from her head to her feet, blessing all of the openings of her body. He would do this for a whole month, every night at bedtime. It was a ritual that really worked. Many people owe the fact that they were conceived and born to this gift of bearberry.

Epilogue

<hr/>

"Four Warriors Find Naanabozho"

<hr/>

I had wanted to tell this story for some time. Keewaydinoquay told it to me. I am not sure if it was in class or privately. She often told me stories because she knew I loved them and because she knew it was the way I learn best. Often when I was working for her, if she wanted to teach me something, she would say, "Close the door of the office, and I will tell you a story." She said it always made her laugh how fast I would close the door. I have loved stories my whole life. This story I thought would make a good last story for the plant book because it has such strong teachings about the consequences of use and misuse of knowledge. It just seems like a good wrap up story to tell at the end of a teaching section. But I was having a hard time remembering the whole story enough to try to tell it. I remembered about the gifts given to the first two of the men and what was given to the last man, but not what was given to the third. I read and reread every book of legends I could find. I reread my notes, and I stewed over the problem. Then, one night I dreamed it. I was in the whole story. I woke several times in the night, and I then went back to sleep and right back into the same story. I realized what was happening, and I was able to say, "I need to know about the third man's gift," or "I need to know about the journey to the island," or "I need to know about how the story ends." And each time I would reenter the story at exactly the right spot to be re-instructed in the part of the story that I needed. It was marvelous! It was like having my own personal tutorial, or a website I could just click on to get to the part I needed to know. I have never been as well prepared to write a story than I am for this one.

Gichi-mewinzha, Naanabozho went missing. The
Anishinaabeg had not seen him for at least two generations.
Everyone wondered what had happened and where Naanabozho's
journeys had taken him that he was so long away from his people.
Four young men from one village fell to wondering where their
Great Uncle had taken himself.

They consulted their elders who all told them, "Oh,
Naanabozho must be off on one of his longer journeys. Do not
worry about him. When he is ready he will come back."

But the young men were impatient, as the young will be. They
said, "If we could find Naanabozho, people would tell stories
about us. We would be famous. And we could ask Naanabozho
for presents. Surely he would grant us our dearest wishes if we
were to journey far and suffer great hardships just to find him and
bring him greetings from his nephews the Anishinaabeg."

So, the four made great preparations to journey far in search
of Naanabozho. They made a great show of hunting game and
drying the meat. They pounded the dried meat into fat and
berries and made cakes of pemmican to sustain them on a long
journey. They took parched corn and popped wild rice and dried
berries, all light foods that would give them strength to go a long,
long way.

They started off with the well wishes of their families and
friends very early in the spring, before the ice was even off the
lakes. They went off on snowshoes so that they could use the
frozen rivers and streams and lakes of their northern home as
highways into the unknown. They set their journey into the
northwest, for their elders had told them that Naanabozho might
well have been traveling to where he was in charge of the Northwest wind.

The young men traveled a very far way from their village while
the lakes were frozen. When Break Up came, they rested and spent
their time making jiimaanan so that they could continue traveling. They peeled birch trees for the skin, gathered spruce roots to
make wadab to sew it onto the frame, and gathered pine sap to
melt with charcoal to make glue to seal the seams. They built two
fine canoes to carry them once the rivers and lakes were clear of
ice. They worked and worked and were ready to embark on their
journey as soon as the waters were free of ice.

On and on they journeyed. They traveled every day, and they
went further and further into the Northwest. They put down their

asemaa and their kinnikinnick, and they asked their Guardians for help and direction and guidance in their search for Naanabozho. Finally after months of journey they came to an island in the middle of a great northern lake that was directly under the *Jiibayag niimi'idiwag,* the flashing, dancing Northern Lights. The men put in to the shore and walked inland until they came to a clearing that was surrounded by high red-stone cliffs on three sides. At the foot of the cliffs were cedar trees in a circle, and in the very center of the clearing sat Naanabozho. He sat as if he were asleep, with his eyes closed. He had been sitting there so very long that a tall cedar tree had grown right on top of his head and the roots hung down the sides of his face like hair.

The young men advanced into the clearing and boldly shouted, "Ahow, Naanabozho! Aaniin! Boozhoo!"

Naanabozho opened his eyes slowly. He stretched one arm after another. Then he reached up and lifted the cedar tree off of his head and set it down at his side. He rose to his feet and heaved a great sigh. Only after a great while did Naanabozho say, "Ahow! Aaniin, my relatives. Have you come to visit your old uncle? Or do you come to ask me for something?"

The young men looked at each other then the boldest said, "Greetings, Naanabozho. We have journeyed far to find you. We have heard all of our lives about the Great Naanabozho and how generous he is. So we thought we would find you to ask you for gifts to help your relatives the Anishinaabeg."

"Yes," said Naanabozho, "You are right, I am a generous uncle who has given his relatives many good things. What more do you want?"

The bold young man said, "I want to be a great warrior. I want to be as bold as my Great Uncle, and I want people to tell great stories about my exploits."

"Howa!" said Naanabozho, "You are a bold one! You have the courage to make this long journey just to find me. I guess you will be a great warrior and one that your people will remember with stories in years to come. Remember when you go into battle that you are a brave man whom your Great Uncle believes will be a famous warrior."

The first young man sat down beaming with pride, and a second young man stood up to say, "Oh, Mighty Naanabozho, son of the West Wind Spirit and the Anishinaabe woman. Aaniin! We have come a very long way and have suffered great hardship to find you. We decided on this journey in the fall of the year. We hunted long hours and brought down much game so that we could leave our families well provided for and so that we could make a large quantity of pemmican to sustain us on our journey. We made strong *aagimag,* snowshoes, to strap to our feet so that we might start out while the lakes and rivers of Anishinaabewaki were still covered with ice. Then we camped during Break Up and made two fine canoes of wiigwaasi-mitig to carry us further. We searched and searched for you. We put down asemaa and kinnikinnick to ask our Guardians for help in finding you. Then one day we saw your beautiful island under the Jiibayag niimi'idiwag. We beached our jiimaanan and walked inland until we found you napping under the Grandmother Giizhik. Oh Great Naanabozho, Great Uncle, I ask that you remember your relatives the Anishinaabeg, and for myself I ask that I may have the gift of oratory, that I may be a maker of speeches that will be useful at the council fires of our Nation. Mii'iw. Miigwech."

"Well," said Naanabozho, "It seems to me that you will make a fine speaker, whose words will be remembered for generations. Be sure to speak with pride and to always urge your listeners to remember the Anishinaabeg of the Seventh Generation in any of their decisions."

"And you," said Naanabozho, turning to the third young man. "What have you come to ask of your Great Uncle?"

"I want Great Medicine Power," said the third young man boldly. "I want Power that will be of use to our people in the time to come so that they will speak about me and honor me."

The words were no sooner out of the young man's throat than he was changed before their eyes into a tall cedar tree.

"There," said Naanabozho. "Now you have your wish. The Anishinaabeg will be able to pick your leaves and branches and use your bark and your roots and all of the parts of you as medicine in the time to come. You have Great Medicine Power."

"And you, my fine young fellow, what have you to ask of Naanabozho?"

Without hesitation the last young man blurted out, "I want to live forever!"

"Granted," said Naanabozho. In the place of the last young man there was a great, gray, granite stone, tall and solid and firm. "There," said Naanabozho. "Now you will live forever, for only the rocks never die."

Then Naanabozho yawned a great yawn and stretched his arms above his head. He sat back down in the spot he had been before the warriors arrived, and he picked up the cedar tree with the long roots and placed it back on his head. He arranged the roots around his face like long hair, and he closed his eyes.

The two young warriors stood for a long time, watching Naanabozho sleep. Then they walked to the cedar tree and the rock who had been their companions. They placed their hands on them and whispered, "*Giga-waabamininim miinawaa,* I will see you later, Brothers." Then they walked slowly back to their canoes to begin their journey home.

Mino-nibaan, sleep well, Naanabozho. Mii'iw. Miigwech.

Recipes

~~~~~~

Wildcat Liniment

Directions for Sharing the Healing Given by the Plants in "Wildcat" for the Relief of Sinus-related Pain

Medicinal Applications of Pines

Use of Pines as Decongestants
Modern Applications of the Use
 of Inhalants
Foot Bath to Enhance
 Circulation
White Pine–Honey Decoction

Tincture of Tamarack and Willow: Traditionally Used to Treat Arthritis

Cattails (*Typha latifolia* or *Typha angustifolia*)

Cossack Asparagus
Cattail-Pollen Pancakes
Golden Cattail Muffins
Making Flour from Cattail Roots
Cattail Corn Bread
Cattail Flour Batter Bread
Cattail Pollen Bread Sticks
Homestead Pudding

Jerusalem Artichokes (*Helianthus tuberosus*)

Sun Root Pickles
Jerusalem Artichoke Casserole
Jerusalem Artichoke Chiffon Pie
Savory Jerusalem Artichoke Pie
Jerusalem Artichoke Salad
Spicy Jerusalem Artichokes
Roasted Jerusalem Artichokes
Jerusalem Artichoke Soup
Palestine Soup

Staghorn Sumac (*Rhus hirta*)

Sumac Tea
Mulled Sumac Drink
Sumac Jelly
Sumac Meringe Pie

Yarrow (*Achillea millefolium*)

Sagamoety

Dandelions (*Taraxacum officinale*)

Little Suns
Boiled Dandelions
Boiled Dandelion Greens in Salad
The Molly Claim Pancakes
Sweet and Sour Dandelions
Dandelion Salad
Dandelion Jelly

Dandelion Hair Rinse
Dandelion Duchess Soup
Dandelion Flower Biscuits
Freezing Dandelion Greens
Scalloped Dandelion Greens
Dandelion Gravy

Plantain (*Plantago lanceolata, Plantago major, Plantago rugelii*)

Beef Plantain Rolls

Pureed Plantain

Roses (*Rosa* spp.)

Uncooked Rose Petal Jam
Uncooked Rose-Hip Jam
Harem Kisses Candies
Bird-of-Paradise Chicken
Rosewater Cookies

Rosewater Cheesecake
Rose Petal Bread
Rose Beads
Rose Petal and Crab Apple
   Jelly

Violet (*Viola* spp.)

Violet Sugar
Violet Honey
Violet Butter
Violet Jam
Violet Syrup
Violet Candy

Violet Syrup on the Rocks
Violet Sherbet
Violet Sundae
Violet Skin Preparation
Candied Violets

Mint (*Mentha* spp.)

Mint Infusion—Mint Tea
Peppermint Lip Balm
Soft Mint Soap
Whole Body Emollient
Cool Mint Body Emollient
Wild Mint Salad Dressing
Mint Sauce

Cucumber-Mint-Yogurt Soup
Honey Mint Carrots
Mint Chocolate Pound Cake
Mint Cookies
Mint Jelly
Mint Jam
Anishinaabe Kinnikinnick

Wildcat Liniment

The following is copied directly from one of Keewaydinoquay's class handouts:

> Dissolve 2 tablespoons of white-pine pitch in vodka to cover.
> Strain when dissolved.
> Add one ounce Vicks Vapo-Rub and stir.
> Add 6 teaspoons cayenne pepper and stir.
> Next, add: 2 ounces Vaseline,
> 15 drops peppermint oil,
> 15 drops eucalyptus oil.
> Stir together well. Store in closed bottle and label.
> Apply externally, massaging until little is left on the skin. This liniment is good for sore muscles, sprains, rheumatic and other local pains, as well as an aid in draining sinus cavities.

Directions for Sharing the Healing Given by the Plants in "Wildcat" for the Relief of Sinus-related Pain

The following is copied directly from one of Keewaydinoquay's class handouts:

> Materials needed: Box of disposable tissue
> 　　　　　　　　　 Clean hands
> 　　　　　　　　　 Wildcat Liniment
> 　　　　　　　　　 Privacy

1. Be seated comfortably. Thank the plants who have given their virtues to this medicinal. Ask all Spirits to help you regain Harmony; say you will try to stay in Balance when it is achieved.

2. Place an amount of the salve at the pineal eye, the depressions at either side of the temples, across the high bones of the cheeks.

3. Place both central fingers at the pineal eye, pressing in with the thumbs and index fingers, begin to massage at the mount of the nose, traveling slowly across the arch of the cheek bones until you come to the temple depressions (This "slowly" means Very Slowly for most persons of this hurry-paced world, using small circular motions sunwise. Do not spare yourself because of tenderness. Think of relaxation in the sinus canals, or force yourself to slow your pace by thinking through the KaWaYaan[1] as you massage from nose arch to temple depressions. That loooooong, eh?) Of course you can blow and wipe and spit whenever necessary. The whole purpose is to get the damn stuff out.

4. Renew salve. Place the thumbs at the temple depressions. Then using either the central fingers and/or index fingers

[1] The KaWaYaan is a prayer that Kee often used in ceremonies.

begin massaging slowly at the pineal eye, working across the bone arch of the brows to the temple depressions. Remember to keep pressure at the pineal eye when working below the eyes on the complete ring around the eyes at the arch of the circum-eye bones. You cannot reverse the procedure. You must begin at the nasal area below the eye in order to unstop the sinus area where it empties into the oral cavity.

5. Place a very light amount of the salve in each ear. If there are any areas about the face, temples, head, which are sore and have not been massaged, do so.

6. Now place central fingers or index fingers at the pineal eye for pivotal balance; with thumbs, search along the inner arch of the bones just above the eyeball until you come to the break in that bone between the socket arch and the nasal ridge. Depress that area hard with the thumbs. It should Hurt! If it does not, you are in the wrong place. Hold that hurting depression while you swing the inner eye to the far extremities in a complete circle. It is easier if you keep the eyes closed for this. You should be feeling the eye muscles stretch. Make it feel as if you had swung the eye clear down to your belly button, out to your ears, up to the top of your head! Sing the Blessing Song[2] inside your head as you do this slowly—or something else which will force you to make the 'Swing Time' of the eye not less than one minute. All the time remember to continue depressing the thumbs so much it hurts.

7. Now place an amount of salve in each nostril. Depress (close) the right nostril with the right thumb. Imagine the passage of the Eustachian tube up to your left ear. Give a big, long, sustained snufffff. (If your irritation is extreme, you may have to grab the edge of the table at this point!)

Depress (close) the left nostril with the left thumb. Imagine the passage of the Eustachian tube up to your right ear. Give a big, long, sustained snufffff.

If nothing has happened so far, just sit relaxed and wait. It will! Chances are, though, you will already have started the sinuses draining. You should feel the progress of the volatile oils across the roof of the mouth in the nasal passages.

Guaranteed you will be relieved from pain for a while. If the infection is severe, you will have to repeat as pain and pressure return. Keep at it until it goes away. And don't be stupid and go out in subzero weather after you have opened all these passages up!

This is also good relief from what you thought was a headache. In that instance, include the muscles at the nape of the neck and up the sides of the neck to the mastoidal area below and behind each ear.

2 The Blessing Song is a song that Kee often used in ceremonies.

Medicinal Applications of Pines

Use of Pines as Decongestants

Euell Gibbons devoted a whole chapter to the pines in his *Stalking the Healthful Herb*, in which he says:

> Dried white pine bark is still a valuable ingredient in cough remedies. It is an official drug in the U.S. *Pharmacopoeia the National Formulary* and in the U.S. *Dispensatory*. Its medicinal properties are expectorant and diuretic. It is most often prescribed in the title role of Compound White Pine Syrup, or as the doctor would write it on your prescription, Syrupus Pini Alba Compositus . . . contains not only white pine bark, but wild cherry bark, spikenard, poplar buds, bloodroot, sassafras root bark and amaranth. If you want to make this remedy at home, there is a complete recipe in the National Formulary . . .
>
> White pine needles have been tested for nutritional benefits, and they gave good yields of vitamin A and five times as much vitamin C as is found in lemons . . . Judging from taste and effects, I believe all white pine products, the staminate catkins, the tender shoots, and the green needles, have the same expectorant and diuretic properties that make the bark an official drug, and I am sure a good cough syrup could be made with any of these tree parts if the bark is unavailable. (119–20)

Modern Applications of the Use of Inhalants

My recipe, after Keewaydinoquay's instruction

> Epsom salts to which is added eucalyptus oil and mint oil and pine or balsam oil. This combination is excellent to use in the bath to break a cold. One can use wintergreen oil as an inhalant, but not in the bath as it attacks mucus membranes. One can add fresh leaves and foliage to Epsom salts and age it a few weeks until the oils in the plant material are transferred to the salts. Food coloring added to this mixture will give it emotional appeal.

Foot Bath to Enhance Circulation

My recipe, after Keewaydinoquay's instruction

1 quart Epsom salts
1½ ounces cayenne pepper
pine or balsam oil

1. Mix ingredients and store in a sealed jar.
2. Dissolve ½ cup in warm water and use to soak feet. Do not sit in this mixture as it does nasty things to mucus membranes.

Alternative/older method: One can push hot peppers and chopped pine or balsam foliage into the Epsom salts and age for a month to transfer the oils instead of using the dried cayenne pepper and the pine/balsam oils.

White Pine–Honey Decoction

My recipe, after Keewaydinoquay's instruction

This is a recipe for a pine-tasting, sweet tea that helps with colds and sore throats.

> **¼ cup inner bark of white pine, cut into small pieces**
> **2 cups water**
> **1 cup honey**

1. Put all of ingredients in a heavy saucepan.
2. Bring to a boil.
3. Turn temperature down and simmer for ½ hour.
4. Strain mixture to remove the bark.

   Serve hot or cold in ½-cup servings. Cooled bark may be chewed as a chewing gum type throat lozenge to soothe a sour throat.

Tincture of Tamarack and Willow: Traditionally Used to Treat Arthritis

Keewaydinoquay gave me this rough instruction. She knew a woman who was an expert with this recipe, and she always meant to set me or another of her Oshkaabewisag with the woman to be further instructed in how to make and use the medicine. She just did not get around to it while I was working with her. One would have to experiment with the dosage if one was to use this tincture. If I had to use it, I would guess that 4–5 drops of the tincture could be used in one cup of hot water, drunk as a tea. I would start off with that and build from there as I saw how the patient reacted. Of course, I would have to drink it first because Nodjimahkwe said never to give a person something to drink that you would not drink yourself. This tincture, of course, could not be used by anyone who was sensitive to aspirin because the willow bark has aspirin in it. This medicine should be remade as often as necessary, but definitely once a year.

> **fresh tamarack needles, chopped**
> **inner bark of willow cut into small pieces**
> **vodka**

1. Put equal amounts of chopped tamarack needles and cut-up inner bark of willow into a sterilized canning jar.

2. Pour enough vodka over the plant material to completely cover it.

3. Cover jar with a scalded lid.

4. Put jar on counter, and every day for three weeks shake jar to stir the contents.

5. Filter out plant material.

6. Bottle and label with contents and date.

Cattails (*Typha latifolia* or *Typha angustifolia*)

Cossack Asparagus

My recipe, adapted from Keewaydinoquay's instruction and Kavasch.

> In spring before the flowering stalks appear on the cattails, pull up on the center of the plant. Remove outer portion, peel the outer leaves the way one peels a banana, and cut off the tops of the leaves. Retain the white, inner tender core. This is the Cossack Asparagus. It can be eaten raw, sliced into a salad, or cooked.
>
> To cook: Cover stalks with boiling water. Simmer 10 minutes or until fork tender. Serve with melted butter. Or lay in a pan next to a nice beef or venison roast before cooking the roast in the oven.

Cattail-Pollen Pancakes

My recipe, after Keewaydinoquay's instruction

> 1 cup cattail pollen
> 1 cup flour
> 3 tsp baking powder
> 1 tsp salt
> 1 tbs sugar
> 2 chicken eggs or 1 duck egg
> (Keewaydinoquay's family used tern eggs. I use duck eggs because I live with a flock of ducks who gift me with a lot of eggs in the spring and summer months)
> 1½ cups milk
> 2 tbs melted butter or margarine
> ½ tsp cooking oil
> butter and/or maple syrup

1. Put pollen through a sieve to remove any debris.

2. In large bowl mix pollen, flour, baking powder, salt, and sugar.

3. In small bowl beat eggs and pour into well in flour mixture.

4. Mix and add melted butter.

5. Heat frying pan. Grease with cooking oil.

6. Pour some batter onto frying pan, and cook 2–3 minutes till little bubbles form.
7. Turn and cook other side for 1 minute.
8. Serve with butter and/or maple syrup.

Golden Cattail Muffins

Adapted from Pringle

1 cup cattail pollen
1 cup flour
2 tsp baking powder
½ tsp salt
1 chicken or duck egg
¼ cup cooking oil
⅓ cup honey
1½ cups milk

1. Preheat oven to 400 degrees F.
2. Line muffin tins with paper cups, or grease the muffin tins.
3. Put pollen through a sieve to remove any debris.
4. Stir pollen in a large bowl with flour, baking powder, and salt.
5. In small bowl beat egg and add oil, honey, and milk.
6. Pour wet mixture into dry. Stir to moisten.
7. Pour into muffin cups, to ½ to ⅔ full.
8. Bake 20 minutes.

Making Flour from Cattail Roots

Keewaydinoquay always taught her students that making flour from cattails was an awfully laborious and unrewarding experience. She said it was not to be undertaken in a survival situation because one could conceivably waste a lot of time and energy for very few calories of food. But if you are one of the ones who wants to try it anyway, this is how you do it:

One can gather the roots at any time from summer and fall into early spring, if you can get through the ice. Dig up the roots with a shovel or rake. Scrub the roots clean and scrap off the outer skin as soon as you harvest. It gets harder to do after the roots dry. Slice the roots and set them out in the sun to dry. Turn them over several times a day and take them inside at night so the dew does not rewet them. It could take a week or more depending on how much sun you get to dry the roots properly. They can, however, be dried in a dehydrator or in a 200-degree or lower oven overnight. Store dried roots in a covered container in a dry place until needed. One grinds the roots up in a food processor or a flour mill or one could put them in a cloth bag like a pillowcase and pound them with a hammer or a stone. Sift out the hard strings and stick-like fibers before using the flour in your recipe.

Cattail Corn Bread

Adapted from Williamson

¼ cup sugar
1 tbs baking powder
½ tsp salt
½ cup cattail pollen
½ cup yellow cornmeal
1 cup flour
1 egg
1 cup milk, soured with 1 tsp lemon juice, or buttermilk
⅓ cup vegetable oil

1. Mix dry ingredients in mixing bowl.

2. Add remaining ingredients and mix until just moist.

3. Spoon into a greased 8x8 inch pan.

4. Bake in preheated oven at 425 degrees F. for 15 to 20 minutes, until golden brown.

Cattail Flour Batter Bread

Adapted from Williamson

1 pkg. active dry yeast
¼ cup warm water
1 tsp sugar
¾ cup milk
1 tbs sugar
2 chicken eggs or 1 duck egg
1 tbs olive oil
1½ cup cattail flour
1½ cup wheat flour

1. Dissolve yeast in warm water with 1 tsp sugar. Set aside until it bubbles.

2. Scald milk, then cool to lukewarm.

3. Add milk, sugar, eggs, oil, and cattail flour to yeast mixture.

4. Beat at high speed for 3–5 minutes.

5. Add remaining flour.

6. Allow to double in size in a warm place.

7. Stir down.

8. Put into greased 9x5x3 inch loaf pan. Brush top with a little olive oil.

   Bake at 375 degrees F. for 50–60 minutes.

Cattail Pollen Bread Sticks

Adapted from Williamson

> **1 pkg. active dry yeast**
> **⅔ cup warm water**
> **2 tsp sugar**
> **1½ cup flour**
> **¼ cup soft butter or margarine**
> **½ cup cattail pollen**
> **1 egg, unbeaten**
> **1 tbs cold water**
> **coarse salt**

1. Sprinkle yeast and 1 tsp sugar into warm water. Set aside to bubble.
2. Add rest of sugar, flour and butter or margarine to the bubbly yeast. Beat until smooth.
3. Mix in cattail pollen.
4. Knead dough on lightly floured bread board until smooth and elastic.
5. Place in greased bowl and set aside to rise in a warm place until doubled in size. Punch down.
6. Cut into 28 pieces and roll each into an 8-inch stick.
7. Place on greased baking sheet, 1 inch apart.
8. Beat egg with water. Brush sticks with mixture. Sprinkle with coarse salt.

   Bake in preheated 375 degree F. oven for 18 minutes or until golden brown.

Homestead Pudding

Adapted from Williamson

> **3 chicken eggs or 2 duck eggs**
> **1½ cups sugar**
> **1 tsp vanilla**
> **⅓ cup cattail flour**
> **2½ tsp baking powder**
> **1½ apples chopped into fine pieces**
> **⅓ cup chopped nuts or peanuts, optional**

1. Beat together eggs, sugar, and vanilla until mixture is thick and lemon-colored.
2. Stir together cattail flour and baking powder.
3. Mix into egg mixture, then fold in apples and nuts.
4. Spread batter into a greased 8x12 inch baking pan.

   Bake in preheated 325 degree F. oven for 35–40 minutes. Serve warm with sweet whipped cream or canned milk.

Jerusalem Artichokes (*Helianthus tuberosus*)

Jerusalem artichokes can be eaten raw the way one eats radishes, or chopped and added to salads. They can be cooked any of the ways one would cook a potato. Keewaydinoquay liked them best either served raw the way we did in workshops, or added at the last in stir fries, or roasted in the same pan with a nice Beef or Venison Roast. She also spoke lovingly of an aunt who made a wicked Jerusalem Artichoke Chiffon Pie. If one really needs specific recipes, the following are gleaned from several sources:

Sun Root Pickles

Adapted from Gibbons, Stalking the Wild Asparagus

Jerusalem artichokes
wine or cider vinegar

1. Peel the tubers.
2. Boil tubers in water to cover for 2–4 minutes. Drain.
3. Pack cooked tubers into clean, sterilized canning jars.
4. Heat wine or cider vinegar to boil.
5. Pour over tubers.
6. Seal jars with scalded canning lids.
7. Boil in hot water bath for 10 minutes.
   Allow to age two weeks before use.

Jerusalem Artichoke Casserole

Adapted from Gibbons, *Stalking the Wild Asparagus*

4 cups Jerusalem artichokes, peeled, boiled, and mashed
2 cups fine bread crumbs
½ cup melted butter or margarine
2 beaten chicken eggs or 1 duck egg
salt and pepper to taste

Mix all of above and pour into a greased casserole dish. Bake at 350 degrees for 30 minutes, at 325 if using glass dish. Serve hot.

Jerusalem Artichoke Chiffon Pie

Adapted from Gibbons, *Stalking the Wild Asparagus*

¾ cup brown sugar
1 envelope unflavored gelatin
1 tsp pumpkin pie spice
3 eggs, divided

½ cup milk
1¼ cups cooked, mashed Jerusalem artichokes
⅓ cup sugar
graham cracker crust

1. In a saucepan combine sugar, gelatin, and pie spice.
2. In another bowl mix egg yolks and milk and add to sugar mixture in saucepan.
3. Cook and stir over medium heat until it reaches a boil.
4. Remove from heat and stir in artichokes.
5. Chill one hour until mixture mounds.
6. Beat together 3 egg whites and sugar until soft peaks form.
7. Fold into stiffened artichoke mixture.
8. Pour into graham cracker crust. Chill until firm.

   I have not made this recipe since they started to tell us that we could not eat raw eggs. I do not know how to change this recipe to make it safer to eat, except to cook both the whites and the yolks and fold the mixture into sweetened and whipped cream, about 1 cup, instead of the egg whites before chilling at the end.

Savory Jerusalem Artichoke Pie

Adapted from Crowhurst

1 pound Jerusalem artichokes
2 tbs flour
1 crushed garlic clove
1 tbs chopped parsley
1 cup onion, finely chopped
⅓ cup milk
pinch of nutmeg
salt and pepper to taste
2 tbs butter or margarine

1. Boil artichokes for 5 minutes in water to cover.
2. Drain. Rub off skins. Chop fine.
3. Blend flour with milk and add to artichokes.
4. Mix in garlic, parsley, onion, milk, nutmeg, salt and pepper.
5. Pour into greased casserole dish. Dot with butter or margarine. Bake at 400 degrees F. for 30 min. Serve hot.

Jerusalem Artichoke Salad

Adapted from Kavasch

1 pound Jerusalem artichokes, scrubbed and cubed
3 green onions, chopped

½ cup salad oil
½ cup cider vinegar
1 tbs honey
1 tbs fresh mint leaves, chopped
2 cups salad greens

1. Mix artichokes, onions, oil, vinegar, honey and mint in a salad bowl.

2. Allow to sit for 1 hour at room temp.

3. Add 2 cups salad greens. Serve.

Spicy Jerusalem Artichokes

Adapted from Kavasch

1 pound Jerusalem artichokes, scrubbed and sliced
½ cup salad oil
2 garlic cloves, chopped
2 tbs chives, chopped or 1 green onion, chopped
2 tbs fresh dillweed, chopped
¼ cup cider vinegar

1. Boil Jerusalem artichokes in water to cover 20 min. Drain.

2. In a skillet mix artichokes, oil, garlic, chives or green onion, dillweed.

3. Sauté for 15 min.

4. Add vinegar and simmer 5 min. Serve hot.

Roasted Jerusalem Artichokes

Adapted from Kavasch

whole Jerusalem artichokes, scrubbed with a vegetable brush
salad oil
butter or margarine
salt and pepper

1. Start a wood fire and reduce it to coals.

2. Wipe artichokes with oil.

3. Wrap individually in heavy-duty aluminum foil and place them directly into the still red coals.

4. Roast for 8 minutes.

5. Turn and roast for 8 minutes more. Unwrap one to check it with a fork the way one tests a baked potato to see if it is cooked. If it is still boney, return it to coals a little longer.

6. Serve hot with butter, salt and pepper to taste.

   In the old days Anishinaabeg did not add salt. They seasoned food either with maple sugar or with hardwood ashes, which give food a salty taste.

Jerusalem Artichoke Soup

Adapted from Kavasch

> **1 pound Jerusalem artichokes, scrubbed with vegetable brush**
> **6 cups water**
> **3 scallions, with tops, sliced**
> **2 tbs dill seed**
> **3 chicken eggs or 2 duck eggs**

1. Boil artichokes in water for 25 minutes or until tender.
2. Drain, reserving liquid.
3. Mash artichokes and return to cooking water.
4. Add dill and simmer 15 minutes.
5. Beat eggs in a separate bowl.
6. Add spoonfuls of hot soup to eggs, then mix and return to pot.

Simmer 1 min. Serve hot.

Palestine Soup

Adapted from *Cuisine*, November 1983

In nineteenth-century England this Jerusalem artichoke soup was called "Palestine Soup" in the mistaken belief that the vegetable came from the Holy Land.

> **4 cups chicken stock**
> **4 tbs butter or margarine**
> **1 large onion, finely chopped**
> **1½ pounds Jerusalem artichokes, pared, cut into 1-inch pieces**
> **1½ tsp salt**
> **½ tsp celery seed**
> **1 bay leaf**
> **ground pepper**
> **2½ cups light cream**
> **¼ cup grated Parmesan cheese**
> **fresh dill, chopped**
> **croutons**

1. Melt butter or margarine in heavy saucepan over medium heat.
2. Add onion and sauté 3–4 minutes, stirring frequently until soft but not browned.
3. Add artichokes, 4 cups chicken stock, and seasonings, except for the fresh dill.
4. Heat to boil. Reduce heat to low.
5. Simmer covered until artichokes are tender, 20–25 minutes.
6. Remove form heat. Remove and discard bay leaf.
7. Puree soup in batches in blender. Return to saucepan.
8. Stir in cream and grated cheese.

Heat over low for 5 minutes. Pour into bowls. Sprinkle with dill and croutons. Serve hot.

Staghorn Sumac (*Rhus typhina*)

Sumac Tea

My recipe, after Keewaydinoquay's instruction

Pick berry clusters on a sunny afternoon after a spell of dry weather. If clusters have few or no insects, place a clump or two in a bowl. Boil water in a kettle, cool for a minute or two to preserve vitamin C, and pour over the berries. Mash the berry clumps a few times with a potato masher. Put top on the bowl and allow the tea to brew for about 10 minutes. Filter the liquid through double layer of cheese cloth or muslin or a coffee filter to remove the tiny hairs and loose berry particles. Serve warm with honey to relieve a sore throat or simply for the pleasure it provides. May be served cold over ice as a lemonade, or used in a recipe calling for sumac tea or infusion.

Mulled Sumac Drink

Adapted from Pringle

8 cups sumac tea
8 whole cloves
2 sticks cinnamon
1 tsp ground allspice
½ cup brown sugar, packed
1 lemon, sliced
1 orange, sliced
grated fresh or ground nutmeg

1. Make sumac tea from berries by pouring boiling water over sumac berries. Filter through cheese cloth or coffee filter to remove little hairs on the berries.
2. Put in clean pan.
3. Add all spices and fruit, except nutmeg.
4. Heat mixture over low heat for 30 minutes.
5. Add sugar, and mix to dissolve.
6. Strain out the spices.

   Serve hot with sprinkle of nutmeg on top.

Sumac Jelly

Adapted from Freitus

4–6 ripe staghorn sumac berry clusters
2 quarts boiling water

1 cup sugar per cup of juice
3 ounces liquid pectin

1. Place berry clusters in pot and cover with 2 quarts boiling water.
2. Mash berries with potato masher.
3. Cover pot and allow the infusion to steep of 10 to 15 minutes.
4. Remove from heat. Strain liquid through cloth or coffee filter to remove solids and hairs.
5. Measure juice. Place in clean pot, combining 1 cup sugar to 1 cup hot juice.
6. Mix and bring to a boil.
7. Add pectin.
8. Bring to boil again and boil 1 full minute.
9. Pour into hot, sterile jelly jars and seal.

Sumac Meringue Pie

Adapted from Carson

4–5 red sumac berry clusters
7 tbs cornstarch
1½ cups sugar
½ tsp salt
3 chicken eggs or 2 duck eggs, separated
2 tbs butter or margarine
1 prepared, baked pie shell
6 tbs sugar

1. In a saucepan, cover berry cluster with water.
2. Bring to a boil. Boil 5 minutes.
3. Strain liquid through cheesecloth or coffee filters. About 2 cups sumac liquid should have been made. If not enough, return to pan, add more water and simmer the heads for another few minutes, re-strain and measure.
4. In the top of a double boiler, combine 1½ cups sugar, cornstarch, and salt with the sumac liquid.
5. Cook over medium heat until the mixture is very thick.
6. In a bowl, whisk egg yolks.
7. Add a little of the hot sumac mixture and whisk to blend.
8. Pour the egg yolks into the double boiler and beat vigorously. Cook 2 minutes, stirring constantly. Remove form heat.
9. Add butter or margarine and set aside to cool.
10. Make a meringue by beating the egg whites until they form stiff peaks. Beat in 6 tbs sugar.
11. Spoon sumac mixture into prepared pie crust. Top with meringue.

Bake in center of the 300 degree F. oven until meringue is browned on the peaks. 15–25 minutes.

Yarrow (*Achillea millefolium*)

Sagamoety

Keewaydinoquay's paternal co-grandmother, Minissing Odahnikwe, gave her this recipe. She told me verbally how to make it, but this written version is from her professor Richard I. Ford, University of Michigan, Ann Arbor; however, his version did not have the vital ingredient, yarrow, used as a cooking spice, and yarrow's inclusion was the reason Kee always told her students about Sagamoety.

> 4 cans kidney beans
> 6 cans of pinto beans
> 1 can Great Lakes navy beans
> 6 cans hominy
> 6 cans whole kernel corn
> 1 34-oz bottle Heinz ketchup
> small amount of brown sugar
> some wild rice
> 1 handful of fresh yarrow, leaves and flowers

Drain and wash beans.

Mix all ingredients and simmer over low heat for a few hours. The bitter taste of the yarrow will be cooked out of finished stew.

Dandelions (*Taraxacum officinale*)

Little Suns

Keewaydinoquay taught me this recipe, and it is her title. We often fried these up in our ethnobotany lab at the University to give our students a taste for dandelions. This is my family's favorite dandelion recipe. We eat it every spring when the yard is covered with dandelions. It means "spring" to us.

> dandelion flowers, with all of the green stems and bitter, white
>   juice removed
> 1 beaten egg
> corn meal
> a little salt
> butter or margarine

1. Remove all of the green stem from the base of the dandelion flowers as you pick them. Use your thumbnail to scoop out the material that grows at the top of the stem into the flower, so that no particle of the bitter juice remains.

2. Wash the flowers and shake them dry.

3. Holding one flower at a time between thumb and forefinger, dip into a beaten egg and then push the flower down into cornmeal to which you have added a shake or two of salt.

4. Place coated flower upright on a plate while you coat the rest of the flowers.

5. Melt butter or margarine in a frying pan over medium heat.

5. Put flower heads face down on the pan and fry to a golden brown. Flip to fry other side.

6. Drain on paper toweling or brown paper bag. Serve warm.

Boiled Dandelions

My recipe after Keewaydinoquay's verbal instruction

Pick whole tops of very young dandelions, picked before they flower. Use a knife to cut the whole plants off just below the surface of the ground. Wash well. Add to an inch or two of boiling water in a sauce pan. Boil for 5–10 minutes. Discard water, or retain to use as a dye for wool. Serve topped with butter and a dash of salt.

Boiled Dandelion Greens in Salad

My recipe

Prepare young dandelion leaves as described in last recipe. Drain and place on top of a mixed salad of spinach and lettuce and tomatoes. Serve with Italian or Caesar or salad dressing of your choice.

The Molly Claim Pancakes

My recipe and title after Keewaydinoquay's verbal instruction

1 cup flour
1 tsp baking powder
¼ tsp salt
1 duck egg, or 2 chicken eggs
1 cup milk
1 tsp melted butter or margarine
More melted butter or margarine to grease frying pan
1 handful dried or fresh dandelion flower petals

1. Mix dried ingredients.

2. Add egg and milk. Mix until it is smooth.

3. Add melted butter or margarine.

4. Melt more butter or margarine in frying pan. Heat until a drop of water bounces on the hot pan.

5. Pour pancakes onto pan. Sprinkle each with dried or fresh dandelion petals.

6. Cook until bubbles start to form on surface of pancake.

7. Flip over and cook other side until light, golden brown.

    Serve hot with maple syrup or sprinkled with sugar.

Sweet and Sour Dandelions

Adapted from Weatherbee

> **boiled, young dandelion leaves**
> **4 slices bacon**
> **1 onion, chopped**
> **1 egg, beaten**
> **¼ cup brown sugar**
> **¼ cup vinegar**
> **¼ cup water**

1. Fry bacon in frying pan until crisp. Drain, retaining grease, and crumble the bacon into bits. Put aside.

2. In the bacon grease, fry chopped onion.

3. Mix in a bowl: egg, brown sugar, vinegar and water. Pour over cooked onions in frying pan.

4. Heat over medium heat, stirring, until the liquid thickens.

5. Pour over drained greens. Top with bacon. Serve warm.

Dandelion Salad

Adapted from http://www.echoedvoices.org/Mar2002/Dandelion _Recipe.html

> **4 cups chopped, young dandelion leaves**
> **3 hard-cooked chicken eggs or 2 duck eggs**
> **3 slices bacon**
> **1½ tbs flour**
> **1 tsp salt**
> **1 egg**
> **2 tbs sugar**
> **¼ cup vinegar**
> **2 cups milk or water**

1. Wash and chop dandelion leaves. Gather them before the flower heads form.

2. Fry bacon until it is crisp. Remove from pan and drain on paper towels or brown paper bag, retaining bacon drippings. Cool and crumble bacon.

3. Mix together flour and salt; add egg, vinegar and milk or water. Stir until blended.

4. Add to bacon drippings in pan and cook until thickened. Cool slightly.

5. Pour dressing over dandelion leaves and mix lightly.

6. Garnish with sliced or chopped hard-boiled eggs and crisp bacon pieces. Serve immediately.

Dandelion Jelly

Adapted from http://www.echoedvoices.org/Mar2002/Dandelion _Recipe.html

> **1 qt dandelion flowers, with all of bitter stems removed**
> **4 cups water**
> **4½ cups sugar**
> **1 tsp lemon juice**
> **1 box Sure-Jell pectin**

1. Cook flowers and water together for 3 minutes. Strain and save the dandelion water.

2. Follow directions on Sure-Jell box using dandelion water.

3. Bring to a boil, then add 4½ cups sugar and lemon juice. Stir until sugar melts.

4. Pour into sterile canning jars. Screw on sterilized lids.

5. Process in boiling water bath for 10 minutes.

Dandelion Hair Rinse

Adapted from http://www.echoedvoices.org/Mar2002/Dandelion _Recipe.html.

Dandelions, like chamomile and marigolds, give a golden glow to blond or light-brown hair. This makes enough rinse for one use.

> **3 cups dandelion flowers**
> **water to cover**

1. Place flowers in large pot and cover with cold water.

2. Bring to boil, turn down heat, and simmer for one hour.

3. Strain and cool liquid before pouring over freshly washed, damp hair.

4. Wrap hair in dark towel for at least 30 minutes.

5. Rinse and dry.

Dandelion Duchess Soup

Adapted from Williamson

> **1½ cups young, dandelion leaves picked before flower head forms**
> **1½ tbs butter or margarine**
> **½ cup onion, chopped**
> **1½ tbs flour**

3½ cup milk
2 tbs grated Parmesan cheese
2 chicken egg yolks or 1 duck egg yolk
1 cup sour cream
½ tsp celery salt
pepper to taste

1. Boil dandelion leaves in water to cover for 10 minutes. Drain.
2. Melt butter or margarine in saucepan. Sauté onion until tender.
3. Blend in flour. Slowly stir in milk.
4. Cook until the mixture thickens slightly.
5. Beat together cheese, egg yolks, and sour cream. Add to soup along with cooked leaves.

Heat gently, season, and serve.

Dandelion Flower Biscuits

Adapted from Williamson

1¾ cups flour
½ cup dandelion flower petals, fresh or dried
dash of salt
2 tsp baking powder
2 tbs butter or margarine
¾ cup buttermilk, or milk soured with 1 tsp lemon juice or
    vinegar

1. Sift together flour, salt and baking powder.
2. Cut in butter or margarine until mix looks like cornmeal.
3. Stir in petals and buttermilk or soured milk.
4. Stir vigorously 3 minutes.
5. Turn onto floured board. Form into ball. Roll ¼ inch thick. Cut with a glass or 2 inch biscuit cutter. Bake at 425 degrees F. for 12 minutes on lightly greased cookie sheet.

Freezing Dandelion Greens

Adapted from Williamson

2 lb young dandelion leaves
3 quarts boiling water to which has been added 2 tsp salt. Salt may be omitted for salt-restricted diets.

1. Pour boiling water over rinsed and drained greens. Let stand for 5 minutes. Drain well.
2. Pack into quart-sized freezer bags, label and freeze.

   May be used in any recipe that calls for cooked dandelion greens.

Scalloped Dandelion Greens

Adapted from Williamson

> 6 cups young dandelion leaves
> water
> 4 hard-cooked chicken or three duck eggs, diced
> 1 cup milk
> 1½ tbs butter or margarine
> 1½ tbs flour
> 1¼ cups grated sharp cheddar cheese

1. Simmer dandelion leaves in water to cover, 10 minutes in a covered pot. Drain well.
2. Make a white sauce with melted butter in saucepan. Stir in flour, then slowly add milk and cheese.
3. Cook over low heat, stirring until sauce is thick and the cheese has melted.
4. Add eggs.
5. Pour over leaves in a baking dish.

Bake at 400 degree F for 15–20 minutes.

Dandelion Gravy

Adapted from *Dining During the Depression*

> 1 handful of young dandelion leaves
> 4 tbs olive oil or margarine
> ⅓ cup flour
> ½ cup water
> 2 cups milk
> salt and pepper
> 1 tsp vinegar
> 2 duck eggs or 3 chicken eggs, hard boiled and sliced

1. Soak dandelion leaves in hot, salted water for ½ hour. Drain.
2. Melt margarine or oil in a frying pan.
3. Add flour and stir with a spoon until it is nicely browned.
5. Stir in ½ cup water. Add milk slowly. Mix until smooth.
6. Add vinegar and dandelion leaves. Mix.
7. Add salt and pepper to taste.
8. Mix in eggs.
   Serve over mashed potatoes.

Plantain (*Plantago lanceolata, Plantago major, Plantago rugelii*)

Plantain leaves contain Vitamins A, C and K as well as calcium. They taste best when leaves are new in the spring. Older plants can be forced to produce new growth later in year by cutting off all of the old leaves, watering the plant, and waiting for it to put out new young leaves. One can also cover an older plant with grass clippings or newspaper or a black garbage bag so that the sunlight can not reach the leaves. In a few days the leaves will have lost a lot of their green colour and bitter taste. They will be blanched like celery, and milder tasting.

In the early spring, when the leaves are still very small and before the flower stalk grows up from the center of the leaves, plantain leaves can be used fresh and green in salads. As the leaves age, they become sharper tasting and much more fibrous. Some people blanch them before adding the older leaves to salads. If the leaves have become too stringy to eat, it is possible to remove the ribs of the leaves, chop the part of the leaves that is between the ribs, soak in salt water for 5 minutes to help reduce the sharp taste and to help tenderize, then use the leaves cooked as one uses cooked spinach.

In late summer, throughout the fall and even into the winter, the seeds of the flower stalk are ready for harvesting. They are, however, very small seeds and arduous to process. One must dry them completely by heating them very slowly in a pan over a low fire, stirring to keep them from scorching. Once the seeds are dry, rub to loosen the outer seed coating, and then winnow the seed to remove the chaff. The resulting seed can then be ground to a flour. It is best used to extend flour supplies. Or one can cook the whole seed as a porridge. The seeds are very high in Vitamin B1 and may be worth the effort in a survival situation.

These are my descriptions based on Keewaydinoquay's instructions.

Beef Plantain Rolls

Adapted from Pringle

> 4 cups plantain leaves
> 1 cup fresh mushrooms, sliced
> 1 garlic clove, peeled and chopped fine
> 3 tbs olive oil
> salt and pepper to taste
> 6–8 thin slices round steak
> 3 tbs butter or margarine
> 2 tbs cooking oil
> 1–1½ cups red wine or red wine vinegar and a little sugar
> 1 tbs flour

1. Wash leaves. Steam or boil for 2 minutes or until tender. Drain. Chop.
2. In large fry pan, sauté mushrooms and garlic in olive oil.
3. Add chopped plantain. Season with salt and pepper.
4. Put mixture on meat slices, roll up and tie each with string or thread.

5. In same fry pan, melt 2 tbs butter and add cooking oil.

6. Brown meat on both sides.

7. Add wine or vinegar and sugar, enough to go half way up fry pan sides.

8. Cover and simmer meat until tender, 15–20 minutes.

9. Remove stuffed meat rolls, cut strings.

10. Turn up heat under fry pan and rapidly boil sauce in pan.

11. In a bowl blend the remaining ingredients of butter and 1 tbs flour. Stir as you add it to sauce. Cook to thicken and pour over meat rolls and serve.

Pureed Plantain

Adapted from Pringle

> **6 cups plantain leaves, either early spring leaves or chopped, deribbed older leaves**
> **2 tbs butter or margarine**
> **½ cup Ricotta cheese**
> **½ tsp ground nutmeg**
> **salt and pepper to taste**

1. Wash plantain. Steam or boil until tender.

2. In large fry pan, sauté the plantain in butter or margarine, then mix in cheese.

3. Heat through.

4. Add nutmeg, salt, pepper, and serve.

Roses (*Rosa* spp.)

Uncooked Rose Petal Jam

Adapted from Gibbons, *Stalking the Healthful Herbs*

> **1 cup freshly gathered rose petals, with whites of leaves cut off**
> **¾ cup water**
> **juice of one lemon**
> **2½ cups sugar**
> **1 package dried pectin**
> **¾ cup water**

1. Put petals, ¾ cup water and lemon juice into blender and blend until smooth. Gradually add the sugar.

2. In a sauce pan, heat pectin and ¾ cup water to a boil. Boil hard for one minute, stirring constantly.

3. Pour the pectin mixture into the blender with the petal mixture and run until completely mixed.

4. Pour into hot, sterilized, small jars.

5. Allow to sit at room temp for 6 to 8 hours to jell.

6. Store in fridge up to one month or in freezer for the winter.

Uncooked Rose-Hip Jam

Adapted from Gibbons, *Stalking the Healthful Herbs*

1 cup rose hips, with stem, blossom ends, and seeds removed
¾ cup water
juice of one lemon
3 cups sugar
1 package dried pectin
¾ cup water

1. In a blender, blend rose hips, ¾ cup water, and lemon juice until smooth. Gradually add 3 cups sugar, blending 5 minutes or until sugar is dissolved.

2. In a sauce pan, heat pectin and ¾ cup water to a boil. Boil hard for one minute, stirring constantly.

3. Pour the pectin mixture into the blender with the rose hip mixture and run until completely mixed.

4. Pour into hot, sterilized, small jars.

5. Allow to sit at room temp for 6 to 8 hours to jell.

6. Store in fridge up to one month or in freezer for the winter.

Harem Kisses Candies

Adapted from Gibbons, *Stalking the Healthful Herbs*

2 cups rose petals, with white part of petals removed
½ cup water
½ pint heavy cream
powdered sugar

1. Mix rose petals and ½ cup water in blender until reduced to a semi-liquid mass.

2. Add cream and mix well.

3. Add enough powdered sugar to make a dough that can be kneaded.

4. Turn out onto a bread board and knead for 2–3 minutes, adding more powdered sugar as needed.

5. Cover with a damp cloth and allow to stand for one hour.

6. Cut off small pieces and shape into balls.

7. Top, if desired, with a pistachio nut or half of a candied cherry.

Bird-of-Paradise Chicken

Adapted from Gibbons, *Stalking the Healthful Herbs*

> 1 roasting chicken
> 3 tbs honey
> 2 tbs melted butter or margarine
> 1 tbs rosewater

Pre-heat oven to 325 degrees F.

1. Mix together honey, melted butter or margarine, and rosewater.
2. Using a pastry brush, paint whole outside of bird with honey, butter, and rosewater mixture before roasting in oven. Use any remaining sauce to baste bird while baking.
3. Bake 2–3 hours.

Rosewater Cookies

Adapted from Louquet

> 1 cup butter
> 2 cups sugar
> 3 chicken eggs or 2 duck eggs
> 1 cup sour cream
> 3½ cups flour
> 1 tsp baking soda
> 2 tbs rosewater
> powdered sugar

1. Cream butter and sugar.
2. Beat in eggs.
3. Add rosewater, baking soda and flour. Mix well.
4. Drop by spoonful onto greased cookie sheet.
   Bake at 350 degrees F. until light brown on edges, 8 to 10 minutes. Dust with powdered sugar while warm. Cool on rack or plate.

Rosewater Cheesecake

Adapted from Louquet

> *Crust*
> 1½ cups graham cracker crumbs
> 3 tbs brown sugar
> 6 tbs melted butter or margarine
> ⅛ tsp nutmeg

1. Combine all crust ingredients
2. Press into bottom of 10-inch spring-form pan.
   Chill in fridge for 30 minutes.

Filling

24 ounces cream cheese
1½ cups sugar
¼ tsp salt
1 tsp rosewater
4 chicken or 3 duck eggs

1. In mixer, blend together cream cheese, sugar, salt, and rose-water. Mix well. Add eggs one at a time, beating well between each addition.
2. Pour cake mixture onto crust. Bake for 50 minutes at 350 degrees F.
3. Remove from oven and increase heat to 450 degrees F.

Topping

2 cups sour cream
¼ cup sugar
2 tsp rosewater

1. Combine topping ingredients and pour onto cake that has been cooked for 50 minutes.
2. Return cake with topping added to the 450-degree oven. Cook for 10 minutes more.
3. Cool and chill cake before removing from pan.

Rose Petal Bread

Adapted from Emery

1 cup lightly packed rose petals, with white parts removed
1 tsp rose extract
3 tsp lemon extract
¼ cup sugar
Add ingredients to a regular, two-loaf recipe for white bread.

Rose Beads

Adapted from Emery

crushed, dried, or cut-up fresh rose petals
rain water
flour
glycerin
sweet oil or rose oil

1. Put enough dried and crushed or fresh and cut up rose petals to fill a cast-iron skillet. A rusty skillet will give the beads a very pretty, velvety black colour.
2. Cover petals with rain water.
3. Bring to a simmer over low heat, and simmering gently for 1 hour.

4. Take it off heat and leave it on stovetop for a day.

5. Next day stir the petals and add more water if too dry, and bring back to a simmer over low heat. Simmer 1 hour.

6. Turn off heat and leave on stove top for one day.

7. Next day repeat procedure, being sure that the petals do not burn as the water level may be very low by this time. Add more water if necessary.

8. Dough should now be stiff, and it will be black if the skillet has rusted. Flour and a few drops of glycerin may be added if necessary to make a dough that will hold together to be shaped into beads.

9. Form beads by hand. Be aware that the beads will shrink a great deal. Try to make the beads as smooth as possible. Pierce each bead and leave on a rust proof pin standing up on a Styrofoam tray to dry, or dry on a thin knitting needle or wire that has been greased to prevent dried beads from sticking to it. Dry completely.

10. Put a little sweet oil or rose oil on hands and rub finished beads in hands to give a fragrant and shiny surface to dried beads.

11. String with other glass or metallic beads if desired.

Rose Petal and Crab Apple Jelly

Adapted from Freitus

> 2 cups rose petals, with white part of petals cut off
> 1 quart ripe crab apples
> 1½ cups sugar per cup of juice
> 6 ounces liquid pectin

1. Fill a pint jar completely with fresh picked rose petals, with whites of leaves removed.

2. Cover petals with boiling water and cover jar with lid. Keep out of bright sunshine. Allow to sit for 24 hours to leach the color and flavor from the petals.

3. Next day strain the liquid and remove the petals.

4. Wash and remove stems and flower remnants from 1 quart of fully ripe crab apples.

5. Cook in a little water until soft. Mash apples to free juice. Simmer for 15 minutes.

6. Strain through a jelly bag and do not squeeze.

7. Combine the rose petal juice and crab apple juice, and add 1½ cups of sugar to each cup of juice. Mix.

8. Bring to a boil for 1 full minute, or until sugar dissolves.

9. Add liquid pectin. Return mixture to a full boil, a boil that cannot be stirred down. Hold at a full boil for 1 minute, then remove from heat.

10. Skim surface and ladle into hot, sterile jelly jars and seal.

Color will be a deep pink. The liquid pectin is necessary because the ripe crab apples do not have enough natural pectin, but they give a lovely color to jelly. Rose petal jelly can be made with this recipe by leaving out the crab apples and adding 1 tsp lemon juice.

Violets (*Viola* spp.)

Violet Sugar

My recipe

> **violet flowers**
> **sugar**

1. Fill a scalded and dry canning jar ¼ full of white sugar. Cover top of sugar in jar with freshly picked violet flowers that have been trimmed of their stems. Cover those flowers with more sugar until the jar is ½ full, Add another layer of flowers then more sugar until the jar is ¾ full. Add yet another layer of flowers and fill rest of jar with sugar, leaving ½ inch of head room at top of jar.

2. Cover with a canning lid and put jar in fridge for 3 weeks.

3. The flavor of the flowers will transfer to the sugar and will become more flavorful over time. The flowers will dry and will be suitable for use to decorate cakes or cookies or just to nibble upon. The sugar will be a nice topping for cookies or cakes or puddings.

Violet Honey

My recipe

> **honey**
> **violet flowers**

1. Heat a jar of honey by putting it, opened, in a Pyrex cup in a pan of boiling water for a few minutes.

2. Fill a clean and scalded canning jar ½ full of freshly picked violet flowers and pour the hot honey over the flowers leaving ½ inch head room at top of jar. Seal and allow to sit at room temperature for 1 week for flavor and vitamins to infuse the honey.

3. After one week, reheat honey by placing canning jar in a pot of hot water to make it easier to pour. Just make the honey warm, not hot, as that would drive off the volatile oils and many of the vitamins.

4. Strain the warm honey into a clean canning jar and seal.

Violet Butter

My recipe

> **1 stick of butter**
> **violet flowers, fresh and chopped fine**

1. Allow butter to sit at room temperature until it is soft.
2. Mix the butter in a mixer or by hand until it is fluffy.
3. Fold in about ½ cup chopped, freshly picked violet flowers.
4. Mold the flower-butter and cover, and chill over night to allow the flowers fragrance and taste to infuse the spread.

   Experiment by using the butter on different vegetables, pastas, rice, fish or chicken as well as a spread for toast, warm buns, pancakes, and scones.

Violet Jam

Adapted from Gibbons, *Stalking the Healthful Herbs*

Uncooked to retain vitamins. Gibbons thought he invented the recipe, but almost identical jam was sold in Charles II's time as a remedy for respiratory conditions, bronchitis, pneumonia, etc.

> **1 packed cup violet flowers**
> **¾ cup water**
> **juice of 1 lemon**
> **2½ cups sugar**
> **1 package powdered pectin**
> **¾ cup water**

1. Put violet flowers in blender with water and lemon juice. Blend until it is a smooth paste. Add sugar a little at a time. Blend until sugar is dissolved.
2. In saucepan on stove, add pectin to ¾ cup water, stirring to dissolve. Bring contents to boil, stirring, and boil hard for 1 minute.
3. Pour into blender with flower mixture, and blend 1 minute.
4. Pour into sterilized jars and seal with scalded lids.

   Will keep in fridge 3 weeks. Freeze for later use.

Violet Syrup

Adapted from Gibbons, *Stalking the Healthful Herbs*

Use in cooking, or as a cough syrup taken 1 tsp at a time, or in larger amounts as a very gentle laxative

> **violet flowers**
> **boiling water**

lemon juice
sugar

1. Fill a hot, sterilized canning jar with violet flowers.
2. Cover with boiling water.
3. Cover jar with a scalded lid and allow to sit on cupboard for 24 hrs.
4. Drain and filter infusion, discarding solids.
5. To every cup of infusion add juice of ½ lemon and 2 cups sugar.
6. Bring to a boil, stirring constantly.
7. Pour into sterilized jars and seal.

Violet Candy

Adapted from Gibbons, *Stalking the Healthful Herbs*

1 package lemon flavored Jell-O
1 tbs unflavored gelatin
1 cup boiling water
1 cup violet syrup

1. Pour Jell-O and gelatin powders into a Pyrex cup or pan. Add boiling water. Stir until dissolved.
2. Add violet syrup. Mix.
3. Pour into a lightly greased, shallow pan and chill overnight or until set.
4. Cut into small cubes and serve in candy dish.

Violet Syrup on the Rocks

Adapted from Gibbons, *Stalking the Healthful Herbs*

2 tbs of violet syrup
ice
water or seltzer water

1. Pour violet syrup over ice cubes in a glass.
2. Fill glass with water or seltzer water.

Violet Sherbet

Adapted from Gibbons, *Stalking the Healthful Herbs*

Do not do this in a city were the snow has had to fall through polluted air. In the city, use crushed ice instead of the snow.

violet syrup
clean, country-fallen snow

1. Pour violet syrup over new fallen, clean snow or crushed ice.
2. Mix to sherbet texture.

Violet Sundae

Adapted from Gibbons, *Stalking the Healthful Herbs*

> **violet syrup**
> **vanilla ice cream**

1. Pour syrup over vanilla ice cream.
2. Top with a fresh violet flower.

Violet Skin Preparation

Adapted from Gibbons, *Stalking the Healthful Herbs*

Said to be good for healing sores

> **1 ounce lanolin**
> **3 ounces cocoa butter**
> **fresh, chopped violet leaves**

1. Put lanolin and cocoa butter in a double boiler or in a Pyrex cup in a pan of water. Melt.
2. Stir in as many violet leaves as the melted fats will cover.
3. Put in a medium oven, 325 degrees F., for 1 hour.
4. Pour through a strainer to remove leaves.
5. Pour into sterilized, small jars. Seal with scalded lids. Label and date jars.

> Rub onto chapped or cut skin. Do not eat.

Candied Violets

Adapted from Crowhurst

Older recipes suggest candying edible flowers by dipping them in a beaten egg white and then into sugar before allowing them to dry. Since uncooked eggs are no longer considered safe to eat due to the danger of E. coli bacteria, this recipe should be a safer alternative. Candied violets retain a lot of their vitamins and just eating 3 or 4 a day would give a person a lot of vitamin C; also, candied violets are so pretty as decorations for cookies and cakes and dessert puddings and custards that this more complicated recipe might just be worthwhile.

> **2 quarts violet flowers**
> **1 ounce gum arabic**

½ cup water
1½ tbs corn syrup
½ cup water
1 cup sugar
powdered, icing sugar

1. Very gently wash individual flowers by swishing them in water, being careful to not bruise the petals.
2. Allow to dry.
3. Put gum arabic and ½ cup water into a Pyrex cup and set it in a pan of water on burner. Stir until gum melts.
4. Take off heat and allow to cool.
5. With a soft, new paintbrush, paint the petals of each flower. Dry flowers completely.
6. In a saucepan, mix corn syrup, ½ cup water, and 1 cup sugar.
7. Bring to a boil and cook until a drop of mixture into a cup of cold water forms a ball.
8. Remove from heat and cool syrup.
9. Dip each flower into the syrup, place face up on a wax paper and sprinkle with powdered or icing sugar.
10. Dry flowers completely and store in an air-tight container.

Mint (*Mentha* spp.)

Mint Infusion—Mint Tea

My recipe after Keewaydinoquay's instruction

Bring 1¼ cups of water to a boil. Remove from heat. Add ½ ounce fresh leaves and stems of *Menthe arvensis* or any mint you prefer. If using dried mint, use less than half that amount.

Allow to steep in a covered pot 10 minutes or longer until the water becomes a lovely golden-green color. Remove the plant material. Enjoy the fragrance and the taste! As well as being a delightful beverage tea, mint helps relieve stomach gas and aids in digestion.

A cup of very strong mint infusion added to the bath is very invigorating and helps to clear the head in a cold and the mind in a quandary.

Peppermint Lip Balm

Keewaydinoquay's recipe from ethnobotany class handout

2 parts olive oil
1 part beeswax
10 drops peppermint oil (or flavoring of your choice)
2% of whole amount benzoin powder (about 1 pinch)
1 tsp glycerin

1. Melt beeswax in a double boiler or water bath. Never heat wax right on a burner. You will not believe how fast one whole kitchen and house can go up in flames, literally.

2. Add olive oil to melted wax.

3. Add benzoin and glycerin and mix quickly and thoroughly as it solidifies very quickly.

4. Take off heat.

5. Add peppermint oil. Mix well.

6. Pour into sterilized containers.

   Note: It is very important to add plant oils right before putting in containers as heat causes the volatile oils to evaporate. Do not use commercial peppermint extract instead of the peppermint oil as it will cause the mixture to separate, producing a poor product. This is the same procedure for the making of various medicinal salves and balms. If more oil is added the produce will be more like a lotion than a solid cream. If the product that results is too hard, remelt and add more oil. If it is not hard enough, remelt and add more wax. More peppermint oil will have to be added if product has to be remelted as the volatile oils will be driven off by the heat, however.

Soft Mint Soap

Keewaydinoquay's recipe from ethnobotany class handout

   15–20 sprigs of fresh mint, cut up
   2 cups water
   2 tbs cider vinegar
   1 tbs glycerin
   4 cups handmade or unscented soap, either liquid or solid (grated)

1. Place mint and water in a glass or stainless steel pan and cover. Boil and reduce the liquid by one-quarter the volume.

2. Pour into a sterilized canning jar. Add 2 tbs cider vinegar and 1 tbs glycerin. Shake well.

3. Allow mixture to stand, covered tightly for 4 hours.

4. Strain through cheesecloth.

5. Pour into a pan and gradually add the soap to this mixture while beating. Beat until creamy.

   Suggestions: A glass coffee pot works well for reducing the decoction, since it usually has the number of cups marked on the side. It is easier to see when the liquid has been reduced sufficiently. If grated soap is preferred, gradually add small amounts of water. Hand mix to avoid a sudsy mess. Mint must be boiled in a covered container to retain the volatile oils. If the scent is lost or not strong enough, try adding peppermint extract a few drops at a time to the finished product.

Whole Body Emollient

This formula was adapted by Keewaydinoquay from Stark's *Formula Book*. I copy it from Keewaydinoquay's ethnobotany class handout.

Glycerin Skin Gel

"Glycerin is an emollient, or softening agent, and is excellent for dry skin. Dissolve 5 tsp gelatin in 2¼ cups hot water, allow to cool to lukewarm and add 3 tbs glycerin. You can also stir in a few drops of any oil-based perfume or essential oil, such as rose oil or oil of rosemary."

Keewaydinoquay instruction: I use these proportions basically, but add a little more hot liquid or less gelatin. The gelatin used should be plain, unscented, and unflavored gelatin. In addition, I dissolve one pinch of benzoin in ½ tsp alcohol, adding this with the glycerin. Before the hot liquid is added, the gelatin should be soaked briefly in a minimal amount of cold water to prevent lumping.

Cool Mint Body Emollient

Keewaydinoquay's recipe from ethnobotany class handout.

Stimulating any time, especially delightful in very hot weather. Steep 2 tbs of mint leaves (or 2 menthol crystals) in the hot liquid of above recipe. Strain or not, according to personal taste. Some folk feel it is more natural if the leaves are visible. Add one tsp of mint flavoring for sweetness of scent and one speck of menthol crystal. Absolutely invigorating!

Wild Mint Salad Dressing

Adapted from Pringle

> **1 cup wine or cider vinegar**
> **4 tbs sugar**
> **½ tsp salt**
> **dash of cayenne pepper**
> **4 tbs chopped fresh mint leaves**

1. In saucepan mix and heat vinegar, sugar, salt, and cayenne. Bring to boil. Remove from heat.
2. Pour over the mint leaves in a sterilized bottle or jar.
3. Chill and store in fridge.

   This dressing is especially nice over sliced tomatoes or cucumbers.

Mint Sauce

Adapted from Crowhurst

> 2 tbs finely chopped fresh mint
> ½ cup white wine or vinegar
> ⅔ cup sugar or honey
> ½ tsp salt
> ¼ cup water

1. Simmer vinegar, sugar or honey, water, and salt for 5 minutes.
2. Pour over chopped mint.
3. Cover and allow to cool.
   Blend before serving. Excellent with roasted lamb.

Cucumber-Mint-Yogurt Soup

Adapted from Richardson

> 2 medium cucumbers, peeled and seeded
> 2 cups yogurt
> juice of ½ lemon
> 3 tbs chopped fresh mint leaves
> pepper
> thin slices of lemon and sprigs of mint for garnish

1. Puree all ingredients, except garnish in blender or food processor.
2. Chill for several hours to blend flavors.
3. Serve cold, garnished with lemon and mint.

Honey Mint Carrots

Adapted from Louquet

> 2 cups carrots, sliced thin
> ½ cup water
> ¼ cup toasted, sliced almonds
> 1 tbs fresh mint, chopped
> 3 tbs margarine
> ½ tsp dry mustard
> ⅛ tsp grated nutmeg
> 2 tbs honey

1. Cook carrots in water over medium heat until tender (8–10 minutes)
2. Drain and add rest of ingredients.
   Heat and serve.

Mint Chocolate Pound Cake

Adapted from Louquet

>   ½ cup cocoa powder
>   3 cups flour
>   3 cups sugar
>   5 eggs, separated
>   ½ cup shortening
>   2 sticks butter
>   1 cup evaporated milk
>   ½ tsp baking powder
>   1 tsp vanilla
>   2 tbs dried, ground mint leaves

1. Sift dry ingredients into mixing bowl. Set aside.
2. Blend shortening, butter, egg yolks, and vanilla in separate bowl.
3. Combine with dry ingredients, then stir in evaporated milk.
4. Beat egg whites until stiff, then fold into batter.
5. Pour into greased and floured tube pan.

   Bake at 325 degrees F. for 80 minutes or until a toothpick comes out clean.

Mint Cookies

Adapted from Shaudys

>   1 cup butter or margarine
>   ½ cup sugar
>   ½ tsp peppermint extract
>   2 tbs crushed dried mint leaves
>   2 cups flour
>   ¼ tsp salt

1. Cream butter or margarine and sugar.
2. Add extract, mint leaves, flour, and salt. Mix thoroughly.
3. Chill dough ½ hour.
4. Form 1-inch balls and roll in sugar. Place on ungreased cookie sheet. Press with your thumb. Bake at 350 degrees F. for 12–15 minutes. Makes 3-dozen cookies or 6-dozen smaller ones.

   Variations: Add chocolate chips or nuts, or roll in mint sugar, or frost with milk chocolate candy while still warm, or glaze with pale green icing.

Mint Jelly

Adapted from Gibbons, *Stalking the Healthful Herbs*

> **2 cups freshly picked mint leaves**
> **2 cups boiling water**
> **¼ cup cider vinegar**
> **4 cups sugar**
> **1 package powdered pectin**
> **¾ cup water**
> **green food coloring, optional**

1. Crush mint in a heavy saucepan with a domed lid using a potato masher.
2. Add 2 cups boiling water.
3. Cover with lid upside down. Fill lid with ice cubes. Put pan on heat and bring to a simmer, remove from heat and allow it to sit 20 minutes. This will be a mini-drip still that will retain the mint smell and flavor for the jelly.
4. Strain infusion and add sugar, cider vinegar, and a few drops of food coloring if desired. Stir until sugar is dissolved.
5. In a sauce pan, dissolve pectin in ¾ cup of water. Bring to a boil. Boil hard for 1 minute.
6. Pour pectin solution over mint infusion and mix.
7. Pour into clean, sterile jars. Seal.
8. Or to make a very pretty jelly batch, filling each jar 1½ full. Allow jelly to set. Take little sprigs of mint and put into center of each jar. Make another batch of jelly and fill each jar to within ½ inch of top. Seal. Cool and store in freezer.

Mint Jam

Adapted from Gibbons, *Stalking the Healthful Herbs*

> **2 cups fresh mint, leaves and stems**
> **½ cup cider vinegar**
> **½ cup water**
> **4 cups sugar**
> **1 package powdered pectin**
> **¾ cup water**
> **green food coloring, optional**

1. In a blender or food processor, blend mint, vinegar, ½ cup water and sugar until well blended and sugar is dissolved. Set aside.
2. Dissolve pectin in ¾ cup water.
3. Bring to boil and boil hard for 1 minute.
4. Pour pectin mixture into blender with other ingredients and blend at slow speed of 1 minute.
5. Add food coloring if desired.
6. Pour into sterilized jars and freeze.

Gibbons cautions that if you make mint jelly or jam with a recipe that requires you to cook the mint that you will lose most of the taste and the vitamins because the volatile oils will be driven off with the heat. He suggests either the use of the drip still as in the jelly recipe or the cooking the pectin separately method used in the jam recipe. These methods retain more of the medicinal qualities when used with other herbs, too.

Anishinaabe Kinnikinnick

This is the handout I wrote for use of my students. The instruction was Keewaydinoquay's that she received verbally from Nodjimahkwe.

Anishinaabe kinnikinnick mixtures will always have cedar, *Thuja occidentalis,* and bearberry, *Arctostaphylos uva-ursi,* as the base, but beyond those two plants the choice of what to add or not add is a personal one. Often people will add one or more or all of the Anishinaabe *Seven Incense Bearers*:

1. Cedar (Atlantic, northern, or white cedar), *Thuja occidentalis,* Nookomis-giizhik, "Grandmother Cedar."

   Foliage is used.

2. Balsam fir, *Abies balsamea,* Nimisenh, "My Elder Sister."

   Needles are used.

3. Sweetgrass, *Hierochloe odorata,* Wiingashk, Wiishkobi-mashkosi.

   All of plant used except the roots. Roots should not be pulled when plant is harvested. If one cuts the plant off with a knife and leaves the roots in the ground, the sweetgrass will just grow back the way lawn grass grows back after it is mowed. Do not buy sweetgrass that has roots attached. Kee said that was a good indication that the plants had just been yanked out of the ground, not treated with respect.

4. Mints, any variety of mint. Genus *Mentha,* several species used.

   Oombendaan: "To open up."

   Stems and leaves are used. Mints give the mixture a sweet, mild, gentle taste.

5. Calamus, *Acorus calamus,* Sweet Flag, Wiikenh.

   Root used. Imparts a spicy taste to the smoke and, because it is a fixative, it helps the mixture retain its oils, smell, and taste for a longer time.

6. Sweet Fern: Kee called it Sweet Non-fern because it is not a fern. *Comptonia peregrina* or *Myrica asplenifolia.*

   Leaves used. Gives the kinnikinnick a sweet, spicy taste.

7. Sweet Gale: *Myrica gale.*

Leaves used. Imparts a spicy taste that is somewhat biting and resembles sage.

Along with the Seven Incense Bearers, a plant must be added to kinnikinnick to help the mixture burn. Any or all of the three following plants are used for this purpose:

1. Mullein, *Verbascum thapsus,* Nookaadiziiganzh.

   Leaves are used. Mullein leaves are covered with little hairs. The hairs trap air to help the mixture burn, but some people have an allergic reaction to them when they break the leaves by hand. Jewelweed tincture is very good for relieving any irritation caused by mullein hairs. When we made kinnikinnick at workshops we always had a bottle of jewelweed tincture on hand in case anyone developed a rash from the hairs.

2. Pearly Everlasting, *Anaphalis margaritacea,* Baasibagak.

   Flowers and leaves are used.

3. Goldenrods, *Solidago canadensis, Solidago odora,* or others of the genus.

   Ajidamoowaanow, Waabanoominens.

   All parts of the flowering plant are used, except roots.

Other plants added to personal preferences commonly include:

2. Roses: *Rosa rugosa,* Oginiiminagaawanzhiig, and other garden variety roses, too.

   Rose petals are used. Save the petals from any bouquets of roses that you are sent. Once the roses begin to droop, take the petals off and dry them in an open basket. They are a beautiful addition to the kinnikinnick and a good reuse of your cut flowers.

3. Sage: Kee used the sage that was sent to her by students in the West. She did not use the sage indigenous to the Great Lakes area as she said it caused nerve damage.

   Use White Sage, white sagebrush, *Artemisia ludoviciana,* Wiingashk, Waabani-wiingwashk, Bebezhigooganzhii-wiingashk. The whole plant above the roots may be used.

   Do Not Use Prairie Sage, *Artemisia frigida,* Bizhikii-wiingashk. It is rare in Wisconsin and protected.

   Do Not Use Wormwood, Southwood, Southernwood, *Artemisia absinthium.* Source of absinthe liquor that causes brain damage.

   Do Not Use Field Sagewort, Field Wormwood, *Artemisia campestris.* Kee called it Sand Sage and said it grew on the sand dunes of the Great Lakes. She thought it a particularly dangerous sage as its nerve damaging properties are released in smoke.

Do Not Use Purple Sagebrush, fabled in old cowboy movies; genus *Salvia.* It is not our sage.

4. Willow, genus *Salix.* Several species. Oziisigobimizh.

    Inner bark used. Used to make a macho, biting blend for smoking in a pipe.

5. Red Osier, *Cornus sericea.* Kee did not use the common name for this plant, "Red Dogwood," because it was not like the southern dogwood. She called it "Bend and Stay Plant,"

    Miskwaabiimizh, Miskoobimizh.

    Inner bark used. Makes a macho, harsh smoke that Kee insisted was an Indian joke on white ethnobotanists. She said it was only used if you wanted to bring someone down who was acting "all snooty and macho 'Male'"[3] and standing up with the pipe in front of a group. One draw on a pipe of red osier and the person would be doubled over coughing. She said the joke just kept being printed and reprinted in botany books until Indians themselves started to believe it, too.[4]

6. White or Yellow Sweet Clovers, *Melilotus alba* (white) and *Melilotus officinalis* (yellow), although now some classify this as two colors of the same plant.

    All parts of the plant are used except the root. Gives a sweet, "fresh cut hay" smell to the kinnikinnick smoke.

7. Yarrow. *Achillea millefolium,* Waabanooganzh, "Plant of the East or Light," "Giver of Knowledge," Waabanoowashk, Ajidamoowaanow.

    All parts of plant are used except the root.

When making kinnikinnick one must remember that one is not making a potpourri. Not all plants are safe to burn. These are the ones in our area that our people have used for millennia and they know are safe.

[3] Kee's description, not mine!

[4] See the section on red osier in chapter 5 for more information on the use of red osier in kinnikinnick.

Ojibwe Word Glossary

Compiled by Wendy Makoons Geniusz

This is a list of the Ojibwe words used throughout this book. The Ojibwe names for plants and trees have been divided into a separate glossary, which follows this one. Unless otherwise noted, these Ojibwe words are written in the double-vowel writing system, also called the Fiero orthography. Anyone interested in learning more about this writing system should consult *A Concise Dictionary of Minnesota Ojibwe* (Nichols and Nyholm) or the newer online version "The People's Ojibwe Dictionary" (http://ojibwe.lib.umn .edu). If the entry is for an animate noun (na), or for an inanimate noun (ni), the first word is the singular form and the second word is the plural form. Animate intransitive verbs (vai), and inanimate intransitive verbs (vii) are also listed. The animate or inanimate designation is important in Ojibwe because one must use an animate verb with an animate noun and an inanimate verb with and inanimate noun. The part of the entry in bold type is the Ojibwe. The italicized portion in parentheses identifies the word type (na, ni, vii . . .) if known. An approximate English translation follows in plain type, and after that there is sometimes a longer explanation as to the meaning or the source of the information provided in the entry. Both of the dictionaries listed above were consulted to ensure accurate spelling of these words. Other print sources consulted are cited in various entries, and the full citations for these sources can be found in the bibliography. Two Ojibwe speakers were consulted on some of these words: Kenneth Johnson Sr. from Seine River First Nation in Ontario, Canada, and an elder who wishes to be identified as "Rose, an elder from Canada." We are grateful to both of them for their assistance. For words that were not as familiar to us, sources are cited.

adaawe (*vai*): s/he trades or buys.

adikameg, adikamegwag (*na*): lake whitefish.

agongos, agongosag (*na*): chipmunk.

ahow: "okay," an expression of affirmation, agreement. Sometimes also pronounced, "Ahaw".

ajidamoo, ajidamoog (*na*): red squirrel.

amik, amikwag (*na*): beaver.

Anishinaabe, Anishinaabeg (*na*): Indian, Ojibwe or Chippewa person. Keewaydinoquay used "Anishinaabe" to refer to an Indian person of one of the Three Fires Nations: the Ojibwe or Chippewa, the Odaawaa or Ottawa, the Boodewaadamii or Potawatomi. In stories "Anishinaabe" is usually thought of as meaning "Mankind."

Anishinaabekwe, Anishinaabekweg (*na*): Indian woman.

Anishinaabewaki (*ni*): Anishinaabe or Indian land, Indian country.

anishinaabe-bimaadiziwin (*ni*): "Indian life," "Anishinaabe life." Kee translated it as "life in the fullest sense," meaning "our good Indian way of life." Some people call it "the Good Red Road" or "the ideal Anishinaabe lifestyle."

anishinaabe-gikendaasowin(*ni*): Anishinaabe knowledge ("Anishinaabe Wordlist").

anishinaabe-inendamowin (*ni*): Anishinaabe mindset, worldview ("Anishinaabe Wordlist").

Anishinaabemowin (*ni*): Indian, Ojibwe, or Chippewa language.

asinaagan: a stone dish used to hold kinnikinnick and asemaa for burning. This word is from Keewaydinoquay, who often pronounced it, "osinaagan." She said it was the original way the Peoples of the Great Lakes prayed before the introduction of the Sacred Pipe, which she said was given to the People by the Dakota.

Aadizookaan, Aadizookaanag (*na*): the spirit of or character in a traditional or sacred story or a legend (Johnson, personal communication). Keewaydinoquay described the Aadizookaanag as traditional stories or the characters in those stories, songs, ceremonies. She referred to them as "The Grandfathers and Grandmothers," and she said they were alive and cognizant.

aajigade, aajigadeg (*na*): coot, mud hen (a type of duck).

aagim, aagimag (*na*): snowshoe.

aamoo, aamoog (*na*): bee.

Aaniin: "Hello," a greeting.

Baambiitaa-binesi (*na*): "Rhythm-beater, pace setter." A character in the creation story of Cedar. Keewaydinoquay wrote this name: Bahmbetah-Benaysee (Keewaydinoquay: 1). Keewaydinoquay described him as a kind of proto-flicker or woodpecker, and she translated his name as, "Flying-around bird." Binesi is a large bird, such as a bird of prey, or a bird with a spiritual connection, such as a thunderbird.

biboon (*vii*): it is winter.

bine, binewag (*na*): partridge.

bineshiinh, bineshiinyag (*na*): bird. Keewaydinoquay translated this word as "small bird."

bizhiw, bizhiwag (*na*): lynx.

Boodewaadamii, Boodewaadamiig (*na*): Potawatomi.

boodawe (*vai*): s/he builds a fire.

Boozhoo: "Hello," a greeting.

Bwaan, Bwaanag (*na*): Dakota; Sioux.

chi-miigwech: "thank you very much," an expression. Also said, "Gichi-miigwech."

Chi-mookomaan, Chi-mookomaanag or **Gichi-mookomaan, Gichi-mookomaanag** (*na*): "Big Knife," a white person.

dagwaagin (*vii*): it is fall, it is autumn.

dikinaagan, dikinaaganan (*ni*): cradle board. Used for an infant who has outgrown the moss bag.

-doodem (*nad*): clan, totem. In Ojibwe this word must be possessive. For example, one may say, Indoodem, "my clan," Gidoodem, "your clan."

esiban, esibanag (*na*): raccoon.

eya' or en': "yes."

gayaashk, gayaashkwag (*na*): seagull.

gekek, gekekwag (*na*): hawk.

Gete-Anishinaabe, Gete-Anishinaabeg (*na*): Old-time Indian, one of the Old Ones, one of the Ancestors.

gichi-mewinzha: a very long time ago.

Gichi-mewinzha, gii-oshki-niiging akiing: a very long time ago when the earth was new. This is the way Keewaydinoquay taught Mary Geniusz to begin telling a story.

Gichi-makwa (*na*): "Great Bear," clan animal, character in the story of the creation of Cedar.

Gichi-manidoo (*na*): Great Spirit; Great Mystery; Creator; God.

Gichi-omakakii (*na*): the Great Blue Frog Spirit who is sent by Frog to visit sleeping people who have shown disrespect to the Aadizoo-kaanag. S/he sucks big, blue welts on the face of a person guilty of disrespect.

Gichigami (*ni*): Lake Superior, often said, "Gichigamiing" (which is the locative form meaning "at, by . . .").

gidagaa-bizhiw, gidagaa-bizhiwag (*na*): bobcat, "spotted lynx."

Gidakiiminaan: our earth. A possessive form of aki, akiin (*ni*): earth, land, ground, country.

Giga-waabamin miinawaa: "I will see you (singular)." Farewell said to one person.

Giga-waabamininim miinawaa: "I will see you all again." Farewell said to more than one person.

ginebig, ginebigoog (*na*): snake.

giigoonh, giigoonyag (*na*): fish.

Giiwedin (*ni*): the North Wind, North.

gookooko'oo, gookooko'oog (*na*): owl.

gwiiwizens, gwiiwizensag (*na*): boy, little boy. The Mide water drum is called this.

Howa!: "Wow," an expression of surprise or exertion.

indinawemaagan, indinawemaaganag: my relative. A possessive form of inawemaagan (*na*): a relative or kinsman.

ininishib, ininishibag (*na*): mallard duck.

ininishibens, ininishibensag (*na*): little mallard; mallard duckling.

Iskigamizige-giizis (*na*): "The Maple Sap Boiling Moon." In the Milwaukee area it is usually in April.

Jiibayag niimi'idiwag (*vai*): they are the Northern Lights (translation from Nichols and Nyholm: 73). "The ghosts or spirits are dancing together."

jiimaan, jiimaanan (*ni*): canoe, boat.

ma'iingan, ma'iinganag (*na*): wolf.

ma'iinganens, ma'iinganensag (*na*): coyote or little wolf (Johnson: personal communication).

makak, makakoon (*ni*): birch bark box or container, box, basket.

makoons, makoonsag (*na*): little black bear, bear cub.

makwa, makwag (*na*): black bear. Keewaydinoquay wrote this word "Muhkwah" and "Mukwah."

Manidoo, Manidoog (*na*): Spirit, Manitou, God.

mashkiki, mashkikiwan (*ni*): medicine.

mashkikiiwikwe, mashkikiiwikwewag (*na*): medicine woman (Johnson, personal communication).

mashkikiiwinini, mashkikiiwininiwag (*na*): medicine man (Johnson, personal communication).

maang, maangwag (*na*): loon.

memengwaa, memengwaag (*na*) : butterfly.

Midewiwin (*ni*): A religious organization of the Ojibwe people. It is also referred to as Medicine Dance or Grand Medicine Society. The members the Midewiwin are often called "Mide."

migizi, migiziwag (*na*): bald eagle.

mindimooyenh, mindimooyenyag (*na*): old woman, old lady.

Minis-kitigaan (*ni*): Garden Island, part of the Beaver Island Chain in the middle of Lake Michigan. Keewaydinoquay spelled this name: Miniss Kitigaan.

mino-nibaan: "sleep well." Command said to one person. From mino-ni-baa: (*vai*) s/he sleeps well

misajidamoo, misajidamoog (*na*): gray squirrel.

Mishi-makwa: The Great Bear. A character in a few stories.

Mii iw : "That's it," an expression.

Miigis, Miigisag (*na*): A type of seashell; the Sacred Shell that brought the People to Anishinaabewakiing.

Miigwech: "thank you," an expression.

Naanabozho: Aadizookaan. Great-uncle of the Anishinaabeg. Son of the West Wind Spirit and an Anishinaabe woman. Called by academics "a Trickster," but that is offensive to those who believe in the old ways. Mary Geniusz says: "I once had a Mide ask me, 'How do you think Christians would feel if you called Christ "a Trickster"?'"

name, namewag (*na*) : sturgeon. Keewaydinoquay described this being as the Guardian of the Great Lakes.

namegos, namegosag (*na*): lake trout.

nigig, nigigwag (*na*): otter. Clan animal, character in the story of the Creation of Cedar.

nika, nikag (*na*): Canada goose.

nimishoomis, nimishoomisag (*nad*): my grandfather.

nindaanis, nindaanisag or **indaanis, indaanisag** (*nad*): my daughter.

ninga (*nad*): my mother. Keewaydinoquay translated this as, "my own mother." Also said, "Inga".

niibin (*vii*): It is summer.

niinimoshenh, niinimoshenyag (*nad*): my sweet heart or my cross-cousin.

nookomis, nookomisag (*nad*): my grandmother.

nookoo: term of address used to one's grandmother. She is your 'noo-komis', but you say, "nookoo" when you are addressing her.

Odaawaa, Odaawaag (*na*): Ottawa. Keewaydinoquay said this name was related to Adaawe: (*vai*) s/he trades.

ogaa, ogaawag (*na*): walleye, walleyed pike.

ogiishkimanisii, ogiishkimanisiig (*na*) : kingfisher.

Ojibwe, Ojibweg (*na*): an Ojibwe person.

ojiibik, ojiibikan (*ni*): root.

omakakii, omakakiig (*na*): Frog.

Onaabani-giizis (*na*): "The Hard Crust on the Snow Moon." In the Mil-waukee area it is usually in March.

opwaagan, opwaaganag (*na*) : pipe.

oshkaabewis, oshkaabewisag (*na*): apprentice, ceremonial helper, medi-cine helper. The description of oshkaabewis duties is much longer that a simple definition can relate. See the Introduction for more information on this word.

ozhibii'ige (*vai*): s/he writes.

Shaawondasee: The South Wind Spirit, from the story "the South Wind and the Maiden of the Golden Hair." This spelling is from Schoolcraft (79–80). The South Wind is also known as Zhaawani-noodin (Nichols and Nyholm: 125) and Zhaawanaanimad (Johnson: personal communication).

Waaban: East Wind spirit, in the story of "the South Wind and the Maiden of the Golden Hair." From Schoolcraft's spelling, "Wabun" (79–80). The East Wind is also known as waabani-noodin, east wind (Nichols and Nyholm: 115) and Waabanaanimad (Johnson, personal communication).

Waabanaaki : original homeland of the Anishinaabeg before the Great Miigis Migration. Kee called it by this name. It was an island in the eastern sea that was destroyed, forcing the People to follow the Miigis to the "Place where the Food Grows Upon the Waters."

Waabanoowin: "The Eastern Medicine" or the "Coming from the East Medicine," sect of the Anishinaabe traditional religion. Members often called "Waabanoo." Kee used both of these names.

waabooz, waaboozoog (*na*): rabbit.

waaginogaan, waaginogaanan (*ni*): dome shaped wigwam or lodge. Kee described this as the traditional home of the Great Lakes peoples.

waapijipizon, waapijipizonan (*ni*): a moss bag, used as a bunting-type bag for an newborn infant (Rose, personal communication).

waawaabiganoojiinh, waawaabiganoojiinyag (*na*): mouse.

waawaashkeshi, waawaashkeshiwag (*na*): deer.

wese'an (*vii*): there is a tornado.

wiigiwaam, wiigiwaaman (*ni*): wigwam, lodge. Kee described this as the traditional, dome-shaped dwelling of the Great Lakes tribes. Some elders describe this lodge as a conical lodge and the waaginogaan as the dome shaped lodge (Rose, personal communication).

wiigob (*ni*) : inner bark of basswood tree used to bind seams of birch bark containers.

wiigwaas (*ni*) : birch bark.

zhiishiib, zhiishiibag (*na*): duck.

zhiishiibens, zhiishiibensag (*na*): little duck; duckling.

zii'amoo, zii'amoog (*na*): wood duck

ziigwan (*vii*): it is spring.

Ojibwe Plant Name Glossary

Compiled by Wendy Makoons Geniusz

These entries follow the same pattern as those entries found in the Ojibwe Word Glossary, except that the italicized names are scientific names provided for plant identification. Whenever known, the singular version of the plant name is followed by the plural version and an identification marker to tell readers if the word is animate (*na*) or inanimate (*ni*). Keewaydinoquay insisted that all plants and trees are considered alive in Ojibwe culture, and the identification of some of these plants as inanimate nouns does not necessarily dispute this teaching. In many cases, a plant name is derived from the name of one part of the plant, such as the berries or the roots, and in those cases, we often find the word considered inanimate, while the plant itself is still considered alive.

This glossary is arranged by the English common names used throughout this book. As with the Ojibwe Word Glossary, *A Concise Dictionary of Minnesota Ojibwe* (Nichols and Nyholm) and "The People's Ojibwe Dictionary" (http://ojibwe.lib.umn.edu) (cited as POD) were consulted to assure accurate spelling, and these texts were sources for some of the names. We used as many plant names as possible from Keewaydinoquay, but, because she did not use a standard system for writing Ojibwe words, we had to check the pronunciation of many of these words with other Ojibwe speakers and with written sources. In some cases we also collected plant names from other sources because Keewaydinoquay said repeatedly that it was important to address all plants and trees by their Ojibwe names, and she often expressed regret at not knowing all of their names. We are grateful to all of the Ojibwe speakers who helped us on this glossary, and we respectfully introduce them here as they asked to be identified: the late Kenneth Johnson Sr., from Seine River First

Nation in Ontario, Canada; the late George McGeshick Sr., from the Mole Lake Sokaogon Band of Lake Superior Ojibwe and chief of the Chicaugon Chippewa of Iron River, Michigan; Dora Dorothy Whipple, Leech Lake Elder; Ma-nee Chacaby, a two-spirit elder from Animikiiwiikwedong, Thunder Bay, Ontario, and a woman who wished to be identified only as "Rose, an elder from Canada."

We consulted the following print sources to create the most accurate list of plant names possible. Full citations for these sources can be found in the bibliography, but we list them here by the abbreviations used to identify them in this glossary and give an explanation for how they were used.

AW: "Anishinaabe Wordlist," collected by Mary Siisip Geniusz from panels of Ojibwe speakers at courses for the Seven Generations Education Institute Master of Indigenous Knowledge/Philosophy Program.

Baraga: *A Dictionary of the Ojibway Language*, by Frederick Baraga. This source was used occasionally to reconstruct names Kee gave to us, as she often used Baraga's writing system, or portions of it, when writing Ojibwe. It is also a source for some of the names. Source includes only English common names.

Densmore: *Uses of Plants by the Chippewa Indians*, by Frances Densmore. In Meeker, Elias, and Heim, Nichols provides reconstructed versions of many of the names collected by Densmore. We cite some of these names in this glossary, along with translations gathered by Densmore, if we have heard Ojibwe speakers use this name or if it is clear that Densmore, who was not an Ojibwe speaker, was not the only researcher to record a specific plant name. Source does include scientific names.

James: *A Narrative of the Captivity and Adventures of John Tanner*, edited by Edwin James. Keewaydinoquay gave Mary Geniusz a 1956 publication of this text, which contains a list of Ojibwe plant and tree names (293–99). Ojibwe speaker John Tanner was most likely a source for the names found in this list, although no one is credited. Source includes only English common names. We retranscribed names cited into the double-vowel writing system.

Johnston: *Honour Earth Mother*, by Basil Johnston. The author of this book is a fluent Ojibwe speaker, and he includes a list of plant names in his glossary. Source includes only English common names. (154–55). We use some names as a comparison for what we found in other sources, and as a source for plurals of some plant names.

MEH: *Plants Used By the Great Lakes Ojibwa*, by James E. Meeker, Joan E. Elias, and John A. Heim. John D. Nichols provided the authors of this text with the Ojibwe names used in this book. In the introduction to this book, the authors provide a brief description of how the list of plant names used in this text were compiled (1–2). Some of these names were Nichols' reconstruction of names from printed sources, and we have used these names in this glossary only when we could verify with an Ojibwe speaker that it was indeed a name for the plant in question or when it was clear that the name had been gathered from multiple written sources, and thus had been heard by multiple researchers. Other names given in *Plants Used By the Great Lakes Ojibwa* are listed as being told to Nichols by Eddie Benton-Benai of Lac Courte Oreilles. We cite these names as well. Source does include scientific names.

MOTN: *Ojibwa Language Manual: Resource Materials and Training Exercises,* by Hannah Maulson, George Oshogay, Earl Thomas, and John Nichols. This manuscript contains an Ojibwe wordlist, and some tree names are on that list. Source includes only English common names. Several fluent Ojibwe speakers contributed to the creation of this manual.

Reagan: "Plants Used by the Bois Fort Chippewa (Ojibwa) Indians of Minnesota," by Albert B. Reagan. Source does include scientific names.

Smith: "Ethnobotany of the Ojibwe Indians," by Huron H. Smith. In Meeker, Elias, and Heim, Nichols provides reconstructed versions of many names Smith collected. Generally, we cite these names in this glossary, along with translations gathered by Smith, if we have heard Ojibwe speakers use this name or if it is clear that Smith, who was not an Ojibwe speaker, was not the only researcher to record a specific plant name. Exceptions are noted. Source does include scientific names.

Zichmanis and Hodgins: *Flowers of the Wild: Ontario and the Great Lakes Region*, by Zile Zichmanis and James Hodgins. The appendix of this book contains a list of Ojibwe names for various plants identified and described throughout the body of the text (259–67). In the appendix, plants are identified only by English common and French names, but it is clear that the authors are referring to the plants listed elsewhere in the text, where they provide scientific names and illustrations for each plant. In their acknowledgements, the authors thank fluent Ojibwe speaker Basil Johnston (they misspell his name "Johnson") for providing them with spellings and translations for these Ojibwe names. They also say that Keewaydinoquay and Sam Ozawamick, whom they identify as "medicine-man and herbalist, Wikwemikong, Manitoulin Island," provided them with the Ojibwe names. Johnston himself might also be a source for some of the names in the list, and he does use the same or similar names in his later publications. The authors do not list sources for the individual names. Some names in this list were retranscribed into double-vowel Ojibwe by Nichols and published by Meeker, Elias, and Heim. Other names we retranscribed. See notes on individual entries.

Balsam fir (*Abies balsamea*)

aninaandag, aninaandagoog (*na*): Rose gave us this name, and she said that the tree and its branches were called this (Rose, personal communication). Word is also in POD.

ininaandag, ininaandagoog (*na*): (POD).

ingiigido'aag: Retranscription of Kee's "Idgigidoag," which she translated as "she speaks for us" or "she stands at prayer for us." A more literal translation might be: "I make them speak." Baraga has "nin gigitoa," which he translates as, "I make him speak" (239). Kee also called this tree "She points out."

Nimisenh, Nimisenyag (*na*): My elder sister or my older, female, parallel cousin. This is one of the names Keewaydinoquay used for balsam fir. Capitalization is used here because this name is addressing the tree and most likely the spirit of the tree directly.

wadab, wadabiig (*na*): Small, flexible root of the black spruce or balsam fir used to bind large containers of birch bark or canoes. Kee said this is also a name for the trees balsam fir, white spruce, and black spruce. Word is on POD, identified as "spruce root."

Bearberry, kinnikinnick (*Arctostaphylos uva-ursi*)

mako-miskomin, mako-miskominag (*na*): bearberry (Chacaby, personal communication).

makwa-miskomin, makwa-miskominan (*ni*): Retranscription of Keewaydinoquay's "Mukwa-miskominan," which she translated as "bear's red berry" (Keewaydinoquay: 10). This name refers specifically to the berry of this plant, although Kee called the entire plant by this name, a common practice with Ojibwe plant names.

Birch, paper birch, white birch (*Betula papyrifera*)

Nimishoomis-wiigwaas, Nimishoomis-wiigwaasag (*na*): "My Grandfather Birch Tree," honorific title used to refer to the white or paper birch. Keewaydinoquay called birch by this name. "Nimishoomis" means "my grandfather." Capitalization is used here because this name is addressing the tree and most likely the spirit of the tree directly.

wiigwaasi-mitig, wiigwaasi-mitigoog (*na*): (McGeshick, personal communication; Nichols and Nyholm: 119).

wiigwaas, wiigwaasag (*na*): (Nichols and Nyholm: 119).

Boneset (*Eupatorium perfoliatum*)

ogaakananiibiish, ogaakananiibiishag (*na*): Ma-nee Chacaby gave us this word, and she said that "ogaak" has to do with "bending" (Chacaby, personal communication). Keewaydinoquay did not give us an Ojibwe name for this plant. She said that her teacher, Nodjimahkwe, called this plant "Shield and Lance Plant."

Bunchberry (*Cornus Canadensis*)

zhakaagomin: name recorded as having been given to John Nichols by Eddie Benton-Benai (MEH: 319).

zhaashaagomin, zhaashaagominag (*na*): This is the name Ma-nee Chacaby uses for this plant. The plural is from her (Chacaby, personal communication; MEH: 319). Johnston has "Zhaushaug-meen," which he identifies by the common name "Bunchberry" (155).

zhaashaagominens: This name is a retranscription of a name Zichmanis and Hodgins recorded (MEH: 319). Zichmanis and Hodgins have "Zhausaugominaehnse," which they translate as "little crushy berry" (260).

Butternut tree (*Juglans cinerea*)

bagaanaak, bagaanaakwag (*na*): butternut tree (MOTN: 318; MEH: 391).

bagaanaakomizh, bagaanaakomizhiig (*na*): butternut tree. Source has "bagaanaakominzh," but we changed the spelling of "minzh" to be consistent with spellings in POD, such as mitogomizh (MOTN: 318).

Catnip (*Nepeta cataria*)

gaazhagensibag, gaazhagensibagoon (*ni*): This name is a retranscription of a name Densmore recorded. They note that another possible pronunciation of this word is "gaazhigensibag" (MEH: 115). Densmore has "gajugĕns'ïbûg," which she translates as, "little cat leaf" (290). Johnston has "Gauzhug-aehnsewi-bug(oon)" and the plural in this entry is a retranscription of the plural he gives (154). This name most closely matches the name that Kee used for this plant. She called this plant by a translation of an Ojibwe name, "Little cat ears."

gichi-namewashk: This name is a retranscription of a name Smith recorded (MEH: 115). Smith has "tci'name'wûck," which he translates as "big sturgeon plant" and "big sturgeon leaf" (372, 405). This name connects this plant to "Name," the sturgeon whose death created many of the mint plants, according to the story Kee told. According to this story, plants were created from his blood when he died, and these plants contain his name.

Cattail, common cattail (*Typha latifolia*) and narrow-leafed cattail (*Typha angustifolia*)

apakway: common cattail; *Typha latifolia*. This name is a retranscription of a name Densmore recorded (MEH: 152). Densmore has "apûk'we" (294). Keewaydinoquay called this plant by a translation of an Ojibwe name: "Defender of the shoreline."

apakweshkway, apakweshkwayag (*na*): cattail or cattail mat (Nichols and Nyholm: 12). *Typha latifolia*: common cattail or *Typha angustifolia*: narrow-leafed cattail. Apakwe is an Ojibwe verb (*vai*) meaning, "s/he puts a roof/thatch on (something)" (Rose, personal communication; Nichols and Nyholm: 12). "Apakwe" may be connected to "Apakweshkway," as cattail mats are often put on roofs of lodges, especially in the summer.

bebaamiseng (*na*): can refer to the fuzz or to the entire plant. Retranscription of Huron Smith's "Bebamasû´n" and "Bebamasûn," which he translates as "it flies around." A more accurate translation might be "the one who flies around," referring to an animate noun. If it was in the inanimate form, we would expect to hear "bebaamiseg," but Smith does not appear to be recording that. Smith specifically identifies common cattail *Typha latifolia* with this name but also lists this as a name for the entire Typhaceae family (390, 423, 432). Ma-nee Chacaby recognized Smith's word, saying that she understood what he was describing, and she gave us "babaaseyaan" (Chacaby, personal communication).

Cedar, white cedar, Atlantic or northern Cedar (*Thuja occidentalis*)

giizhik, giizhikag (*na*): (Nichols and Nyholm: 61). Keewaydinoquay always said this word with the Ojibwe name for "my grandmother" in front of it: Nookomis giizhik.

Nookomis-giizhik, Nookomis-giizhikag (*na*): "My Grandmother Cedar," honorific title used to refer to the cedar tree. Kee always called Cedar by this name. "Nookomis" means "my grandmother." Capitalization is used here because this name is addressing the tree and most likely the spirit of the tree directly.

Dandelion (*Taraxacum officinale*)

doodooshaaboojiibik, doodooshaaboojiibikan (*ni*): "milk root" (Rose, personal communication).

mindimooyenh, mindimooyenyag (*na*): dandelion. This name is a retranscription of a name Zichmanis and Hodgins recorded. (MEH: 134). Zichmanis and Hodgins have "Mindemoyae," which they translate as "Old woman" (262). Johnston has "Mindemoyaehn(*uk*)," and the plural in this entry is a retranscription of the plural he gives (154).

wezaawaaskwaneg (*ni*): "yellow light." From ozaawaaskwane (*vii*) "yellow light" (technically it is a changed conjunct form). Retranscription of Smith's "wesa'usakwûnek," which he translates as "yellow light" (366), and "weca'waskwûne´k," which he translates as "yellow light" (399). Kenneth Johnson said "ozaawaaskwane" means "yellow light" (Johnson, personal communication). This name is closest to Kee's name for this plant, "little suns."

Equisetum, Horsetail, Meadow Horsetail (*Equisetum pratense* and *Equisetum arvense*)

aanikawishkoons, aanikawishkoonsag (*na*): Rose gave us this word. She was specifically identifying *Equisetum arvense* at the time (personal communication).

otadimoomitigoons, otadimoomitigoonsag (*na*): Ma-nee Chacaby gave us this word and simply identified it as "Equisetum, horsetail" (Chacaby, personal communication).

zhiishiibinashk (*Equisetum arvense*): Retranscription of Smith's "Gîji'bînûsk," which he translates as "duck food," "duck round" (368, 400). Although we question the accuracy of all the plant names recorded by Smith, who by his own admission did not speak Ojibwe, we were reluctant to omit this name from the glossary because it does record the connection that ducks have with this plant. Our pet ducks used to be very interested in eating this plant. Whenever they had the opportunity to go to the side of the yard where it was growing, they would race over and eat it. We believe it was providing them with necessary calcium because once we started to give them calcium supplements in their diet, they were no longer as interested in this plant.

Goldenrod (*Solidago Canadensis*) or others of the genus

ajidamoowaanow This name is a retranscription of a name Densmore recorded (MEH: 349). Densmore has "a'djidamo'wano," which she translates as "squirrel tail" (293).

Waabanoominens, Waabanoominensag (*na*) Ma-nee Chacaby gave us this word. (Chacaby, personal communication). It is capitalized here because Kee often spoke about plants that were connected to the Waabanoo religion, and it appears that this name is one of those. See Waabanooganzh for an example of a plant name that Kee specifically connected to this religion.

Goldthread, mouth root, canker root (*Coptis trifolia*)

giizisoomashkiki: Retranscription of Zichmanis and Hodgins's "Geez-isomuskiki," which they translate as "Sun medicine" (260). Johnston has "Geezisso-mashki-aki," which he translates by the common name "Goldenrod" (154).

ozaawijiibik: This name is a retranscription of a name Densmore recorded. Authors note similar names from other sources (MEH: 375). Densmore has "oza´widji´bĭk," which she translates as "yellow root" (288).

Heal-all, Self-heal (*Prunella vulgaris*)

ingijibinaa: Retranscription of Keewaydinoquay's "Ingitchibiina," which she translated as "very great drawing out one" or "the great draw-er-outer." Ma-nee Chacaby recognized this name for this plant but said she uses a slightly different version of this name; see below.

ogijibinaan This name is from Ma-nee Chacaby. She said this name and the one used by Kee refer to sucking something out and that this plant can really suck things, like poison, out of one's body. Chacaby also used the name "ogiji'obinaa" (Chacaby, personal communication).

Hemlock: eastern hemlock (*Tsuga Canadensis*)

gaagaagiwanzh or **gaagaagiwinzh:** Authors note both as possible pronuncations (MEH: 309). Huron Smith has "gagagi'wîc," which he translates as "raven tree" (380). "Gaagaagi" is a raven. Kee called this tree: "porcupine, his tree."

Jack pine (*Pinus banksiana*)

akikaandag, akikaandagoog (*na*): (POD)

okikaandag, okikaandagoog (*na*): (Rose, personal communication; Nichols and Nyholm: 201; POD). Kee spelled this word "Oo-ke-ca-dug," and translated it as "He Is Crippled With Arthritis."

wakikaandag (*na*): Jack Pine (Nichols and Nyholm: 201)

Jerusalem artichokes (*Helianthus tuberosus*)

ashkibwaa, **ashkibwaag** (Rose, personal communication).

giizisoojiibik, **giizisoojiibikag**: "sun root." Retranscription of Keewaydinoquay's "Gissisajeebikeg," which she translated as "Sun Tubers" or
"Root of the Sun." It appears that Kee's word is in the plural form,
and the plural on this entry was retranscribed with this assumption. In her lectures she used the Ojibwe name and both English
translations interchangeably. Kenneth Johnson said that "sun root"
would translate as "giizisoojiibik" in Ojibwe (Johnson, personal
communication).

Jewelweed, touch-me-not; spotted jewelweed, spotted touch-me-not (*Impatiens capensis*)

omakakiibag: Jewelweed, spotted touch-me-not, *Impatiens capensis*.
Retranscription of Zichmanis and Hodgins's "Mukikeebug, which
they translate as "Frog petal" (263). Johnston has "Muk-akee-bug,"
which he identifies only by the common name: "Jewel weed" (154).
In her class lectures, Kee often told a story about how Omakakii,
Frog, taught the Anishinaabeg how to use this plant.

Joe Pye, gravelroot (*Eutrochium purpureum*); and spotted Joe Pye (*Eupatorium maculatum*)

bagizowin: "Bathing." Joe Pye, gravelroot; *Eutrochium purpureum*.
Retranscription of Huron Smith's "Bû´gîsowe" (364). Bagizo is a verb
meaning (*vai*) s/he bathes, swims.

meskwaanakwak-bagizowin: spotted Joe Pye; *Eutrochium maculatum*.
Retranscription of Densmore's "Me´skwana´kûk bû´giso´wĭn,"
which she translates as "swimming" (289). Most likely from "Misk-
waanakwad" (*vii*), it is a red cloud, and "Bagizo" (*vai*), s/he bathes,
swims.

Juniper, bush or common juniper (*Juniperus communis*) and red "cedar" (*Juniperus virginiana*)

gaagaagiwaandag, **gaagaagiwaandagoog** (*na*): bush or common juniper;
Juniperus communis (Rose, personal communication). Word is also
on POD.

miskwaawaak, **miskwaawaakoog** (*na*): red "cedar;" eastern red "cedar," pasture juniper, pencil "cedar," baton rouge-red stick; *Juniperus virginiana*. This name is a retranscription of very similar names recorded
from three different written sources (MEH: 77).

Labrador tea, swamp tea (*Rhododendron groenlandicum*)

mashkiigobag, mashkiigobagoog (*na*): Rose gave us this name, and the plural is from her (Rose, personal communication; MEH: 196). Densmore has "muckig´obûg," which she translates as "swamp leaf" (290). Word is also on POD but with the plural "mashkiigobagoon."

Maple, sugar maple tree (*Acer saccharum*)

ininaatig, ininaatigoog (*na*): (Nichols and Nyholm: 68).

ishkaatig, ishkaatigoog (*na*): George McGeshick referred to the maple when he used this name, but he also translated it as "a hardwood." (McGeshick, personal communication).

Mint: wild mint (*Mentha arvensis*) and mountain mint (*Pycnanthemum virginianum*)

oombendaan (*na*): *Mentha* spp. Retranscription of Keewaydinoquay's word "Oombayndahn," which she translated as "to rise up or open up the interior" or "opener upper." Ma-nee Chacaby recognized this name for mint, but she also said that she usually adds "dakaasa" to the beginning of it to refer specifically to mint: "dakaasabendaan." She said that dakaasabendaan could be pluralized because this word is used when talking about mixing mint with other medicines, but that oombendaan could not be pluralized because it only refers to mint when "it's all by itself" (Chacaby, personal communication).

dakaasabendaan, dakaasabendaanag (*na*): *Mentha* spp. (Chacaby, personal communication). Chacaby added that the "dakaasa" refers to "the cool part of the mint."

aandegobagoons, aandegobagoonsan (*ni*): wild mint; *Mentha arvensis*. This name is a retranscription of a name Smith recorded (MEH: 343). Smith has "andego'bîgons," which he translates as "little crow leaf" (405). The plural is from Johnston, who has "Aundaeg-bugoohnse" (*un*), which he identifies by the English common name "wild mint" (154).

namewashkoons, namewashkoonsag (*na*): mountain mint; *Pycnanthemum virginianum*. This name is a retranscription of a name Densmore recorded (MEH: 179). Densmore has "name'ûckons," which she defines as, "little sturgeon plant" (290). This name contains the Ojibwe word "name," sturgeon. Ma-nee Chacaby recognized this plant and this name for it. The plural form is from her (Chacaby, personal communication).

Motherwart (*Leonurus cardiac*)

niibiishikaabijigan, **niibiishikaabijiganag** (*na*): Ma-nee Chacaby gave us this name and said that "kaabijigan" refers to a tea that "pulls out what's wrong" with a person (Chacaby, personal communication). It is likely also pronounced "aniibiishikaabijigan."

Mullein (*Verbascum thapsus*)

nookaadiziiganzh, **nookaadiziiganzhiig** (*na*): Retranscription of Keewaydino-quay wrote this word: "Nokadisigunzh," but she did not give a trans-lation for it. This name appears to contain the verb "Nookaadizi," meaning s/he is meek or mild-mannered (Nichols and Nyholm: 102). Ma-nee Chacaby recognized this name for this plant and gave us the plural ending. She said that this name describes the soft leaves of this plant. She said it was related to the verb "nookizi" (Chacaby, personal communication). Nichols and Nyholm define "nookizi" (*vai*) as "be soft, be tender" (102).

Naanabozho's Squeaky-Voice Plants

What Kee called all of the following plants: wolf claw or stag horn moss (*Lycopodium clavatum*) and princess pine, tree club moss (*Lycopodium dendroideum*) and running cedar, ground cedar, Christmas club moss, and ground pine (*Diphasiastrum complanatum*)

miishiwiiganens, **miishiwiiganensag** (*na*): Wolf claw or stag horn moss, *Lyco-podium clavatum*. This name is from Ma-nee Chacaby, who identifies this plant as "wolf club moss" (Chacaby, personal communication).

mitakamig-giizhikaandag: running cedar , ground cedar, Christmas club moss, ground pine, *Diphasiastrum complanatum* (Rose, personal communication).

gaagaagiwaandagoons, **gaagaagiwaandagoonsag** (*na*): princess pine, tree club moss, *Lycopodium dendroideum*. This name was given to us by Rose. She said that the "gaagaagi" part referred to the raven and that this plant was almost the same as juniper, only smaller and not sharp (Rose, personal communication). Keewaydinoquay referred to the entire *Lycopodium* genus as "Naanabozho's Squeaky-Voice Plant."

zhingonaakwaan, **zhingonaakwaanan** (*ni*): princess pine, tree club moss, *Lycopodium dendroideum*. George McGeshick gave us this word and he also said that "zhingonaakwedaa" means "let's go pick greens." "Zhingonaakwe" (*vai*) means "s/he picks greens" (McGeshick, per-sonal communication)

Oak: white oak (*Quercus alba*) and northern red oak (*Quercus rubra*) and black oak (*Quercus velutina*)

mitigomizh, mitigomizhiig (*na*): Rose added that the acorn is called "miti-gomin, mitigominan" (Rose, personal communication; Nichols and Nyholm: 88; MEH: 224, 304, 393). POD lists it as specifically white oak, *Quercus alba*.

Oswego tea, bee balm (*Monarda didyma*)

aamoogaawanzh: Retranscription of Zichmanis's and Hodgins's "Amogawuhnshk," which they translate as "bee plant" (264). The ending (gaawanzh) on this word is questionable because of the final "k" in the original spelling.

Pearly everlasting (*Anaphalis margaritacea*)

baasibagak: This name is a retranscription of names recorded by Zich-manis and Hodgins and Smith (MEH: 14). Zichmanis and Hodgins have "Basibuguk," which they translate as "Narrow-leaved" (264). Smith has "basi'bagûk," which he translates as "small leaf" (362).

Plantain: native plantain (*Plantago rugelii*), common plantain (*Plantago major*), and English plantain, narrow leaf plantain (*Plantago lanceolata*)

Note on plantain names: It is probable that all of the following Ojibwe names actually refer to the plantain that is indigenous to North America, *Plantago rugelii*. Or that both *Plantago major* and *Plantago rugelii*, which look very similar, go by these Ojibwe names. Kee gave no Ojibwe name for this plant, but she often called it by the translation of an Ojibwe name, "white man's footprint." Kee's name for this plant probably refers to one or both of the imported species: common plantain (*Plantago major*) and narrow-leaf plantain (*Plantago lanceolata*). Kee never spoke about a native species of plantain. The plants in the entries below are identified as they are listed in the original sources.

ginebigowashk: common plantain (*Plantago major*). This name is recorded as having been given to John Nichols by Eddie Benton-Benai. "Ginebigwashk" is also listed, and this name is a retranscrip-tion of a name recorded by Densmore (MEH: 119). Densmore has "gine'bigwûck," which she translates as, "snake-like" (291). Ginebig is an Ojibwe name for snake.

mashkiigobag: common plantain (*Plantago major*) and English or nar-row-leaf plantain (*Plantago lanceolata*). Retranscription of Huron Smith's "Jimûcki´ gobûg," which he translates as "sort of a swamp leaf" (381). Kenneth Johnson said he did not recognize the "ji" Smith writes in his entry, but that "mashkiigobag" meant a "swamp plant" (Johnson, personal communication).

omakakiibag: common plantain (*Plantago major*). This name is a retranscription of a name Densmore recorded (MEH: 119). Densmore has "o'mûkiki'bûg," which she translates as "frog leaf" (291).

Plant of the Great Sturgeon: possibly *Satureja arkansa labella* or *Satureja arkansa arbella*

namebiniganzh, namebiniganzhiig (*na*): Retranscription of Kee's "Nahmahbinigunzh," which she translated as, "The Plant of the Great Sturgeon." Another translation might be "plant of the sucker fish." From the story we know that this plant was created when the Great Sturgeon died. Namebin, whose name appears in namebiniganzh, is usually identified as a sucker fish. This plant is most likely *Satureja arkansa labella*. Kee said it was a subspecies, and another of Kee's apprentices said it is a calamint. Ma-nee Chacaby recognized this plant and this name for it. The plural form is from her. She said this plant grows by bodies of water, such as rivers and lakes (Chacaby, personal communication).

Poison ivy (*Toxicodendron radicans*)

animikiibag, animikiibagoon (*ni*): This name is a retranscription of similar names recorded in two written sources (MEH: 135). Possible translation, "thunderbird leaf." Ma-nee Chacaby said she uses this name for poison ivy. The plural in this entry is from her (Chacaby, personal communication).

doodamakiibag, doodamakiibagoon (*ni*): Ma-nee Chacaby said she also uses this name for poison ivy (Chacaby, personal communication).

maji-aniibiish, maji-aniibiishag (*na*): (Rose, personal communication).

Poplar, quaking aspen, popple tree (*Populus tremuloides*)

azaadi, azaadiwag (*na*): (McGeshick, personal communication; Nichols and Nyholm: 15; Meeker, Elias, and Heim: 253).

Red osier (*Cornus sericea*)

miskoobimizh: This name is recorded as having been given to John Nichols by Eddie Benton-Benai (MEH: 340). Keewaydinoquay called this plant by the translation of an Ojibwe name, Bend and Stay Plant.

miskwaabiimizh, miskwaabiimizhiig (*na*): (Nichols and Nyholm: 87). Densmore has "mĭs'kwabi'mĭc," which she translates as "reddish" (288).

Red pine (*Pinus resinosa*)

apakwanagemag, apakwanagemagoog (*na*): (MEH: 219; MOTN: 303). Huron Smith has "abakwanûgi'mûg," which he translates as "bark in plates" (421). Keewaydinoquay gave only English translations of one Ojibwe name (or possibly two Ojibwe names) for this tree: "He Scalps Himself" or "He Flakes Himself Off."

bakwanakendag, bakwanakendagoog (*na*): (Chacaby, personal communication).

bapakwanagemag, bapakwanagemagoog (*na*): (POD).

Roses: wild prairie rose (*Rosa arkansana*), prickly wild rose (*Rosa acicularis*), smooth rose (*Rosa blanda*), and wild rose (*Rosa virginiana*)

bizhikiwigin, bizhikiwiginiig: wild prairie rose (*Rosa arkansana*). The authors note this word specifically refers to the "fruit" of the plant and they give the name only in its plural form. This name is a retranscription of a name Densmore recorded (MEH: 53). Densmore has "bi'jikiwi'ginig," which she translates as "cattle rose" (292). Bizhiki means cow or buffalo.

ogin, oginiig (*na*): rose hip; also means "tomato" (Nichols and Nyholm: 105).

oginii-waabigwan, oginii-waabigwaniin (*ni*): rose (Nichols and Nyholm: 105). Genus *Rosa*. "waabigwan," refers specifically to the flower.

oginiiminagaawanzh, oginiiminagaawanzhiig (*na*): prickly wild rose (*Rosa acicularis*), smooth rose (*Rosa blanda*), and wild rose (*Rosa virginiana*). This name is a retranscription of similar names recorded in several written sources (MEH: 82, 225,394,). The plural is from Baraga, who has "Oginiminagawanj," "rose-tree, rose bush; pl. ig" (317).

Sage: white sage (*Artemisia ludoviciana*) and prairie sage (*Artemisia frigida*)

bebezhigooganzhii-wiingashk: white sage (*Artemisia ludoviciana*). This name is a retranscription of a name Smith recorded (MEH: 66). Smith has "bebeji'goganjî wîngûshk," which he translates as "horse hollow tube" and "horse medicine" (363, 417)

bizhikii-wiingashk: prairie sage (*Artemisia frigida*). This name is recorded as having been given to John Nichols by Eddie Benton-Benai.

bizhikii-wiingwashk, bizhiikii-wiingwashkoon (*ni*): prairie sage (*Artemisia frigida*). This name is a retranscription of a name recorded by Densmore (MEH: 65). Densmore has "bi'jikiwĭn'gûck," which she translates as "cattle herb" (287). Another possible translation is "Buffalo herb," as bizhikii is a cow or buffalo.

waabani-wiingwashk: white sage (*Artemisia ludoviciana*). This name is recorded as having been given to John Nichols by Eddie Benton-Benai (MEH: 66).

wiingashk, wiingashkoon (*ni*): white sage (*Artemisia ludoviciana*). Plural is from Baraga, who defines this as an "aromatic herb" (MEH: 66; Baraga: 419). Word is also on POD, but there it is identified as sweetgrass (*Hierochloe odorata*).

Shaga (birch fungus)

zagataagan, zagataaganag (*na*): fungus burned to use as a cleansing smudge ("AW"). This fungus grows on the birch tree. Keewaydinoquay just called this fungus "Shaga." Word is on POD, but identified as "tinder, punk." The plural is from POD.

wiigwaasitaagan, wiigwaasitaaganag (*na*): (Chacaby, personal communication).

Sphagnum moss (*Sphagnum* spp.)

aasaakamig, aasaakamigoon (*ni*): Sphagnum moss (Rose, personal communication, AW). Densmore has "asa′kŭmĭg," identified as *Sphagnum* spp. Word is on POD identified as "moss." Kee just taught students to call this moss "sphagnum."

Spruce: white spruce (*Picea glauca*) and black spruce (*Picea mariana*)

gaawaandag, gaawaandagoog (*na*): white spruce (Nichols and Nyholm: 52) Keewaydinoquay called white spruce and black spruce "He Cuts Himself Down."

mina'ig, mina'igoog (*na*): white spruce, highland spruce (*Picea glauca*) (Rose, personal communication; Johnson, personal communication). Word is also on POD.

wadab, wadabiig (*na*): small, flexible root of the black spruce or balsam fir used to bind large containers of birch bark or canoes. Kee said this is also a name for balsam fir, white spruce, and black spruce. Word is on POD, identified as "spruce root."

zesegaandag, zesegaandagoog (*na*): black spruce (*Picea mariana*) (Rose, personal communication). Word is also on POD.

Sumac, staghorn sumac (*Rhus hirta*)

baakwaan, baakwaanan (*ni*): (Rose, personal communication). Baraga has "Bakwan," which he defines as "the fruit of the vinegar-tree" (67).

baakwaanaatig, baakwaanaatigoon(*ni*): retranscription of a similar word from several sources (MEH: 28). Baraga has "Bakwanâtig, bakwanâti-gon," which he translates as "vinegar tree" (67). Huron Smith has several variations of "bakwana'tîg," which he translates as "binding tree" (354, 397, 424). Word is also on POD, and plural is from there.

gookooko'oo-miin, gookooko'oo-miinan (*ni*) Dorothy Whipple gave us this word, but she only says it in its plural form. One might expect to hear "minan" and not "miinan" but she repeatedly said it this way. (Whipple, personal communication). Possible translation: owl berries.

Sweet flag, calamus (*Acorus calamus*)

wiikenh, wiikenyag (*na*): (Whipple, personal communication; MEH: 154). Also on POD, and plural is from there.

Sweetgrass (*Hierocholoe odorata*)

wiingashk, wiingashkoon (*ni*): (MEH: 168) Plural is from Baraga, who has "wingashk," which he defines as an "aromatic herb." (Baraga: 419). Word and plural form are also recorded on POD.

wiishkobi-mashkosi: sweetgrass. This name is a retranscription of a name Densmore recorded (MEH: 168). Densmore has "wicko'bimûcko'si," which she translates as "sweet grass" (294).

Tamarack (*Larix laricina*)

mashkiig-mitig, mashkiig-mitigoog (*na*): Retranscription of Keewaydino-quay's "Mashkigmatig, mashkigmatigoog," which she translated as "swamp or medicine tree."

mashkiigwaatig, mashkiigwaatigoog (*na*): (Rose, personal communication; Nichols and Nyholm: 78).

mashkikii-mitig, mashkikii-mitigoog (*na*): "medicine tree." Keewaydinoquay said that her grandfather, MidéOgema and his friends used to argue about whether this tree was mashkiig-mitig or mashkikii-mitig.

Tobacco (*Nicotiana rustica*)

asemaa (*na*): tobacco. Keewaydinoquay said that real Anishinaabe asemaa is *Nicotiana rustica*. The tobacco commercially grown, and sold today in cigarette and pipe tobacco form is *Nicotiana tabacum*. They are two different species of the same genus. They are two different plants!

Violet, American dog violet (*Viola conspera*)

waawiyebag, waawiyebagoon (*ni*): Retranscription of Huron Smith's "Wewaîe´ bûgûg" (392). We looked at Smith's word with Kenneth Johnson, who said that this word describes the round appearance of a plant, and it is used as a name for some plants. The plural given in this entry is his assumption of what the plural would be (Johnson, personal communication). Basil Johnston has a similar word, "Wae-wauwiyaeyau-bugug," which he identifies by the common name "violet" (155).

White pine (*Pinus strobes*)

zhingwaak, zhingwaakwag (*na*): (MEH: 220). Baraga has "Jingwak ... -wag" and the plural is from him (173). Word is also on POD. Keewaydinoquay spelled this word "Gingguck".

Willow, Genus *Salix*

oziisigobimizh, oziisigobimizhiig (*na*): Willow (Nichols and Nyholm: 112). Several species (MEH: 200, 201, 348, 369, 386). Word is also on POD identified as *Salix* spp.

Yarrow (*Achillea millefolium*)

ajidamoowaanow: This name is a retranscription of similar names recorded Densmore, Smith, and Zichmanis and Hodgins (MEH: 93). Densmore has "a'djidamo'wano," which she translates as "squirrel tail" (286). Smith has "adjidamo'anûk," which he translates as "squirrel tail" (362). Zichmanis and Hodgins have "Ojidumowaunoh," which they translate as "Squirrel's tail" (267).

Waabanooganzh: Retranscription of Keewaydinoquay's "WabanoGungh," which she translated as "Plant of Light or from the East." She also called this plant "Giver of Knowledge." Kee said this plant was connected to the Waabanoowin religion, and out of respect for that religion, the plant names containing "Waabanoo" are capitalized.

Waabanoowashk Retranscription of James's "Waw-be-no-wusk, "Wawbeno medicine" (299).

Bibliography

Allen, Melinda. 1980. "Cattails Plants against the Cold." *Mother Earth News.* July/August. Retrieved from http://www.motherearthnews .com.

America's Fascinating Indian Heritage. 1978. Pleasantville, N.Y.: Reader's Digest.

Anderson, Edgar. 1971. *Plants, Man, and Life.* Berkeley: University of California Press.

Angier, Bradford. 1974. *Field Guide to Edible Wild Plants.* Harrisburg, Penn.: Stackpole Books.

"Anishinaabe Wordlist." Collected by Mary Siisip Geniusz from panel of Ojibwe speakers at courses for Seven Generations Education Institute Master of Indigenous Knowledge / Philosophy program, Ontario. For more information on this program, see www.7generations.org.

Baraga, Frederick. [1887] 1992. *Dictionary of the Otchipwe Language.* Reprint, *A Dictionary of the Ojibway Language.* St. Paul: Minnesota Historical Society Press.

Bates, John. 1995. *Trailside Botany: 101 Favorite Trees, Shrubs, and Wildflowers of the Upper Midwest.* Duluth, Minn.: Pfeifer-Hamilton.

Benyus, Janine M. 1989. *Northwoods Wildlife: A Watcher's Guide to Habitats.* St. Paul: North Central Forest Experiment Station, USDA Forest Service.

Bown, Stephen R. 2003. *Scurvy: How a Surgeon, a Mariner, and a Gentleman Solved the Greatest Medical Mystery of the Age of Sail.* New York: St. Martin's Press.

Bremness, Lesley. 1994. *Herbs.* New York: Dorling Kindersley.

Bulfinch, Thomas. 1964. *Bulfinch's Mythology: The Age of Fable, or Stories of Gods and Heroes.* The Center, Feltham, Middlesex: Hamlyn House.

Carson, Dale. 1996. *New Native American Cooking*. New York: Random House.

Coffey, Timothy. 1993. *The History and Folklore of North American Wildflowers*. New York: Houghton Mifflin Company.

Crockett, Lawrence J. 1977. *Wildly Successful Plants: A Handbook of North American Weeds*. New York: Collier.

Crowhurst, Adrienne. 1972. *The Weed Cookbook*. New York: Lancer Books.

Densmore, Frances. [1928] 1974. "Uses of Plants by the Chippewa Indians." *Forty-fourth Annual Report of the Bureau of American Ethnology, 1–274*. Reprint, *How Indians Use Wild Plants for Food, Medicine, and Crafts*. New York: Dover Publications.

Duffy, David Cameron. 1990. "Land of Milk and Honey." *Natural History*. July.

Economic Research Service. USDA. 1996. "Interest Increases in Using Plants For Environmental Remediation." IUS6. September. Available at http://www.ers.usda.gov/publications/IUS6/ius6g.pdf

Emboden, William A. 1974. *Bizarre Plants: Magical, Monstrous, Mythical*. New York: Macmillan.

Emery, Carla. 1977. *Old Fashioned Recipe Book: An Encyclopedia of Country Living*. New York: Bantam Books.

Encyclopedia Britannica. 1951. Chicago: Encyclopedia Britannica, Inc.

Favel, Eleanor and Hank Goodsky. "Ojibwe Language Curriculum." St. Paul's Public Schools. Indian Education Program. American Indian Culture and Language Enrichment Program.

Foster, Steven and James A. Duke. 2000. *A Field Guide to Medicinal Plants and Herbs of Eastern and Central North America*. The Peterson Field Guide Series. New York: Houghton Mifflin.

Freitus, Joe. 1977. *Wild Preserves: Illustrated Recipes for over 100 Natural Jams and Jellies*. Washington, D.C.: Stone Wall Press, Inc.

Geniusz, Wendy. 2005. "Keewaydinoquay: Anishinaabe-mashkikiikwe and Ethnobotanist." *Papers of the 36th Algonquian Conference* (Winnipeg: University of Manitoba), 187–206.

Gibbons, Euell. 1966a. *Stalking the Good Life: My Love Affair with Nature*. New York: David McKay Company.

———. 1966b. *Stalking the Healthful Herbs*. New York: David McKay Company.

———. 1962. *Stalking the Wild Asparagus*. New York: David McKay Company.

Graves, Robert. [1955] 1981. *Greek Myths*. London: Penguin Books.

Grieves, Mrs. M. 1931. *A Modern Herbal*. Recopyrighted 1995–2000. Available at http://www.botanical.com.

Hall, Alan. 1973. *The Wild Food Trailguide.* New York: Holt, Rinehart and Winston.

Hart, Jeff. [1976] 1996. *Montana Native Plants and Early Peoples.* Helena, Mont.: Montana Historical Society Press.

Harvey, Gail. 1995. *The Language of Flowers.* New York: Gramercy Books.

Headstrom, Richard. 1984. *Suburban Wildflowers: An Introduction to the Common Wildflowers of Your Backyard and Local Park.* Englewood Cliffs, N.J.: Prentice-Hall, Inc.

Hyam, Roger and R.J. Pankhurst. 1995. *Plants and Their Names: A Concise Dictionary.* Oxford: Oxford University Press.

James, Edwin, ed. [1830] 1956. *A Narrative of the Captivity and Adventures of John Tanner (U.S. Interpreter at the Sault de Ste. Marie) during Thirty Years Residence among the Indians in the Interior of North America.* Minneapolis: Ross & Hanes, Inc.

Johnson Sr., Kenneth. Interview. (Fluent Ojibwe speaker from Seine River First Nation.)

Johnston, Basil. 1976. *Ojibway Heritage.* Lincoln: University of Nebraska Press.

Jones, William. [1917] 1974. *Ojibwa Texts.* Vol. 1. New York: G. E. Stechert, Publications of the American Ethnological Society.

Kavasch, Barrie. 1977. *Native Harvests: Recipes and Botanicals of the American Indian.* New York: Vintage Books.

Keewaydinoquay. 1977. *MukwahMiskomin or KinnicKinnick, Gift of Bear: An Origin Tale Never Before Recorded How to Use BearBerry for Teas, Emergency Food, Treating Diabetes and Internal Infections, Making Non-narcotic Smoking Mixtures.* n.p.: Miniss Kitigan Drum.

Kelly, Cecilia. 2000. Letter to the Editor. *Discover,* March, 10.

King, Frances B. 1998. "American Indian Plant Use: An Overview." In *Stars Above, Earth Below: American Indians and Nature.* Edited by Marsha C. Bol. Niwot, Col: Robert Rinehart Publishers.

Leighton, Anna L. 1985. *Wild Plant Use by the Woods Cree (Nihithawak) of East-Central Saskatchewan.* National Museum of Man Mercury Series. Toronto: McClelland and Stewart.

Lowe, Patty. 2001. *Indian Nations of Wisconsin.* Madison: Wisconsin Historical Society Press.

Longford, Elizabeth, ed. 1991. *Oxford Book of Royal Anecdotes.* New York: Oxford University Press.

Magic and Medicine of Plants. 1986. Pleasantville, N.Y.: Reader's Digest Association.

Ma-nee Chacaby. Interview. (Fluent Ojibwe speaker, two-spirit elder from Animikiiwiikwedong, Thunder Bay, Ontario.)

Marrone, Teresa. 2004. *Abundantly Wild: Collecting and Cooking Wild Edibles in the Upper Midwest.* Cambridge, Minn.: Adventure Publications.

Maulson, Hannah, George Oshogay, Earl Thomas, and John Nichols. 1986. *Ojibwa Language Manual: Resource Materials and Training Exercises.* Wisconsin Department of Public Instruction.

McGeshick Sr., George. Interview. (Fluent Ojibwe speaker from Sokaogaon Mole Lake Band and Chicaugon Band of Iron River, Mich.)

Meeker, James E., Joan E. Elias, and John A. Heim. 1993. *Plants Used by the Great Lakes Ojibwa.* Odanah, Wis.: Great Lakes Indian Fish and Wildlife Commission.

Meister, Judy Osahmin. 2004. *The Spirit of Healing: A Journal of Plants and Trees.* Wisconsin: Minaden Books.

Nichols, John D. and Earl Nyholm. 1995. *A Concise Dictionary of Minnesota Ojibwe.* Minneapolis: University of Minnesota Press.

Niederhofer, Relda E. 1985. "The Milk Sickness: Drake on Medical Interpretation." *Journal of the American Medical Association* 254, no. 15 (October): 2123–25.

Niering, William A., and Nancy C. Olmstead. 1979. *The Audubon Society Field Guide to North American Wildflowers, Eastern Region.* New York: Alfred A. Knopf.

The Oxford Dictionary of Quotations. 1979. New York: Oxford University Press.

The Oxford English Dictionary. http://dictionary.oed.com

"A Possible New Source of Food Supply." *Scientific Monthly,* August 1919.

Peterson, Lee Allen, and Roger Tory Peterson. 1977. *A Field Guide to Edible Wild Plants: Eastern and Central North America.* Peterson Field Guide Series. Boston: Houghton Mifflin Company.

Pringle, Laurence. 1978. *Wild Foods: A Beginner's Guide to Identifying, Harvesting, and Cooking Safe and Tasty Plants for the Outdoors.* New York: Four Winds Press.

Reagan, Albert B. 1928. "Plants Used by the Bois Fort Chippewa (Ojibwa) Indians of Minnesota." *Wisconsin Archeologist,* n.s., 7 no. 4: 230–48.

Quilter, Jeffrey. 2005. *Treasures of the Andes: The Glories of Inca and Pre-Columbian South America.* London: Duncan Baird Publishers.

Schoolcraft, Henry R. [1856] 1984. *The Hiawatha Legends: The Myth of Hiawatha and Other Oral Legends, Mythologic and Allegoric, of the North American Indians.* AuTrain, Mich.: Avery Color Studies.

Shakespeare's Flora and Fauna. 1995. London: Pavilion Books Limited.

Smith, Huron H. 1923. "Ethnobotany of the Ojibwa Indians." *Bulletin of the Public Museum of Milwaukee* 4: 327–525.

Smith, Norman F. 1978. *Michigan Trees Worth Knowing.* Hillsdale, Mich.: Hillsdale Educational Publishers, Inc.

Smith, Virginia A. 2005. "Fruit of the Vine: Kudzu Extract May Help Binge Drinkers Cut Consumption in Half, Study Hints." *Milwaukee Journal Sentinel,* May 18, 3A.

Stokes, Donald W. 1989. *The Natural History of Wild Shrubs and Vines.* Chester, Conn.: Globe Pequot Press.

Tekiela, Stan. 2000. *Wildflowers of Wisconsin, Field Guide.* Cambridge, Minn.: Adventure Publications, Inc.

Thibodeau, Karen, Julie Buchasbaum, and Mike Beno, eds. 1996. *Dining during the Depression.* Greendale, Wis.: Reminisce Books.

Trees of North America. 1970. New York: National Audubon Society.

Weatherbee, Ellen Eliott, and James Garnett Bruce. 1982. *Edible Wild Plants, a Guide to Collecting and Cooking.* n.p.

Weatherford, Jack. 1988. *Indian Givers: How the Indians of the Americas Transformed the World.* New York: Crown Publishers, Inc.

Williamson, Darcy. 1995. *The Rocky Mountain Wild Foods Cookbook.* Caldwell, Ida: Caxton Printers, Ltd.

Wilson, F. G. n.d. *Forest Trees of Wisconsin: How to Know Them.* Madison: Wisconsin Department of Natural Resources.

Zichmanis, Z.. and J. Hodgins. 1982. *Flowers of the Wild: Ontario and the Great Lakes Region.* Toronto: Oxford University Press.

Index

Mary Siisip Geniusz (1948–2016) was of Cree and Métis descent and a member of the Bear Clan. She worked as an oshkaabewis (a traditional Anishinaabe apprentice) with the late Keewaydinoquay, an Anishinaabe medicine woman and ethnobotanist from Michigan. She taught ethnobotany, American Indian studies, and American multicultural studies at the University of Wisconsin–Milwaukee, University of Wisconsin–Eau Claire, and Minnesota State University Moorhead.

Wendy Makoons Geniusz is assistant professor at the University of Wisconsin–Eau Claire, where she teaches Ojibwe language courses. She is the author of *Our Knowledge Is Not Primitive: Decolonizing Botanical Anishinaabe Teachings* and coeditor (with Brendan Fairbanks) of *Chi-mewinzha: Ojibwe Stories from Leech Lake* by Dorothy Dora Whipple (Minnesota, 2015).